A Northern Confederate
at Johnson's Island Prison

A Northern Confederate at Johnson's Island Prison

The Civil War Diaries of James Parks Caldwell

JAMES PARKS CALDWELL
edited by George H. Jones

with an introduction by James D. Hardy, Jr.

McFarland & Company, Inc., Publishers
Jefferson, North Carolina, and London

LIBRARY OF CONGRESS CATALOGUING-IN-PUBLICATION DATA

Caldwell, James Parks, 1841–1911.
    A northern Confederate at Johnson's Island Prison : the Civil War diaries of James Parks Caldwell / James Parks Caldwell ; edited by George H. Jones ; with an introduction by James D. Hardy, Jr.
       p.   cm.
    Includes bibliographical references and index.

    ISBN: 978-0-7864-4471-7
    softcover : 50# alkaline paper

    1. Caldwell, James Parks, 1841–1911—Diaries. 2. Johnson Island Prison—Biography. 3. United States—History—Civil War, 1861–1865—Personal narratives, Confederate. 4. United States—History—Civil War, 1861–1865—Prisoners and prisons. 5. Prisoners of war—Ohio—Johnson Island—Diaries. 6. Hamilton (Ohio)—Biography. 7. Caldwell family. I. Jones, George H., 1922– II. Title.
E616.J7C35   2010
973.7'82—dc22   2010010423

British Library cataloguing data are available

©2010 George H. Jones. All rights reserved

No part of this book may be reproduced or transmitted in any form or by any means, electronic or mechanical, including photocopying or recording, or by any information storage and retrieval system, without permission in writing from the publisher.

Front cover: inset—James Parks Caldwell circa 1880, from the Sigma Chi archives; background—text from Caldwell's diary

Manufactured in the United States of America

McFarland & Company, Inc., Publishers
  Box 611, Jefferson, North Carolina 28640
    www.mcfarlandpub.com

Table of Contents

Preface and Acknowledgments — 1
Introduction (by James D. Hardy, Jr.) — 3

Caldwell's Life — 7
Caldwell the Classicist (by Kenneth Kitchell) — 49
"In Durance Vile" — 68

The Diaries — 71

Appendix: Letters, Poems and Essays — 203
Notes — 239
Bibliographic Essay — 261
Index — 267

Preface and Acknowledgments

This book was a labor of love for many years. When the Sigma Chi fraternity moved its headquarters, William T. Bringham, Sr., executive secretary, found and showed me a folder that contained some letters from James Parks Caldwell — the only one of the seven founders of Sigma Chi who served in the Confederate Army — and some pictures of him at various ages, along with two diaries from his prison years during the Civil War. Most of this came from his sisters after his death. Joseph Nate, in his 1930 history of Sigma Chi, used some of this material, along with information he collected from people who knew Caldwell. This work is deeply indebted to Nate's fine study. Caldwell had fallen in love with a girl whose family was from the South, and he moved to north Mississippi not long after graduating from university. When the war came, he joined the Mississippi army as a lieutenant in the artillery. He was captured at Port Hudson, Louisiana (fifteen miles from my home), when it was surrendered in July 1863. He was then imprisoned in the U.S. Custom House in New Orleans before spending the rest of the war in Johnson's Island Prison in Ohio. He wrote a letter to his sister from New Orleans, titled "In 'Durance Vile,'" which piqued my interest.

The diaries have never been published except for short excerpts, and it seemed to me that these diaries would be of interest to the public as part of Civil War history. Douglas Carlson, grand historian of the fraternity at that time, through his constitutional authority to encourage such work, made the diaries and other materials available to me to publish with all the necessary permissions. Thus began fifteen years of work on this book. The diary page is 4 by 3 inches. The ink had sometimes bled through the thin pages, which were occasionally best read with a mirror, reading the image on the next page mixed with that page's own writing — some of it very small writing, which required a super magnifying glass. A daunting task.

Roger Long of Port Clinton, Ohio, an expert on Johnson's Island Prison, had read many diaries of prisoners there. Long knew so much about the prisoners that he was a treasure trove of information. His notes on the prison and prisoners added enormously to understanding the diaries and life in prison. He conducted me on a walk through the grounds and cemetery of the prison. He also obtained records of Caldwell at Miami University and details of his involvement with the Moon family. I owe him a deep debt of thanks.

Kenneth Kitchell, then chair of the Department of Classical Languages at Louisiana State University, translated and annotated the Latin in the diaries. Kitchell also supplied a chapter, "Caldwell the Classicist," discussing Caldwell's education and use of Latin. He playfully pointed out to me how fortunate I was to have a translator who knew the word "bedbug" in Latin. All his efforts add an immeasurable richness to the book.

James D. Hardy, Jr., professor of history at Louisiana State University, encouraged me to publish this work because of its value as history. I had run out of steam, so I am especially indebted to him for his assistance in keeping me on line to stay the course. His introduction puts this material in its proper place in history.

Charles Elliott, of the history faculty at Southeastern Louisiana University, read the manuscript and gave me many helpful suggestions, for which I am grateful. My thanks to Gerard Jorda, teacher of Romance languages, who assisted my reading of the French and Spanish words in the text of the diary. David Leister and Colin Leister kept the computer functioning and directed me in using it while moving on to a new computer. Alisa Plant organized and edited the manuscript. Many others gave help and encouragement as well. Anyone who has ever attempted anything of this sort knows how many seemingly hopeless obstacles there can seem to be. To all my heartfelt thanks. All errors remain, of course, my sole responsibility.

My undying gratitude goes to my wife, Klileen, who for most of two years labored on further deciphering the diaries. She integrated the notes of Kitchell and Long into the diaries, researched books read by Caldwell, and found the source of many of the quotes that Caldwell used in the diaries. She also made suggestions and did some editing and organizing of the book.

Introduction

by James D. Hardy, Jr.

As the votes in the presidential election of 1860 were counted and published, Abraham Lincoln emerged as a minority president. Three-fifths of the voters had cast a ballot for one of the other three candidates in the race, the Democrats Stephen A. Douglas or John Breckinridge, or the Unionist, John Bell. Lincoln had also been a regional candidate. He had carried all of free America, but not one of the fifteen slave states. The political and psychological divisions between slave and free states, exposed in the Compromise of 1820 and cast into permanent public consciousness by the Compromise of 1850, had reached their logical conclusion. National politics had finally come to be fixed, permanently as far as anyone could see, on the issues of free soil and slavery, abolition and popular sovereignty, Dred Scott and John Brown. There were not quite yet two American nations, but there were two national parties representing increasingly incompatible societies.

The election of 1860 had not, by itself, divided the American people so sharply, nor had it alone been the messenger that revealed such divisions. National and state politics and climate of opinion had been moving steadily toward sectional animosity, as opposed to sectional differences, at least since the Mexican War (1846–1848), perhaps since the emergence of abolitionism in the 1830s. Many in public life had warned of possible dissolution of the Union, and not a few, including abolitionist William Lloyd Garrison, welcomed it. In 1856, the new Republican Party, drawn from those who opposed the extension of slavery to the western territories and those who were not Democrats, ran its first presidential candidate, John C. Frémont. Frémont lost, but the new party did not break up since its basic issue of slavery remained. Its power and presence grew in the free states, and, in 1860, the Republicans tried again. They ran a strong candidate, Abraham Lincoln. Lincoln's victory in the election of 1860, at least in the south, shouted aloud that the house divided could no longer endure.

As this stark and simple political reality sunk in, men and women on both sides of the freedom line began to think that they lived in interesting times. Perhaps they should keep a record. Thousands decided to start journals or diaries. Both soldiers and civilians took part in the effort to record and remember. Journals described day-to-day life at home and in camp, commenting upon military and political events both close at hand and far away. Many journals and diaries showed the fear of loss of loved ones, and almost all reflected a sense that the war was changing personal and national life forever. By what they recorded and left out, they reflect the gap between individual lives and the great events of war and politics. Taken together, the journals and letters help define the tensions and flavor of life lived (and endured) within social and military conflict.

Diaries could come from unusual venues, and these included prisoner-of-war camps. For prisoners, the boredom of camp routine differed only in detail from bivouac and garrison, while danger from disease, exposure, and malnutrition replaced enemy bullets. They were still far from home and unable to return, still in the army but unable to fight. Early in the war prisoners were routinely paroled or exchanged, but by the last year of fighting men were often sent to camps. Prisoners' narratives can have a special tone, not only about deprivations, but also about life lived on hold, so to say, apart from the great events and issues that had filled their lives. They had once been part of the big show; now they were passive observers only.

One of these prisoner diaries was written by James Parks Caldwell, a Confederate artillery lieutenant, held on Johnson's Island at Sandusky, Ohio, on Lake Erie, in 1864 and 1865. Caldwell, a doctor's son, had been born in Ohio, a free state that went for Lincoln in 1860. Although there were many northern Democrats, and many of those sympathized with the South, comparatively few northerners went into the Confederate army. Caldwell was more likely to join the Confederacy than most from a free state, however. He was from Monroe County, a part of Ohio south of what political sociologists call the "accent line," the southern tier of counties near the Ohio River where sympathy for the South and approval of slavery was fairly strong. Of course, for those living near the freedom line, family ties and social loyalties often led both north and south. Many in the Ohio Valley had property and business on both sides of the river that then divided the nation. The border states, and the Virginia counties that seceded from secession and became West Virginia, stayed in the Union, though they sent men to both armies. Still, James

Parks Caldwell was something of an anomaly in the Confederate army, as was Andrew Johnson of Tennessee in the U.S. Senate and General George Thomas of Virginia in the Union army.

Caldwell was distinct in another way. He attended Miami College at a time when college attendance was rare and generally confined to children of the prosperous who wished to enter a learned profession, such as law or the ministry. Miami was an important educational center for the Upper South as well as for Ohio, with students from the Mississippi Valley and the free states of the Northwest Territory. While at Miami, Caldwell was in school with Benjamin Harrison, later a Republican president. Caldwell was also a founder, in 1855, of Sigma Chi, one of the older college fraternities and certainly the most famous of them all. Few undergraduates have had such a lasting impact on student life and traditions in American higher education.

After graduation Caldwell went south to Memphis and on into Mississippi, where he started a school for the children of planters and began to study law. And then came war. Rather than return north, Caldwell joined the Confederate army, fought at Shiloh, and was captured at Port Hudson. A fellow prisoner from Port Hudson was Edward Douglass White of Louisiana, who also studied law, and who later became the Chief Justice of the United States. White was paroled to his mother, but Caldwell was held at the old Customs House in New Orleans and was then sent to his natal but no longer home state of Ohio.

When Caldwell was captured in July 1863, the war had already been lost by the Confederacy. Fighting was far from over, and the exceptionally sanguine campaigns of 1864 in Virginia and Georgia lay ahead. These campaigns could only extend Union victory, already secure on the sea and in the Mississippi and Ohio valleys, to the rest of the Confederacy. Moreover, there was no longer any real possibility of British or French intervention on the Southern side. For the Confederacy, the only remaining hopes were war weariness in the north and a Democratic victory in the elections of 1864. Neither happened. As Caldwell watched from captivity, his adopted side lost the war and then ceased to exist. By the summer of 1865, Caldwell was an American again.

Caldwell's decision to join the Confederate army affected the rest of his life. His service in the Confederate army could not be finessed or explained away, certainly not in the immediate aftermath of the war. He saw no advantage in returning to Republican Ohio, where there could hardly be a place for him. Even with his leadership skills, his social presence, his education, his family connections, how could he now rise to respect and prominence? Taking Horace Greeley's advice, Caldwell went west. For a time he became a newspaper man in California, and, along with Mark Twain, contributed to

Bret Harte's *Overland Journal*. He later returned to the South he had fought for. Settling in Biloxi, Caldwell rose to a prominent position in the Mississippi bar, an appropriate profession for a man with a college education. It was also an appropriate comment on late nineteenth-century America, where every career and every profession and every life was profoundly affected by the Civil War, which lasted long after the fighting had ended.

Caldwell's Life

The Caldwells had settled in the Carolinas in the late 1600s. They moved north into Pennsylvania where W. W. Caldwell, the father of James Parks Caldwell, was born and reared in Carlisle, graduating from Dickinson College there. He then moved west and settled in what is now southeastern Ohio. He graduated from the Ohio Medical College and set up his practice in Monroe, in Butler County, a quiet, rural setting. Soon afterwards he married Isabella H. Parks. Land records indicated they were neighbors.

The Caldwells had eight children all of whom reached maturity. Their first child, James Parks Caldwell, whom they called Parks, was born on March 27, 1841. There were four boys, who predeceased the four sisters. Isabella Parks Caldwell and Rebecca Caldwell remained in Hamilton, Ohio, where the family had moved in 1858, to care for their aged parents. When the last parent died in 1906, the two sisters moved to Los Angeles to be with their other two sisters. Isabella, the one in the family who remained closest to Parks throughout his life, lived to be ninety-nine years old. In 1926, she wrote to Joseph Nate, who was writing the history of Sigma Chi, giving the following data about the family:

> James Parks Caldwell, born in 1841, died in 1911, called Parks. Samuel Wilse Caldwell, born in 1843, died in Los Angeles in 1921, called Wilse. Isabella Parks Caldwell, born in 1846, known as Bella and later Aunt Bep. Mary Caldwell, born in 1848, married James Beatty, a federal judge in Idaho who retired to California. Benjamin Rush Caldwell, born in 1849, died in Little Rock, Arkansas in 1883, called Rush. He was named for a famous Pennsylvania physician and signer of the Declaration of Independence. The rest of the family was born after the 1850 census was taken: Joseph H. Caldwell, called Joe, worked in Alaska and retired to Los Angeles. Ida Caldwell, the widow of C. M. Jones and mother of Isabella Caldwell Jones Davis, the niece who gave Nate most of the material and information about the Caldwell family. Rebecca Caldwell, who lived in Los Angeles. She outlived all the others.[1]

Oil painting of James Parks Caldwell at age 4 when he was living in Monroe, Ohio. It was given to the Sigma Chi Fraternity by his family in 1955 and hangs in the fraternity headquarters in Evanston, Illinois. It was photographed by Douglas Carlson who was Grand Historian at that time.

Butler County was the center of a community of Shaker families, and it presented a moral though somewhat austere environment for a child. There were few children in the area, and Parks learned to be self-reliant and to invent his own games. His association with older people gave him a maturity beyond his years, and as other siblings joined the family, he became even more grown-up. Dr. Caldwell enrolled Parks, age five, in the educational academy in Monroe, where he excelled. In 1854, the school's principal told Dr. Caldwell that the boy had covered everything that the academy offered in study, which included much Latin and advanced mathematics. Dr. Caldwell decided to send Parks, age thirteen, to Miami University in Oxford, Ohio, which was fairly close to his home.

Miami University

Miami University, named for the Miami River, had a reputation for excellence. Founded in 1809, the second school established west of the

Allegheny Mountains, it had achieved the status of a fine institution of higher learning. Students came from surrounding states, some traveling up the Mississippi River to Cincinnati from as far away as Memphis, Tennessee. Although a land-grant school, Miami University was a noted training ground for Presbyterian ministers. All the presidents of the school, from its founding till after the Civil War, were Presbyterian ministers.

The faculty at Miami University was a distinguished one. Professor William H. McGuffey, a member of the faculty before young Parks arrived at the university, produced the series of *Eclectic Readers*, which are still famous today, known as *McGuffey's Readers*. Professor David Swing founded the famous Central Church of Chicago. Many of Parks's classmates were also important men later in life. Benjamin Harrison became president of the United States. Whitelaw Reid was a noted journalist and ambassador to the Court of St. James. Benjamin Pyatt Runkle, one of the seven founders of the Sigma Chi Fraternity, became a major general in the Union Army in the Civil War. Calvin Brice was a U.S. senator. These were fellow students Parks associated with daily, a marvelous climate for a thirteen-year-old boy.

Dr. Caldwell kept exact and careful records of family affairs. He chronicled the events of Parks's education, noting:

"September 2nd, 1854. James Parks Caldwell, aged 13 years, 5 months and 6 days left home (for the first time) for Oxford and entered the Second Class of Miami University, September 2nd, 1854. Expenses first time [term], $54.00. January 18th, 1855. Accompanied him to Hamilton, took supper together at the Hotel — then he took stage for Oxford. He was keen to get to his studies. About ten of his fellow students were in the stage. Expenses second time, $50.00. September 11th, 1855. Parks left for Oxford to enter the Junior Class. Expenses 3rd time, $71.00. Nov. 9th, I went over for Parks and brought Tom C. Bell along with us the next day. Expenses, $75.00."[2]

College Days at Old Miami, published by Miami University in 1984, is a diary of T. C. Hibbett, a student at the university between 1851 and 1854. This gives a good picture of university life at the time Parks was there. In 1852, the 29th Annual Circular of Miami University was published. The student body was made up of 28 seniors, 23 juniors, 34 freshmen, and 48 sophomores. Campus consisted of two large brick buildings. One had classrooms, and the other was used as housing for the faculty, which consisted of six professors and the president. There was also a preparatory department of 45 students, presumably pre-college men, and a normal school to train teachers that had 63 students, who "practice taught" in a model school of 25 students. Parks was not associated with any of these departments because he was pursuing the college program for a bachelor of arts degree. The course of study was heavy in the classics but also contained much mathematics and some

Photograph of Caldwell at age 13, probably made at Hamilton, Ohio, before he left to enroll in nearby Miami University, considered the Yale of the West, at Oxford, Ohio. He entered the second class or sophomore level on September 2, 1854.

physical sciences and physical education. Parks avoided physical education whenever possible. (The rheumatoid arthritis that he suffered from later in life may have been a cause.)

The Annual Circular of Miami University detailed the four-year curriculum. The freshman year included Herodotus, ancient history and geography, Oriental history, Livy, Roman history, algebra, the *Iliad*, Greek history, Horace's odes and satires, trigonometry, and surveying. This required knowledge of Latin, much more than one would be expected to have today. The sophomore class studied Thucydides, Horace's epistles, Cicero, modern history, analytical geometry, Eschines, Tacitus, and mechanics. The junior year studied Demosthenes, Cicero, differential calculus, natural philosophy, mental philosophy, and logic. Seniors closed out their education with Aeschylus, Terence, chemistry, physiology, dynamics in analytical mechanics, spherical trigonometry, analogy of religion, moral philosophy, astronomy, geology, political science, political economy, and the history of modern Europe.

Three literary societies at Miami played an important role in the life of the campus. To be chosen to represent one of the societies in the school's yearly literary contest was an honor, and to win the contest was the greatest honor of the campus. Throughout the year the societies held frequent debates, and their members often erupted into fistfights all over the campus, even in classes. Along with the literary societies there were men's social fraternities. Membership in these was small, due to the size of the student body. Most of the students belonged to both groups, but the fraternity ties were closer, with opportunities for more intimate friendship and the mysteries surrounding each fraternity's rituals, handshakes, and secrets. The fraternities were also oriented to electing one of their members as the orator of the literary society.

An event in January 1848, called the "Great Snow Rebellion," brought about the abolition of fraternities on campus for several years. This is chronicled in several international fraternity histories and in student diaries of that period. There had been serious differences between the president of the university and the student body; the cause of the friction remains unknown. A heavy snow fell on the night of the rebellion, and after a caucus of students, a brilliant plan was conceived. Giant soft snowballs were rolled up and placed against every door and window of the college building. An unexpected hard freeze turned the snowballs into solid blocks of ice, denying access to the building for days. Finally, a thaw removed the ice blockade. The discipline that followed was severe. Expulsions caused an exodus of students, and attendance numbers at the university did not recover for several years.

In 1852, fraternities were again allowed on the campus. The fraternities were splitting like amoebas; as soon as one had a dozen members or so, they argued and split to form another. A new fraternity, Delta Kappa Epsilon, known as "Deke," had just split from a chapter of Phi Delta Theta. When Parks came to Miami in 1854, he became part of this still perhaps unsettled situation. The Dekes invited Franklin Howard Scobey, the son of a Dr. Scobey from Hamilton, Ohio, to become a member, and he accepted. His father and Dr. Caldwell were good friends, and Parks was in his same class in the university, so Scobey suggested Parks as a potential member, as well as two other friends. They were all invited to join the Dekes, and all accepted. The other two were Benjamin P. Runkle and Isaac M. Jordan, country boys who were able to debate and write essays, skills of major importance in college life. They also loved to fight and would assault anyone who seemed to question their integrity. Daniel C. Cooper and Thomas C. Bell were also invited to join. These six brought the membership of Deke to twelve, and it was decided to limit the membership to that number. The young men roomed or boarded around Oxford and ate at a home where meals were served for students. Social life, usually limited to Oxford, was quite lively. The town girls and students at a recently opened women's seminary provided the social focus of the students at Miami. The next year Parks was joined in Oxford by his sister Isabella, who enrolled in the college for women, along with a town girl named Virginia Moon. She would become the rebel spy whose love changed Parks's life.

The fraternities, politically active on campus, tried to elect their members to all positions of importance—most notably, to represent one of the three literary societies at the Annual Exhibition. During Parks's sophomore year, the six newest members caucused and agreed upon a nominee for the Erodelphian Literary Society. Though he was not a Deke, the six agreed he was the most qualified. When the vote was taken, there was a tie. The other six Deke upperclassmen were incensed that the youngest members would take it upon themselves to make this important decision, and it became a cause célèbre in the chapter. The Deke chapter was split six against six, and neither side would make any concessions. The older six called upon a valued alumnus from Hamilton, Ohio, named Minor Millican to come and straighten out the disagreement. Millican (later a Civil War hero who was killed in the war) demanded that the younger six recant. They refused and, after a heated discussion, walked out. The six who withdrew, along with another student, William Lewis Lockwood, formed yet another new fraternity, which became Sigma Chi. Lockwood, the relatively wealthy son of a clothes merchant from New York City and well-educated in elocution and writing, brought new talents into the group. Parks's fellow charter members, outstanding young men, became prominent in later years. Daniel Cooper, the oldest at twenty-five, was looked on as the fraternity's leader and became a Presbyterian minister. Thomas C. Bell, twenty-three, became a major in the U.S. Army and later a college president. Isaac M. Jordan, twenty, served in the U.S. Army and later was elected as a congressman from Ohio. Benjamin P. Runkle, nineteen, rose to the rank of major general and was later a Presbyterian minister. William Lockwood, nineteen, a captain in the U.S. Army, became a successful businessman, who eventually died of his war wounds. Franklin Scobey, eighteen, served in the U.S. Army and returned to Hamilton after the war, where he became a farmer. For a fourteen-year-old boy, these were inspiring role models.

In 1908, Runkle wrote of Parks, his roommate: "Our holidays were spent in the fields and along the streams, one of us carrying a gun, or fishing rod, but Caldwell, his copy of Poe or his Shakespeare. His contributions, essays, poems, plays and stories read in literary halls, in the chapter meetings and on Saturdays before the whole corps of students were the most remarkable productions that I ever heard. Few of us escaped the pointed witticisms that flowed from his pen or ever lost the nicknames that he gave us in his dramas. He never seemed to study as other boys. What he knew appeared to be his intuitively. He wrote Latin and Greek poetry, and he was more widely versed in literature than any other student in the college. He left the university with the respect and whole-hearted affection of every soul from dear old Dr. Hall

Room where Caldwell lived with Ben Runkle in 1854 and 1855. The room is considered the birthplace of Sigma Chi and is owned by the fraternity. It is on the second floor above a commercial office. The furniture is not the original but is of the same period (photograph by the editor).

(the President) down to the janitor." Isaac Jordan, then a U.S. congressman, said of Parks at an alumni banquet in 1881, "Caldwell — the most precocious intellect I have ever known."[3]

Dr. W. W. Caldwell, his father, recorded in his records, "Parks graduated on Friday, May 15, 1857, aged 16 years, one month, and 18 days."[4] Dr. Caldwell was well-known for his skill in the practice of medicine and for his scholarly interests. In 1858, he moved the family to Hamilton, a much larger town, and became a member of the Hamilton County Medical Society, serving as its president in 1869. Dr. Caldwell was an influential man and involved in community affairs. He was a staunch Presbyterian and an unyielding Democrat in national politics. In the stirring political events in Ohio occurring in this period before the Civil War, he became what was known as a War Democrat. As Isabella Davis, the only niece of Parks, said in a letter, "Southern Ohio was close to the Kentucky line where feelings were very tense. Thousands were Southern sympathizers. Dr. Caldwell was a believer in States Rights. The whole thing we all knew was States Rights and principal and principle!"

After graduation, Parks spent a short time at home and then decided to go west, where his Uncle Ives lived in Burlington, Iowa. For a young man on horseback or carriage, this distance, nearly three hundred miles as a crow flies, must have been a few days' journey. At sixteen years of age, the adventurer Parks began the life of a man freed from his former ties. We learn that he planned to study with a preceptor and become a lawyer. A letter to his father shows the thinking of this young adult. The letter came in a small packet marked "50 cents" and without an envelope.

This picture of Caldwell after graduation from Miami University at 16 years of age in 1857 is a copy of a daguerreotype preserved by the family and printed in Nate's *History of the Sigma Chi Fraternity*. After graduating Caldwell went to Iowa to visit an uncle thinking maybe he would settle there but he returned to Hamilton, Ohio, and read law with Judge Clark until he went to Mississippi in 1858.

Burlington, Sep. 28th, 1857
Dear Father,

Yours of the 23d reached me when I was last in town. (day before yesterday) That enclosure astonished me, the facts were these. I wrote the letter, as you know by this time. I took it over to Dr. Hayden intending to send it thence to town, and having neither money nor stamps, I merely handed it to Uncle as it was and asked him to mail it telling him that I had no stamps. He did so but forgot to prepay it, hence that notice. I was very sorry to hear that you were not coming to Hawkeye State, as I did from Mr. Law before your letter reached me, but perhaps it is best to wait awhile. Money matters are very tight here also and the panic has just begun. Green Thomas & Co. Bank (the most reliable in Burlington, or hitherto consider'd so at least) has suspended payment and on account of their failure the Trust Co. has also suspended. These will come up again, however, in a few weeks at most. Their Eastern debt came due before they had time to collect. But "those who ought to know" say that next Spring will be a very good time to invest money in or about Burlington as things will be very low and then probably double again in a year.

As to prosecuting my studies. Where! And when! Uncle's Law, Hayden and Mr. Oviatt (I had almost said Uncle) think that I had better remain here for several reasons. 1st I intend to be a western man and therefore should thoroughly study and understand western ways. 2nd The difference in Statutes of Ohio and those of Iowa, which will cause a year's study additional as well as one year's useless study if I should study in Ohio. 3rd The advantage of seeing and being enabled to study more thoroughly those Land Cases and Disputed Titles which occur so frequently in the western courts and so seldom in those of Ohio. 4th The advantage of studying where I intend to practice instead of studying one place and going off among strangers to practice. Here, if I am at all adapted for a lawyer, I might grow into a reputation. 5th I have a good many friends hereabouts. It would, of course, be more pleasant to be at home but the future must be looked at, as I will be when studying law but girding on my armour for the Great Battle of life.

So Robertson and Lethe are married at last after a long war of intrigue. Ike wrote me more than a month ago that they would be married on Sep 15th. Perhaps you will hear of an about-to-be wedding soon but Aunt Rebecca said that she was giving to write soon, so I will say nothing about it!

If you wish and think it would be best for me to come home, please let me know in time for me to "visit around" a little as I have staid at Uncle Ives' almost entirely. We heard from Uncle Howes day before yesterday. I suppose he will be at Monroe this week and I suppose you will send out my diploma by him. My love to all.

         Believe me ever your loving son,
               Parks

P.S. I intend to go into town tonight to take Mr. Law's horse in for him to come out with tomorrow.

For whatever reason, perhaps the financial recession, after a short stay in Iowa, Parks returned to Hamilton, where his family had moved. He began his law study in the office of Judge James Clark in Hamilton. Clark was one of the best lawyers in Ohio, widely respected, and the candidate of both political parties for judge of the Common Pleas Court. In 1857, he had decided to return to the private practice of law. Clark was a brilliant man and involved in politics. He married Charlotte Moon, better known as Lottie. (This is not the famous Baptist missionary named Lottie Moon, who was Charlotte's first cousin.) The Moon family had moved to Ohio from Virginia with the opening of the Western Reserve and had settled in Oxford. There their children were educated, the boys at Miami University and the girls at Ohio Women's College, where Isabella Caldwell and Virginia Moon were classmates and friends. Parks was associated with the dynamic personalities of Lottie and her husband and was bound to be influenced by their thinking. Shortly after this time, Clark was noted as a Peace Democrat, which meant he was against the oncoming war. He was the leader in Butler County of the Copperheads, who were southern sympathizers. Their opponents gave them the name, as copperheads were a dangerous breed of snakes. The Copperheads accepted the name as a badge of honor. They even carved the large copper penny so that only the head remained and affixed a pin to the back, wearing the emblem for all to see. Clark believed that states had the right to secede but he was against slavery. He reasoned that slavery would disappear, as it was uneconomical.

There is much folklore concerning the Moon sisters. Although they were flamboyant beyond belief and their antics have been enhanced over the years, they were clearly a lively bunch. Lottie, the judge's wife, was born in 1829. Mary Beeler Moon, better known as Mollie, was born in 1834 and became a faithful correspondent to Parks while he was in prison. Virginia Bethel, who was known as Ginnie, was born in 1844 and thus was three years younger than Parks. By this time she and Parks had developed a romantic attachment.

The Moons had family connections in Memphis, Tennessee, and Panola County, Mississippi. Dr. Caldwell dutifully recorded in his family notes, "J.P.C. Left Hamilton Oct. 7, 1858 for Mississippi. Reached Memphis October 16. Left Memphis for Panola, Oct. 21. God bless my dear son."[5] Parks stayed as guests of the Moons in Memphis and in Panola, and decided to settle in the South.

He reasoned that he was not fully prepared to practice law in his new home; but, as he considered himself an expert in the classical languages of Latin and Greek, he decided to teach. He sought employment with local plantation owners and was employed by Colonel Freeman Irby, who owned and worked a large plantation. The title of colonel had been granted to Irby as an honorary title and had no relation to any army.[6] The 1860 U.S. Census of Panola County, Mississippi, listed one F. B. Irby as 38 years old, from

Virginia, a planter by occupation, with real estate worth $40,000 and a private net worth of $39,000 (over $2 million today). The Irby family was listed as wife M. L., 35 years old, and children Wm. B., 14 years, Mary, 12 years, Bettie, 10 years, George, 6 years, M. L. (f), 4 years, and Sallie, 4 months. Next appeared James P. Caldwell, 19 years old, from Ohio, a teacher of languages. The census records that F. B. Irby had 33 slaves. Parks lived with the Irbys and thus knew from first-hand experience the use and conditions of the slaves on the plantation. Yet as far as is known, he never made any mention of slaves in his papers, diaries, or in any of his talks throughout his life.

Parks soon organized a school that he named the Palmetto Academy, where he taught the Irby boys as well as the male children of other plantation owners. The Palmetto flag of the state of South Carolina was a symbol of opposition to the North. It was the Palmetto flag that was raised in Charleston when the South fired on Fort Sumter, since there was no southern flag at that time.

Days on the plantation of Colonel Irby were happy ones for Parks. He wrote that he was trying his hand at breaking a colt using the South American method of blindfolding the animal until he was mounted and then removing the blindfold. He wrote, "After removing the blindfold the astonished filly stood dazzled by the sunlight and neatly deposited me over her head." And once he tried teaching Sunday school in the cabins of the slaves "with as surprising results." Later letters from Parks to his family showed his enthusiasm for his pupils and his awareness of the approaching war. The following is an example:

> Panola, Miss. Sept. 11th, 1859
> Dear Father;
>
> Your last three letters were received, all at once, yesterday and I opened the last one first and thereby obtained nothing but good news. I am very sorry indeed to learn of the severe illness of my dear Mother and earnestly hope that she may soon fully recover. A day or so before the letters, I received a box containing the packages for which please accept my warmest and most sincere thanks and present them to Mother for the taking of her affection therein contained and to sisters for theirs. For the stationery, pens, &c I am particularly grateful to you, as I was more in need of them than of any of the other things, excepting those nicely marked handkerchiefs. I was also thankful for the newspapers as well as those of which I am in weekly receipt. The packages were placed in a box at Memphis & shipped by Jimmie Curtis to Sardis, where Mr. Irby receives all his freight. I also received a letter from him (J. C.) detailing an account of his adventures in Hamilton. He is certainly one of the best young men I ever knew. I am very sorry to hear of the death of Uncle Jo. Parks' little boy. Ellen wrote me that he was very "proud of it." I will try to write to Mr. Oviatt some of these days. I am very glad to hear that they are getting along so well. I will also try to write once a week to someone at home.

The box found me in bed with another chill or rather the effects of one. The quinine preparation shall be fully attended to next time. The chills do not come regularly, but every time a little sooner than the time before, but I will make allowances for all that next time, too.[7]

Peaches seem to be very cheap in your market. I didn't know they ever got down to even $5.00. Your assurance that you will be glad to see me whenever I "cannot teach," is appreciated and I thank you for it; also for your offer of "the needful" & concerning debts, the two letters I am happy to say, I have no need of, but am just as grateful as if I had. I do not consider "teaching" as my "business" by any means, but my present intentions are, if everything suits, to resume the study of law in Hamilton and, when admitted, to come South, where there are no reasonable doubts of my ultimate success.

This is one of the reasons why I proposed going further South so that I might see the different portions of the country which I intend to adopt. But I will lay the whole thing before you just as it came about. A little more than four weeks ago, while on a visit to the "upper neighborhood I staid all night with a young man, Edwin Walton, a member of my Secret Society [Sigma Chi] who graduated some 5 or 6 years since at the University of Mississippi. In the course of conversation we spoke of the gallant, but somewhat mythical, Davy Crocket of Tenn. And Edw. Walton, the young man, gave me a description of a visit to the Alamo fortress in Texas where the redoubtable Davy was killed. From this we got to talking of Texas and he advised me to go there saying that, if I wished, he would write to a correspondent there, and he knew that there was a situation for a classical scholar in the family of his correspondent, which, if it were not already taken, he could secure for me, adding that it would be a very lucrative one (Said planter owns upwards of 100 "working hands" which in Texas is a "very large force.")

Now at that time I felt very much depressed on acc't of the chills, and Texas being such a salubriously healthy country, can it be wondered at that I accepted his offer? The place alluded to is near Bastrop on the Colorado river, the next county below that in which the Capital is situated and in a notoriously — almost fabulously healthy country. Now, since I have received your advice on this point, I shall not go if there be any honorable means of escape. (and I expect there will be such) Besides, they want me to stay here and (I suppose,) can and will if I desire it, get me a little larger school next year, but I should like a situation where I could teach the higher classics of which (& of which only, I fear,) I myself am very fond, and which I consider myself well-qualified to teach.

Your good opinions of the South are so correct and true to the life that they must certainly have been formed from & based upon experience. If ever there was an honorable, high-minded & generous people on the earth, "The Southerners" are one, and should I be sick (I have had "nothing but chills yet,) I will be as well taken care of, as I could be anywhere, of this I have had experience already.

I will write next week to Belle [sister Isabella] and Rush [brother Benjamin Rush] and soon after to Mollie [Ginnie's older sister] whose longer letter deserves and answer "all to itself." I will endeavor to write once a week. Give my love to all and especially my love & filial regards to My dear Mother & for whose speedy recovery my sincerest wishes are framed.

Very respectfully,
Your loving Son.
J. P. Caldwell

P.S. What do you think now of my "going further South," you said that it would be an evidence of my not looking "far ahead:" if I were to go with an eye to my ultimate law-establishment there, would it not rather be an evidence of the contrary? — of my looking too far ahead?

Parks continued teaching, and the Palmetto Academy flourished. His routine was teaching, writing letters, and continuing his self-education, while all the time he was aware of the gathering clouds of war. He realized that the threat of war was a reality, and even though he enjoyed teaching, he also thought of "the injustices exhibited toward the South." His letter to his father dated December 17, 1860, stated that he was "thinking of joining the division of Gardiner, Loring, Breckenridge and Bowen." This does not appear to be a correct alignment of names, but as he said the injustices had "taken fire in his soul."

April 1st 1861
Dear Mother;

I now seat myself to write you, at the completion of my twentieth year, renewed assurance of my love and respect, and of my gratitude for that care and kindness which you have ever bestowed upon me, and for that training to which I owe all that I am and shall ascribe all that I may ever become. This duty should have been performed last Wednesday, but on that, and several successive days, I was prevented by complaint from writing to you, and on Saturday I went down to the "lower neighborhood" whence I returned only last night.

In lieu of something better to write about I shall first assure you of the continuance of my excellent health and then proceed to tell you something about my school, both which topics, I trust will not prove wholly devoid of interest to you. The Palmetto Academy is still in its flourishing condition, and I expect, in the course of a week or so (i.e. when Will Moon arrives,) accession to my number of, at least, twelve or fourteen pupils. My pupils are the best behaved and best-bred I have ever seen. Scarcely one is of other than a first-rate family. The spirit of the boys is high, as their conduct is honorable. To illustrate it, I shall relate what occurred last Friday: on that day, they, of themselves organized a military company (and at least eight of them are capable of serving their country to a good purpose,) called the Palmetto Cadets and composed of fifteen boys every one of whom has his gun and knows how to use it. They then by subscription raised ten dollars on the spot where with to purchase a Confederate States Flag, to be hoisted at our school house. It has been sent for to N. Orleans & will be raised as soon as rec'd, on which occasion we will have holiday, and perhaps a speech, or something of the kind. Two companies of volunteers left this county for the Army last week but one was forced to return home crestfallen as the required number of volunteers had already been obtained. Fifteen hundred Missippians [sic] are now at Pensacola and fifteen thousand more will start before the reverberation of the first battle has died away. I know one lady who has a son at Charleston, a son and husband (the latter more than 50 years old) at Pensacola, and still another son who is preparing to go, while a fourth will go as soon as the first blow is struck, thus leaving her in charge of her youngest son (1 ½ years of age) and servants. This was the stuff our revolutionary grand-mothers were made of and their spirits still animate the soul of their descendants. I shall enclose this letter in an envelope representing, on its face, the Southern Flag: it is not so pretty as yours, but we hope to make it as glorious and never to stain its fair folds with disgrace or dishonor.

Accept my sincerest thanks for the present, which, Father informs me, is in preparation for me. The linen I do not now need, but it will someday come into use and as to the other, to you, more important gift, it shall be read and regarded for the sake of the love I bear her who gives it. Give my love to all. I have weak eyes, and write by lamplight. With the utmost respect, I am as ever

Your affectionate son,
J. P. Caldwell

Thoughts of war permeated all levels and ages, and southern culture was nowhere more evident than here. In this letter, Parks reveals a distinct bravado and heroism, as well as the natural excitement of a young man. War is for the young. It is interesting that the mail was going through the border of the Confederate States and on to Ohio. It seems it went through normally. This letter to his mother carried the date April 1, 1861. Fort Sumter would be fired upon on April 12, just eleven days later. The Civil War had begun.

In 1929, Joseph Nate, historian of the Sigma Chi fraternity, asked Norman Monaghan of Memphis to go to Como, Mississippi, and attempt to find what he could about Caldwell. Monaghan reported in a letter dated March 13, 1929, that he had interviewed several of the older men who remembered Caldwell and were Caldwell's pupils in the Palmetto Academy. E. P. Coleman and John Wallace of Como were taught by him and remembered him well. They said that he taught there until "the war" and then closed the academy. They declared that "he [Parks] came to Mississippi with a family named Moon from Ohio and that he was in love with a young lady in that family named Miss Ginnie Moon, and on that account when the family moved South from Ohio, he came South." In his prison diaries, Caldwell wrote of his love and longing for Virginia or VBM, a beautiful and vivacious young woman and always the "Girl of his Dreams."

On April 5, 1912, in Caldwell's obituary, the *Gulfport (Miss.) Daily Herald* said, "He had told intimate friends of a love affair during the Civil War, when he had made an effort to get a leave of absence to go and claim his bride. An engagement with the enemy was imminent and the leave of absence was denied him. Just why the marriage did not take place after the war was never explained, but it is said that the girl, who was to have been his wife, has never married." Ginnie Moon never did marry. Parks's life from seventeen years of age was changed completely because of his love for a rebel spy.

Isabella Caldwell's niece wrote in a letter that "Aunt Bella (who adored Uncle Parks & visited him in Biloxi) was once threatened with being expelled from Oxford College and she and his 'girl friend,' Miss Ginnie — transported much needed opium, etc. via the petticoat express to the tragically suffering South. Grandpa (Dr. W. W. Caldwell) nearly impoverished himself sending supplies from his drugstore in Hamilton, Ohio." When the war started, Ginnie had requested to be sent home from college and was refused. It is said that she shot all the stars from the flag flying over the campus. The story is still told, but the flag is not in evidence. While obviously a fable, it serves to show Ginnie's flamboyance. She said that she had promised to marry sixteen Confederate soldiers during the war, saying afterwards, "I thought if they died, they would die happy, and if they didn't, I didn't give a damn."

Judge Clark's home was the local collection place for messages to go to the Confederates, and the question then became, "Who will take them?" Lottie Moon Clark, his wife, volunteered to take dispatches to General Kirby Smith in Kentucky, which required her to pass through the Union lines. The story is told that she did so disguised as an Irish washerwoman. This was the first of her many forays across the lines. One time, so the story goes, she portrayed herself as a helpless rheumatic cripple on her way home and was offered transportation by President Lincoln's party.

While visiting Jackson, Mississippi, in December 1862, Ginnie volunteered to carry a message from General Sterling Price to Judge Clark in Hamilton. The message was to the Knights of the Golden Circle, a secret group, who were attempting to arrange a plan to get Ohio, Indiana, and Illinois to secede from the Union. The secret group also went by the names of American Knights and Sons of Liberty. It was reported that there were 40,000 members in Ohio, 88,000 in Illinois, and 60,000 in Indiana. The group had a secret constitution, and its members planned to secede and form a third country called the Northwest Confederacy, with Clement Vallandigham, U.S. congressman from Ohio, as its president. The story goes that Ginnie succeeded in delivering the message. She made many passages across the line but was suspected of being a spy and Clark's house was under constant watch.

One day, Ginnie and her mother, accompanied by Judge Clark, boarded a boat in Cincinnati. Clark left after attending to the luggage and Captain Harrison Rose appeared and handed Ginnie a message declaring her to be a

Confederate spy and carrying contraband goods and dispatches. The letter from General Rosencrans at Nashville, Tennessee, said, "Arrest Miss Virginia B. Moon. She is an active and dangerous rebel in the employ of the Confederate government. She has contraband goods, rebel mail, and is the bearer of dispatches."[8] Ginnie wrote years later that she ate the dispatches containing the names of the Knights, and the plans for the Confederacy to unite with the Knights of the Golden Circle.

She was turned over to Captain Andrew Kemper, whose letters are in the library of the Historical and Philosophical Society of Ohio. Kemper was a member of the chapter of Delta Kappa Epsilon at Miami University when he was a student. Kemper recognized the Moons and inquired about her sister Mollie, who was about Kemper's age. Kemper's papers carefully document all of the material found in a trunk, consisting of ordinary garments and "6 pcs. of opium in rolls and 40 bottles $\frac{1}{8}$ oz morphine." Carson, the surveyor of customs, gave a receipt for this material. A packet of letters was taken and read. Captain Kemper stated that "those intended for the South are written systematically without names or places or dates. Those that do bear place or date show that the fair mail carrier is widely known in her business. They were from Philadelphia, Montreal, and Murfreesboro, Tenn. They show that she had traveled diligently, and been engaged for some length of time in this way." The Moons, Ginnie and her mother, were sent to General Ambrose Burnside, once a suitor for the hand of Lottie Moon, Ginnie's sister and the wife of Judge Clark. The general paroled them to Jones Station, the home of Judge Clark. Ginnie was further paroled to her uncle in Memphis.

After the Civil War, the Clarks moved to New York City, where Clark developed a successful law practice. Isabella Caldwell later wrote that Clark and Caldwell kept up a correspondence, much of it in Latin. Lottie became the Paris correspondent for the *New York World* and appeared in many of the European courts. Judge Clark said, "She is the damnedest, smartest woman in the world." She also wrote several books under the pseudonym of Clay. Ginnie returned to Memphis with several adopted children, operating an elite boarding house and devoting herself to "good works." It was said that it was easier to give her a check than to argue with her. She always referred to herself as "an unreconstructed rebel, a political rebel because she loved her South with its traditions, a social rebel because she reserved the right to think, to speak, to act with directness and sincerity, and she admitted of no compromise."[9]

Ginnie's foster daughter, Viva Warren Jones, married and became an actress. In 1919, at age seventy-five, Ginnie showed up in Hollywood to live with her daughter and son-in-law and sought a job in the movies. When asked what parts she could play, she said, "I've played them all," as indeed she had. She appeared in *Rustle of Silk* and *Robin Hood* with Douglas Fairbanks and in *The Spanish Lady* with Poli Negri. She followed her daughter and husband to New York City in 1924 to be with them and lived in her own apartment in Greenwich Village, where she died at the age of eighty-one in 1925, after having lived a "full" life, according to her obituary in the *New York World*. It is not known if she ever met Parks again after the Civil War.

But to return to the story of Parks. He had developed a friendship with Fred Brennan, another Ohio man and southern sympathizer, and together they joined the Confederate Army. The records of the Confederate Veterans in Jackson, Mississippi, show that Parks enlisted as a private in Captain Hoole's company of Mississippi Light Artillery. No further mention can be found in Parks's writings of Fred Brennan's fate.

Parks joined the division of generals Loring and Gardiner, and by the early summer of 1862 had been promoted to a second lieutenant. He was an artillery officer, and kept a small diary in which he wrote the weights of the shells and amount of powder necessary to send these shells various distances. He also made some arithmetic calculations interpolating the distances between known points.

Parks wrote to Ben Runkle, his old roommate, on April 16, 1896, and exchanged reminiscences of the war. Parks recalled an incident that occurred at Jackson, Mississippi,

> connected with an attempt of mine to discover if perchance some old college friends might be among a lot of officers waiting for exchange at Jackson. Having brought dispatches to Headquarters (which by the way, was a kindly way of granting me leave enough to furnish myself with a new uniform on my fresh promotion to the lofty position of Second Lieutenant) and delivered them, I found my way to the prison front, and rode up so that my horse's forefeet rested on the sidewalk. I then shouted at a group of officers in the second story windows, "Any Ohio men up there." "Lots of 'em," came the reply. I then asked for one to come to the window. In response, a gentleman who announced himself as Major Van Horn (I forget what command) came forward. I inquired for anyone who had been at Miami, and for certain regiments which I knew to have been raised in Butler County. I was rather glad to be disappointed of finding any acquaintances. The amusing feature of the interview was the reply of one of the officers to my statement, "I am from Ohio, myself," which was, "Those are d___d queer clothes for an Ohio man to wear."
>
> The sentry at the door, hearing me say that I was from Ohio, took upon himself to order me away, and the officer of the guard refused to listen to my request for admission to the prison, but, somewhat impertinently ordered me off. I galloped to Headquarters, where I was remembered by reason of my recent errand there, and asked to speak with General Pemberton, to whom I stated the case, and went back with written authority to visit the prisoners

unaccompanied. This I accordingly did (first getting a supply of smoking tobacco), taking great pleasure in humiliating the hypercritical officer on guard.

Shiloh

The battle of Shiloh, sometimes called the battle of Pittsburg's Landing, brought the two former roommates together, but they never knew it until after the war. Ben Runkle was a major with the Thirteenth Ohio, having

Photographed from the original daguerreotype of Caldwell as a second lieutenant. He joined Captain Hoole's Battery of the Mississippi Light Artillery. He was soon promoted to second lieutenant. The inscription 61 is clearly written across the original tintype. He was 20 years old.

come through the Western Virginia campaign under generals McClellan and Rosecrans. General Grant was gathering forces in western Tennessee to cut the armies of the South in two parts. Runkle's unit made a forced march from Virginia to join General Don Carlos Buell in Kentucky. They then continued on to Shiloh. Without any rest they joined the battle, which was loosely contested by both sides, the armies of which were composed of many untried soldiers. It is reported that large groups of men simply wandered back and forth, finding targets of opportunity as they appeared. Runkle and his regiment faced the Washington Battery of New Orleans and led the attack that captured the entire battery. During the counter-attack by the South, Runkle was shot through the feet but continued until he was wounded again with a shot through the face, which caused the major loss of his jaw on the right side, as well as part of his tongue. He was left for dead on the field of battle. Wounds in those days usually resulted in death because of infection.

Whitelaw Reid, Runkle's opponent in the split of the Delta Kappa Epsilon chapter at Miami University, when told of Runkle's death, reported as correspondent of the *Cincinnati Gazette,* "He died a hero. Green grow the grass above his grave." But as the saying goes, "His death was greatly exaggerated." Runkle returned to Ohio and recovered from his wounds. He wore a beard from that time. He was appointed colonel of the 45th Ohio Infantry, reaching the rank of major general in the United States Volunteers in 1865. Along the way, he was on the staff of Governor Tod of Ohio.

Parks during this same time was also involved in fierce fighting. He was in the assault of Battery Robinette, which resulted in great slaughter. Three times the South attacked, only to be repulsed with losses that forced withdrawal. The Union forces moved south in a heated battle, taking Corinth, Mississippi, which had been evacuated by the South. Parks was in the forces that were designated to slow and hold back the Union army. His adversary was General McPherson's division, an extremely formidable foe, which led the pursuit. Parks fought in the attempt to retake Corinth and the Battle at Iuka. In *Battles and Leaders of the Civil War,* General Rosecrans states, "The whole assault was as good fighting on the part of the Confederates as I ever saw."

In his 1896 letter to Runkle, Parks wrote, "I find that General Bowen in his report of the Corinth campaign has done me the honor to class me among those conspicuous for coolness and courage during the action and on the retreat. I, of course, knew what kind of a military record I had, every man does, but felt some reluctance to assure you of my own merit, without support of more disinterested writers.[10]

Following the defeat at Shiloh, the southern forces found it necessary to regroup for further combat. According to Parks's diary, his troops were gathered at Greenwood, Mississippi, on December 29, 1862. They left Greenwood for Vaiden, Mississippi, on January 20, 1863, and were examined at Jackson, Mississippi on February 14, 1863. Parks's unit of Captain Hoole's Mississippi Light Artillery was decimated at Shiloh, and he transferred to the Watson Battery of Louisiana Artillery as a second lieutenant in 1863.

Port Hudson

Port Hudson, Louisiana, a Mississippi River port a few miles north of Baton Rouge, was a key spot on the river together with Vicksburg, Mississippi. These two strongholds of the Confederacy kept the route to the West via the Red River open because they controlled the use of the river. So long as the South held these spots, the Confederacy could not be cut in half.

Why has the battle of Port Hudson been forgotten? In his book *Port Hudson, Confederate Bastion on the Mississippi,* Lawrence Hewitt has listed several reasons. Port Hudson surrendered a few days after Vicksburg surrendered because it then was not needed, as the North had cut the supply lines to and from the West. Grant had captured Vicksburg and Banks had captured Port Hudson. Lee had just lost at Gettysburg. This took away the news value.

Still, several things about this battle were of importance. It was the longest siege of any American force anywhere in history. It was the first time Negro troops were used in battle. They fought but had no training so were not very effective. This led to 180,000 Negros, former slaves, being used by the North in the rear, which freed 180,000 soldiers from duty behind the lines and moved them into battle during the war. If General Banks of the U.S. had been able to break through and advance to Vicksburg then he, as the ranking general, not Grant, would have taken Vicksburg. Maybe he would have become president of the United States after leading all the U.S. forces. Admiral David Farragut commanded the Union gunboats that were attempting to go past Port Hudson on the Mississippi River. Lieutenant Dewey, later Admiral Dewey, who opened Japan to the world, was on one of the ships. Port Hudson is not a national park although recently it has become a state park and may be headed toward becoming part of the Vicksburg National Park. After the war, the river changed course a bit and left the town of Port Hudson, so much so that the town has disappeared. Perhaps these are the reasons the battle remains largely unknown.

The Confederate forces occupied a large bluff along the Mississippi River just as the river makes a 90-degree turn to the left. This made any vessel in the river a fitting target for the cannons of the South. The bluff had been fortified with mounds of dirt and some cotton bales. To encounter the southern forces face-to-face, the North would have to climb a 30-degree hill in the open and without protection. It proved to be an impossible task.

The Watson Battery of Lieutenant Parks Caldwell had six guns. These were cannons, some of which now are part of the regular decorations of the U.S. Military Academy at West Point. Major General Gardner commanded the Confederate defense of Port Hudson. He divided the defense into three commands. The southern wing was commanded by Colonel William Miles, the center by Brigadier General William Beall, and the northern wing by Colonel Isaiah George Washington Steedman. The Watson Battery was divided: four guns were assigned to the center and two guns to the northern wing. These were the guns to which Caldwell was attached. The strength of the Confederates at Port Hudson was about 7,000 men, and the Union army and navy consisted of 30,000 men. Wives, slaves, and others came and went into the area from behind the lines, but at the height of the final weeks of the battle, there was a mass exodus of this support group.

Colonel I. G. W. Steedman is an important figure in this story. He not only was Parks's commander at Port Hudson but also was the surgeon in charge of the hospital at the prison on Johnson's Island, where Parks spent one and a half years. Steedman was born in 1835 in South Carolina, where three generations of his family had lived. In March 1862 he was commanding the heavy batteries of artillery at Island 10 on the Mississippi during the battle of Shiloh and was captured. He had pneumonia at the time and was sent to St. Louis, where he recovered after six weeks. He was then sent to Columbus, Ohio, and paroled for a month within the city limits, after which he was sent for the first time to Johnson's Island. He was a prisoner there until September 1862, when he was exchanged for a matching U.S. Army officer at Vicksburg. He rejoined his regiment and returned to the war.

Steedman was ordered to Port Hudson with his regiment and placed in charge of the flank with the part of the Hudson Battery to which Parks was assigned. After the siege and surrender, he was sent with all of the officers to New Orleans and kept in the Custom House, which is still extant. He returned to Johnson's Island Prison for the second time by way of ship to New York then across land by train to the prison. At the request of the prisoners, he became surgeon in charge of the prison hospital until his second exchange in the spring of 1865.

Watson Battery, with Second Lieutenant Parks Caldwell, arrived at Port Hudson in March 1863 and, as noted, was split into two parts. Parks's two guns were assigned to Colonel Steedman on the northern flank of the defenses with the assignment to destroy the U.S. gunboats that were attempting to run the blockade and go to Vicksburg. The Confederates occupied very high ground and looked down on the river, anticipating the advances of the gunboats. On March 14, 1863, the bombardment from the Union gunboats began. There were seven Union boats that hoped to get past Port Hudson.

The battle of the attempted passage was so intense that the river was covered by smoke, so much so that neither side could see clearly. Farragut decided to attempt to pass at night, which was a wise decision, although only two boats — the *Hartford* with Farragut aboard and the *Albatross*— made the passage. In the long run this was not significant because two vessels could do only a little of what was needed to blockade the Red River. The Confederate batteries were tilted down and fired directly into the remaining five Union vessels. The six hundred artillery rounds that were fired into the vessels disabled the *Richmond*, the *Genesee*, and the *Kineo*. The *Mississippi*, which was the largest and slowest of the Union gunboats, was crippled and sank in the river. Lieutenant Dewey, later the hero of the Spanish American War, was aboard and was one of the last to leave the sinking ship. This river battle was a huge Confederate victory.

On May 21, the Union troops began advancing from the river side and attempted to climb the steep slope up to encounter the Confederates. On May 25, the fight in the woods of Port Hudson began with the "grand charge" on May 27. This was also disastrous for the Union forces. Black troops were used but, although willing, they were poorly trained. The charge on June 14 was labeled as the "greatest charge of all," but it again ended with the repulsing of the Union troops. Had the Union forces examined the terrain, they would have realized the futility of the attack. At about this same time, on June 12, the *Albatross* lay at anchor in the Mississippi River, having shelled the town of St. Francisville upriver from Port Hudson. An incident occurred that is emblematic of the strangeness

First Lieutenant Caldwell after the Battle of Shiloh April 7, 1862, where Captain Hoole's Mississippi Light Artillery had been decimated and at some point, Caldwell transferred to the Watson Battery of the Louisiana artillery. The troops were at Greenwood, Meridian, and Jackson, Mississippi, before being transferred to Port Hudson, Louisiana. They arrived in early March 1863 at Port Hudson, Louisiana, becoming part of the longest siege in American military history, ending July 9, 1863.

of this war between "brothers." A boat approached the shore with a flag of truce from the *Albatross*. Lieutenant Commander John E. Hart of the *Albatross* had taken his life in a "fit of delirium." He had been a Freemason and had requested that he be given a Masonic burial. The request brought a response that there were several Masons there in the town, and there were also several on the *Albatross*. It was agreed that he would be buried in the cemetery of Grace Episcopal Church, where his body rests today. Appropriate Masonic services were conducted by the Masons present. The officers of the *Albatross* and a troop of Marines were present from the ship. After the services the Union forces returned to the ship, and the war continued.

The siege also continued, but the Union had apparently decided that it would not be worth losing men to attempt the capture of Port Hudson. The Confederates were down to eating rats and mule meat or other available material but showed no sign of capitulation. On July 4, 1863, Vicksburg surrendered, making Port Hudson of no consequence in defending the river and Vicksburg. On July 8, 1863, a flag of truce was raised and cessation of firing occurred. Officially, on July 9, James Parks Caldwell became a prisoner of war. All of the officers at Port Hudson were sent to New Orleans on July 15 and placed in the police jail, which was the Custom House on Canal Street. It is a large structure of several floors, and Parks was kept on the ground floor. It was not equipped to be a prison, however, and the sanitary facilities were almost nonexistent. The men were paroled to the city of New Orleans during the day, where they probably found help from its citizens.

Nine days after the surrender of Port Hudson and while a prisoner in New Orleans, Parks wrote a lengthy letter to his sister. Written in pencil at the top of the letter in his sister's handwriting is the word "smuggled." Apparently he had someone mail the letter so it would not appear to have come from him. That letter, "In Durance Vile," appears in this book before the diary itself.

After the War

Parks was lovingly received at home. After a recovery period from the ravages of prison life, he pondered his future. Judge Clark and his wife Lottie Moon Clark had moved to New York City, and Ginnie was in Virginia with Mollie, her older sister. He journeyed back to Panola County, Mississippi. He found plantation life in shambles, with many men killed in the war and no slaves. Reconstruction was intolerable to him, and his being an ex–Confederate officer was a problem. Still, the Palmetto Academy was reestablished and he served as its principal from 1865 to 1866. His fine background working with Judge Clark allowed him to progress in his law studies, and in a letter to his family in Ohio on November 25, 1866, he reported, "I was admitted to the bar yesterday in Panola County, Mississippi."

Parks had a small, unrewarding law practice and a bit of income from writing for the newspapers, but he felt there was no hope of success for him in the South. He had always wanted to be a "western man," and he decided that now was the time. He wrote (in Latin) to Judge Clark in New York, to say he was arriving there on his way west. His old friends greeted him warmly. They had secured a berth for him on the ship Santiago de Cuba sailing for California in June 1868.

A newspaper clipping saved by Caldwell's family is self-explanatory. It is the sort of prank that Caldwell did — of course he is the one who is writing his own recommendation. It was sent to a publication, but there is no record of whether or not it was published.

A Touching Ode,

The following lines, composed by a young Confederate officer during his incarceration as a prisoner of war on Johnson's Island, in the winter of 1863, are too good to be lost. A copy of them was furnished from memory to a friend by the author, while here, a few days since, on his way to California, and they are now made public without consultation with him. They were written by James P. Caldwell, Esq., a young member of the Mississippi bar, whose brilliant talents, united to a character every way estimable, will not meet their due reward, if they fail to secure him, in his new home, the same high regard and esteem in which he is held by the friends he has left. Mr. Caldwell has sailed for San Francisco. Our friends in California will find in him a gentleman of high qualities, in every respect. Throughout the whole of the recent struggle, the cause he espoused had no more honest, devoted, or gallant defender. A thorough scholar, soldier, and gentleman, may success attend him!

Parks was admitted to the bar in Tennessee, Texas, and California. The 1870 U.S. Census for San Bernardino County, California, lists "James Caldwell, 29 years old, profession, lawyer." He practiced law for several years in San Bernardino and Los Angeles, interspersing his legal practice with literary work and teaching. He wrote that he was trying the California climate to see if it agreed with his rheumatism. He did not develop a sustaining law practice, but a letter of recommendation indicates that he did teach, probably in classical languages or writing, at a collegiate level.

While in California, Parks wrote several articles for Bret Harte's *Overland Monthly*. The table of contents lists some of the other authors: Mark Twain, Bret Harte, and others distinguished by M.D., Prof., and Rev., as well as a name that surely must be a pen name, Socrates Hyacinth. Parks wrote an article published in the June 1869 issue that appears to be typical of his humor shown earlier in his school and diary writings; it is a tongue-in-cheek article about an insignificant event but written as classical criticism. The article is entitled, "Some Account of a Great Western Poet" and praises the banjo song "Lament of Joseph Bowers." In the article, Parks discusses each word and line of the song, even comparing it to "Paradise Lost" and other great works, using several references from Vergil's *Aeneid*. He stated in the article, "The words derive additional grandeur from their very simplicity and directness" and then quoted the first verse:

> My name is Jo Bowers,
> I have a brother Ike;
> I come from old Missouri,
> And all the way from Pike.

Toward the end of the article, he expanded his argument and quoted from the "Dictionary of American Antiquities," prepared three thousand years hence by some learned pundits and, after seducing the reader into accepting a learned article, broadsides the reader with very funny extrapolations. (See Appendix.)

Caldwell was in his 30s when he was editor of a newspaper in San Bernadino and contributing author to the *Overland Monthly*. He lived in California most of this time. He returned to Mississippi about 1875 and settled on the Gulf Coast in 1888.

In February 1870, Parks published "The Rationale of Slang" in *Overland Monthly*. He wrote, "I have termed Slang the illustration of history" and discussed the influx of terms and phrases from Roman and Greek works, Chaucer, and the languages of other countries. He concluded, "Great is the power of words, and when the power works evil, or the idea is mean and sensual, let the word be unhesitatingly condemned; but when either a new word, or a new application of an old, increases the facility of expression, let us use it, remembering that all precedents were once innovations." (See Appendix.)

Another article in the July 1870 issue was entitled "Through the Lower Coast Counties," and related the tale of travel with a companion on horseback from the foothills of the Santa Cruz Range and beyond. The route that they rode on their "plug" horses made for a heroic venture of about four hundred miles from just below San Francisco to Los Angeles. The article gave a picture of the country, stressing its beauty, loneliness, and character. He colored the article with "a pack of dogs, palpable of the 'yallar' variety," adding that "we consulted our friend Ishmael, who had encamped near by, like a land-

Noah, 'with his wife and his sons, and his sons' wives,' and many varieties of living things." He referred to the "seventeen million coyotes" he heard one night and concluded with, "Not here shall I essay to describe the impressions which brighter weather brought me of the City of the Angels, as she sits, dowered with wealth and decked with marvelous beauty, throned amid her groves and gardens, undoubted queen of all the southern land." (See Appendix.)

Parks had a facility for language and a soul that appreciated beauty. This, coupled with his knowledge of classics and history and punctuated with humor, give one pleasure in reading these writings even now.

Apparently, it was the practice of colleges to grant advanced degrees to their graduates who had achieved success in their endeavors in business. The archives of Miami University have the following letter from Parks to Professor R. H. Bishop, professor of Latin languages and literature, in answer to a missive from Professor Bishop:

San Bernardino, Cal.
Mar. 5th 1870

Prof. R. H. Bishop,
Miami University:

Dear Sir,

Yours of 7th ult. has been received. I thank you for the early attention you gave my note, as well as for the kind inquiries you make. I should like very much to receive the second degree and believe myself entitled to it on the terms you mention; certainly, I deserve it more than I did the first.

1. Continued study after graduation: I diligently kept up my studies — both classical and literary — until the breaking out of the war. Indeed I commenced studying almost immediately after my graduation. Since the surrender I have resumed the habit. I will endeavor to furnish such evidence as may be required to support my statements, of whatever kind it be. I believe I can write a Latin thesis on any given subject of which I know anything <u>in English</u>, and would prefer doing so if any of my classmates obtained his degree by presenting such a voucher. I do not say that the Latinity might not be somewhat canine, but it would evince study.

2. Activity and usefulness in business: Since '57 I have been practicing it a little, and have taught long (some six years in all); the rest of the time I wasted in the war — on the losing side, as you doubtless know. And here, Professor, <u>puce tua dixerim</u> ["if I may speak frankly"], in your opinion such discontinuance of <u>civil</u> business would be at all likely to prejudice my case before a literary senate, I do not wish this to be considered an application or preparatory step thereto. I hope you will pardon what I have just written, but it is redeemed from the charge of being preposterous by events, which <u>have</u> occurred. I know that during those years I was removed from opportunity for study, — that, in fact I was scarcely reminded of literary pursuits (save on one occasion of the Horatian maxim "<u>non cuivis contingit adire Corinthum</u>"

["everybody doesn't get a chance to go to Corinth"], but I also know that any objection on this score would arise rather from the nature of my employment during the interval than from its occurrence.

3. As to the application to the Faculty: please tell me whether any special form is required or not. I would wish now to apply through you — unless you think the Faculty may be influenced by considerations arising from the 'war,' 'rebellion' or quodcunque if dici jus fasque est ["whatever is just and proper to call it"]. If this can be considered an application, I desire it to be so. Lastly, the fee: I enclose a post office order for the money. In case either of failure or of your deeming it inexpedient for me to apply, please give the money to some educational charity — any which may need it. I do not wish it returned.

Please excuse my rambling and somewhat redundant letter. I am highly sensible of your kindness and grateful for your good wishes, and shall now endeavor to reply to your inquiries, so far as they have not been answered already.

I have not settled here: on the contrary I expect to leave during the coming summer: I am as yet not quite certain whether I shall go either to San Jose or Los Angeles, however. I have been teaching since coming to Cal.—on acc't of the difficulty of commencing at the bar without sufficient means to enable one to wait—but expect to resume the practice when I leave this place. I am not married.

My success in life has been moderate: I have not made a fortune, yet I have always been able to live comfortably and enjoy as much luxury as is good for one who cannot afford more. But I fear I have trespassed too much upon your time already, and will therefore desist. I remain, Professor, with renewed thanks and assurances of sincere respect.

Very truly yours,
James P. Caldwell.

On June 29, 1857, the faculty minutes of Miami University record that J. P. Caldwell was nominated for the first degree along with other classmates. The second degree referred to in the preceding letter apparently was not granted, for the 1910 Miami University Catalog lists James Parks Caldwell, Lawyer, Biloxi, Mississippi, with an A.B. degree, admitted to the bar in 1866, in California from 1867 to 1875, and then in Mississippi, where he lived the rest of his life.

Another example of his literary work was introduced rather mysteriously by J. C., who might well have been Parks himself. There is no record of Parks being in New York at that time. For the full story and Latin poem, "Admuscam Molestam," as well as a translation, see the following chapter, "Caldwell the Classicist."

In 1873, *The Union,* a San Bernardino newspaper announced the establishment of a rival, local paper. *The Union* stated, "The services of J. P. Caldwell, a gentleman of rare culture and literary attainments, and an accomplished and graceful writer, have been secured as editor-in-chief." *The Union* further prophesied warm journalistic times in the city during an oncoming campaign.[11]

After his time in California, Caldwell returned to his home state of Ohio, where he edited several papers in small towns near his birthplace. Sometime around 1875, however, he finally settled where his heart was: Mississippi. He again did editorial work in Jackson, Mississippi, with an old friend of Confederate days.

A letter responding to an invitation to a fraternity reunion was found in Sigma Chi fraternity archives. It was written on March 27, 1881.

Parks wrote, "I have a knack of hoping. Memory leads me back to the long ago, when life was fresh and all was fair before me as it is for my young fraternity brothers. I will not be able to attend the reunion due to my health. I have been laid up with rheumatism for some time. Six weeks this time. Seven would have been worse." It seems that he had spells of illness and remissions, which are characteristic of the condition.

The next letter, from Louisiana, carries no explanation of why he was there. He must have been involved in some legal practice from Mississippi, since there is no record of his being licensed in Louisiana. It is a poignant letter of consolation to his mother on receiving news of his brother's death. (Benjamin Rush Caldwell had died in Little Rock, Arkansas, in February 1883.)

> Loreauville, Iberia Parish, La.
> March, 27th 1883
>
> My very dear Mother:
>
> I have been thinking of you all day, and of this letter — which I know I ought to write because you expect it, though I can say little to cheer and nothing to console you. Death has at last invaded our family circle, so long spared, and brought bereavement which makes other evils light. It is something, that his coming was so long delayed. The news of brother Rush's death was startling to me and made me feel more sensibly than I ever did before, the uncertainty of life and the transitory nature of all earthly things. I have often thought of my own death but have never dreamed of his — yet he has gone from us, and I not only remain but am physically stronger than I have been for years. This I know you will rejoice to hear, as your recent loss must cause you to feel greater anxiety about your other children, especially those who are so far away. How I wish I could talk to you instead of writing! It has long been my firm resolve to see you as soon as it may be possible, and up to a few days ago I had hoped it might become so at some time not very far distant. At present, however, I am again uncertain as to my future. I do not like to think, much less to write much on this subject. My health is good, my rheumatism not having been very severe at any time since I came here, where I have been

well and kindly cared for. I shall not venture to leave until all danger from the damp spring weather is over, and when I do go I shall not leave you long in ignorance of my movements. I ought, I know, to have written oftener than I have but have had so little to write that you would have cared to hear over and above the mere fact of my health. I shall enclose in this a likeness — taken about two weeks ago by one of the boys here who has a camera; everyone says it a good one, and it will give you an idea of my present appearance.

Give my best love to all at home, especially to Father — of whom and yourself I have thought almost continually for many days. I know you both are patient and hopeful, but you have so many troubles to bear that you must require all your fortitude. All my hope for the future — and I still cherish a little — centers on you but hope is a slight thing and I sometimes think that even love, like faith, "without works, is dead," or might as well be.

With love to all, I am as ever and more than ever your
Affectionate Son,
Parks.

The following is a letter of recommendation for Parks, who taught in California when he sojourned there. Apparently he did so at the college level, since he carried the title of professor in this letter of recommendation.

The Christian Advocate
Official Organ of the M. E. Church, South
Office of O. P. FITZGERALD, D.D., EDITOR

Nashville, Tenn. May 1, 1883

To Whom It May Concern:

Having known Prof. J. P. Caldwell as an educator in California, it gives me <u>sincere pleasure</u> to bear testimony to his professional fidelity and ability, and to his character as a gentleman of unblemished honor, culture and refinement. He stands high in my esteem as a man and as a teacher. As Superintendent of Public Instruction of California during the term of his professional service in that State, I had good opportunity to learn what was his worth and standing.

Very Respectfully
O. P. Fitzgerald

The following letter was published in the Joseph Cookman Nate's *History of Sigma Chi Fraternity*. President Jefferson Davis was then living in Beauvoir, on the Mississippi coast. Caldwell was writing for the newspaper in Jackson, Mississippi, at the time and sent his diaries to Davis for the former president's perusal. Davis's comments expressed his personal feelings and values twenty-nine years after the Civil War.

Beauvoir, Miss.
June 15, 1885

J. P. Caldwell, Esq.
My Dear Sir,

I this day mail to your address the Diaries which you kindly gave me the opportunity to examine. To me, as to others who, like you have had prison experience, they revive buried memories, and the value of such exact records will increase as years roll away, unless, which God forbid, future generations shall prove recreant to the principles which our Fathers established and we faithfully strove to maintain.

Accept my thanks for the consolatory manner in which you call my attention to the political dawn.

I have trusted, as you do, in the power of truth and as Job said of his Maker, "though He slay me yet will I trust Him."

With sincere regard and my heart's best wishes for your welfare, I am

Yours faithfully,
Jefferson Davis

When Jefferson Davis died on December 9, 1889, one of the most circulated tributes to his memory was written by Parks as an editorial for the *Commonwealth* of Jackson, Mississippi.

In 1886, there was much land fraud occurring in Wyoming. Lawyers were hired by the government to go to Wyoming and investigate the situation. Parks was hired by President Grover Cleveland to perform this mission. In a letter to his family in December 1886, he wrote, "We saved about 65,000 acres for the state." In March 1888, Parks was still in Wyoming, where he was employed in the U.S. Land Office and also as editor of the *Cheyenne Daily Leader*. He reported on the events of the railroad going through Wyoming to the West. At that time, coal was being mined for the railroad but it was difficult to get miners. It was found that Chinese men would work for a pittance, trying to save money to bring their families to America. He wrote a story about this, reporting that ten thousand Chinese men were miners for the railroad.

In 1888, Parks again returned to Mississippi and began the practice of law in Mississippi City, Gulfport, and Biloxi. He wrote that this was his last move. He said the climate was the best of any he had experienced. He made a detailed study and record of the land titles of south Mississippi, which had been a part of west Florida and under Spanish rule before 1810. Consequently the original land grants were in Spanish, but this proved to be no problem for Caldwell. He became the recognized authority in legal circles for his work on Spanish-language titles. He served as consulting counsel in litigation arising from the titles, especially after the Spanish American War. Later, when the abstracts of Harrison County were organized, Caldwell's work served as the basis for the county records.

Runkle, Parks's roommate in college, wrote the following in his tribute to his former classmate in 1896: "Caldwell is naturally a literary man, and the thing to be regretted about his military service is that the labor and trials of war changed the course of his career. His articles written for magazines and other periodicals are marked with the stamp of ability.— He is an old-fashioned democrat, but he is not a politician; is a supporter of the present administration, and an inveterate enemy of the spoils system.— He holds that Gen. Robert E. Lee and Gen. George Henry Thomas were the great soldiers of the war."

Parks wrote to his sister in January 1898, when he had occupied a small house just beyond the beach of the Gulf of Mexico. He said, "I have suffered more with cold weather the past few days than any three — Johnson's Island excepted. Levi [his old and loyal black servant] wilted with the first blast of cold and didn't appear for a week, during which time I carried coal for my little house here on the gulf. I was beginning to lose heart a bit under these small miseries." He was then fifty-seven years old and burdened with more than moderate rheumatoid arthritis, especially in his hands. Writing or carrying anything was difficult.

On March 25, 1898, another letter to his sister gave his opinion on the developing Spanish American War. He wrote, "I cannot bring myself to believe there's going to be a war. Spain had done nothing so far — unless we accept as true the wild assertion that she is responsible for the Maine incident — or accident." This is an interesting observation from a veteran and experienced editor of newspapers.

On June 1, 1898, he wrote, "General Ben Runkle [his old roommate] kept writing for 'material' but I referred him to my Confederate Veteran Dicking Samp at Sardis, Mississippi for my war record. It establishes my presence on the line. Runkle certainly did his work in a very kindly spirit which I appreciate."

He continued to write his sister:

Mississippi City, Miss. _____ 189__

I have a lot of old "Confederate Veterans" [a publication concerning those who had served in the Confederate Army], I have gathered them together and only wait until I shall have glanced over them and perhaps made marginal notes before sending. They contain a good deal of "rot," but some history. I shall send by express, soon after the "warm weather" shall have been with us for a reasonable time.

By the way, this date [March 17] is memorable. Thirty-six years ago tonight, the frigate Mississippi was destroyed in her attempt to pass the batteries at Port Hudson. Lieut. Geo. Dewey was her executive officer and I am heartily glad that he escaped on that occasion. <u>We</u> were stationed above, and only got a parting shot at the <u>Hartford</u> which led the column, and which got safely past us all the way due to the intelligent valor of Farragut, whom the later Dewey has taken for a pattern.

While I am at it, and have made the allusion, I may as well give you an account of my experiences of that night.

We had been ordered inside the works for the first time and late in the night reached the place designated for us. Lieutenant Barlow — a very gallant officer and in many respects the most efficient I ever served under (now Commander of the Confederate Home at Higginsville, Mo. having come out of the war a field officer) was in command. The bivouac was forward in the dark, pieces stationed, not parked regularly, and the men generally held on the alert. Barlow and I — with our heads resting on our respective saddles, and smoking our pipes — were lying before a smoldering fire. The enemy had been firing mortar shells for ten or twelve days but we were out of range and it didn't matter much anyhow.

Now, however, all at once something broke loose and the air was filled with streaks of light and bursts of flame. The enemy had been trying to steal by and had been discovered and fired upon. Their broadsides in reply were to us the first note of warning. Barlow jumped to his feet ordering "Boots & Saddles"— I don't remember what I did but a few minutes afterwards when we were all "hitched up" & galloping to the front I said, "Mr. Barlow, where are we going?" His answer was, "To the bank, somebody will show us where." Sure enough, before we had got there or near there, we met a staff officer with orders for the battery. Had we waited his arrival, the whole thing would have been over without our participation. Barlow, soldier-like, had moved toward the firing, without orders, and trusted to meet them (the orders). I don't think we hurt anybody that night, as the Hartford was nearly past before our beacon (the other side of the river) was lighted, and she, with Farragut on board, escaped with small hurt. But the Mississippi was burned, most of her officers & crew escaping, but they lost that night more men than the whole U.S. Navy has lost during the Spanish War. I wonder if Dewey happens to think of it, to-night.

With love to all, affectionately your brother,

J. P. Caldwell

The following is the heading on the stationery used by Caldwell when writing the next letter:

COUNSELOR
SOLICITOR
CONVEYANCER
Has a complete abstract compiled by him of all the records of Harrison County, affecting title to real estate.
J. P. CALDWELL

Mississippi City, Miss., October 8, 1900

My Dear Sister, I have several times been at the point of commencing a letter to you but each time have procrastinated because I really did not know how to write concerning my physical condition — of which you would expect me to write something or you would proceed to infer the worse. Not that I yet know but I have a well grounded belief that I am better, after nearly a month's fluctuation or alternation of indications and conditions. I would be for some days convinced that I was on the eve of a "spell" when the alarming expectations would disappear for a short time, only to return again and again to become less violent: they seem

[The bottom of this page is missing. On the back of the above part, the letter is finished as follows:]

I shall write again in the course of a few days and to Beppy soon — with love to all I am

Affectionately yours,
J. P. Caldwell

I regret that Joe's letter has somehow got soiled — I had it with a lot of others on the mantelpiece in my bedroom. Excuse me for not having been more careful.

[Part of a letter, page 2, seems to belong at this place.]

... sizes and sorts, which seek a light the moment it appears, on this account, I usually go to bed "in darkness and, leaving door and windows open, enjoy a refreshing sleep."

I haven't sent you any "Veterans" [*Confederate Veterans*], since the receipt of your letter, though I have a number on hand, because I would like to make comment contemporaneously, and besides I suppose you have some still on hand unread. By the way, let me call your attention to the character of Sam Davis — it is the finest, greatest and best, developed by the war.

[Another partial letter of the same time:]

Besides, I feel sure that you will have said the right thing, as you have some intuition that way.

I work almost daily among the records and shall have my abstract down to date before the evil days come when no rheumatic man can work without serious discomfort. Only within the last three days have I realized that summer is over, but the aboriginal variety may abide with us for some weeks. There has been no indication of frost (there being no question this year none is anxiously looked for,) nor have fires been kindled yet in sitting or sleeping rooms, but for three nights past I have had to crawl under the blankets before morning. In the daytime the sun warms all.

Thanks for the tea, which I like very much though I have concluded to drink that beverage more sparingly. While not so plainly injurious as coffee, I fear the effect of continuous use and intend to limit myself to a cup when I get up in the morning. It had been my habit for many years to make coffee as soon as I rose, and unless I get something hot, feel badly. Tea mitigates this feeling, though I shall not soon grow fond of it on the ground of its own intrinsic merit. It stimulates, however, "cheers" is just the right word.

I have laid out three Veterans to send you, but find my mucilage all dried up and will, unless I forget, take them to the Court House with me tomorrow. I have ascertained that one stamp (2 cents) will furnish the right postage for three. I will give those next to be sent a cursory turning over to-night and note any suggestions or explanations needed and give you any possible benefit desirable therefrom.

I am almost persuaded that Sam Davis was — and is — the hero of the war. Certainly he was the only approach, I can recall, to the character of martyr — a word generally misapplied by glib tongues & reckless pens. Davis could have saved his life at the sacrifice of something better.

Sam Davis, Caldwell's unparalleled hero, was a young Confederate private and scout in the Tennessee infantry. On November 20, 1863, he was gathering information on Union troop movements toward Chattanooga, Tennessee, when he was stopped by two Union troops in Confederate uniforms and exposed. He had papers in his boots. He was court-martialed and condemned to death by hanging. The Union general offered him his freedom if he would reveal the source of his information. Sam Davis replied, "If I had a thousand lives, I would give them all here before I would betray a friend or the confidence of my informer." This exemplifies the fidelity of Parks to his vows and beliefs.

Summing Up

It was difficult to keep up with the activities of his siblings. In a letter to his sister, he wrote, "If any news comes from Brother Joe in Alaska or from our little Presbyterian Missionary cousins in China, transmit to me at once."

His interest in politics remained keen, as evidenced by this letter on November 4, 1900: "I shall still vote for Bryan. Am reading 'With Fire and Sword' by Sienkiemoz (which for convenience, I call Ferguson)."

His sister announced that she would visit him, and Caldwell replied:

Mississippi City, Miss., Jan. 15, 1901

My Dear Sister,

Seldom into my bleak and barren life has greater gladness come than when I received Beppy's letter answering that you would soon be with me, and abide for a time. I know I shall greatly enjoy your visit and will do all in my power to render it a pleasure for you as well, so far as the conditions permit. These are not very favorable, as you know. There is a pleasant boarding place almost within a stone's throw of my office, but its mistress is temporarily absent. Mrs. Ramsay — wife of our Sheriff — will receive you and lives now a little farther, and is about to remove to the place formerly occupied by Mrs. Davis, which Mr. Ramsay has bought and had repaired, the need of which action you may remember. My own little house affords no fitting quarters at least in winter.

I fear I shall have to go to Jackson about the 21st to remain a very few days. I shall try to obviate the necessity, but the chance is that I must go, to be back here by the 25th of this and other matters I shall write later.

The commencement of the new century was unpropitious to me. I had swollen feet & swollen hands and was not altogether well myself. We have had no cold weather yet but much damp, and "fog & mist" which are worse. Within the past few days matters have gradually mended until in to-day we have had glorious sunshine and spring weather without a flaw, fire needed only at night and now as I write the room is too warm. I have not had a pain today and am writing with a pen, something I have not tried before for several weeks, except just to sign my name. I may not have rheumatism again for months and that is the most painful of my maladies.

I would like to have you write me something as to your proposed route, that is, by what road. The L&N [Louisville and Nashville] would be more direct but not to be preferred to the Q&C [Queen & Crescent] if other advantages offer as I can meet you in N.O. [New Orleans] There should be a reduction of cost in Southward travel at this season.

I have been working in the Clerk's Office most of the day and am writing this just after supper, and Sam will be here shortly to take it to the mail by tonight (10 P.M.) train. I hear his slow & stately approach and hasten to close, with love to all. I shall answer Sister Ida's letter tomorrow, and will write you again in a few days (this time, sure).

Affectionately yours,
J. P. Caldwell

He wrote on September 29, 1901,

Lamentable assassination of President McKinley was a great shock. This ought to call public attention to the urgent need of suppressive legislation against enemies of the human race, which proclaim their murderous doctrines of anarchy. Murder as a cult is entitled to no constitutional privileges.

I was disappointed at not being able to attend the Confederate reunion. I was to have made the address. It is consoling to think that nothing is likely to prevent my attendance on Haley's comet next month. (It has already put in a dim appearance; and its presage of wrath begins to affect the colored mind.)

My friends, Mrs. Davis and Miss Winnie with Judge Kimbrough recently came to consult me re. the abstract on Beauvoir [the last home of Confederate president Jefferson Davis, only a short distance from where Parks lived on the Gulf Coast].

On May 11, 1902, he wrote, "I was able, by great and somewhat painful effort, after weeks of work, to get the Beauvoir abstract in shape. This is my last service to the Confederacy, making it a Confederate Home."

In 1903 Parks became bankruptcy referee for the Southern District of Mississippi, a position he held until 1912. His work was reported to be fair and thorough by all he served.

In 1905, at the fiftieth anniversary of the founding of the Sigma Chi fraternity, the four living founders met with the convention at Miami University, where Parks made a speech about the three founders who were dead. Perhaps it serves a summation of the values that controlled his life.

> Here have we met, my brethren, to celebrate the jubilee of a great Fraternity, whose principles and purposes we hold in reverent honor, and in whose progress and prosperity we feel a common pride; rejoicing at the lofty place

attained and held by Sigma Chi among the moral and intellectual forces which "make for righteousness" and, all unseen of men, exert far-reaching influences for the betterment of the social and political world. For each of us knows that, in the mind of the eager-hearted youth who for the first time assumes its blazon on his breast, the White Cross of our order becomes at once a shrine for the culture of that love to which both Paul and Plato have lent the music of their words — an emblem of self-respecting manhood, and a perpetual monitor inculcating, as the sole basis of honor, the lesson of truth, of courtesy, and of courage.

Four of us, surviving founders, have proudly come at your behest to share the general triumph, and to receive as well the highest mark of honor which one of us, at least, has yet attained. It should be noted, too, that we severally come from diverse and distant regions of this broad, beautiful, and abounding land of ours: from the utmost continental West, "where rolls the Oregon and hears" far other sounds than his own dashing, long since lost in the multitudinous murmur of industry and trade; from the capital city of the greatest republic of all time, where the glad Potomac glides along to mingle unvexed waters with the advancing tide; from the sinuous shore of the Mare Clausum of the western world, where gentle breezes ripple into infinite laughter, or angry storms arouse to fatal fury the many-tinted waters of the Mexican sea; and (dean of the founders, still abiding near the home of his youth) from the mighty commonwealth within whose boundaries all four of us were born, and in whose progress and promise we must ever hope to feel both interest and pride.

We were seven, we founders; but not all of us are here to greet you in the flesh today; three noble brothers have gone from us. Whither? or where? are questions to answer which would transcend the ever-expanding and nearly infinite limits of human knowledge. With the little cottage girl who utterly fails to understand why her brothers, under the sea or under the sod, should not still be reckoned as of her kindred, seven — I for one — feel deep sympathy. Where dwell the soul of the departed we know not, nor shall know until we shortly join them in the world beyond. Enough that underneath us all are the everlasting arms of the Eternal God.

The place selected for this reunion, only to a less degree than the occasion,

This is the last known photograph of Caldwell, taken on June 28, 1905, at the celebration of the fiftieth year of the founding of the Sigma Chi Fraternity. He was 64 years old. Four of the seven founders were still alive. The speech he gave shows his keen mind. He suffered from years of rheumatoid arthritis and died in 1912 at 71 years of age.

awakens tender memories of the days of old. This venerable seat of learning, pioneer of education in all the mighty West, looks back upon a storied past, rich in the achievements of her sons in every field of effort known to man. We, of her class of 1857, come back to "Old Miami," not to stand as casual strangers within her gates, but as grateful and loving sons, acknowledging the potent force and abiding effect of the training here received; though returning to assist in the commemoration of an incident, not the most notable in her history, but to us the dearest, associated so intimately with the best and brightest phases of our college life. Our Alma Mater has been the nursing mother of statesmen, soldiers, and patriots, whose names are interwoven in the earlier history of our country, and whose fame has descended as a common heritage of pride to us their successors. Of old, during the first period of her career, and in her most high and palmy state, and for a time much shorter in duration than the golden age of Pericles, she gave to the Republic more devoted sons than gave the Academic Grove to the City of the Violet Crown.

This reunion of classmates after half a century is of itself and event so unusual that a feeling of wonder mingles with the memories it recalls, and a certain sense of unreality pervades the mind:

Can such things be, and overcome us Like a summer's cloud, without our special wonder?

That this happy meeting should have been promoted by the Fraternity and take place, as it were, in its visible presence, is another overpowering fact, thrilling the heart as with a new and strange emotion of exulting joy, while setting in sharp contrast that weak beginning which we celebrate today. I almost persuade myself, however, that the splendid loyalty to the fraternal idea, which I have noted as characteristic of Sigma Chi, has given to its founders a more exalted place than they deserve. Not to them only, nor even chiefly, have been due the amazing growth and wonderful progress of our fair Brotherhood, and its magnificent position in the fraternity world — results too marvelous for me to recognize as the natural outcome of any work in which I have consciously borne part. True it is that without the sowers there had been no hope of harvest; but this abundant fruitage betokens later efforts, when ours had gone to waste amid the turmoil of troublous times. Those who came after had a harder task, out of which their native energy has wrought a notable success. Men of constructive intellect, it was theirs to conserve the spirit by a radical change of form, to repair and remodel the crumbling foundations, and to rear thereon the stately structure, which we now behold. By historical analogy, the Declaration was our part, while they have brought the Constitution, without which all results of patriotic achievement had been lost in the petty bickering of internal strife. The eminently practical system which these master-minds devised exactly fits the purposes in view, leaving wide liberty to the individual chapter, while bringing the Fraternity into an effective union, at once harmonious and strong, and based upon the very principles to which our country largely owes its greatness and its power. It is pleasing to reflect that two of our original number (foremost among us and leaders from the beginning)—the lamented Jordan, and Runkle here present—were privileged to share the honors of our renaissance. As the least active of the founders, I tender my homage to the real makers of Sigma Chi, content for my own part, having witnessed the planting of the acorn, to rest rejoicing in the far-thrown shadow of the mighty oak.

Fifty years ago, for all its wide expanse and <u>ocean</u> boundaries, our country had scarcely attained the rank of a second-rate power, and the nation, in the wider sense which now obtains, had not yet been born. Instead there were jealous sections, snarling at each other, each sneering at the other's worth and boastful of its own. One might almost say that it was but the Saxon heptarchy writ large. For more than a generation the highest hope of statesmanship had been to postpone the evil day, the swift approach of which only the willfully blind could fail to see. It came at last, with the bursting into flower of "the blood-red blossom of war with its heart of fire." Then followed four eventful years of storm and stress, which, whatever else they brought, have left a common heritage of valor as an abiding inspiration through all coming time. My brothers here and I viewed the shield from opposite sides, each equally sure that his vision was clear; and quite as sure am I that not one of us would be willing, were it possible, to undo his action in the past. At the end, the greatness of the victor brought some solace to defeat. The great soldier who led the conquering hosts set a bright example, which might have become the rule, had not a mad assassin stilled the kindly heart that prompted those noble words at Gettysburg. But purblind Fate had other things in store, and it appears to have been foreordained that a descent into hell should precede the resurrection. Both the war and the worse that followed have passed into history, and are remembered without bitterness; and I am glad to know that the most faithful upon the defeated side have brought back to the flag of their fathers the same loyalty with which they followed the starry cross, remembered now with tender pride, but without sorrow, and certainly without a shadow of regret.

Those evils which always follow in the wake of war have gradually been dispelled, until their influence is scarcely felt in public life. The latter half of the period under consideration has seen such marked improvement in popular ideals of right that there seems reason to hope for the coming of a time when parties shall be held to their proper function of passing upon questions concerning which good men honestly differ, without attempt to stifle conscience where all honest men agree. It is something for Americans to be proud of, that twice in one generation, and almost of their own accord, the people have honored themselves by calling to the highest office men of widely different political views, each of whom has deserved and received the support of patriotic citizens irrespective of party lines. That public office is a public trust is no statement of party creed; and it is not on party grounds that faith and sympathy go out to the great American who is even now striving to put in practice his gospel of a "square deal." A succession of such men would place the country on a lofty plane—"great, strong men, men who can rule, and dare not lie."

Fifty years hence it is more than probable that another and greater assembly will gather here to commemorate the centennial of Sigma Chi,[12] and it occurs to me as not impossible that among the younger brothers attending this convention some may happily survive to be present on that occasion. There is more than one whose expectancy of life is great enough to justify a further look into the future, and the number of whose years falls easily within the age-limit of the founders when the Fraternity began. Through them I would transmit a greeting, with a hand-clasp, to a generation yet unborn, with an expression of fervent hope that they may look back upon a career less checkered than that which we have seen; that the Brotherhood may have attained, by the accretion of like to like, the utmost growth consistent with its ancient maxim, Non quot, sed qualis; and that the great Republic, her peace secured by floating battlements, shall have long established throughout her broad domain the absolute supremacy of law.

Parks selected the following motto to precede his "Reminiscences," which he gave at the fiftieth anniversary of Sigma Chi and have been included in preceding pages. It is placed here to give his thoughts on his part in the war. It was taken from Ovid and was an amazingly apt sentiment for him to choose as he recollected his thoughts about what he had endured.

Quis enim sua proelia victus
Commemorare velit? referam tamen ordine; nec tam
Turpe fuit vinci, quam contendisse decorum est:
Magnaque dat nobis tantus solacia victor.—Ovid, *Metamorphoses* IX, 4–7
   (*Who would care to relate how he was conquered in battle? Still, I will tell all in order. Neither was it so much a disgrace to be conquered as it is an honor to have striven in the first place and the fact that the victor was so great gives us great consolation.*)

By this time, Parks was living at the Kennedy Hotel in Biloxi, near the railroad station, so he could travel along the Mississippi coast easily. After the Sigma Chi centennial in 1905, many persons made the pilgrimage to see him. Visitors to the hotel always sought out "Judge" Caldwell, as he was known, finding him friendly, courteous, and extremely witty. He was always full of reminiscences. He remarked that he was never a judge but had once been introduced as bishop, a title he might prefer. Among those who came to see him was Whitelaw Reid, his fellow student at Miami University and a correspondent for a newspaper at the time of the battle of Shiloh. Caldwell and Reid spent several days enjoying themselves. One of the most prominent men in Mississippi was quoted as having said, "Caldwell was the most highly cultured, the most deeply learned and, take him all in all, the most remarkable man I have ever seen or of whom I have ever read."[13]

He wrote to sister Bep on August 9, 1905, "Yellow fever here. It is the lady mosquito that does the devilment. What a pity Noah didn't leave this creature out of the Ark."

He wrote another epistle on the letterhead of Kennedy's Hotel, "John J. Kennedy. Proprietor First class accommodation. Café in connection. Opposite Depot. Biloxi, Miss.":

December 25, 1908

I have been for long, neglectful,—because I <u>could</u> have written, and <u>could</u> oftener write,—though generally at the sacrifice of convenience and the risk of pain, but feel that I must send Christmas greetings. I have not gone to Gulfport to-day (it is now 9 P.M.), where I might have done a little marketable work,—which however, may as well be done tomorrow, or the day after. I really don't like to work on Sundays, and I positively will <u>not</u> work on Christmas,—if I can possibly help it. The elements have been kindly toward me this winter. We have had some cold weather, but, so far, very little dampness; and, for ten days past,—with the exception of one fog, more demoralizing than ten rains,—have not had or needed fire. I do not object to cold weather, however, so long as it is <u>dry</u>: that is the main thing.

Of course, as I have no other matters of common interest to write about, I must give an account of my health. I have not had a cramp for nearly three weeks,—in testimony whereof this scrawl, in my own handwriting (holographic—wholly written with my own hand,) and decipherable. There have been many months during which I was disabled from work; this has naturally and not improperly lost me much business, though I am not yet entirely stranded. Fortunately, I am like an Irish colonel to whom I once carried a very drastic order from my General, and who replied, "My compliments to the general, and I perfectly comprehend the situation,"—which meant all that was desirable under the circumstances.

I found in a recent press dispatch a statement that a Miss Henrietta Gras [?] was one of the party of young ladies, who so greatly aggrieved the president by passing his own cavalcade. I think I can find the clipping when I go up to my room (I am for greater ease, writing in the Hotel office), and will enclose it. Sister will remember Sallie Irby, whose daughter <u>Henrietta Gras</u> is. To descend into politics, permit me to say, that Roosevelt is (in my opinion) a great, good and sincere man, but lacks self-control, and has lost prestige by descending into the arena of vituperation. The wonder is that he did not establish a Sapphire annex to his Ananines Club, on account of the published statement of the teacher-chaperone of the young ladies.

I hope you are enjoying the holiday season, and are in health, with as much happiness as circumstances permit, and with best love to sister Ida and all her household,—having written the most extensive letter perpetrated for many years,—I remain.

Affectionately your brother,
J. P. Caldwell.

Parks wrote to his mother on his birthday for as long as she was alive. In one of his last letters, on March 27, 1911, he wrote his sister, "Today I have reached the Biblical three score and ten that seems to limit the ordinary span of life, that several of our ancestors, namely Noah, went far better. I had an unexpected visit from Newman Miller, my fraternity brother who is with the University of Chicago Press, and we talked all night. I enjoyed his 24 hour visit very much."

When Parks died on April 5, 1912, he was memorialized in many publications. The *Gulfport (Miss.) Daily Herald* on Friday, April 5, 1912, carried this headline: "James P. Caldwell, Lawyer, Veteran, and Founder of a Fraternity, Dead." The account said that "during the evening he suffered considerably from gastritis, which caused his death."[14]

This caused Roy Harmon to write in the *Sigma Chi Quarterly*, "Caldwell the gentle, the true, is dead."[15]

The memorial adopted by the Harrison County Bar Association had this to say:

> — No finer scholar has ever graced our Bar, and fortunate indeed were those of us who knew him well, and who enjoyed the enlightening influence of his conversation. Modest almost to a fault, never seeking to exploit himself, he still delighted in the companionship of his friends, and sharing with them the stores of his learning. The same thoroughness that marked his scholarship characterized his legal reading—
> Above all he was a kindly gentleman in all that the term means and implies. He was the soul of honor. He abhorred wrong and to have wronged another would have pained him inexpressibly. Yet he was positive in character, and unyielding as the rock when principle was involved, and courageous and

Caldwell's burial site "The Old French Cemetery" Biloxi, Mississippi, on the Gulf Shore Road on the Gulf of Mexico. The monument was erected by the Sigma Chi fraternity in 1930. He lived nearby from 1888 until his death (photograph by the editor).

chivalrous to a degree that would challenge the admiration and emulation of the Knights of the Round Table.—

He was buried in the Biloxi Cemetery named "The Old French Cemetery," which is near the Lighthouse landmark. The street leading to the cemetery is appropriately named Caldwell Ave. In the neutral ground of the highway between the cemetery and the gulf is an historical marker that reads: "— Here — lies the body of James Park [sic] Caldwell, a founder of Sigma Chi Fraternity." In 1930, the fraternity erected a marble monument on the spot. One side gives his Confederate soldier history: "James Parks Caldwell, March 27, 1841 — April 5, 1912; Lieutenant of Artillery — Confederate States of America 1861–1865; Member of Mississippi Bar —1866– 1912." The other side says, "Founder of the Sigma Chi Fraternity." This is followed by the simple phrase that perhaps sums up his life: "ONE WHO WAS FOUND FAITHFUL." It concludes: "This granite stone is the outer symbol of the fraternity's regard, but the real monument to James Parks Caldwell is erected in the hearts of the thousands of Sigma Chis throughout the length and breadth of this land. ALL HONOR TO HIS NAME."

Caldwell the Classicist

by Kenneth Kitchell

In one sense, the name of this essay is deliberately misleading, for despite the great amount of Latin and the smattering of Greek that one finds in Caldwell's diary, he was not a classicist in the strictest sense of the word. That is to say, Caldwell had neither the training nor the inclination to make his profession the lifelong study of the literatures and the material cultures of ancient Greece and Rome. Yet he did pursue a lifelong love of these subjects, a love he acquired as he pursued the normal liberal arts education of his day. But James Caldwell also went quite beyond what we would expect the average undergraduate to retain from his undergraduate studies. To read Caldwell's diary and to trace his use of his classical training is to be given a wonderful opportunity to study both the training in classics demanded of students the years just prior to the Civil War and the long-term effects this training had on their lives.

We can be fairly sure that Caldwell studied both Latin and Greek as he quickly exhausted the educational resources of the Monroe, Ohio, high school. The secondary curriculum of the day was driven by college entry requirements and these specifically laid out the authors which an entering freshman should have already read.[1] We are secure, then, in estimating that as a secondary school student Caldwell had studied Caesar's *Gallic Wars* in his second year, and, in his third and fourth years, had read some selection from the authors and works most in vogue in his day: Cicero's *Orations*, Ovid's *Metamorphoses*, and Vergil's *Aeneid* and *Georgics*.[2] While Sallust's histories were often part of the secondary readings, we learned above that the curriculum Caldwell pursued at Miami was heavy in the classics. He had studied Herodotus, ancient history and geography, Livy, Roman history, the *Iliad*, Greek history, Horace's *Odes, Epistles*, and *Satires*, Thucydides, Cicero, Aeschines, Tacitus, Demosthenes, Cicero, Aeschylus, and Terence. The list is as telling from what it includes as it is from what is omitted. There is a strong bias, for example, toward ancient historians (Herodotus, Thucydides, Livy, Tacitus) and to orators (Cicero, Demosthenes, Aeschines). One can also detect a certain moral bias. Homer's *Iliad* is here, but the less tragic and more frivolous *Odyssey* is not. Likewise, the stiffer and quite moral playwright Aeschylus is represented, but the less overtly religious Sophocles (generally regarded today as the master of ancient tragedy) and the outright skeptical Euripides are absent. None of the erotic Roman love poets, such as Propertius or Catullus, was offered to the Miami students, but all three major works of the more staid Horace were studied.

While the list is a bit quirky by modern tastes, the amount of Latin and Greek that was read by the average undergraduate pursuing a degree surpasses the requirements of many modern classics B.A. programs. Indeed, given the changes that have occurred in contemporary high school and college curricula, many young men and women today begin their Ph.D. programs with less actual work in the languages than Caldwell had. Intensive programs exist at prestigious universities to ensure that the graduated doctoral student is still up to par, but the discrepancy remains an interesting indicator of educational change.

It is not merely that young Caldwell managed to sit through a series of courses in his Miami years, for there is ample proof that he emerged quite competent in the use of the Latin language, a language for which he seems to have a genuine love that lasted all his life. His college roommate Runkle is an excellent source for how Caldwell learned his Latin and Greek. In a tribute to Caldwell delivered in 1908, Runkle reported, "He never seemed to study as other boys. What he knew appeared to be his intuitively." He could not parse the Greek and Latin, but he wrote Latin and Greek poetry.[3] To a Latin teacher, Runkle's observation is very telling. When he claims that Caldwell could not "parse," he means that Caldwell was incapable of answering the battery of questions which has been posed to Latin students ever since non–Romans began to study the Latin language. Any reader who has studied Latin will recognize the sort of question I mean: "What is the tense, mood, voice, person, and number of that verb?" "What is the gender, number, and case of that noun?" "What is the name of that use of the ablative?"

Apparently Caldwell could do little of this. Yet we hear that he was writing Latin and Greek poetry at an early age and his later works, as found in the diary, show an intense familiarity with the language even though they may not be great literature. From the evidence we have, then, it seems that Caldwell learned his Latin in an instinctive way, more like the original speakers did than in any formulaic manner. Since there are far more entries in the diary in Latin than in Greek, I will concentrate on that language in the analysis that follows. Typically, Caldwell would have started his Latin quite young and would have added Greek later. Moreover, Greek is a more difficult language, and few ever attain the fluency in it that they acquire in Latin. It is thus not surprising that Greek in the diary is largely confined to the whimsical jottings of the "Fasti Jacobi" of May 24, 1864.

Caldwell's Latin

It is important to stress from the start that by the time we first see Latin in Caldwell's diary, on January 2, 1864, he had not studied Latin in a formal way for six and a half years. He had been busily engaged first in the study of law and then with the necessities of making a living as a teacher and as a soldier. Yet he had apparently kept his Latin alive, for in the 1860 U.S. census, the nineteen-year-old James P. Caldwell of Ohio was listed as residing in Panola County and making his living as a teacher of languages, where, as we read above, he tutored many children from neighboring plantations and eventually established the Palmetto Academy near Como, Mississippi.

Very tellingly, in a letter to his father dated September 11, 1859, Caldwell neatly sums up the ambiguity of his situation:

> I do not consider "teaching" as my "business" by any means, but my present intentions are, if everything suits, to resume the study of law in Hamilton and, when admitted, to come South — A little more than four weeks ago, while on a visit to the "upper neighborhood" I staid all night with a young man, a member of my Secret Society.... We got to talking of Texas and he advised me to go there saying that, if I wished, he would write to a correspondent there, and he knew that there was a situation for a classical scholar in the family of his correspondent, which, if it were not already taken, he could secure for me, adding that it would be a very lucrative one. Now at the time I felt very much depressed on acc't of the chills, and Texas being such a salubriously healthy country, can it be wondered at that I accepted his offer? Now, since I have received your advice on this point, I shall not go if there be any honorable means of escape (and I expect there will be such). Besides, they want me to stay here and (I suppose) can and will if I desire it, get me a little larger school next year, but I should like a situation where I could teach the higher classics of which (& of which only, I fear,) I myself am very fond, and which I *consider myself* well-qualified to teach.

Here, in words over a century old, we see the portrait of many a Latin student populating our Latin classrooms today. In the current academic framework, when Latin is less and less studied in the secondary schools, most students come to college unacquainted with Latin and first encounter the language while dealing with their language requirement. It then frequently happens that a student is quite good at the language, having discovered a hitherto undetected talent and appreciation for its beauty. Yet this is not why the student came to college. In today's view, college is where one receives career training and today, as in Caldwell's day, the life of the teacher is poorly remunerated. In the words quoted above, we can hear Caldwell's heart arguing with his reason. His reason tells him to be a lawyer, for here lies prestige and financial security. His heart pulls him in the direction of teaching his beloved Latin and in being able to go beyond the basic levels, introducing his charges to the authors we mentioned earlier.

As we know, reason won out and Caldwell pursued a career which generally lay outside of the classroom, though there are hints that he taught sporadically in California. Yet the love he bore for Latin and classical antiquity would not allow him to abandon his studies. We have ample evidence that he continued to read and write Latin throughout his life. The evidence from the diaries is the most extensive, and we will discuss this in some detail below. But after the war, in the 1869 *Overland Review*, Caldwell wrote a whimsical article analyzing a banjo tune as if it were a great piece of literature, and in so doing makes many references to the *Aeneid*.[4] On March 5, 1870, in a letter written from California, Caldwell wrote to Professor Bishop of Miami, a Latin professor, vividly describing his post-baccalaureate studies:

> Continued study after graduation: I diligently kept up my studies — both classical and literary — until the breaking out of the war. Indeed I commenced studying almost immediately after my graduation. Since the surrender I have resumed the habit. I will endeavor to furnish such evidence as may be required to support my statements, of whatever kind it be. I believe I can write a Latin thesis on any given subject of which I know anything *in English*, and would prefer doing so if any of my classmates obtained his degree by presenting such a voucher. I do not say that the Latinity might not be somewhat canine, but it would evince study.[5]

On May 23, 1870, Caldwell produced the poem "Ad Muscam Molestam," a spoof once more of a current banjo tune (discussed at length below), and Caldwell's sister related that after the war Caldwell continued to write his friend Judge Clark after Clark moved to New York and that much of their correspondence was in Latin.

The Latin in the Diary

But the strongest evidence of Caldwell's classical training is to be seen throughout his diary and writings. As was the custom of his day, he liberally sprinkled his narrative with stock quotes from ancient authors. While this may seem affected to modern ears, we should not be too quick to condemn, for such a custom was the norm for those who claimed to have had a proper education. By quoting Vergil, for example, and by expecting your listener to catch the quote, you were at once showing off your learning and also acknowledging the intellectual achievements of your listener. In an interesting scene in the recent film *Tombstone,* two gunslingers try to outduel each other, not with pistols, but with quotes from the Latin, and in so doing move from antagonism to grudging respect.

A reader today is struck by the aptness with which Caldwell applies his quotes. Thus, on January 13, 1864, when the despair and boredom of his situation on Johnson's Island was just beginning to sink in, he resorted to Vergil for appropriate words to the effect that perhaps, someday, it would be a pleasure to remember even those things. In a lighter vein, Caldwell even used the classics to discuss the weather. On January 19, 1864, Caldwell complained about the interminable winter on Lake Erie by citing Horace's *Odes*; later, on March 5, just when he thought winter might finally have left, Caldwell expressed his unhappiness over its return by quoting and wryly altering yet another Horatian line.

His uses for apt lines from the classics were many. On August 23, 1864, he changed another common phrase to preach universal caution in the battle of the sexes. A single quote of Seneca is used to help console him in the beginning of his second year of imprisonment (July 19, 1864), and one line from Ovid served the same purpose (May 10, 1865) as he considered a self-imposed exile to Mexico. Such aptness goes far beyond mere citation for effect and testifies to Caldwell's intimacy with classical texts, which, for him, were often far better at summing up his feelings than he was himself.

Such a use of quotes also had a side effect that was very useful for Caldwell as he wrote in his tiny diary — they saved space. We find him using stock phrases from the Latin, some of which remain to this day. Thus we find "verb sat." (February 25 and April 25, 1864) to mean "A word to the wise is sufficient," or "ultra meam crepidam" (July 9, 1864) to mean "The cobbler should stick to his last." On March 29, 1864, instead of writing a paragraph on the perfidy of a fellow who offered to take the oath of allegiance to the Union and then was caught, all Caldwell had to do was note, "O tempora, o mores," and the fellow was instantly compared to one of the greatest traitors in all Roman history. A quick citation of Horace's *Epistles* was all that was needed to cast doubt on the competence of a general (June 22, 1864) and two words, "rara avis," served as great praise for his sister (December 8, 1864). Perhaps most tellingly, as Caldwell neared the end of his ordeal (April 11, 1865) and as the futility of his position became unavoidably clear, two words from Livy, "vae victis" ("woe to the conquered"), spoke volumes about the lack of choices available to those on the losing side of any war.

While these uses of Latin and the classics presuppose an audience as equally erudite as their author, Caldwell's Latin jottings ironically often imply an audience incapable of reading them, thus ensuring secrecy. On April 19, 1864, for example, Caldwell complained that Beldin might not have mailed a letter as promised and exclaimed, "Timeo Danaos —." As the notes to that passage indicate, he was evoking Vergil to insult Beldin, saying that he is not to be trusted, even when offering to do something nice. This is another instance of the apt brevity such quotes could impart, but by being in Latin, and by being a literary reference to boot, it also reduced the probability that Beldin would ever know of the insult. The case of Peccary (September 9, 1864) provides an interesting parallel, for here Caldwell used Latin purely as a cryptographic device without any literary overtones. Peccary, perhaps a minister, had fallen out of favor with Caldwell, who then wrote, in Latin, "Peccary is that pastor/shepherd about whom I said good things, but now I take them back." December 7, 1864, provides a telling contrast to this case. On this date, Caldwell reported that someone named George Chany shared his quarters, adding the notation, "De quo quae mala antea scripsi nunc revoco," or "I now take back the bad things I said about this man previously." Even though this statement revealed that Caldwell now liked the man, he was afraid that Chany might learn that he once wrote badly about him and thus hid his change of mind beneath the Latin. As Chany is not mentioned elsewhere in the diary, Caldwell's first unflattering reference was presumably in a letter. Sometimes the reason for secrecy is unknown, but tantalizing. What was in the letter from his sister that caused Caldwell to report to himself, in Latin, "The letter which came yesterday got to me to-day. It was written by my sister"? Finally, we turn to the case of the Fasti Jacobi, the strange little vignette Caldwell wrote on May 24, 1864, using English written in Greek characters. Much is illegible, but on the surface it would appear to be a fairly harmless bit of drollery. Does it hide some personal feelings (the word "love" can be made out fairly often) or does it perhaps satirize members of the camp? Or might it be simply the result of a man desperate for something new and challenging to do?

There is no such ambiguity about the very first Latin entry in Caldwell's diary. This day was during an intensely cold period on the lake, and Caldwell spoke movingly about huddling in bed in the face of weather below twenty degrees, writing his journal with numbed fingers, heating his pen in order to dissolve the frozen ink. On January 2, 1864, quite fed up with this uncongenial weather, he wrote, "Hodie frigoris dies est congelare testes simiae aeneae"—"Today is cold enough to freeze the balls off a brass monkey." The "monkey" is a brass plate on which cannon balls were stacked. They would fall off in freezing weather; what is most interesting here is that Caldwell used Latin in this instance to cover his off-color remark.

One question remains to be addressed before we move on to Caldwell's reading agenda. Johnson's Island was used almost exclusively to house officers,[6] and one might at first think that most of them would have had the same educational background as Caldwell and thus the same ability to read his comments, obviating any secrecy he may have obtained by using Latin in his diary. Surely the educational level of the officers at Johnson's Island would have been higher than at a prison camp for enlisted men, but not all officers had the educational background of Caldwell. Some, of course, would have risen through the ranks, relying on their abilities and courage rather than on any privileged background to attain their rank. Moreover, the liberal arts background was not supported by all educational institutions at the time. There was increasing demand for a "practical" education, and the military academies such as West Point and VMI were adamant in cutting back on the amount of classics they taught, stressing mathematics, tactics, and engineering instead. There was, then, some degree of privacy to be obtained from writing in Latin.

Caldwell's Reading Habits

It is a rare privilege to have such detailed information about Caldwell's reading habits. A mere list of the authors he read might indicate the breadth of his tastes, but the information contained in the pages of his diary allows us to understand Caldwell's choice of authors, whether he had a reading agenda, and his daily routine.

Caldwell spent much of his time reading Vergil and Horace, two authors he had studied in school and who are beyond doubt the authors most commonly cited by him. He seems to have had works by both authors with him from his earliest days at Johnson's Island, and it is likely that he had taken his school texts with him to war. The reader will recall that Caldwell did not read Vergil in college but that the *Aeneid* was the acme of secondary school Latin studies in his day. Clearly Caldwell had kept up his reading of this masterpiece on his own, and his diary entries tell us that he would return to reading it throughout his incarceration. On May 27, 1864, for example, he reported that out of boredom he picked up the *Aeneid* and read some three hundred lines of the poem, a very fine pace. Horace's *Odes* and *Satires* had been read by Caldwell in college, and it was this textbook that he probably brought with him to the front.

But Caldwell was apparently not content with rereading the works from his classroom days. We have several hints that he consciously sought to expand his repertoire by seeking out and reading authors new to him. On April 1, 1864, he first expressed his interest in reading Lucretius and noted that he had sought in vain for a copy. Later, on August 9, he reported that he had sent to Harper & Bros. for a copy of Lucretius, which made its way from New York to Ohio in admirable time.[7] Titus Lucretius Carus lived in the first century B.C. and gained well-deserved fame for his *De Natura Rerum* or *On the Nature of Things*, a philosophical poem that popularized the doctrines of Epicureanism to Rome. The poem, generally admitted to be unfinished at Lucretius's death, is in six books and consists of some 7,400 lines of archaic, sometimes dense hexameter verse. Caldwell understood what lay before him; on the day the book arrived (August 21, 1864), he stated that "in it I have a task before me for it is altogether untrod open ground." By this he meant that he had never read it before and had not the benefit of classroom experience to fall back upon.

Lucretius was to prove to be Caldwell's favorite ancient author, but it did not come easily to him. On September 13, just 33 days later, Caldwell reported that he had finished the first of the six books, a book containing 1,117 verses. Very excited about what he had read, he was effusive: "I am delighted with him though sometimes he shows too much of the philosopher (& that too, of an obscure philosophy) & too little of the poet for my taste. Among the many dicta he sets forth are to be found the germ of a true philosophy than any other ancient, or at least any other Roman dreamed of." Inspired, he apparently attacked the text in earnest. On September 15, he disclosed that he read Lucretius every morning. He also apparently became more familiar with Lucretius's style and mannerisms, for on September 21 he wrote that he had finished Book 3. Books 2 and 3 comprise 2,268 lines, and we can thus see that Caldwell has progressed from about 33 lines a day to 283.5 lines a day. This is excellent progress and is well in accord with his newfound enthusiasm. But on September 29, he admitted that he has not been keeping to his plan of reading Lucretius every morning. Instead, to divert himself, he has begun writing the Hymn to the Confederate Flag, which we shall discuss below and which he finished on October 6. His focus on Lucretius still wavered, for on both October 3 and 14 he admitted to having neglected the author for several days. Significantly, on October 26 he wrote away for a play of the comic playwright Plautus,[8] as if seeking lighter fare to read next after the heavier philosopher. Still, five days later he announced the completion of Book 5. Again we can compare his progress, for Books 4 and 5 comprise 2,744 lines, which he read in forty days. Only five days later, on November 4, he finished the last book, 1,286 lines long. In all, it took Caldwell almost exactly three months to read the entire work of this complex author, no small feat for a prisoner of war who probably lacked a Latin lexicon (see below).

He probably hurried to finish because his Plautus had arrived on November 3.

Plautus does not appear on the curriculum that Caldwell pursued in college; instead, the more proper Terence, the other surviving Roman comic playwright, was studied. Terence, though decidedly less funny than Plautus, was also less scurrilous, and he has always been taught as an example of elegant style. Plautus, it should be noted, is also an author from the early Roman period (he lived in the middle of the second century B.C.), and we can now see that Caldwell's plan in reading Lucretius and Plautus was to fill some specific gaps in what he had read in college. Moreover, since the *Captivi* treats an old man named Hegio who is seeking his two sons, one captured by pirates and the other a prisoner of war, it is clear that the play had specific resonance for Caldwell. He must have heard of it when studying at college and now seemed an excellent time to read it.

He began reading the *Captivi* on November 11 and finished it, pacing himself at about an act a day, on November 17. Plautus is in a form of archaic Latin that can be difficult, but Caldwell had been exposed to this when studying Terence. The dialogue and monologues of the play must have seemed blissfully easy after the dense thoughts of Lucretius and indeed he called it "delightful." Soon thereafter, on Christmas Eve, Caldwell began Sallust (a contemporary of Lucretius and thus still part of Caldwell's plan), stating that he has "never read this before." He finished the *Catilina*, some forty pages of fairly straightforward prose, in six days. As usual, there is more to Caldwell's choice than at first meets the eye, for Catiline (Caldwell generally misspelled his name), more properly Lucius Sergius Catilina, was a disgruntled nobleman who fomented rebellion against the Roman state, doing so in 62 B.C. when Cicero was consul. The resultant publicity helped boost Cicero's career, but it is likely that Caldwell was more interested in the civil unrest that Catiline represented than in Cicero. Sallust castigated Catiline, of course, but he also went on at some length about the need for dignity, courage, and integrity among the nobles. That Caldwell too cherished these virtues is clear from the next reading program we will study — his fascination with the story of Nisus and Euryalus.

It is clear that Vergil was one of Caldwell's favorite authors. As early as January 7, 1864, Caldwell employed a Vergilian description to describe "Rumor" as "many-tongued," and his first quote from Vergil was entered on January 13, just two days before he stated that he had nothing to read other than Vergil and Horace. But on or about April 9, 1864, Caldwell embarked on a special project that would have a special meaning for him. On this date we have our first set of quotes from Book 9 of Vergil's *Aeneid*. It is quite possible that this book was not read in Caldwell's secondary curriculum, for since the earliest days of American education all of Vergil was not required for college entrance. In the eighteenth century as few as three books were required, with the norm being six of Vergil's twelve books,[9] and, as we have seen, Caldwell did not read Vergil as part of his college curriculum. He may thus have been reading this book as he had read Lucretius, Sallust, and Plautus — to fill out his college education — but in it he soon found more than he expected.

As the book opens, the Trojans, having left Troy under Aeneas's guidance to seek a new land, have established a camp on Italian soil. This will ultimately lead to the founding of Rome by Aeneas's descendants, but for the moment all is not well. Aeneas is out of the walled camp, visiting King Evander, who lives on the site of what will eventually become Rome, and Turnus, the local hero, has taken this opportunity to attack the Trojans Aeneas has left behind. The Trojans take refuge behind their walls and realize that all will be lost unless Aeneas can be made aware of their plight. Nisus volunteers to sneak out at night and inform Aeneas of his comrades' plight. But his staunch friend, Euryalus, will not hear of his going alone and insists on accompanying his older, more cautious friend. They present their plan to the Trojans in assembly and an older Trojan, one Aletes, praises their virtue. The warriors slip out, slaughter several drunken Italian soldiers as they sleep, and take some of the dead men's armor as a prize. But the moon flashes on the helmet Euryalus has taken and a passing group of Italian horsemen spots him. The two young men flee and are separated. Nisus faithfully goes back for his comrade, only to find him captured by a band of Rutulians. From the darkness Nisus throws his spear, killing a few Italians, but this only seals Euryalus's fate, and his death is described in memorable lines. Maddened at the younger man's death, Nisus shows himself, attacks, and dies bravely.

For the average reader, the scene is very moving, and it is filled with interesting contrasts such as the craven slaughter of sleeping warriors and glorious displays of courage. But for a man in Caldwell's situation, the passage bore heavier meaning. He too was a soldier encircled by the enemy. He too had seen both the good and the bad side of war. He too had seen countless comrades sacrifice themselves for the love and devotion that only comrades in arms develop for one another. As he read Book 9, the number of lines he copied into his diary increased. I should point out here that this was a habit he probably developed in school, for from time immemorial Latin students were encouraged to keep reading diaries in which they made note of such prosaic things as rare turns of phrase and unusual vocabulary (see his entry of April 2, 1864). But they also noted down interesting or useful quotations. Many successful professionals later went back to these books from their student days and mined them for appropriate sayings with which to improve their writings or speeches.

The first few Vergilian jottings of Caldwell seem fairly random, merely containing a nice turn of phrase or some interesting rhetorical phrase. He did not enter any Vergil from Book 9 for three days, and on April 11 his entries from Vergil (Book 6), Horace, and Dante were decidedly gloomy. One can almost sense the depression he was feeling. But on the next day he returned to Book 9 and appeared to have found words there to cheer him, for he began to put in his diary longer passages of Latin, all of which stressed the glory of selfless sacrifice during war[10]: "Gods of our fathers, beneath whose protection Troy ever is, you are not ready, it seems, to blot out the Trojans completely from the earth, for you have brought forth this sort of spirit and such stout courage in our youth." "What rewards, gentlemen, could I possibly think worthy to pay back such praiseworthy deeds? The gods and your own characters will sooner provide the fairest of all." "Here, here is a spirit that scorns the light of life and which thinks that that honor, for which you strive, is well bought with a life." On the same day, he also recorded Nisus's telling Euryalus to stay behind and be safe — "I would prefer that you survive; your age is more worthy of life" — and on April 15 he copied out Nisus's attempt to save his friend Euryalus through the sacrifice of his own life — "Turn your weapons on me, on me, oh Rutulians. I am the one who did it. The guilt is all mine. That fellow dared nothing, was capable of nothing. I swear this by heaven and the stars who see all. All he did was love his ill fated comrade too dearly."[11] Such noble sentiments, spoken by two young men of about Caldwell's age, lost nothing of their relevance or emotional impact for being two thousand years old. Caldwell, hunched over his book in the middle of a prisoner-of-war camp, might well have recalled them from his days in the field, and he knew that as the cause of the South grew grimmer, they were increasingly spoken by his comrades who had not had the misfortune of being captured. Such must his feelings have been also as he copied out (April 24) the lines spoken by Euryalus's mother. How many mothers' sons had he seen die? As is indicated in the notes for April 15, there is even some evidence that Caldwell was so moved by what he read that he went back, reread, and marked down further quotations. I encourage each reader of this essay to find a copy of the Aeneid and read Book 9 through the eyes of Caldwell — it is as close as we can come to sitting with him in his alternating days of hope and despair.

Caldwell the Author

We have seen that Caldwell read his Latin for many reasons. He revisited old friends such as Horace, filled in gaps in his education, and found relevance in texts by authors long dead. If this were all that one found in the diary, it would still be worth the insights into the man. But in this case we are privileged to have some of Caldwell's original Latin compositions in the unexpected form of a Latin translation of two banjo tunes and a hymn to the Confederate flag.

Caldwell was very prone to write in Latin. In fact, as pointed out above, he had been composing poems in Latin and Greek from his school days. This too was a common part of Latin education in the era, but Caldwell seems to have had a special talent in this direction. Let us begin with his Latin hymn to the Confederate flag, surely his most ambitious project and one of which he himself was justifiably proud.[12]

Since the Latin text has been printed in the 1864 diary and the translation in Appendix 1 we will not reprint them here, but a few notes on its composition are in order. From his diary entries, we know that Caldwell began to compose the poem on September 29, 1864, and finished it on October 6. An early attempt to transcribe the poem is found on October 9, but it appears in its fullest form on June 2 of the same year. As I will discuss below, there is some evidence that Caldwell worked without the aid of a lexicon.

The rhyme scheme is AAB CCB. A stanza consists of two groups of three lines each, wherein the first two lines of each stanza rhyme with each other, but the last lines of the two stanzas rhyme with each other and not with the lines just preceding them. Thus the last words for each line in the first stanza give us "crux ... lux ... lumen ... fortis ... mortis ... numen." There is no discernible metrical pattern to the piece, and lines have varying numbers of syllables. This normally would make one think that the piece was designed to be sung to some preexisting tune; and, since Caldwell's other compositions fit this description, it seems a fairly safe assumption that *Ad Patriae Vexillum* was meant to be sung. Moreover, its subtitle, *Carmen Militaire*, also gives this impression, for a *carmen* is a song.

While the hymn is not great literature, it does have several nice touches to its composition and it was very clearly written by someone under the influence of classical antiquity. For example, ancient gods are mentioned in three places, giving the piece a decidedly Roman tone — Mars (l.7), the household god called a Lar (l.23), and in l.53 "Lucifer" is to be read not as the Christian Satan, but as the Roman name for the Morning Star. Caldwell's overt imitation of Vergil and Horace in various spots also makes clear his indebtedness to the ancients, and his dating its completion in the Roman fashion is a clear indication of how he wants his poem to be viewed. Caldwell was also fairly adept at Latin alliteration: "nostrae nationis lucida lux" (l.2); "decus dulce" (l.25); "pro patria moriuntur ... morte ... memoriae" (l.31f.). A few other touches are noteworthy. For example, lines 37–38 show some clever internal rhyme, as each of the successive lines begins with a rhyming two-word phrase and ends with a single rhyming word: "In belli fulminibus/ in leti grandinibus." On a grimmer note, Caldwell's word choice is revealing. While the poem is ostensibly optimistic and proud, it is interesting to note that while it begins using forms of the word for "glory" three times in the first thirteen lines (l.1, 10, 13), the word does not appear after that time, whereas words formed from the stem meaning "bloody" appear throughout the poem's end (l.42, 49, 61). The realities of war were never far from Caldwell's mind.

Yet the other examples we possess of Caldwell's original Latin compositions are of a much lighter nature. We have seen his sense of humor as displayed when he altered an existing Latin quote for his own purposes (March 4, 1864), and he sometimes lapsed into Latin for effect over something as trivial as a recipe. His lighter side is also evidenced in the two other long Latin compositions we have from him, each modeled on a popular song.

The first is his version of "Old Uncle Ned," a traditional banjo and minstrel tune, made most popular in a version of Stephen Foster published in 1848, though it existed in the public domain before this time. It is important to print the song's original words, offensive though they may be to modern ears, as these were as the words Caldwell had to work from[13]:

Old Uncle Ned

Oh there was an old nigga and dey calld him Uncle Ned
Hes dead long ago, long ago
And he had no wool on de top ob de head
De place wha de wool ought to grow.
Refrain:
Den lay down the shubble and de hoe
And hang up de fiddle and de bow.
No more hard work for poor ole Ned
He's gone wha de good niggas go. (last two lines twice)
His fingers were long like the cane in de break
He had no eyes for to see.
He had no teefe to eat de oae cake[14]
So he had to luf dat oae cake be.
Refrain
On a cold frosty morning poor Uncle Ned died
Masters tears down his cheeks ran like rain,
Case he knew when poor Ned was under de ground
Hed neber see his like again.[15]
Refrain

This is a fairly typical minstrel song of the period. It does not dwell on the realities of slavery, but stresses the nobility of the slave and the affection borne him by his owner. Caldwell took the song and did more than merely translate it, for he adapted it completely into a "classical" context. We are fortunate in being able to see earlier versions of the translation in his diary so we can see his technique in process. Let us first look at the text:

De Morte Edwardi:

I

Jampridem[16] erat senex niger
(Haud dubito atque piger),
Qui solitus[17] "Ned" vocari:
Et nihil erat laneum
In summum ejus craneum,
Ubi solet vegetare.

II

Similes arundinibus,
Qui florent in fluminibus,
Et debiles exercendo
10 Huius erant digiti
Ut, prae servi rigidi
Casu, oculi videndo

III

Defuerunt far edendo
Dentes, itaque depsendo
15 Non huic opus far:
Quam ob rem atque far et panem
Et quae pertinent ad sanum
Prohibuit quisque Lar.

IV

Pastinum eius nunc depone,
20 Abjecto etiam ligone,—
Quae viris Faunus dedit.
Pariete nunc dependeat fides
Ornetur atque plectro aedes,
Nam silentium his insedit.

V

25 Edwardo labor erit nullus
Nec ei dolor erit ullus
In saecula saeclorum:
Elysios campos nam advenit,—
Nobis coelum eum tenet
30 Ethiopum et bonorum
Carceri militari Ins(ulae) Johnsoni Die, Sept. IVa

Translation:

I. Once there was an old black man, (and I have no doubt he was slow as well), who used to be called "Ned." There was no wool on the top of his head where it usually grows.

II. His fingers were like the reeds that grow in rivers, and they were weak from working, just as his eyes were too stiff to see due to the hardship of being a slave.[18]

III. He had no teeth to eat his spelt with, and so he didn't have to knead it. For this reason too no cupboard offered him spelt and bread and the things that contribute to good health.

IV. Now lay down his shovel and his hoe — the gifts Faunus gave to humans. Let his lyre hang on the wall and let the house be decorated with his pick, because silence has fallen over them.

V. There will be no more work for Ned and neither will there be any pain for all of time. For he has come to the Elysian fields. The Heaven of good Ethiopians now holds him for us.

(Written) at the Military Camp on Johnson's Island, Sept. 4.

In general outline the song is close to Foster's version, of course. But there are significant differences as well. First of all, the poem shows an interesting sort of dualism in its attitude to the old slave. Much of the description is decidedly sentimental, stressing the humanity of the old man, blind, crippled with arthritis, and lacking the teeth to enable him to enjoy simple food. Yet in line two Caldwell also inserted a completely new line, stressing the fact that the slave was undoubtedly "piger." While "piger" is translated here as "slow," it tends to carry a negative overtone, more akin to "lazy" than merely slow, and Caldwell's social views seem to break through in his word choice.

But another aspect of his poem is even more intriguing, for he has completely translated the poem into the world of antiquity. Note first that the Latin song can not be sung to the tune — the meter is wrong and it is simply too long. Caldwell could have done that, of course, but he chose instead to create a new poem, half contemporary, half ancient. For example, "hoe cake" or "corn cake" has been rendered as "far," or spelt, a grain much eaten by the ancients. Caldwell went on to say that Ned's cupboard did not offer him the right foods for healthy living. But for "cupboard," Caldwell uses "Lar," a Roman household god.

In the next stanza (l.19f), he translates the refrain with some remarkable words, for "pastinum" and "ligo" are not words found in the linguistic arsenal of even the most professionally trained classicists. A "pastinum" represents in fact an English word not found in the arsenal of most Americans, for it is a "dibble" — a two-pronged stick used in planting certain plants such as grape vines — and "ligo" is actually a mattock rather than a hoe. Caldwell further enhanced the ancient atmosphere by saying that these two tools are the gifts to humankind by Faunus, a Roman agricultural deity. So ingrained is Caldwell's archaizing that Ned's fiddle and bow have become an ancient lyre and the pick used to strum it (l.22f.), and the slave, once dead, goes to the Elysian Fields, the place of eternal bliss in Vergil's concept of the afterlife.

We see, then, that this poem was more than a casual song for Caldwell. It was a chance to use, and indeed to flaunt, his learning, not just by writing in Latin, but also through the use of the obscure words and allusions he had acquired in his vast reading. It is this fondness for the recondite that leads us to one final comment on "Uncle Ned." The use of "pastinum" raises interesting questions, which, while ultimately unanswerable, nonetheless yield interesting insights into the depth of Caldwell's learning. "Pastinum" is a very rare word, found only in a few recondite ancient authors on agriculture, such as Columella. It is not to be found in authors such as Horace or Vergil, who formed the core of Caldwell's education. The fact that Caldwell used it here begs the question of whether he had a lexicon at his disposal as he read and wrote his Latin. No mention of a lexicon was made throughout the pages of his diary other than the fact that on November 12, 1864, he reported that the great scholar Porson thought that the thesaurus of Gesner was the best,[19] and it is highly unlikely that Caldwell had this 1749 imprint with him on Johnson's Island. Caldwell was just jotting down a reference for the day when he could leave the island and once more enjoy the services of a good dictionary. Another bit of evidence indicates he did not have a lexicon to consult. On April 2, 1864, Caldwell jotted down notes to himself asking about the meanings of two words in a Latin quote he had found. The meanings are not that unusual, and the only reasonable conclusion is that he did not have a lexicon in which to look them up.

Such evidence is not conclusive, but it is highly evocative, for it would seem that Caldwell not only read complex authors such as Lucretius without a lexicon, but that he also composed "Mors Edwardi" and the "Ad Patriae Vexillum" without the benefit of an English to Latin lexicon. Such were his training and his natural talents.

The final bit of extended Latin composition that we have from the pen of Caldwell comes after his incarceration. In a letter dated May 23, 1870, Caldwell wrote to James Alphonsus McMaster, the editor of the New York *Freeman's Journal,* an influential Catholic newspaper[20]:

> Mr. McMaster:—Please insert the following, clipped from a recent No. of "The Overland Monthly,"[21] in the Freeman's Journal, where all good things ought to be. The archaeological introduction is from the pen of your and my young friend, James P. Caldwell, Esq. of San Bernandino, California. The Latin bears unmistakable marks of the fossiliferous period. The promulgation of this classical treasure trove, pretty effectually silences a class of pretenders who have been squabbling for the original authorship of a very absurd imitation of it—in fact, convicts them of being nothing but a pack of Shoo-fliars.

> In excavating for the foundations of a corral, in San Bernandino County, there was recently exhumed one of the lost decades of Livy graven on tinplates in the reformed Egyptian character. Among the many time honored fictions of Roman history which it destroys, is the sublime reply of Caius Marius to the officer who sought him amid the ruins of Carthage. The hero's genuine answer is to be found in the following verses, which he is said to have chanted with much pathos. They have been transcribed from the new-found MS., (which — it is but just to the historian to state — contains an apology for their Atellan rudeness)[22] and are offered to the public, not only as illustrating history, but as indicating the classical dignity of American statesmanship.

Caldwell's tongue is firmly in his cheek here. First of all, as we will see below, he concocts a Roman date for the excavation of the manuscript ("MS. EFFOSSVM KAL. APR. MDCCCLXX"). This works out to be April 1, 1870, and is a sure giveaway. Moreover, by claiming that the text was discovered by being excavated and that it was written on tin plates in reformed Egyptian characters, he is having fun at the expense of the Mormons, whose sacred texts, written on gold sheets in "reformed Egyptian" script, were dug up by Joseph Smith just prior to 1830. Just as his joke with the date was predicated on a common education, so too did Caldwell expect his readers to know the story of Caius Marius, the famous general who was at the heart of some of Rome's most bloody civil wars. As reported by the ancient biographer Plutarch,[23] Marius was nearing the end of his career and was on the run from his enemies. He landed in Carthage seeking asylum, but the local commander met him at the beach and forbade him to land. Marius was silent for a while and simply told the soldier to go tell his general, one Sextilius, that he had seen Marius sitting on the ruins of Carthage, apparently comparing his own fallen status with that of the city, once proud but now in ruins. Caldwell suggests that the real words of Marius are preserved on the tin plates and that Marius in fact told the soldier, "Shoo fly, don't bother me, I am a soldier from company G!" The poem he appended is in fact a translation of "Shew Fly Don't Bother Me," a song whose authorship is a bit in doubt, but whose popularity was intense. The song, subtitled "A Comic Song & Dance," was published in 1869 in Boston and clearly had made its way to California in rapid order, no doubt traveling by way of the minstrel circuit, where it was very well received.[24] Here are the verses from the original:

> I think I hear the angels sing (3 times)
> The angels now are on the wing.
> I feel, I feel, I feel.
> That's what my mother said,
> The angels pouring 'lasses down, upon this nigger's head.
> Chorus:

Shew! fly, don't bother me, (3 times)
I belong to company G.
I feel, I feel, I feel, like a morning star (3 times)
If I sleep in the sun this nigger knows (3 times)
A fly come sting him on the nose.
I feel, I feel, I feel.
That's what my mother said,
Whenever this nigger goes to sleep, He must cover up his head

In attempting to render this nonsense song into Latin, Caldwell faced many hurdles, of course, not the least of which was its purely silly nature.

Ad Muscam Molestam.
Mihi videtur ut angeli cantent
Pennisque celeribus item volent,
Ac eos sentio, bis terque sentio,
(Genitricem hoc olim dixisse scio)
Theriacen diffudisse nuper
Nigri hujus in caput desuper.
   Abi, musca, ne inquietes me,
   Sum enim miles de manplo G.

2.

Itemque sentio, mentis per vim,
Ut Phosphorus ipse egomet sim,
Sed tamen existimat Aethiops hic-
Apricetur sicubi dormiens sic
Ut adesset musca punctura narum —
Sibi, tegendum caput tam charum.
   Abi, musca, ne inquietes me,
   Sum enim miles de maniplo G.
(MS. EFFOSSVM KAL. APR. MDCCCLXX.)

1. It seems to me that angels sing, and likewise fly on swiftest wing. And I know, two and three times I know (because my mother told me this once) that they recently poured down Theriac on the head of this black man.
   Go away, fly, don't bother me, I am a soldier from company G.
2. Likewise, I know, by the power of my mind, that I am the Morning Star.
   But nevertheless this Aethiopian thinks — as he lies sleeping sunning himself there — that a fly will sting his nose and that his head has to be covered.
   Go away, fly, don't bother me, I am a soldier from company G.
(Manuscript dug up on the Kalends of April, 1870).

Once more we see Caldwell showing off his erudition on a trivial subject. Theriac, for example, is actually a potion made in antiquity that functioned as an antidote against snakebite and is a fairly obscure reference. Using "Phosphorus" for the morning star is still more posing, for the two elements "phos" and "phorus" are Greek equivalents for "luci" and "fer," that is, "light bringer."[25] Read by itself, the Latin poem is almost senseless, but to his contemporaries, Caldwell's version must have seemed a very clever party trick indeed.

Conclusion

What, then, are we to make of James Caldwell the classicist? In many ways, he was emblematic of his age. Raised in an educational tradition that cherished the Greek and Roman classics, he grew up firmly believing that his ability to read and write Latin fluently was the hallmark of a cultured person. Seen in this light, his quotes and popularizing pieces can be seen as a form of affectation, designed more to impress than anything else. On the other hand, we have strong hints that this was a man who firmly believed in the educational aims of his day. He sought to further his knowledge of the classics in an organized way and, through the dark years of his imprisonment, constantly turned to them for counsel, comfort, and insight into the often confusing events surrounding him. It is fair to say that in many ways his love of and his devotion to the classics were a great part of his world view. He was incapable, it seems, of merely looking at contemporary events through contemporary eyes. He constantly held them up to the mirror of antiquity and studied what was reflected back at him. It is no accident that in 1905, when he was sixty-four years old, he still tended to describe his wartime experience in classical terms: "My brothers here and I viewed the shield from opposite sides, each equally sure that his vision was clear; and quite as sure am I that not one of us would be willing, were it possible, to undo his action in the past."[26] In the same speech he expressed his wish for the future of his fraternity with a Latin maxim, "Non quot, sed qualis"—"Not how many, but of what sort"—a motto that has resonance for us today as well.

In many ways, then, Caldwell was ordinary—the predictable product of his educational system and social environment. Yet this ordinary man also had an extraordinary talent with the Latin language and was thrust into an extraordinary existence on Johnson's Island. This combination of the ordinary and the extraordinary come together in the pages of the diary kept by "Caldwell the Classicist."

"In Durance Vile"

"In Durance Vile," New Orleans, La.
July 18th, 1863

Dear Sister Belle,

Maj. Gen. Gardner surrendered Port Hudson & its garrison to Gen. Banks on the 9th inst. This scrap of chronology will account for the date of my letter, and now for a bit of history. The Siege of Pt. H. lasted for 47 days and the defense was the most obstinate of the war. Gen. Banks, himself, having *written* that "The courage and gallantry evinced by the garrison would in any *other cause* be termed heroic." (We are much obliged for the compliment but beg leave to demur to the saving clause.) Right sorry am I to say that I cannot express any such opinion of the Federal troops who were to us numerically as ten to one and who allowed *one simple line* of rifle pits (constructed in a great measure after the commencement of the siege) to keep them at bay. We had *one man* to every *twenty* yards of works. Finally, after we had tasted viands unknown to epicures, we were forced by Gen. Starvation into a surrender. By the way, mule meat & broiled rat are very good *in their way*. As to Horseflesh I could not bring myself to taste it; it seemed too much like banqueting on the remains of some departed friend.

I am confined, along with almost all the other officers of our command, in the custom house. In our room are 40, in several others nearly or quite as many, and we are not allowed to smell fresh air. Thus far our daily bread has been sour, and nothing else has been issued but *very* salt beef & coffee. I am in very ill health and I fear the breaking out of a pestilence, generated by the filth & close atmosphere to which the kindness of our discarded Uncle Samuel has consigned us. I shall say nothing of my private wants & grievances, because you are too distant to afford any relief, as I was told by the Provost Sheriff that we wouldn't remain here long enough for me to receive a letter from you. Whither we are to go is a mystery, whether Pickens, Tortugas, The River forts or some stronghold in Yankeedom is a mere matter of conjecture. I hope the latter, however, but any place to escape this Black Hole. Whenever we become so located as to enable me to hear from you I shall write for some pecuniary assistance, hoping that Father will be ready to forget the rebel in the son. Greater than all our physical grievances is the sight we must witness daily from our windows, of our pride, the glory of the south, the city of the crescent crouching cowed but not *conquered* at the feet of the despot, to see citizens & ladies when they dare to pause for a moment looking, perhaps, for the face of a long unheard from son or brother, ordered with *menacing gestures* by the white-livered Massachusetts's sentinels to "disperse." These guards, who never dared to face us manfully in battle, are exceeding brave when their warrior ire is excited by old men, ladies & little boys. As long as we were in the hands of those who had fought us we met with very gentlemanly & respectful treatment, but we had not yet disembarked here, when we heard the *gallant* garrison murmur at our being allowed to wear our swords,—a privilege by the way, rather unusual in this war but one which our defense won for us from Gen. Banks, who agreed to it as one of the conditions of the surrender.

 I write things here which wouldn't pass muster at the office, so I shall endeavor to have my letter smuggled to the P.O.—, but hereafter I shall write merely commonplaces. I wish I could tell you all about the Pt. Hudson affair, for to my *own knowledge* a great part of the published account is absolutely false, about the negroes fighting, for instance, & about our numbers & the strength of our works. Give my best love to Mother, bidding her not to be distressed about me as I shall doubtless come out all right. I take the matter philosophically and try to content myself with things as they are. That was a very silly bird which beat out its brains against its prison wires rather than endure captivity, whereas had the poor misguided fowl but waited its time, it might have again filled the free forest air with songs of deliverance. The starling, too, which sat on its perch and cried all day long: "I can't get out, I can't get out," though very sentimental was a perfect ninny. I shall neither butt out my brains against the custom house walls, nor sit whiningly bemoaning my fate, but with cheerful mind & hopeful heart, await the time when I shall strike many a good blow for the cause I love. With us *National* & *personal* existence are synonymous. All are as yet hopeful, and faithful; confident that the end will be glorious though we may not live to see it. Yes, the bright St. Andrew's Cross which ever waves in the "vanward of our fight" shall yet float over our homes in peace, reminding us by its tattered folds that "through much tribulation we have received our reward." My Love & regards to Father, Sisters & Brothers,— Kind remembrances to Aunt Dovey & Uncle Joe. To

Mr. Clark my affectionate regards. Tell him I would give all my Confederate Scrip could he see me in my present position as "your Nation's guest," and witness the workings of Yankee abolitionism in my surroundings — I shall write a few lines as often as I get a stamp.

Your loving Jail-bird,
J. P. Caldwell

When I last heard (Aprl. 26th) from Va. M., Clark, Frank & Miss Mollie Moon were well. I haven't seen Will M. since Jan'y but heard since the Yazoo Pass affair.

The Diaries

For his 1864 diary Caldwell used an 1863 Pocket Diary published by Denton & Wood, Cambridgeport, Mass. It is 4 and ¾ by 3 inches. He carefully changed the day each day, always using <u>day</u> as printed but, for instance, marks out Tu., replacing it with Wedn., as well as leaving 186 but changing the 3 to 4. Perhaps this helped him keep up with the passing of time. In the early pages there is a good bit of bleed-through, making his entries extremely difficult to read. Indeed, the diaries have been deciphered rather than edited—everything is exactly as he wrote it as far as can be determined. Some pages may have as few as 65 words and others 295—tiny writing but sometimes quite legible. Caldwell was meticulous in his use of commas, spelling, and grammar, though not always according to today's *Chicago Manual of Style*. He always hyphenated to-day, spelled Shakespeare as "Shakspeare," and occasionally used quotation marks around titles of books but more usually around quotations, of which there are many. Beginning on February 19, he often drew a line after the day's happenings and quoted from various books he was reading, sometimes extensively over several pages—anywhere he can find a bit of blank paper. These asides have been labeled and set off in a different typeface to improve usability but their interruptive sequencing has been retained.

For his 1865 diary, Parks used an 1860 Pocket Diary, 5 and ¾ by 2 and ½ inches, but there were 3 days to each page, so he had no room to quote as he did in 1864. He only had to change the 0 in 1860 to a 5 until he reaches February 29, which he scratched out. He then carefully changed the days again as he did in the 1864 diary.

[On the first recto after the cover is opened:]

Jas. P. Caldwell
Lt Artillery

P.A.C.S.
Rec'd at Johnson Is.
Nov.7th 1863

[Next verso is the title of the diary]
Pocket Diary
1863
published annually by
Denton & Wood,
Cambridgeport, Mass.
MDCCCLXIII

JANUARY 1864

Friday, January 1, 1864

An inauspicious commencement "for the new year." About twelve o'clock last night the weather turned suddenly cold with a wind which threatened to topple our old barn over our heads.[1] The bay was frozen over solidly and exhaling a steamy vapor from its entire surface. My ink froze, in a stoneware bottle, forced out the cork, and found its way over my best pr. of breeches. The thermometer is outside and stood at 10 below zero during the day and is now at 20 degrees.[2] Have been in bed all day to keep warm and expect to remain here as long as the very cold weather lasts. My fingers are numbed with writing this.[3]

Johnson Island Prison from vol. 4, page 10, of Nate's *History of the Sigma Chi Fraternity*.

Saturday, January 2, 1864

"Hodie frigoris dies est congelare testes simiae aeneae."⁴ Thermometer 20 below zero, colder say the inhabitants, than it has been in sixteen years. Been in bed all day. Rec'd a letter from Sister Belle with a photograph of an old friend. Six of "us" are supposed to have escaped last night. Many more attempt it to-night. I think I shall try it tomorrow night myself. One of those who tried to escape last night was compelled by the cold to deliver himself up to Col. Pierson and seek readmittance.⁵ "O most lame & impotent conclusion."⁶

Sunday, January 3, 1864

Weather (now the most important thing) moderates somewhat, yet far from moderate and somewhat intensely cold. Out of about the hundred who attempted, or prepared to attempt, to escape only 3 or 4 got out of the Bull Pen, each eventually captured and taken back to the yard. One of them who escaped night before last was brought back this morning, [illegible half page]

Monday, January 4, 1864

Weather comparatively pleasant, tho still colder than I like. Went up to Block 3, to-day, to see Maj. Taylor, who had told Col. Chauvin that he wished to see me.⁷ He is a cousin, once removed on the mother's side of Miss Emma, the lady who had written to him that she had a "little friend" here and had given him such a good description that he recognized me before leaving my family. Saw photographs of Miss Emma & [illegible word] which recalled old & pleasant days to my mind. I have a great mind to write to Miss Emma. Played chess with Manly to-day⁸; [two illegible lines]

Tuesday, January 5, 1864

Several inches of snow fell last night, but the temperature is much warmer. Wrote to Sister Belle, a "long letter."⁹ I now begin to look for a letter fr. Dixie as I wrote to Miss Mollie many a month ago.¹⁰ Had an oyster stew to-day. The last of the edible contents of my box, except for one can of peaches.¹¹ Played chess with Manly (2nd N. C.) with a favorable result, now I stand two games ahead. I begin to experience friendly feelings for M. thinking of the "nicest" felicities for this well bred gentleman. News from the Sandusky paper that the cold during one late spell was of a much greater intensity than even my imagination had envisioned, & that the mercury ranged much lower than had been thought.¹²

Wednesday, January 6, 1864

Weather turns colder again. There is, to-day, a huge grape concerning exchange.¹³ Operators on this line go so far as to state that 500 are to leave for Pt. Lookout to-morrow,[14] but even if this prove true, I doubt whether we will be sent with a view to exchange us, or only to some worse prison. Finished reading the History of British [illegible word], which I found very uninteresting compared with Lord Mahon & with Macaulay's Essays on Clive & History. Carlyle gave one more insight in the subject than any mere history could have done.[15] Loser at chess. The game standing even, we quit playing.

Thursday, January 7, 1864

Rumor, many-tongued, is the goddess of the day, and many various oraculam are the dicta asserted to-day by the ministers at her shrine, the "grapevine telegraph" operators.[16] Nobody has left as yet but all believe that five hundred or so will leave to-morrow. If for exchange, I should like above all else to go, but if it be merely a change of prisons, I would rather be excused. Maj. Sanders, my "bunky,"[17] having gone to sit up with the sick "Old King Burns"[18] declares his intention of taking his place for the night. What a dull life is this of ours when such things form my sole item!

Friday, January 8, 1864

The Hero of to-day's sensation is one Daugherty, (Docharty or something of the sort) of the same mess & room with myself, who wrote out to a Yankee official, signifying his desire to return to his allegiance.[19] The Yankee Lieut. to whom he gave his letter, being drunk, lost it. It was found, brought to our room and read, whereupon D. bolted but did not escape until he was unmercifully kicked and beaten. The Yank off. who came to his rescue threatened to order his men to fire on us but his threats were rec'd with curses and jeers. Woe to the luckless wights who fire upon 2000 men. I wish they had though, as we would either have been free now or at least have had the satisfaction of killing many Yankees. (continued) Received this (Friday) evening a letter from brother Wilse enclosing photograph of Sisters Mary & Lizzie and advising me of a coming box.[20]

Saturday, January 9, 1864

Three years ago to-day my state withdrew from the accursed Union[21]; no different were my feelings then than from my feelings now, though my hopes are still as sanguine as ever. Then I rejoiced over the birth of a new nation; now I grieve over the perils which surround its growing infancy and only console myself with my firm belief in the certainty of our ultimate success. In this weary prison life I stand in need of consolation; each day is a blank and life has become mere animal, or rather vegetable existence. "Give me to drink mandragora, that I may sleep away this gap of time."[22] Threw dice to-day to decide which of our trinity should bring water for the next two weeks;

the lot fell upon me.²³ Besides, Manley is six games ahead of me at chess. Quite a "run" of ill "luck" though there is no "luck" about chess.

Sunday, January 10, 1864

Col. Luce, who escaped in Yankee guise, on the wood wagon, several days ago, was brought back to-day. He got as far as Newark, Ohio, but not being well enough posted to sustain the character he had assumed, he was detected.²⁴ I read, to-day, half of the little book father sent me with my valise, called "The [illegible word] of Time." A devotional work, well written but very uninteresting, which I only read because my Father sent it.²⁵ Weather much warmer to-day and the snow melting a little. I rejoice in even so slight a change for the better.

Monday, January 11, 1864

Received a box to-day containing an excellent overcoat, a blanket & quite an assortment of comestibles. I shall now be able to enjoy my wanted <u>nightly</u> collation of coffee & some "breadstuff" accompaniment. I begin to-night on coffee and mince pies and do not expect to enjoy balmy slumber in consequence, the Arabian berry being, in its effect, quite the reverse of the much desired "Mandragora." Rumor of the day: <u>1600</u> officers already exchanged (& a proportionate number of men) including the Gettysburg and Pt. Hudson prisoners. Whereas my reason murmurs "Bunk," even while my strong and credulous desire is inciting me to *hope* that the rumor may have some slight foundation in truth.

Tuesday, January 12, 1864

Wrote to brother Wilse & rec'd letters from Joe and Rush, & Sisters Mary & Lizzie — all good letters and evincing ability I am proud to see in my brothers & sisters. Joe's in particular, is an excellently written letter, better than many a man can write, while Lizzie writes with a childish and charming naïveté. The letter from Rush, rec'd in my Xmas box though, beats them all. He is certainly, what he wishes to be thought, a "white boy." I forgot to record the reception of a good photograph of Gen. Bowen in Wilse's letter.²⁶ My box yesterday: quite a striking proof of the interest those at home take in pleasing me. Alas, he is gone and "I shall never look upon his like again."²⁷ Rumors still firm, with full market & heavy demand.

Wednesday, January 13, 1864

A mild, almost spring like day; wrote to Brother Jo — a short letter.²⁸ Our guards reinforced by the arrival of a brigade of four regiments.²⁹ Such is the culmination of all the rumors, which, I believe, have been kept afloat for the purpose of keeping us quiet until the garrison might be strengthened. The dullness of this our life may be imagined, when even this small page proves difficult to fill with passing mention of occurrences. "How weary, flat, stale, and unprofitable are all the uses"[30] of this our prison life, yet "forsan et haec olim meminisse juvabit."[31]

Thursday, January 14, 1864

Temperature soft and balmy, like that of yesterday, but having one disagreeable effect, viz, thawing the frozen ground and converting our solid, but rough, pavement into a deposit of the most adhesive mud I ever trod on.[32] "They say" that the Hoffman battalion is to be sent to the front, being relieved by the new comers (old soldiers from Meade's army.) Woe to any luckless wight who may be captured since they will be known in every brigade of our army and their brutality and studied disposition to insult duly remembered to their great discomfort. From <u>soldiers</u> who fight in the field, better treatment is to be expected.[33]

Friday, January 15, 1864

Finished reading "Jane Eyre,"[34] a book I have been trying for the last five years, to get at and finally stumbled on unawares. I like it very well;—Women seldom write novels so interesting and free from "romance" and namby-pamby.

Snow fell last night to a moderate depth, and to-day, in the sunshine the glare is quite painful to the eyes. Have nothing to read now except Virgil and Horace,—and find it difficult to while away the time.

Took dinner with Capt. Johnson, to-day. First time I have yet dined out. "Gavroche"[35] is still four games ahead of me at chess. Water carrying is a great bore, and has procured me the Soubriquet of Cosette.[36] Wrote to brother Rush to-day a long letter—"technically, but really of very moderate length."

Saturday, January 16, 1864

Rec'd a "letter" from Sister Belle, very racy and hitting one rather "palpably" on several weak spots. She quotes a drunken lyric of mine (of whose very existence I had supposed her ignorant) in return for my insinuation that she had obtained her Shaksperian distich from a dictionary of Poetical Quotations.

A fine day—gained <u>one game</u> at chess from Gavroche. I shall say no more about our games, however, until I shall have recovered equilibrium. Passed away a little time, to-day, in the composition of an elegy on Gavroche supposed to have been written "Pur sa Fianca deloreuse,"[37] on the news of his supposed death.

Sunday, January 17, 1864

A dull day, dull as only Prison Sundays can be. The ice hasn't broken up in the lake yet though — but I said I wouldn't write anything more about the weather. Began reading "Rutledge" to-day but haven't gotten far enough along to be interested much in the narrative. Here is an opinion, however, expressed by the (as yet) nameless heroine, in which I heartily concur, "Though Mr. Macaulay is probably the most brilliant writer of the century, he is the one who has done the least good. I don't think anyone who has the least faith, reverence or loyalty can <u>read</u> him except under protest." "A very Daniel come to judgment."[38]

Monday, January 18, 1864

Finished "Rutledge:" I like this book very much, though it would puzzle me to assign any reason for so doing. (Bosh! 1865)[39] A letter from Father containing three photographs, his own, Mr. Clark's & Bro. Jo's. The letter was a long one. Last night the last of my edibles disappeared so that I shall have to depend, in future, for nightly solace on coffee alone. How great a contrast is afforded between my situation this time last year, & that in which I now find myself. Then I was in presence, daily, of my best friend and was almost happy.[40] "A year ago and I was happy! No not happy — yet encircled by deep joy which though twas all around I could not touch. But it was ever thus with Happiness. It is the joy tomorrow of the mind, that never comes."

(Barry Cornwall)[41]

Tuesday, January 19, 1864

"Iam satis terris nivis atque dirae, Grandinis miset Pater,"[42] though Pater doesn't seem to think so. Wrote a long letter to Father. Bread issued to-day too late for dinner much to the general discontent. Snow fight this evening between another Block and ours. Gavroche, in his youthful ardor, plunged into the midst of the foe, engaged their color bearer, but, overwhelmed by numbers, was so "worried" and "sacked" — in the Scotch Presbyterian signification of the word — that he had a hemorrhage in consequence. I begin to feel certain ominous twinges about the left knee, which may, I fear, presage an attack of Rheumatism, my old enemy, he with whom I have had, till now, a long armistice.[43]

Wednesday, January 20, 1864

A year ago today the W. B. left Grenada for Vaiden.[44] Just before leaving, I went to Mr. McLean's to bid my friend farewell, & much to my disappointment, found her gone. I have not seen her since. Been reading "At Odds" all day,[45] and don't like it, though it does to while away time in prison.

More snowball fights to-day, & now, at night, Colonel Bullock is "raising a company" for a grand battle to-morrow.[46] Our block is to furnish a battalion to Gen. Archer's brigade,[47] in the conflict imminent between the upper-endions and the lower-endions.[48] Each room is to furnish a company.

Thursday, January 21, 1864

Battle over: Block One, Capt. Fellows — Two, Col. Scales, Three, Col. Wood, Four, Col. Lewis, Five, Col. Blacknall, and a detachment from Seven, constituted our Brigade com'd by Gen. Thompson.[49] The enemy, the respective battalions of blocks 8, 9, 10, 11, 12, & 13 were com'd by Col. Maxwell.[50] We were victorious, though our block lost its colors early in the day (stolen) we captured two stands from the enemy, and never once gave back except when those in our flanks had given way. Exciting fight though, some hard hits were given. I received one in the mouth. I like it much better than the real sure-enough fighting.[51]

Friday, January 22, 1864

Wrote to Sister Mary a short letter.

The little corporal, who has been calling our role ever since my arrival at this island, bade us farewell this morning. His place is to be filled by a Lieut., one of the regiments lately sent here. I rejoice at the change, for the Corporal — though better than most of his class — was impertinent, while the Lt., having seen service, will behave as nearly like a gentleman as can be expected. The Corp. rejoiced that he is still to remain "outside" for it seems that these Hoffman fellows have no desire to be sent to the front; not much to be wondered at.

Saturday, January 23, 1864

On the "room detail" to-day; some experience of wood sawing, which, tho' by no means to be considered in the light of a diversion, I did not find very hard.[52] A long — though not technically so — letter from home from Bro. Wilse containing the usual amount of inquiries concerning my "wants" and evincing a desire to supply them all. It is very gratifying to think that not one word has been written by those at home to discourage me in the least in that course which they know I am determined upon. On the contrary, I am led to believe that they approve of the stand I have taken, explicitly, in some letters, and inferentially in all. I answered the letter immediately & have just mailed my reply.

Sunday, January 24, 1864

Wrote to Sister Belle, a long letter: "Dixie" mail came to-day, but brought me no letter.[53] I fear my letter must have miscarried; if the next Flag-of-Truce mail brings it not, I shall feel certain of it and write again. Have been reading <u>at</u> "Sketches by Boz" but having the bad taste not to admire Dickens overmuch, I have not enjoyed the perusal much.

The meat they give us here is detestable and unfit to eat, while the bread though generally good, is sometimes sour and always insufficient in quantity. These are they who prate of the <u>horrors</u> of Libby Prison.[54]

Monday, January 25, 1864

I must somewhat alter the statement I made yesterday concerning our rations, inasmuch as the meat is sometimes palatable, especially on pork days, though never yet of really good quality. Besides we receive beans & hominy, by far the most acceptable portions of our diet. I do not wish to be caught, even by <u>myself</u>, uttering any Yankee-like complaints, but am willing to endure anything that may be put upon me, consoling myself in the thought that there's a "better day coming," one in which we shall enjoy the sweets of revenge, though not of one visited on prisoners; it would be bad enough, were it not for war crimes, to kill the poor cowardly creatures whom we meet in the army.

Tuesday, January 26, 1864

Yesterday I finished reading a very ludicrous book, entitled "The Color Guard," being a "corporal's notes" of service in the 14th Army Corps. The writer is a Yankee preacher, & was a "nine month's man." verb. sap.[55] Hard tack (seven small squares) issued to-day instead of bread.[56] Misc. Dixie mail, and a letter from Miss Mollie, dated "Richmond, January 6th" giving me welcome assurance of the well being of my friends, and containing messages to some of her Va. friends in here, one of whom, Capt. Holland, I at once called upon.[57] The others, Col. Carrington and Capt. McCulloch,[58] I am deterred from visiting by my terror of <u>mud</u>. Wrote to my little sister to-day.

Wednesday, January 27, 1864

On "kitchen detail" to-day; i.e. I am one of those whose duty it is to lay the tables, carry 'round the viands, saw the wood for the kitchen, & to sweep the dining room. Wrote to Miss M., filling the prescribed page. Rumors of our removal hence are again becoming current: this time Ft. Delaware is indicated.[59] They seem to bear the appearance of truth much more than did the others. However, I suspend my judgment for a while, as they cannot remove us until the ice in the lake is either broken up by thaw or strengthened by another freeze. We have no fire to-day, the temperature being balmy as that of May.

Thursday, January 28, 1864

Somewhat unwell to-day, having a slight fever and a "splitting" headache, probably the effect of more exercise yesterday & combined with indigestion & cold caught by taking a cold bath last night—

Rumors rampant, now designating Craney Island, Norfolk Bay as our probable destination. I have heard so many rumors during the course of my captivity, that I am naturally more incredulous. "Credat Judaeus Apella, non Ego."[60]

> [Literary aside] "You unloose, in asserting your own liberty,
> A knot, which, unloosed, leaves another as free."
> (Lucille)[61] "The dark air with odors hung heavy & rich
> Like a soul that grows faint with desire."

Friday, January 29, 1864

Toward evening, yesterday, I grew worse and by nightfall had quite a high fever. In the latter part of the night, however, I fell into a sound slumber and this morning was much better, in fact, well — except a sensation of extreme lightness. I felt as though, "I had died in sleep and was a blessed ghost."[62] I now feel quite well and hope that my sickness may return no more. Another "Dixie" mail to-day but no letter for me. I begin to have serious apprehensions that my last letters home have been miscarried, since it is full time for answers to arrive. It came.

Saturday, January 30, 1864

More mail matter to-day, but no letter for me: this is very strange.

Though I have been very well all day, slight, though acute, pains in the back of my head this evening betoken a system still out of order. Having an unusually good dinner, I probably ate too much. I am beginning to be subject to frequent attacks of the "blues." The dismal appearance of things out-doors, combined with this tedious imprisonment, is having its natural effect. I feel as though six months more of this life would set me crazy.

Sunday, January 31, 1864

Another dull, dismal day. Finished reading "Anne of Guerstein" begun last night. The only one of the Waverlies I had not read before.[63] The ice is breaking up in the bay and communications are consequently cut off, no mail having come to-day. The lake has been free from ice for several days but that in the bay has such tenacity, that I think it doubtful whether it is entirely broken up before another freeze renews it; especially as there seem some signs of colder weather this evening. Rumor does not hold such unrefuted sway as she did a few days since, though most believe we are to leave as soon as may be.

February 1864

Monday, February 1, 1864

No communication with Sandusky to-day. Ice still breaking up but not as fast as one would suppose. My shoes are in such bad order that I don't go out in the mud to roll-call.[1]

Capt. Moseley of Florida was visited by some friend, a sister I believe[2] — and while outside asked whether he would remain here long enough to receive some clothing from N. Y. and rec'd a reply in the negative, being told that nothing but the state of the bay prevents our removal. Nevertheless I am so incredulous, as to believe that we will not all be sent away.

Tuesday, February 2, 1864

A mail to-day, bringing me a letter at last — from Bro. Rush. It appears that my letters have, several of them, been miscarried. No doubt but that the infernal Yankees, seeing that they contained certain requests, stopped them. These miscreants are known to be in the habit of doing these little things. I had written to Father before the arrival of Rush's letter complaining of the silence of those at home. I have just answered R's letter repeating my requests, which might cause my letter to stop this side of Sandusky Bay.

Wednesday, February 3, 1864

Another letter from home to-day, from Sister Mary, and containing a photograph of myself — taken from a daguerreotype I gave, in my salad days, to Miss Emma, — sent for the purpose of having my autograph appended. My letter to Mary was miscarried, but she wrote regardless of that. The letter to Wilse, was, after all, duly rec'd, but not so that to Lizzie to-day. I procured from Capt. Taylor the 2nd vol. of "Ten Thousand a Year" which I read with pleasure,[3] the thread of the story being already known to me, I do not much miss the first volume. Here is a passage which pleases me. "What is difficulty? Only a word indicating the degree of strength requisite for accomplishing particular objects; a mere notice of the necessity for exertion; a bugbear to children and fools; only a mere stimulus to men."

Thursday, February 4, 1864

Wrote to Sister Mary last night but dated the letter "to-day," lest offense should be taken at two letters bearing the same date since I dated Rush's letter — ahead. Have been quite ill this evn'g, a complication of my patrial[4] &

my personal maladies, chills & neuralgia. My <u>chill</u> was a very severe one, but the fever was alleviated by some ginger tea, prepared for me by Capt. Johnson. To-morrow I shall take quinine which will, I trust, prevent a recurrence of the attack.[5]

Friday, February 5, 1864

Steamboat came over to-day, first time this year. "Our Indian," Capt. Hamilton, of the Choctaw Nation, died last night at the hospital. He was, by all accounts, a brave & worthy man, as well as an educated one.[6]

I am to take "Cook's pills" tonight, and quinine tomorrow morning, by which nostra I hope to evade my chill. Major Durr, (39th Miss.) prescribed for me.[7] He acts as physician for all sick in the block. Wrote to Father today, announcing the final culmination of our rumors in "air, thin air."[8]

Saturday, February 6, 1864

On this day I was so under the influence of Quinine that I felt in no mood for writing, so fill this up on the 7th. All my quinine, however, some twenty-three grains, did not keep off my chill which came back with redoubled malignity.[9] The drug in its effects is worse than the malady, for I heard a noise like the rush of many waters & when this ceased could hear nothing except sounds proceeding in my immediate vicinity. I know nothing more disagreeable than these chills; especially so in prison. Wrote to Father this day a letter which I already regret.

Sunday, February 7, 1864

Well enough to-day except this sensation of extreme <u>lightness</u> before alluded to. I am to take medicine again to-night. Day before yesterday the rumors about our removal were all contradicted by a Yank officer, but to-day, they are afloat again with unusual appearances of probability. I had so far succumbed as to write that my box should not be sent, but on the strength of the contradiction I wrote to have it sent for this site. Now, should we leave, I will lose it. "Verily I said in my heart, all men are liars."[10] Of Yankees this may be said more openly, at least, <u>here</u> in this prison."

Monday, February 8, 1864

This has been the only <u>merry</u> day of my life at Johnson's Island. Capt. Berkeley rec'd 10 gallons of good whiskey—which passed express by some hocus-pocus,—which sufficed to render us all as happy as kings.[11] The miseries of prison life were all forgotten. In my own case, it kept off my chill effectually, and enabled me to pass one day without feeling miserable. I am very glad, however, that ardent spirits aren't allowed us here, as we have no inducements to restrain ourselves from intemperate use of them. Outside, in freedom one can employ all the good things of life moderately & there is no danger except to weaklings.

Tuesday, February 9, 1864

Last night quite a number were notified that they would leave to-day, names beginning with A, B, C, & D. I was omitted, but to-day it was published that all having those letters as initials, would be taken. I have packed & am ready. Col. Berkely, Col. Bullock, Maj Blacknall, Lt. Bond, Apperson and several others from this room have already gone outside.[12] Two 'lots' have been taken out & we are ordered to return to the gate at the tap of the drum. It may be that they have as many as can be taken at once already & that I may still remain. I wish, however to go, as Frank Battle[13] has quite a plausible plan of escape on foot for him, a friend & myself.[14] No bread to-day.

Wednesday, February 10, 1864

The ice which rendered navigation difficult yesterday, now — having been strengthened last night, precludes it altogether. Hence nobody leaves to-day. Capt. Barnes, chief of mess, having gone off, my bunk-mate has been chosen to fill his place.[15] Wrote to my brother to-day. I fear those at home think I have gone off as no letters have come for some time back.

I read Longfellow's new book, "Tales of a Wayside Inn" within the past few days. The design is evidently taken from old Geoffry Chaucer's Canterbury Tales and the pieces bear no stamp of originality, though they contain some striking factual beauties as "The Birds of Killingworth." Tales like the "Saga of King Olaf."

Thursday, February 11, 1864

A letter to-day from Bro. Wilse announcing that a box would be expressed "next Wednesday," which was yesterday, so that, unless delayed by some of my letters, it is now in Sandusky, & will be brought over as soon as the ice permits. It seems that my last letter to Sister Belle has also gone astray. Oh, these infernal Yankees! Began "Fantine,"[16] to-day, intending to read the whole series, when I shall have nothing else. I have read them once, but think them well worthy another perusal. Pickle beef is now issued to us instead of fresh beef, though we fare better now than we did formerly.

Friday, February 12, 1864

On "police detail" to-day very dirty work; making one realize the trials of a scavenger's life.

What a bore this <u>diary</u> is getting to be! Nothing to write about, and if I had, I would be in no humor for writing. But since I have undertaken it, I shall even "persevere unto the end,"[17] hoping that the present dearth of incidents may be followed by a plentiful harvest when I shall have been exchanged and launched into the exciting scenes of a "rattling campaign." How I long for active service! even more than I do for scenes of quiet peace. It is so wretchedly dull here that when I am free, I must have something unusually strong to strike a balance and make up for lost time.

Saturday, February 13, 1864

On "kitchen detail" to-day, probably the last detail I shall serve on upon Johnson's Island, since the ice is melting in the bay, and so soon as navigation opens another lot of prisoners will be sent away and I will most likely be one of the number. Last night a great floe was carried out lakeward, and, judging from appearances, the bay will be open enough to allow the boat to come over to-morrow. Owing to the state of the bay there has been no communication with Sandusky to-day & consequently no mail.

Sunday, February 14, 1864

This day is to be "marked with a white stone"[18] as the date of the arrival of a box of "eatables" from home: "Gibbon" also came, an invaluable book.[19] Contents of box, besides were crackers, ham, chickens, pies, bread, cakes, coffee, etc. A letter from Father accompanied it, and two dollars in greenbacks which were admitted.[20] The day, though a fortunate one in the above respects, has been marked by one calamity: the consignment to solitary confinement of Capt. Frank Battle — to irons, also, I suppose as a hostage for somebody. He was once before in irons for eight weeks at Nashville.[21] These things are not calculated to make us love our enemies.

Monday, February 15, 1864

Another box from home to-day, being in some sort, supplemental to that rec'd yesterday, containing some articles — butter, for instance, — in which that was deficient. A book also was in it, M. Ernest Renan's "Life of Jesus," which I shall take to Mr. Clark, as it has been published since he left this country.[22] I have only read the introduction — which I like very much, — and shall read no further at present: Why should I? It is my own book and may be read at any time, besides, some of my friends are very anxious to read it. I also rec'd a letter from Sister Belle to-day containing quite a supply of p.o. stamps. Wrote to Father.

Tuesday, February 16, 1864

Last night a high wind arose by the agency of which the weather has become much colder. The stove is much crowded, and a dance is kept up besides, yet many suffer constantly from the cold. I regret to say that there are some who manifest a spirit of mean and petty selfishness, unworthy not only of Confederate officers, but of men of any sort of breeding. I feel quite unwell this evening being troubled with sundry twinges in the "forepart of my back" which reminds me painfully of "the bellyache of my boyhood."

> [Literary aside] (Lucile)[23] "Women learn by an instinct men never attain, to discern each others true nature" Miss Mollie's doctrine.

Wednesday, February 17, 1864

I was quite ill last night, slept little and spent the night miserably. To-day I remained in bed till one o'clock, and feel "all right" again. I attribute my derangement to pudding eaten at dinner yesterday. This morning the bay was found again solidly frozen, so that the mail was bro't over on the ice. It is very cold and we are very uncomfortable. Dancing is kept up almost all day. My ink is solid and I only write by plunging my pen, heated in the candle-blaze into the inkstand, and heating it again before the ink has time to freeze upon it. Hoc opus & c.[24]

Thursday, February 18, 1864

Letters arrived to-day from Capt. Barnes and others of our ci-derant[25] comrades, by which we learn that they are at Point Lookout, Md., and that the change is for the better, as they are able to procure anything they may need at "reasonable prices and no pictures."[26] So much for the Ft. Delaware bug-bear. I rec'd a letter from Brother Wilse (which I have already answered) informing me of a box which came three days in advance of the letter. Dr. McElwee sent me Renan's "Life of Jesus." Father is daily expecting to receive a pass. My right knee has been seriously affected with the rheumatism since yesterday, giving me great pain.

Friday, February 19, 1864

A letter from Bro. Rush, which I have already answered: also wrote to Sister Belle but dated one of the letters a day ahead. My rheumatism somewhat better & the weather somewhat less cold.

> [Literary aside] "Mill on the Floss," a novel by the author of "Adam Bede"[27]; a queer book and one, to which, I believe the oracles of the novel reading world have assigned a high position. I am in danger, therefore, of incurring the reproach of "bad taste" when I unhesitatingly say that I don't like the book. It possesses, however, great terseness and vigor of expression and great originality: the latter quite a commendable quality in these days of feeble feminine imitation of

Saturday, February 20, 1864

The weather has again become soft and spring like, though there is a sting about the morning air. A letter from Sister Mary enclosing a better photograph than the one sent several weeks ago. My knee troubles me no longer. A comfortable bath to-day at the bathhouse.

the great & inimitable Miss Bronte.[28] Some of the expressions and comparisons are not what we would expect to find in the pages of female writers, e.g. "Who has not felt the beauty of a <u>woman's arm?</u> The unspeakable suggestions of tenderness that lie in the dimpled elbow and all the varied gently lessening curves down to the delicate wrist...."[29] A woman's arm touched the soul of a great sculptor two thousand years ago, so that he wrought an image of it for the Parthenon, which moves us still as it clasps lovingly the timeworn marble of a headless trunk. Maggie's was such an arm as this and it has the warm tints of life." In this I think "<u>George Eliot</u>" manifests an appreciation which <u>Mrs. Evans</u> could not have felt. The woman is lost in the author. I like this. "She glared at him like a wounded war-goddess," a fine expression for the angry looks of an insulted woman. The authoress manifests an intimate acquaintance with two subjects, viz: classical literature and common life. She does not attempt to soar higher than that phase of existence to which, perhaps, her experience has been limited — and I like her the better for it.

Sunday, February 21, 1864

A slight snow fell last night, but had disappeared by ten o'clock. Attended roll-call this morning, first time for many days. I stumbled upon an old book this morning which I hope to find interesting, M. de Fenelon's "Dialogues on Eloquence."[30] I haven't read anything so solid for a long time. Finished "Mill on the Floss" last night. Wrote a letter to Miss Mollie Moon to-day "her Flag of Truce." also to Sister Mary.

[Literary aside] Here is another passage showing a woman's idea of man's heroic devotion to her sex, as well as a most commendable ignorance of the subject: "The days of chivalry are not gone, notwithstanding Burke's grand dirge over them. They live still in that far off worship paid by many a youth and man to the woman of whom he never dreams that he shall touch as much as her little finger or the hem of her robe." It may be owing to my practical, commonplace nature that I am incapable of appreciating such devotion, or of feeling it. To my mind, hope and love go hand in hand, though one sometimes cherishes a sentiment of deep reverence and lofty honor toward a lady who has been his firm friend and has shown noble and elevated qualities,—without a thought of self-interest. It is not to the lady of his love. This has been my experience. I said I did not like the book. I haven't shown why nor shall I. There are many good things in it and one doesn't regret having read such a book.

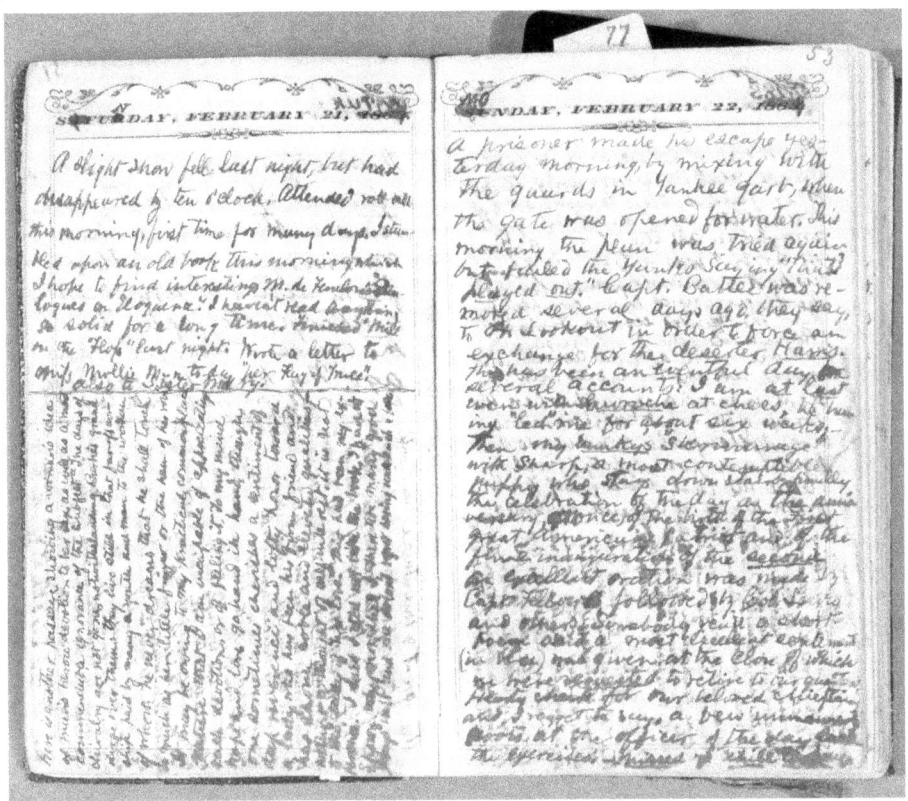

Pages from the diary show the difficulties in deciphering sometimes because of Caldwell's handwriting and "bleed through." Most of the time the writing is very legible except for a word or phrase. At the lower left is one of his asides.

Monday, February 22, 1864

A prisoner made his escape yesterday morning, by mixing with the guards in Yankee garb, when the gate was opened for water.[31] This morning the plan was tried again but failed the Yankees saying, "That's played out." Capt. Battle was removed several days ago, they say, to Pt. Lookout in order to force an exchange for the deserter Harris. This has been an eventful day, on several accounts: I am at last even with Gavroche at chess, he has "led" me for about six weeks. Then my bunky's "scrimmage" with Sharp, a most contemptible puppy who stays downstairs[32]; finally the celebration of the day as the anniversary, at once, of the birth of the First Great American patriot and of the final inauguration of the second.[33] An excellent oration was made by Capt. Fellows followed by Col. Lewis and others.[34] Somebody read a short poem and a most excellent sentiment (in verse) was given at the close of which we were <u>requested</u> to retire to our quarters. Hearty cheers for our beloved chieftain and I regret to say a few unmannered hoots at the officer of the day and the exercises[35] — <u>missed my chill to-day.</u>

Tuesday, February 23, 1864

One, or two, it seems <u>did</u> effect an escape yesterday morning, though others failed. This morning a Col. Kyle, of Ala. went out of the gate arrayed in all the glory of a "Yank" officer, but was detected.[36] He played his part admirably, and looked the officer much more completely than the Yanks ever do. Finished "Leonnes, a tale of the first Crusade," a Catholic novel as good as religious novels are apt to be; but with the scene injudiciously laid where the touch of the great magician has already stamped his own success and precluded possibility of rivalry. Read the last Dialogue of Fenelon from which I append sentences.

> [Literary aside] Isocrates employed ten or fifteen years in smoothing the periods of a panegyric, which was a discourse concerning the <u>necessities of Grace.</u>[37]
> "Nescire enim quid autem,
> quam natus sis, acciderit,
> id est semper esse puerum." Cic. Orat. 1.84[38]
> "A low conceit in pompous words expressed
> Is like a clown in regal purple dressed."
> A fine comparison of the Gothic with the Grecian architecture, & a lively to different style of eloquence. Dialog. III Speaking of the superiority of the taste of Linginus[39] over that of Isocrates;—many think it impossible that such should be the case inasmuch as the former dwelt in a politer age even in the day of the Glory of Athenian letters. Many, nowadays, form their opinions similarly in other matters.

Wednesday, February 24, 1864

I am now engaged in reading the Life of Steuben, by Friedrich Kapp.[40] It is quite an entertaining book, and one which my military experience — or rather, observation, renders more readable than it would otherwise be. The want of discipline and the trials of the first Inspector Gen'l are well set forth and the effects of that discipline which he forthwith instituted.

This evening I had a chill followed, of course, by fever. It seems that I am not to be rid so easily of my former guest. Three Yanks drowned yesterday crossing with the vessel from Sandusky.[41]

Thursday, February 25, 1864

Boat over from Sandusky this evening and I had another chill. This is the sum of the day's events & so ends my record.[42]

[Aside] By means of the frequent boxes sent me from home, I have been able to enjoy my nightly luncheon quite regularly since Christmas. These little collations to me represent the "noctes, coenaeque deorum" on a small scale. Those, quibus datur accumbere epulis, are Bunky, Gavroche, and Rufus Cantridge, though one Des Caises, once asked, still attends.[43] (I heard him with great nonchalance relate, the other night, the contents of some letters which had passed between an old college acquaintance and his father and which had been thrown accidentally in his way by the fortunes of war. Verb Sat.)[44] I like four; it is a companionable number, though if [illegible word] would attend it would not be displeasing to me but he fears the "evil eye & tongue." Vide Supra.[45]

Friday, February 26, 1864

Another chill to-day, despite the quinine that is in me, a very high fever. Dr. Lewis called in[46]: prescribes, for tomorrow dover's powder & cinchona (quinine being "out"—to-night I take Blue mass. I fear I shall be ill.[47]

[Aside] To illustrate the selfishness of uncurbed humanity, I shall explain. When coffee first became a "regular thing" with me, I determined to drink it at night. My pot holds five cups. There are nine in my mess, & my bunky, Gav., & myself were to be three to a certainty. My messmates in this room, when asked, refused and much to my joy, I was left to select companions who knew the difference between obscenity and wit, ribaldry & table-talk. But, my comrades are offended because I reserve ham & other eatables for supper use, though I have ever furnished my share to the general table. This is an illustration of their character. Skimpole rec'd a box[48] not

Saturday, February 27, 1864

By the joint assistance of Blue Mass, Cinchona, Dover's powders & Epsom Salts, I escaped my chill, but was afflicted with more sickness than it would have caused me. Major Saunders having abdicated, Capt. Carter was chosen to succeed him at a mess-meeting to-day.[49]

[Aside continued] long since: its contents were consumed in the privacy of Capt. Calvin Knowles' bunk[50]; the Dutch Hog never receives a box though ever so boastful & I believe he's written for enough to start a wholesale grocery. His people, in their assessment of honor, wish him to take the oath. Q. S. Fitz Lucedale & Le Conubrini are not noble fratres. Heartcent is the only respectable man in the lot though Amaryllis kept to his own interests would be gentlemanlike,[51] mon vieux camarade de la batterie W, holds his acceptance place in any opinions on food only. Hope I may hereafter.

Sunday, February 28, 1864

Am to-day under the influence of cinchona, slightly alleviated by draughts of citric acid lemonade. Missed my chill so that I may now consider myself freed for two weeks more. A letter from Father wherein he gives up all hope of obtaining a pass.

Monday February 29th 1864.[52]

The intercalary day.—I spent it in bed, not exactly ill, but not having entirely recovered my health. Some Dixie letter yesterday & none to-day; if I receive none this mail, I shall write for I <u>know</u> that my friends have written to me ere this.

> [Literary aside] "Our duty down here is to <u>do</u>, not to know,
> Live as though life were earnest and life will be so." Lucille

March 1864

Tuesday, March 1, 1864

Wrote to Father to-day. Feel quite weak and enervated and fear that I am still liable to have an attack of some severe illness. Last night I finished "Roland Cashel," which I found as good as Lever's Novels are apt to be.[1] This is a kind of reading of which I should feel ashamed were I otherwise situated; but here anything serves to while away the time. "Steuben" is still on hand but I do not feel adequate to the perusal of anything heavier than trash, as yet. March "comes in like a lamb," tho by reason of cloudy weather the day is not pleasant.

Wednesday, March 2, 1864

Rec'd photograph of Sister Belle, which I have placed vis-à-vis with that of her friend: a note came in the envelope with the phot. to this effect "The letter accompanying this photograph was contraband and has been destroyed," signed by the examiner. By these, and like precautions the govrm't of the U. S. is preserved intact. Various reports of the success of our arms in different quarters, are in circulation to-day, and I'm disposed to believe that most of them are essentially true. A few victories will bring about an exchange: afterwards we can bear <u>our</u> part in achieving that independence of which we are certain. Wrote to Sister Belle.

Thursday, March 3, 1864

I have finished the Life of Baron Steuben, and have enjoyed its perusal very much. There were troubles in the old war[2] worse than ours, and we should draw inspiration and encouragement from the success of our Fathers. A letter was rec'd here the other day from Capt. Frank Battle; he did not go for exchange, as reported, but is at Ft. Warren in irons.[3] A large Dixie mail, to-day, but no letter for me: this is very strange for I feel certain that letters have been written. The box from home, of which I was advised, though due yesterday, has not come yet.

Wrote to Miss V.B.M.—(Virginia)[4]

Friday, March 4, 1864

A box of good things arrived from home to-day; also two letters, one from Father, the other from Sister Mary. I am sensibly reminded of the enduring love and kind recollection of those at home and hope that I may not be so base as to forget them. Even in the God-forsaken "mob led" Yankee land true hearts still beat. My wants are anticipated for I seldom make any requests. The weather is now beautiful & spring like & sails again give to the bay the appearance of life & bustle. A few of us (ΔKE)[5] met together to-day. These old associations are very pleasant.

Saturday, March 5, 1864

Ingrata vice, rediit acris Hyems.[6]

This morning snow lay upon the ground and it has continued to fall during a great part of the day. What a "changeful clime" is this. Wrote to my Mother to-day. Letters rec'd from our former room-mates, now at Pt. Lookout, state that they are guarded by negro troops. I hope I may not be sent thither, though I should think the "mild Nubians," "blameless Ethiopians," would both be more corruptible & less efficient than even New England Yankees. There has been much complaint of late, concerning the insufficiency of our rations. Several petitions have (I believe) been sent out on the subject.[7]

Sunday, March 6, 1864

For my own part I do not see that they are any worse, in this respect, than they were formerly and besides, I, for one, would rather live on half viands than ask a favor of our enemies. I have often been hungry: in fact, when I have had nothing more than the rations, I am almost always so until dinner time. Each must, however, think for himself re this & blame no one.

[Aside] Weather somewhat more moderate, but unpleasantly cold still [illegible word] being muddy. Yankee chaplain came in & preached to-day. Believe he had an audience. Several indignation meetings were held, in view of his coming, and many violent & Puritanic resolutions adopted, though they were merely "sound & fury."[8] I think it would have been well for no one to have attended & this is the only kind of proscription I believe in. All others are Yankee-like.[9]

Monday, March 7, 1864

On Police — scavenger duty — again to-day. My illness excused me from the other details, as my turn came while I was unfit for duty. Wrote a letter to Father. The great dearth of events induces me to leave my paper blank, to be filled when circumstances permit.

"Nature never made a heart all marble, but, in its passions; [illegible word]
The wild flowers love; from whom rich seeds spring forth;
A world of mercies and sweet charities."   Barry Cornwall
I know a lady fair to see:
Take care!
She can both false and fancy be,
Beware! Beware!
She is [illegible word]
She has two eyes, so soft and brown,
Take care!
She gives a side glance & looks down,
Beware! Beware!
Trust her not
She is fooling thee!
She has a bosom white as snow,
Take care!
She knows how much its [illegible word]
Beware, Beware!
(Hyperion)

Tuesday, March 8, 1864

Somebody broke a lamp over the Sutler's[10] head in return for some of his impudence; the lamp is a dead loss but it is feared that the Sutler was not injured seriously. It is not known who did this praiseworthy deed, as — with heroic modesty, he mingled with the crowd and sought concealment. I fear the Yankees may yet ferret him out. A letter has come from Pt. Lookout stating that 200 of those who left here — among them several from our room, — have been selected by lot to go to City Point.[11] They hope an exchange will be the result of the processing. Having procured "Heart of Midlothian,"[12] I shall desist from my literary labor of writing quotes from Coleridge's novel, with which I have been amusing myself for want of better employment.

Wednesday, March 9, 1864

"The bleak winds of March" come with great bluster upon the scene: the surface of the lake is white with fields of ice, detached from the Canadian shore, and the bay is dotted with drifting floes.

On detail today, to dig sinks,[13] a most disagreeable occupation and one which causes my nose to share the indignation of Trinculo's.[14] Finished my third reading of "The Heart of Midlothian," a most exquisite novel but already too familiar to be very interesting. What would I not give for free access to a good library!

Thursday, March 10, 1864

The day mild, though sunless, despite the threatening aspect of yesterday. A letter to Sister Mary.

> [Literary aside] The English officer to whom Sir James Turner was prisoner after the rout at Uttoxeter, demanded his parole of honor not to go beyond the walls of Hull without liberty. "He brought me the message himself,—I told him I was ready to do so, provided he removed his guard from me, for, fides et fiducia sunt relativa[15]; and, if he took my word for my fidelity, he was obliged to trust it, otherwise, it was needless for him to ask it, and in vain for me to give it, and therefore I beseeched him either to give trust to my word, which I would not break, or his own guards who, I supposed, would not deceive him. In this manner I dealt with him because I knew him to be a scholar." Turner's Memoirs, pg. 80. The English officer allowed the strength of the reasoning but that concise reasoner put an end to the discussion by deciding that "Sir James Turner must give parole or be laid in irons." Note to Legend of Montrose.[16] Cromwell was the great original Yankee.

Friday, March 11, 1864

I chanced upon an old number of the Atlantic Monthly, wherein I have found some good reading. An article on Darwin's "Origin of Species," another on Shelley, and a few chapters from "The Professor's Story" (Elsie Venner)[17] which I regard as the best novel yet written for the Atlantic. The Atlantic was the best review on the continent despite its Jacobinical & Abolitionist (or radical) tone and tendencies. I speak, of course, merely from a literary point of view. Wrote a letter to Brother Wilse. Last of my coffee consumed. Dark, stormy weather, rain in the forenoon.

Saturday, March 12, 1864

Two letters from Father and sister Belle,— the latter a most excellent one, so much so that I wonder at its passing the ordeal of examination.[18] This being the fourteenth day, I expected to have a chill, but have been agreeably disappointed. Father's letter contained a photograph of Sister Belle. Some of the officers who slept here—among them Capt. Bullock & Blacknall— have already been exchanged. It seems probable that an exchange has been effected, so that in the course of time, we shall be restored to our country and her course. Though not credulous, I believe that in two months I shall be free.

Sunday, March 13, 1864

Day very disagreeable, though not very cold; snowing all day. Began Renan's "Life of Jesus," find it thus far, delightful.

[Literary aside] "I have seen falsehood veiled by the virginal cheek of a child. I have seen the immaculate meek Desdemona false; Imogene wanton; have seen Juliet faithless; and she, the chaste Ithacan queen, choose a swine from her suitors, and, from his embrace, rise to write to her [illegible word] that she pines for his face in a tender Ovidian strain."

"For let a man once show the world that he feels afraid of its bark and it will fly at his heels.
Let him fearlessly face it, it will leave him alone.
But 'twill fawn at his feet if he flings it a bone."

"The face that most fair to our vision allowed
Is the face we encounter and love in the crowd
The thought that most thrills our existence is one
which, before we can frame in language, is gone."

"and is it too late?
No! for Time is a fiction and limits not fate
Thought alone is eternal. Time thralls it in vain.
For the thought that springs upward and yearns to regain
The pure source of spirit, there is no Too Late."
(March 27 + + + "Lucile" + +)

Monday, March 14, 1864

Changed my "table" in the mess to-day, leaving Shannon, Blount, Van Cracey, Elkins,[19] et id genus omne,[20] and transferring my attendance to the table of Saunders, Johnston, Manly and Turner.—"Set free from daily contact with the things I loathe,"[21] I rejoice at the change. Major Jos. H. Saunders, 33rd N.C.—Chapel Hill, N.C; Capt. W. H. Johnston, 23rd N.C, Charlotte, N.C; Lt. Matt. Manly, 2nd N.C. Newberne, N.C.—Capt. Henry Turner, also of the 23rd N.C. but a citizen of Georgia. The last I know not intimately as I do the others. I like their society better than that of any other of my fellow prisoners.

Tuesday, March 15, 1864

Wrote a letter to Father to-day.

A "grape" is in circulation to the effect that France has recognized the Confederate States.[22] I am very skeptical upon all such gossips, though I believe that when recognition <u>does</u> come, as it must one day, our first welcome into the family of nations will be from that power whose greatness and glory constitutes her first among enlightened nations or mayhap from Spain, stately embodiment of conservatism, — free anti-Jacobian conservatism, such as that for which we war to-day.

Wednesday, March 16, 1864

On two "details" — kitchen and room; read some of the "Sermons by the Paulists," or sermons preached in the Church of St. Paul the Apostle. An excellent work, and <u>convincing</u>, if one admits the postulate upon which it rests.

Had a chill, to-day, and also think I have done enough for one day. These chills do not trouble me much during their continuance, but I find them very <u>wearing</u> in their effects, and difficult to break up, even with assiduous dosing oneself with unpleasant remedies. I don't believe I shall ever rid myself of them until I can obtain the right amount of the right medicine, i.e. quinine.

Thursday, March 17, 1864

St. Patrick's day! There are associations to which my memory recurs on this day, and a reminiscence connected with it, <u>Eheu effrenata inventas!</u>[23]

Finished Renan to-day, have derived both pleasure & profit from its perusal, <u>pleasure</u> from its beauty of style and the mildness of its polemics: <u>profit</u>, because I am led to a more exalted opinion of humanity, a higher conception of religion (<u>true</u> religion) than I had ever realized before. I shall read it again, however, and with care. Am reading the "Sermons" in Latin.[24] A letter to Sister Belle.

Friday, March 18, 1864

Another chill, more severe than usual.

I have been very much amused by my late perusal of "The Household of Bouverie, or the Elixir of Gold" by a Southern Lady,[25] the most ludicrous book — yet unintentionally so — I have met for a long time. In any other situation, I shouldn't have thought of reading it, but here anything not absolutely <u>Rosamutilda</u> or <u>Emerson-Bennetly</u> may be read. The authoress takes great credit to herself for accuracy in quoting Shakespeare giving "a looker-on in <u>Vienna</u>" as a proof yet within a few pages has the audacity to write "to the <u>manor</u> born" and "give me some drink, <u>Titania</u>." A beam in <u>her</u> eye <u>surely</u>.

Saturday, March 19, 1864

Spent the greater part of the day in bed. Read "Legend of Montrose," and found it as interesting as it was when I first read it. The character of Sir Dugald Dalgetty gives a raciness, a flavor, as it were, to the whole story.

I am to begin taking cinchona tonight at bedtime,— to-morrow I will be miserable through its influence, yet it is only in this way that I can break up my chills even for the brief fortnight which they are content to allow me to enjoy.

Sunday, March 20, 1864

Bay frozen over — no communication with Sandusky. Very ill last night or, rather, <u>sick</u> with such <u>nausea</u> as I have experienced since I went to sea.[26] Don't know whether I have had a chill to-day or not, I have been either in a sleep or stupor all day and my brain has been reveling in a confused medley of dreams like those of an opium-eater. I had a slight fever in the evening however. Haven't been out of bed or even dressed. Took cinchona and Dover's powders[27] and calomel has been prescribed for tonight, but shall not take it till morning & by advice of my "bunky," shall throw away <u>one</u> pill as 10gr. seems too heavy a dose.

Monday, March 21, 1864

Still in bed: took my calomel this morning and expect to be sick enough in consequence, before night. Bay still frozen over. Finished reading another worthless book "Darien, or the Merchant Prince" by Eliot Warburton.[28] I rejoice that I derive no pleasure — other than the <u>negative</u> one of mere <u>occupation</u>— from such books, else I should deplore the <u>demoralization</u> of my taste.

Not so sick, after all, from the effects of the medicine, only slightly nauseated. A mail is said to have come over the ice this evening but no matter has been brought in for distribution.
STHENOSCOPE[29]

Tuesday, March 22, 1864

Missed my chill, so that I am rid of the malady for a fortnight, at least. I feel very weak, and much worn by my slight sickness. Have spent the day in bed. Weather very cold. Another mail but nothing as yet has been distributed; except, "papers." It will be strange if I do not receive a letter from home. Have been reading Lever's "Martins of Cro' Martin," which I find like all the rest of his work, abounding in improbabilities, feminine & equine, and replete with errors, grammatical, historical and geographical, yet, full enough of incidents to make it <u>readable</u> in this hole. Elsewhere I'd not descend to it.

Wednesday, March 23, 1864

Day warmer: ice in the bay so strong that it has again become a thoroughfare. A letter from Brother Rush announcing a box, to be sent by next

Sunday, my birthday. I felt sure of some such token of remembrance on that day. Answered the letter at once. Am still far from well;— indeed I don't think I have any chance of recovering my health until I shall be landed free in Dixie. Confinement, prison fare, and worse than all, that depression of spirits which is the very atmosphere of captivity, will keep me down. Have at last, I believe, got hold on a good book.

Thursday, March 24, 1864

This morning I awoke with a slight pain in the abdominal regions: By breakfast time it had culminated in a decided case of cramp cholic. Opium, camphor, morphine & mustard plaster were resorted to in vain, and I passed a day of great suffering followed by a night of nervous dreams.[30] I think I suffered more for the length of time, than I ever did before. (this I write March 25th) A polite Yank Captain came in to-day, at a general roll-call in the evening, and took the full name, rank and command of each. This looks to me somewhat like preparations for exchange. The day was a beautiful one, very mild & balmy though the bay still "closed solid"— I wish it would break up.

Friday, March 25, 1864

Pleasant day: ice, so rotten that no communication has been held with the main land. I feel "myself again," except in regard to strength, for I am very weak, so that I cannot walk across the room without great fatigue. Wrote to Father to-day for ale or porter. Hope he may send it soon. Am reading Owen Meredith's "Lucile."

[Literary aside] "The great mortal combat between human life,
and each human soul must be single. The strife
none can share tho' by all its result may be known,
when the soul arms for battle, she goes forth alone."–
"Cling to one faith and die with it, though earthquakes
may shatter the shrine."
"The man who seeks one thing in life, and but one,
may hope to achieve it before life is done."–
"For the world's a nettle, disturb it, it stings;
Grasp it firmly, it stings not."
"As there gleams in the thyrsus[31] that Bacchanals bear,
Thro' the blooms of a garland, the point of a spear."
"Tis the half empty vessel that freest emits the water
that's in it. Tis thus with men's wits,
or at least with their knowledge."

"In the distant Savannah a talisman grows, that makes all men brothers that use it."

Saturday, March 26, 1864

Beautiful day — ice still in the bay, but loosened up by the thaw, is very rotten, so that it is likely the boat may yet come over this evening. Walked, this morning, the whole length of the "bullpen," but was greatly wearied by the exertion. Shall begin to take exercise very gradually.

The boat <u>has</u> come over; working her way around and through the ice in a manner interesting to witness. I watched her passage from one of our bay windows. I suppose we'll have "her mail" tomorrow and express on Monday. I feel an interest in both. Finished <u>Lucile</u>, like it very much though the style is not that which I like best in poetry. It, I suppose, might be termed a <u>conversational</u> epic.

Sunday, March 27, 1864

Easter, and my birthday: a day ever to me full of memories of the past. Wrote a letter to my dear Mother, as long as the rules would permit: this is one of the duties of the day.[32] The ice is now out of the bay, and the dark waters roll unfettered nor again to be so, I trust and believe, while I remain a prisoner. No <u>letter</u> mail to-day; except one of newspapers,— nor has the express yet come in; the latter I long for with all the eagerness of a hungry man, for I believe that I have a 'box' outside. The head Sutler came in to-day & issued checks. Tomorrow he begins to sell & to sell <u>eatables</u>. This will be a great relief.[33]

Monday, March 28, 1864

Finished Bulwer's "Strange Story" and only regret that it had not been longer.[34] I read it once before during the siege of Pt. Hudson[35] but the circumstances then surrounding me were not those most favorable to the proper appreciation of a literary work. To my having been, yesterday, deeply absorbed in the most interesting portions of the above named work, I attribute the origin of an exquisitely delightful dream, which, last night, blessed my vision,— full of pleasure, intellectual — I almost say <u>psychal</u>— it was a strange medley of thrilling thoughts & beautiful forms; of familiar faces (or rather <u>one</u> familiar face) in strange scenes; for those great issues of strange yet powerful phantoms with which Bulwer abounds, seemed intermixed with my life & with one still dearer. There was nothing merely physical in my dreams,— it was a vision of the <u>soul</u>. A letter from Father dated 22nd inst. The box was sent on the 24th and has not yet arrived, express not having been issued. When it does come a part, at least, of the edible contents will be found spoiled.— — — Just my luck.

Tuesday, March 29, 1864

A dull, damp, dark, dirty, disagreeable day; a very Sunday in its gloom and irksomeness. Nothing to do, nothing to read, and almost nothing to think about. I wrote to Father. The only incident of the day is a very disgraceful one.

One Stevens, an Arkansas Captain,[36] made application to be permitted to take "the oath" but was detected & severely "punished" by one of his officers, as well as turned out of his mess. He went around begging entrance into another, but met only insult, contempt and rougher usage. He openly avowed that he had intended to

Wednesday, March 30, 1864

take the oath only for the purpose of "getting out," and he did not intend to keep his oath, thus, pleading perjury as an apology for an equal crime. O tempora, O mores.[37]

> [Aside] A day, the very counterpart of yesterday. About three hundred boxes of express matter came in to-day, and so late that but few have been issued: Mine, coming in the second hundred, will have to wait a day longer, or till to-morrow by which time everything spoilable will have been spoiled. A large Dixie mail to-day but, as usual, no letter for me. This is strange for I know that some must have been written.

Thursday, March 31, 1864

March "goes out" in a manner characteristic of her latter days, for this is but another of a seemingly endless category of disagreeable days. Box came in to-day. Nothing spoiled. Everything topsy-turvy; salt, vinegar & pepper lost,—spilled. The beets & cabbage in cans are fresh and afford us a great luxury. Potatoes, tomatoes, butter, molasses, apple-butter, eggs, coffee, ham, chickens & beef, crackers, smoking tobacco, pies, cakes, beef-steak & fresh pork, with canned peaches & quinces about complete the list. A new & fitting pr. of shoes. A letter fr Wilse.

April 1864

Friday, April 1, 1864

Wrote to Brother. Lucretius, it seems, was not to be found in [illegible word]; so I didn't receive it, but, instead, Bulwer's novel "Lucretia," which I have read but shall read again. I find my whole system still out of order, and I fear indulging my appetite as I should like. I am taking—or supposed to be taking, for I often forget it,—a tonic preparation of iron and quinine. I found among the envelopes sent me the other day, <u>one</u> filled with quinine, so that I am independent of the druggist on this point.

Saturday, April 2, 1864

Weather begins to look spring like again. Unwell, weakness of stomach. System wants tone, not yet recovered from debilitating effects of my pet tertian.[1] Navigation seems to be permanently resumed, as both steamers & sailing craft frequently make their appearance bearing out from the bay, lakeward.

Versus Monachi, ap. <u>Kames</u>

De planctu cudo metrum cum carmine nudo

Mingere cum bombis res est saluberrima lumbis."

Quid significat "bombis," quid "<u>cudo</u>"? nonne iste "<u>ferio, ut nummum</u>"? Quaestio Clerico propositurus.[2]

Sunday, April 3, 1864

Day delightful. Quite unwell & in bed all forenoon — Walked up to Capt. Isbell's room in the evening and got Wilkie Collins' "No Name,"[3] which I at once attacked. Wrote a letter to Uncle Joe.

> [Literary aside] Speech of Viscount Dundee to the Chiefs & gentlemen of his army, before the battle of Killiecrankie (Macpherson's "State Papers.")[4]
>
> "Gentlemen—you are come hither this day to fight, and that in the best of causes, for it is the battle of your king, your religion, and your country, against the foulest usurpation and rebellion, and having,

Monday, April 4, 1864

A letter from Father. Finished "No Name;" quite readable, tho' not a first class novel. To the incidents the interest is due. A dull drizzly day. Answered Father's letter.

> [Literary aside continued] therefore, so good a cause is in your hands, I doubt not but it will inspire you with an equal courage to maintain it;—for there is no proportion between loyalty and treason, nor should there be any between the valor of good subjects and traitors. Remember, that, today, begins the fate of your king, your religion and your country. Behave yourselves,

Tuesday, April 5, 1864

Began Romola, by George Eliot. Like it thus far very well, but doubt the author's power to sustain herself throughout; displays great learning, much more than the one would expect from a woman.

> [Literary aside continued] therefore, like true Scotsmen, and let us by this action, redeem the credit of this nation, that is laid low by the treachery

and cowardice of some of our countrymen,—in which, I ask nothing of you that you shall not see me do before you, and if any of us shall fall on this occasion, we shall have the honor of dying in our duty, and as becomes men of valor and conscience;

Wednesday, April 6, 1864

A great shout at roll-call this morning proclaiming the arrival of glad tidings; the arrangement of preliminaries whereby a general exchange may be expected. <u>Nous verrons</u>.[5]

[Literary aside continued] Such of us as shall live, and win the battle, shall have the reward of a gracious king, and the praise of all good men. In God's name, then, let us go on, and let this be your word—King James and the Church of Scotland, which God long preserve!"

Thursday, April 7, 1864

Finished Romola. The report about exchange seems to be approaching confirmation.

[Literary aside] "O day thrice lovely when at <u>length</u> returns the soldier home into life;
when he becomes a fellow-man among his fellowmen.
The colours are unfurl'd; the cavalcade marshals, and now the buzz is hushed.
Now the soft peace-march beats, home brothers, home:
The caps & helmets are all garlanded with green boughs, the last plundering of the fields.
1st Pt. Wall Act I.S.4.[6]
"With light heart the poor fisher moors his boat
And watches from the shore the lofty ship
Stranded amid the storm."
- -
"In vain the human being institutes free action;
He is but the wise-world's puppet of the blind power,
which out of his actions creates for him a dread necessity."

Friday, April 8, 1864

Fast-day and as such generally observed. If the Yankees were <u>looking</u> I would fast, myself, to show my respect for Mr. Davis, but the general observation answers that purpose. Suffering from inflammation of my right eye, brought on by five minute's <u>walk</u> in the wind.

[Literary aside] "For fable is love's world, his home, his birthplace:
Delightedly dwells he 'mong fays and talismans, and spirits,

and delightedly believes Divinities, being himself divine.
The intelligible forms of ancient poets,
The fair humanities of old religions
The power, the beauty and the majesty,
That hath their haunts in dale, or piny mountains,

Saturday, April 9, 1864

Rainy, disagreeable day. An "April day," without the sunshine; unvaried shower. Eye still gives me pain.

[Literary aside continued] Or forest, by slow stream, or pebbly spring,
Or chasms and watery depths; all these have vanished.
They live no longer in the faith of reason!
But still the heart doth need a language, still
Doth the old instinct bring back the old names,
And to you starry world they now are gone,
Spirits or gods, that us'd to share this earth
With man as with their friends
Yonder they move, from yonder visible sky
Shoot influence down; and even at this day
'Tis Jupiter who brings whatever is great,
And Venus who brings everything that's fair!"
Wall II, 4
Et iam prima novo spargebat lumine terra
Tithoni croceum linquens Aurora cubile.
"an sese medios moriturus in hostes—
Inferat, et pulchram properet per vulnera mortem?"
"Euryale auden sum dextra; nunc ipsa vocat res."[7]

Sunday, April 10, 1864

Wrote to Brother Wilse. Reading—Kames Elements of Criticism. Eye almost well.

[Literary aside] Boston Puritanism in Sandwich Isles
From 1830 to 1837, and especially in the latter year, Puritanism was rampant in the Sandwich Islands, where under the auspices of Yankee Missionaries a dreadful persecution was maintained against the Catholics. I transcribe herewith a few incidents from Simpson Journey Round the World,[8] as I may not see the book again and would like to have the "authority" at my command. "The persecution now raged more fiercely than ever, while new varieties of torture were invented. A party of 60 or 70 Catholics, having brought before the governor, they all recanted but 13; and the recu-

sants also were induced to see the error of their ways, and to exchange the Pule Pulani[9] for the <u>Pule Mr. Bingham</u>, by being suspended in pairs by the wrists,"

Monday, April 11, 1864

"John Halifax, Gentleman;" quite a pleasant days reading.[10] I have long been eager to read it on account of praise lavished upon it by Miss MM, who is not one of those who praise too freely. The book has however some tedious chapters and the conduct of some of the dramatic persona, though <u>most</u> <u>Christian</u>, is strange.

"Sedet aeternumque sedebit"
verb. secund., qd seg.?[11]

[Literary aside] "Lasciate agni speranza
Voi che entrate"—In Inferni portis[12]
"Scandit aeratas vitiosa naves
Cura: nec turmas equitum relinquit[13]
Post equitem sedet atra cura[14]

Tuesday, April 12, 1864

Four letters — in one envelope from three younger sisters to-day. The letters were all <u>written</u> yesterday. Nothing new concerning exchange. I still hope. Wrote to Sister Mary.

[Literary aside continued] "His annis gravis, atque animi maturus Aletes;
Di patris, quorum semper sub numine Troia est,
Non tamen omnino Teucros delere paratis,
Cum talis animos iuvenum, et tam certa tulistis pectora.
Quae vobis, quae digna, viri, pro laudibus istis
Prarmia posse rear solvi? pulcherrima primum
Di moresque dabunt vestri" (IX)
Multi patri portanda dabat mandata: sed aurae
Omnia discerpunt, et nubibus inrita donant."
"Est hic, est animus, lucis contemptor; et istum
Qui vita bene credat emi, quo tendis honorem."
Te superesse velim tua vita dignior aetas.[15]
(-- 1p.) Ms. & Eus.

- -

[aside] across the top of the wall seven feet high with their ankles in irons. On another occasion, two women, respectively 30 and 50 years of age, were similarly treated, excepting that they were not tied together and

after the miserable wretches had been hanging about eighteen hours, all night in the rain and all the forenoon in the sun, some

Wednesday, April 13, 1864

Box of ale arrived—but I have not yet rec'd the necessary "permit" to get it. Maj. Beldin (U.S.) has just told me that if my Father apply to Gen. Terry he will rec. permission to see me. I have just written this to Father & shall expect him in a few days, though the word of a Federal officer is a very frail reliance. Maj. B., however, is, at least, a gentleman<u>like</u> man.—

[aside continued] of the foreign residents applied in their behalf to Mr. Bingham who refused, however, to interfere, alleging that the sufferers must have been condemned for some offense against the law. Of course they were, as the judge very clearly explained to the aforesaid party of 60 or 70. They were not, he told them, to be punished for repeating Catholic prayers, or believing Catholic doctrines, but because in so doing, they had disobeyed the orders of the king." Capt. Laplace of the [illegible word] stopped the persecution with spirit in 1837.

Thursday, April 14, 1864

Got my ale—13 bottles, scotch also, 1 bourbon whiskey, 1 brandy, 1 gin, 1 Mad.wine. This medicine will seem more palatable than "[illegible word.]" 42 prisoners arrived last night, old captures brought from other prisons. Mostly Arkansians. My box lost by "stealage," of course.

[Literary aside] "Non vinum, ut vinum, appetitur, sed tale Bonumque—
Sic et vita, ut vita, est nil, nisi bona: quod si(?)
Est misera, ut vinum corruptum despiciatur
Esse quidam, per se nec amandum nec fugiendum est,
Quippe habet hoc quamvis vilissima rerum, vermis,
Musca, lapis, cortex nihil est optabile <u>adempta</u>
<u>Conditione boni,</u> nisi est tale esse bonumque
Non vides cur optari cur possit amari."[16]
Quoted in Palingenius by Ch. Canot.

Friday, April 15, 1864

Weather cooler—unfavorable news concerning exchange; to the effect that no <u>general</u> exchange has yet been agreed upon. I fear that this may have some truth in it. Macaulay's History of Eng. 1st volume with Rufus Centuris: wish we had the whole of that interesting romance.

[Literary aside continued] "Me, me, adsum, qui feci; in me convertite ferrum,
O Rutuli! Mea fraus omnis, nihil iste nec ausus;

> Nec potuit; caelum hoc, et conscia sidera testor:
> Tantum infelicem nimium dilexit amicum."
> "Volvitur Euryalus leto, pulchrosque per artus
> It cruor inque humeros cervix collapsa recumbit:
> purpuerus veluti cum flos, succisus aratro,
> Demisere caput! pluvia cum forte gravantur."
> "Fortunati ambo! Si quid mea carmina possunt,
> Nulla dies umquam memori vos eximet aevo:
> Dum domus Aeneae Capitoli immobile saxum
> Accolet, imperiumque pater Romanus habebit,"
> Hic amor unus erat, pariterique in bella ruebant."
> (Eneid. IX. Nisus Euryalus)[17]

Saturday, April 16, 1864

Rain, snow & gloomy weather. Letter from Father. Reading "Very Hard Cash." Excellent book, so spirited & entertaining. Charles Reade excels all his contemporaries in felicity of expression[18] and is without a superior in the [illegible phrase] yet is he something of a "criticaster"— his own words withal; for despite his fling at the grammatical inaccuracies of others; he indulges in expressions that are at least inelegant, if not inaccurate; frequently on [illegible word] whether such a line occurred or not, ran to & fro, or citable instance.

Sunday, April 17, 1864

Finished "Very Hard Cash." Shall look for (<u>am expecting</u>) Father to-morrow.

To-day, during the consumption of our fancy repast, <u>facetiously</u> called <u>dinner</u>, Capt. Turner asked me "If I intended to settle permanently into the pedagogical gown," and, upon my affirmative answer, "If I would like to settle in Ga." I replied that I 'didn't care'. Then he offered me a "place" at $1500 the first year, & an increase proportionate to my subsequent success. I told him this would suit me. Now this little table-talk may have some influence on my life. Quien sabe?[19]

Monday, April 18, 1864

Box of <u>eatables</u> arrived from "<u>home</u>"— i.e. my father's house. Also a jar of brandy peaches which prove delightful & a few additional bottles of ale. All these are for the nonce to be understood as comprehended within the term <u>eatables</u>. The ale and liquors have already wrought wonders for me & I feel quite strong again: this may however, be but a temporary relief but I hope otherwise. In the box— written on the back of an envelope on a package— was an excellent letter from my "sympathysing brother."

Tuesday, April 19, 1864

I have been expecting my Father, but begin to fear that Beldin did not mail my letter, despite his promise. "<u>Timeo Danaos</u>."[20]

An order has come in to the effect that all sick & wounded shall present themselves for examination, that they may be exchanged. Had this come a week ago I might have had some chance. Two weeks ago I would have been certain of success. I now wish my ale had not come & my chills had not yielded to treatment. I regret to see many officers coolly preparing to "pass off" for sick by means of deception & falsehood.

Wednesday, April 20, 1864

News of a great victory in La., and news too, so seemingly authentic that I believe them. Banks' Army is & ever will be miserably demoralized.[21] This is due, in part, to us of Port Hudson. Apropos. Capt. Cyrus Dickey, a.a.g. to the Yank Gen. Ransom is reported killed — How strange that I should feel no grief for my old college friend — "Tempora mutantur et nos mutamur in illis."[22] Wrote to Father in reply to a letter rec'd to-day. He is not coming here, deterred by some reason which he cannot explain by letter; at least, this is the conclusion to which I arrive from his letter. A medical examination this evening — much base humbug.

Thursday, April 21, 1864

A "<u>lovely</u>" day; — one which would justify the whole vocabulary of feminine adjectives. Finished a re-perusal of Bulwer's "Lucretia," an interesting book, but dark and sombre: what a relief to read after it Coleridge's lines to his Genevieve (those entitled "Love.") Subscribed to the circulating library this evening and took out Coleridge. On kitchen detail: water & wood & in addition "small rations." A general scrubbing up of rooms & airing of the bedding. Feel rather tired. Think the sick & wounded will leave tomorrow. Mem. an address: Capt. Henry G. Turner — 23rd N.C., Quitman, Ga. or Henderson, N.C.

[Literary aside] Tum super exanimum sese proiecit amicum confossus, placidaque ibi demum morte quievit.
(En. IX.)[23]

Friday, April 22, 1864

The sick & wounded who were "passed" by the examining board left us to-day. among them Capt. Turner, of our table, & "Governor" Smith & Capt. Sharp, (N.C. Cav.) from our room. Gen. Hutchison 8 Va. also. Capt. Taylor, Miss Emma M's kinsman, also left. They will all be in "Dixie" in a short time. If this business had come on a month ago, I would have gone, but I have recovered too soon. I would gladly be sick or have a severe wound, to get back to my own country. I rejoice that many who attempted to lie their way out, failed;— though some succeeded. "Ancient Mariner and Wallenstein," my reading to-day. Day rainy, & such as none but Yankees would have chosen.

Saturday, April 23, 1864

"Moved" my lodging to the bunk left vacant by Capt. Turner. The weather will soon be too warm to sleep "double". Reading "Old Mortality,"[24] for about the sixth time, & again as much interested as I was the first perusal. A letter from Dixie, & better still, from "V.B.M."— This cheers me more than all the ale & liquor. I feel in better spirits than I have since my captivity, & more eager for exchange than ever since I now know I shall see my friend in Richmond as soon as I can. I mark this day with a white stone.

Sunday, April 24, 1864

A letter to Brother Wilse. A very disagreeable & gloomy day. I have the worst fit of 'blues' I have had for a long time, brought on, I believe, by thinking of exchange and believing it remote. Yesterday's letter now renders me only more dissatisfied with my lot and eager to be where it came from. Passed off the afternoon by reading "Woodstock," or rather by skipping along through it.

[Literary aside continued] "Aut tu, magne pater Divum, Miserere, tuoque
Invisum hoc detrude caput sub Tartara telo,
Quando aliter nequeo crudelem abrumpere vitam"
"Non illa virum, non illa pericli, telorumque memor"
"Femineo ululatu." (En. IX 490+)[25]

Monday, April 25, 1864

Read the episode of Nisus & Euryalus in the ninth book of the Eneid,— to my mind the finest episode in Epic Poetry — Wrote a letter to V.B.M. full-page, but not such as I could wish to write. A squad of prisoners came in to-night. Tennessee cavalry.— verb. sup.

from Milton's Comus.
"Behold this cordial julep here,
That flames and dances in his crystal bounds
With spirits of balm and fragrant stands of night
Not that Napenthes, which the wife of Thone
In Egypt gave to Jove-born Helena
Is of such power to stir up Joy as this,
To life so friendly, or so cool to thirst."

> [Literary aside] Si cui videor non iustus, inulto
> Dicere quod sentit, permitto"—Hor.
> (sed ubit–)[26]

Tuesday, April 26, 1864

More prisoners arrived to-day, but most of them are old captures; those who are not belong to that numerous class who are "captured at home" and are no loss, whatever, to the service. The news this morning's papers bring is very cheering: our prospects are everywhere brightening. Several important captures made recently by our troops will also tend to hasten exchange. Reading: Journey round the World, Simpson (Sir George, I believe, superintendant of the H.B. Co.— tho' the covers & title page are torn off. I shall elsewhere inscribe some passages relative to the persecution in Sandwich Islands.[27]

Wednesday, April 27, 1864

A letter from Father, which I have already answered. Read "Midsummer Nights' Dream"[28] & finished "Simpson." The latter work is an authority upon the effects of Boston missionary enterprise— their Sunday laws & Seventh-Commandment bills are all given, as well as their persecution of Catholics, & that too by one who seems, elsewhere, almost bigoted in favor of Protestantism. Yet he acknowledges that the Catholic schools, which he visited, were doing good & that in a more Christianlike way than those of their guardians & would-be persecutors.

> [Literary aside] "The paramount gentleman of Europe, the soldier, scholar, and statesman in one—England's Sir Philip Sidney"[29] (Coleridge)
> "Un homme capable de faire des dominos avec les os du Saint Pere."[30]
> Le Pere Garoh

Thursday, April 28, 1864

"Merry Wives of Windsor"— Took out "Hawthorne's Marble Faun" from the library— or at least, the first volume of it. This work I have long desired to read, impelled more by the recollection of commendations bestowed upon it by a very dear friend, (VBM), perhaps, than by any predilection in favor of the Author or his book. I have finished the volume: the language is good, the style elegant, but the book is, so far, very unsatisfactory. Rumors of speedy exchange are very prevalent. I see much reason to hope, but am far from being confident of a speedy release.[31]

MAY 1864

Tuesday, May 3, 1864

Anniversary of Chancellorsville,[1] and of Gavroche's capture in celebration of which event we had a great dinner. Weather still unpleasant, and eye still troublesome.[2] Obtained 2nd vol. of Hawthorne's "Marble Faun,"[3] and finished the story, which is, upon the whole, very unsatisfactory. The style is good enough, and the scene is laid in a country, which is of all countries, richest in the treasures of romance. Yet is something wanting, withal.

> [possibly continued from April 29–May 2; pages missing] and German auxiliaries, (who still remained with him) in a long speech calculated to excite their ardour and animate their courage. It had evidently no effect. They listened without interest or attention" (vide May 11th)

Wednesday, May 4, 1864

Two letters from Brother, & Sister Mary. Very fine day. "In the Tropics," by a settler in St. Dominge — a thoroughly <u>Yankee</u> book, the author of which is imbued with the thirst for filthy lucre to the exclusion of more generous emotions: he reveals it naïvely, & without intention. Why he seems to believe that nature, the all-bountiful Mother, endowed the soil & climate of the tropics with the rich gifts of fertility and luxuriance, merely that <u>he</u> might make a few pitiful dollars. There is Yankee energy, too, in the book. Answered Brother's letter.

Thursday, May 5, 1864

An almost summer day: no fire in the stove & all windows open. I noticed a tree beginning to turn green. Wrote Sister Mary. Read Bulwer's Night & Morning. My eye has almost recovered from its inflammation.

> [Literary aside] The <u>Everlasting</u> Hills
> "There rolls the deep where grew the tree,
> Oh Earth! what changes thou has seen!
> There where the long street [illegible word], hath been
> The chillness of the central sea.
> The hills are shadows, and they flow
> From form to form & nothing stands;
> They melt like mists, the solid lands,
> Like clouds they change themselves again"
> (Tennyson)

Friday, May 6, 1864

Finished "Attaché in Madrid,"[4] a very entertaining book. "Behind the Scenes," by Lady Bulwer: — a silly lucubration of a (seemingly) silly woman;

spiteful, affected & pedantic, all this judging from her book. I should pronounce her to be Tupper & Theology. Horace, (misquoted,) & writers of a less pure latinity attest her learning: strictly on church, state, & landed gentry evince her deep political wisdom, as well as laudations of America: having all these great gifts, then what a pity that she writes her native tongue with ruthless disregard for grammar.

She canonizes [illegible word] at the sacrifice of his name.

Saturday, May 7, 1864

Many reports are current of a battle already commenced in Virginia. The Enquirer has dispatches to that effect. There is little doubt, at all events, but that there will be a great battle ere many days. We must remain on the qui-vive,[5] annoyed by all sorts of careless rumors and anxiously awaiting the returns from the battle. Of the issue, I feel as certain as if I already had before me the few lines, signed R. E. Lee, General, which will so modestly announce it, but of the cost at which we are to gain the victory, I cannot think without fear. "Waverly"[6] _____ On kitchen detail.

Sunday, May 8, 1864

Wrote to Sister Ida. Read "Much Ado about Nothing"— No news comes in to-day, it being Sunday. There is much anxiety manifested by the prisoners, though no doubt as to the result. 23rd Penna. one of the old soldier regiments which has been here for several months leaves to-morrow for the front. It is the last to go, leaving us to the tender mercies of the "Hoffmanns." Bon fires are burning, cheers resounding, music playing, etc. in honor of the occasion. Our Lieutenant belongs to this regiment.

Monday, May 9, 1864

This day is memorable for affording me the sorest trial I ever had to undergo. The incident, nothing at all wonderful in itself, occurred as follows: a Yank came in to prepare the bunk immediately beneath mine for a bed, our mess things were in it, he asked whose things they were; being at the farther end of the room, I knew nothing of the affair until he came up to me. Then as I was going to remove the things he said. "It takes you a long time to get it through your wool,— get to work right away." My first impulse as I turned to face him was to strike, but I restrained myself, though had I struck, he would have been torn to pieces ere he could have got out of the yard, for all around were eager for such a denouement, though in the end a blow from me would have brought trouble on us all. Personally, I would strike such a man only as I would one whom I could kill. A blow like such a one degrades the giver. I have no fear but that every one capable of appreciating my motives will understand them. To those who doubt I can afford practical demonstration.

Tuesday, May 10, 1864

It is sad that gentlemen have to endure such things, but not at all out of keeping either with the general policy of the Yankees or with my own N. O. experiences.[7]

May 10th, 1864[8]

Cold day —sleet & rain — The news that comes from the front is not of a discouraging nature though it comes through Yankee sources and it is intended to be favorable to them. The past offers a standard by which we may judge the truth of their bulletins. After the battle of Chancellorsville, it was confidentially announced that the flag was over the rebel capital. "As You Like It"

Wednesday, May 11, 1864

"Winter's Tale" Bulwer's "Leila," (one of his earlier works.) Go to hospital tonight to 'sit up' with Lt. T. Ruffin. Wrote to Sister Lizzie. "News of

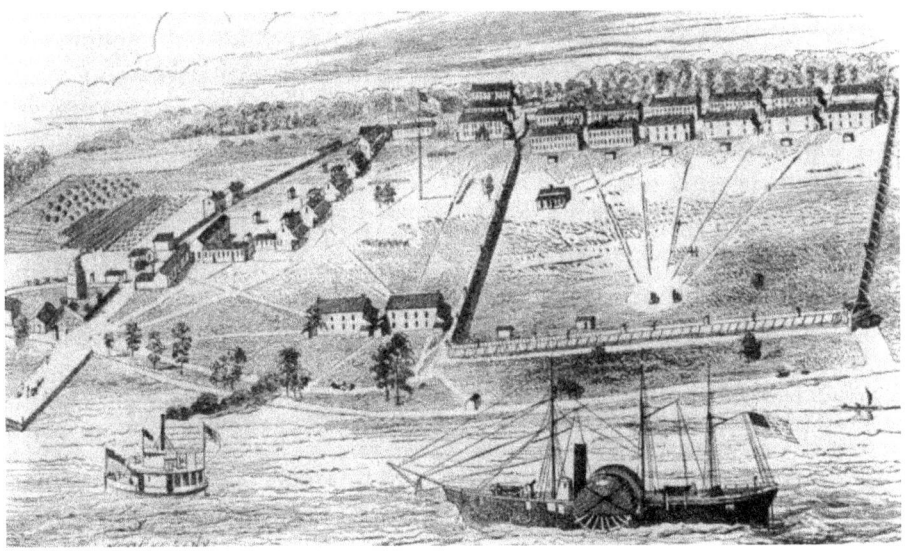

This schematic drawing of the prison shows the locations of the prison wall around the barracks. The sutler's house is shown standing alone inside the walls. To the left without the walls are the guard barracks, the entry, and the cemetery with headstones. The lake steamer and USS *Michigan* are drawn below. Today a bridge connects the island of 300 acres with Port Clinton, Ohio, and about half of the left half of the drawing is now a housing development.

battle," to-day, is more favorable. Lee's defeat is like to prove a success and his <u>retreat</u> is <u>probably</u> a change of front to meet a flank movement.

> [Literary aside] Nettled at his want of success, he galloped up to the French line in very ill- humour and said in a caustic tone, "Francais! Je n'ai rien a vous dire: vous avez Jure'de vaincre ou de mouirir; faites votre, devoir"⁹— Told by an old soldier to T. Ruikes.

Thursday, May 12, 1864

Bulwer's <u>Ernest</u> <u>Maltraves.</u> Wrote to Br. Jo. to-day. The papers are full of reports from the front where fighting is still going on. Seventeen General officers are hors de combat. The Federal attacks are all disputed, many of them repulsed: They, however, claim victory as usual, nous verrons.¹⁰ Began Lady Morgan's Diary, impelled there to by recollection of an excellent essay lent me — of the British Review (by Macaulay, I believe)

Friday, May 13, 1864

I find it an entertaining book, many good things intermixed with much pure "veal" X — —

The reports to-day aver that Johnson's Div'n, of ours, has been captured. I do not, of course, believe it, but even <u>if</u> it should prove correct, what of it? Was not Malvern Hills among the Richmond battles? Besides, there are many divisions left to dispute every inch of the way to our capital — but, to indulge in a strain of remote contingencies, even <u>should</u> our capital fall — a thing impossible under existing circumstances, we are still in no danger of subjugation. Nothing can blight my confidence in our ultimate triumph, but even if I <u>knew</u> that our grand attempt would end in disaster, I would not falter on that account, but would adhere unto the end. Reading Irving's Alhambra — delightful <u>almost,</u> as when I first read it, in the dreamy days of boyhood. A squad of prisoners brought in to-night, but none of them from Lee's army. desultory captures.

Saturday, May 14, 1864

Finished "Alhambra" — read "Love's Labour's Lost." — We can make out nothing certainly rec'd yet from the news reports concerning the battle in Virginia. It is dreadful to be cooped up here at such a time. Our anxiety is much more intense than that of our gallant comrades who are actors in the drama which interests us so much. The battle of — whatever it may be called has passed into history, though we knew it only by the most mythical tradition.

Sunday, May 15, 1864

"Taming of the Shrew" & "Two Gentlemen of Verona" — A letter to Sister Belle. I have not received any letters for several days, and think that my correspondents are neglecting me more than they should. Capt. Turner has written back twice. He is still at Pt. Lookout. Of the sick who left, only one from our block, Probst, has "gone through." No papers — i.e. <u>late</u> papers — come in <u>to-day</u>, the "Sandusky" not issuing on Sunday; & therefore, we hear no news.

Monday, May 16, 1864

No letters, nothing to read — From the <u>trend</u> <u>of</u> <u>the</u> <u>day</u>, though we obtain it only from Yankee sources, — I derive much comfort, as I believe that before another week comes in the whole truth will have leaked out and our victory will be acknowledged.

> [Literary aside] Porson's Charade—
> My <u>first</u>, tho' the best, most faithful of friends,
> You ungratefully name as the wretch you despise;
> My <u>second</u> (I speak it with grief) comprehends,
> All the good and the great, & the learned & the wise,
> Of my <u>whole</u>, I have little or nothing to say
> Except that it marks the departure of day.
> [CUR X FEW][11]

Tuesday, May 17, 1864

"Views Afoot;" Bayard Taylor's first book of travels, by no means equal in style or in the entertainment offered the reader, to his later efforts. The Jacobin & the Yank occasionally peer out from beneath the <u>traveler</u>. "Morte d'Arthur" by Tennyson. These beautiful nights render it almost a temptation to turn night into day. We have music after taps from the "balconies," of the blocks. Also by night the Yank band played a few beautiful strains by way of serenade. "Robert le Diable"[12] would suit their present feelings and conditions.

Wednesday, May 18, 1864

"The Abbot"
(Roland Grame & Catharine Seyton)[13]

A small squad of prisoners, less than a dozen, brought in — recent cavalry captures in the West.

> [Literary aside] Whenever his enemies wished to taunt <u>Horace</u> with his humble birth, they would observe, "Quoties vidi patrem tuum cubito emungentem?"[14] This is explained by the fact that his Father was a Sulsainant or fish-salter & his <u>hands</u> always briny.

Thursday, May 19, 1864

A letter from Sister, from which I learn that those letters have been written which I have not rec'd.

"Monastery"— Scott's failure, despite ridiculous Sir Percie Chafton. Our mess has a new roll-caller (Chs. Starr, 128 Ohio) the most stupid officer, and the meanest, most Yankee looking man (but one,) I have ever yet seen. A general "muster" to-day.

> [Literary aside] "Tout ça est bien gentil, mais qu'est qu'on fait de ça à a la maison."
> Horace Walpole on a yng lady's accomplishments.[15]

Friday, May 20, 1864

Finished "Monastery," and with it, my month's subscription to the circulating library—Wrote a letter to Sister. Our old attendant the Gunboat "Michigan" made her appearance again to-day, but only for a short "call."

<u>An Enigma.</u> (The initial letters form the name of an ancient city of renown.)

The noblest object in the works of art,
The brightest gem that nature can impart,
The point essential in the lawyer's case,
The well-known signal in the time of peace,
The farmer's prompter when he drives the plow,
The soldier's duty & the lover's vow,
The planet seen between the earth & sun,
The prize that merit never yet has won
The miser's treasure & the badge of Jews,
The wives' ambition & the Mason's dues.[16]

Saturday, May 21, 1864

"Tempest" Began Gibbon's Artillerists Manual. The Glorious News from all quarters renews our hopes.

1st Apollo Belvedere,Parthenon
2nd Diamond,Emerald
3rd Evidence,Reason
4th Bell,G
5thS
6th Fidelity,Protection
7th O—(impossible)
8th J
9th Gold, GaberdineS
10th Show & Salary(s)S

> To while away the time, I have been endeavoring, vainly, to solve this enigma—I can make nothing of it.

Sunday, May 22, 1864

Merchant of Venice, & Comedy of Errors.
On kitchen detail

[Literary aside] Buff Coat[17]—Note C. app. to Rokely + No. of peasantry taught to read & write, greater in Ireland, than in England.—Archbishop of Cashel, apud[18] E. L. Bulwer's "England & the English." ++____
Two thirds of the British army composed of Irish. Id+
The ablest defenders of a religious establishment—Chalmers & Hume, one a Dissenter, the other a Deist—I. D.

- -

Nice & dear the ΤΟ ΠΡΣΠΟΓ & the ΤΟ ΚΑΛΟΓ[19] of English feminine conversational morality. I.D.

Monday, May 23, 1864

Thunder last night. No letters, whereat I marvel.
A few prisoners from Gen. Johnston's Army.

[Aside] Every now and then we should examine ourselves; self-[illegible word] is the offspring of self-knowledge. But foreigners do not examine our conditions; they only glance at its surface. Why should we print volumes on other countries, and be silent upon our own? We travel the world and neglect the phenomena around us? Why should [5 illegible lines]

Tuesday, May 24, 1864

"Troilus and Cressida"
A letter to Father —

[Aside] FASTI JACOBI[20]
A[21]
Wednesday, May 25, 1864
A letter from Sister Mary. A suit of clothes has been sent me, which has not been heard of. Sent on 13th inst.
Bulwer's "Godolphin"[22]
On Police detail.

Thursday, May 26, 1864

Clothes came at last, having been detained outside for more than a week. Letter from Father. Letter to Sister Mary. The few lads from here were sent off for exchange. Two from our mess. D.S. Potter and Ware, both captured at home in Tennessee.

Friday, May 27, 1864

Box came, containing eggs, ham, etc. besides a few bottles of very good ale.

Look up, for want of more entertaining reading, Virgil's IV book Aeneid — read about three hundred lines. I didn't read much this day last year.[23]

[Aside] Names of some of Mess 2, Block 5 (July 31st 1864)	
Blount, T. W.	Texas © P.H.
Cherry, G. O.	N. C. (l) Cav. N.C.
Dillard, J. W.	Miss.2.r. (l.) G.
Garland, J. C.	Ark. (c.) Helena
Johnston, W.	H.N.C. (c.)
Manly, Matt.	N.C. (l.)
Saunders, J. H.	N.C. (m)

Saturday, May 28, 1864

Letter to Father.

[Aside] Ruffin, Thos.	N.C. (l) 4 cuv.
Novès, J. E.	La. P.H.
Munson,	Tenn. ©
Carter, J. R.	Va. (c.) G.
Chilcut, J. W.	Tenn. (–)
White, M. B.	Va. (c.) cav.(–)
Van Pracy, H. A.	Ala. (l) (-) P.H.
Roberdeun, J. D.	Texas © G.
Trevilian, C. B.	Va. (l.cav.)
Williams, J. B.	N.C. (c.) G.
Draughn, H. H.	N.C. (l) G.(–)
Duphy, T. H.	Va. (l.) G.
Robertson, C.	Va. (l.) G.
Gold, J. E.	Tenn. (l.)
Moseley, Alex.	Fla. (c.) M.R.
Moseley, A. S.	Fla. © M.R.
Odum,	N.C. (l) G.
Bowen,	Tenn. M.R.

Sunday, May 29, 1864

Letters fr Sister & Br. Rush. Both answered, Rush's being dated a day ahead. Big fuss at roll call: petty stealing: searching carpet-bags for scaling ladders. Cold weather, the removal of our stoves much regretted.

[Aside] Rawlings, J. J.	Tenn. l M.R.
Tune, J. H.	Tenn. l M.R.
Glover, S. H.	Tenn. c cav.
McCarty, F. M.	La. + c M.R.
Davis, R. C.	Tenn. l M.R.
Stevens,	Fla. L. Rea—
Redout,	Tenn. l M.R.
Oliver, J. B.	N.C. l. G.
Hickey, A.	N.C. l. G.
Oliver, C.	Tenn. C cav.
Richard, L.	N.C. l. G.
Haley, Frank	Ala. l. G.

Monday, May 30, 1864

Letter from Bro. Wilse, answered immediately.

[Aside] Smith,	—l.
Bailey,	Ky. l.
Kendrick,	N.C. l. G.
Inman,	N.C. l. G.
Shepard, J. A.	Texas l. cav. La.
Gibson, "Bob"	Va. l. G.
Leslie, S. D.	Va. l. G.
Philpot,	Md. l. Va cav.
Dawson, C.	Va. l. strag.
Long,	N.C. c & a.c.s.
Jones, B. H	Va. col.—valley
Shephard, E. C.	Va. ex.—l.
Quin, Joseph	Md. md. but (l)
Jordan, C. S.	Texas c.cav. La.
Dartz, J.	Texas l. cav. La.
Phillips, J .M.	Miss. l. G.
(second room)	
Porter,	N.C. l. G.

Tuesday, May 31, 1864

Very warm day. et praeterea nil.[24]
(The above are in our room)

Riley, A.   Texas m La.
Clark, J. B.   Miss. c G. (Jackson)
Dences, W. P.   Miss. l G.
Cordray, C. S.   Texas (l, La. inf) P.H.
Elkins, J.   Texas l cav La.
Hall, H. H.   Texas c cav La.
Mitchell, W. H.   Texas l cav La.
Tyler,   Texas l cav La.
Lurtchell, W.   Fla. l G.
Moore, W. R.   Fla. m G.
Patterson, E. D.   Ala. l G.

> [Literary aside] An old French ballad has this line characteristic of the French penchant for glory.
> "Le premier des rois fût un soldat heureux."[25]

June 1864

Wednesday, June 1, 1864

Very cold day.

Letter from Father.

Col. Boyd, who left this block for exchange in January was killed in the recent battles. Six prisoners brought in last night.

> [Literary aside] "De toutes les bouffonneries la plus serieuse est le mariage." (Figaro.)[1]
> "Bien como quien se engendro en una carcel, donde toda incomodidad tiene en assiento y todo triste ruido hace eis habitacion." Cervantes, preface to Don Quix: Did not the great Satirist have a prophetic eye to Johnson's Island? Trans.—"Like one you may suppose born in a prison where every inconvenience keeps its residence, & every dismal sound its habitation."

Thursday, June 2, 1864

Day pleasant — another change non ingrate[2]

> [Literary aside] Ad Patriae Vexilluam
> Carmen Militare[3]
> SEE I PAGE 375[4]

Friday, June 3, 1864

Began Hawthorne's House of the Seven Gables (Finished June 4th)— Ten years since I read this book for the first time. I liked it better then — than

I do now — though there is much quick wit and genial humor scattered through chapters which I can still appreciate.

> [Literary aside] Non iam, prima peto, Mnestheus neque vincere certo;
> Quanquam O!—sed superent, quibus hoc, Neptune dedisti—
> Extremos pudeat rediisse: hoc vincite cives,
> Et prohibete nefas." AE n. v. 194[5]
> "Abiit ael planes"
> Who said this? "Emori nolo; me esse mortuum nihil estimo."[6]

Saturday, June 4, 1864

Went down to block 11 to see the wooden tombstone designed for the grave of Capt. S. F. Hamilton, Co. B. 2nd Choctaw Battalion. The design is appropriate and much better executed than some would expect. It represents a blasted trunk, with a few stunted branches broken, as if by some tornado. A bow hangs from one of these, a quiver lies at the base, & arrows, broken, are scattered on the ground. The whole surrounded by

Sunday, June 5, 1864

a wreath of forest leaves, a masterpiece of carving. The Indian name of the departed "brave" should have been given, but after all, it matters little as the whole is to be left out subject to Yankee desecration which evinces a malevolence against the dead only equalled by cowardly insolence toward the living.

> [Aside] YANKEE CHIVALRY
> A few nights ago the authorities without were informed by some spy of the tunnel in progress under the hospital.

Monday, June 6, 1864

An officer with a squad of men came in stealthily at the time when they might expect to find the culprits at work, intending to surprise them. Without a word of summons the gallant Lieutenant walked straight to the hole, placed his pistol in it & discharged it. Fortunately the alarm had been given by a sentinel posted for the purpose.

> [Aside] "The City of the Czar," a very entertaining series of letters by T. Raitces, an Englishman, written in 1829—(Lea & Blanchard, 1838.)
> One of the militia regt's left this morning.

Tuesday, June 7, 1864

Weather unpleasantly cool again: <u>fires</u> would not be uncomfortable, Oh, what a climate! On kitchen detail — but almost nothing to do. Our rations of sugar, candles and (so called) coffee are stopped, and an order appears on the bulletin board to the effect that rations are to be stopped as a punishment for "tunnelling" to attempt escape and damage done to public property. Chiefs of messes are also ordered to report all persons injuring

Wednesday, June 8, 1864

government property, or attempting to tunnel out, that their rations alone may be stopped: otherwise, all will suffer diminution of rations or such other punishment as may be deemed necessary. It is the "weakest" document I ever saw: the absurdity of expecting anyone (except their own paid spies who live undetected among us) to turn informer is most palpable. xxxx

Read G. P. R. James' Leonora D an evidence of great dearth in the literary "line" — but I cannot again be so reduced that I read [illegible word]

Thursday, June 9, 1864

Two letters, from Bro. Rush & Sister Belle. The fellow Stevens who applied to take the oath some time ago, having been discharged from the hospital, where he sought refuge, has been causing trouble again. All the messes refuse to allow him shelter. A Yankee officer delivered him to the Chief of a Mess in B.7, saying that he would be held responsible for his safety. Notwithstanding he was turned out to sleep on the ground as was right & proper.

Friday, June 10, 1864

A letter to Brother Rush. To-day I enjoyed quite a pleasant talk with Capt. Moreland, (17th Ala.) formerly Capt. of the Beauregards[7] & an intimate friend of Mr. Moon. He was captured at Revoca [?] and gave me much interesting news of our common acquaintances in Dixie. R. A. M.'s business in Europe is procuring a vessel for privateering purposes. Will is to join him on his arrival at Wilmington.[8] O Utinam et Ego?[9]

Capt. M. "Stags" in the other end of B.5 (Mess)

Saturday, June 11, 1864

Worked an hour this morning on sink-digging detail.

[Literary aside] (Criterion of Manhood,—and Proper Reverence for the Character of Womanhood.)

(De Quincey)

One such criterion, and one only, as I believe, there is—all others are variable and uncertain. It lies in the reverential feeling, sometimes suddenly developed, towards woman and the idea of woman. From that moment when women cease to be regarded with carelessness, and when the ideal of womanhood, in its total pomp of loveliness and purity, dawns like

Sunday, June 12, 1864

A letter to Sister
Milton's Comus

> [Literary aside continued] some vast aurora upon the mind, boyhood has ended; childish thoughts and inclinations have faded away forever; and the gravity of manhood, with the self-respecting views of manhood, have commenced.
> "Mentemque priorem expulit atque hominem toto sibi pectore." (Lucan.) Cedere iussit[10]
> I do not wish, in paying my homage to the other sex, and in glorifying its possible power over ours, to be confounded with those thoughts and trivial rhetoricians who flatter woman

Monday, June 13, 1864

A continuation of the unpleasantly cold weather we have been having for several days. No letter, though this is nothing unusual.

> [Literary aside continued] with a false lip worship; and hold out to them a picture of their own empire, built only upon sensual or upon shadowy excellences. We find continually a false enthusiasm, a mere bacchanalian inebriation, on behalf of woman, put forth by modern verse writers, expressly at the expense of the other sex as though woman could be of porcelain, whilst man was of common earthen ware, for though the sexes differ

Tuesday, June 14, 1864

A Spring-like day — quite warm & pleasant, — something unusual, though, I suppose, when Summer does "set in" fairly the heat will be as extreme as the cold has been during the winter.

> [Literary aside continued] characteristically, yet they never fail to reflect each other; nor can they differ as to the general amount of development; never yet was woman in one stage of elevation, and man (of the same community) in another. Thou, therefore, daughter of God and man, all potent woman! reverence thy own ideal; and in the wildest of

Wednesday, June 15, 1864

A squad of prisoners, the third since I last mentioned the arrival of any. "Fair Maid of Perth."[11] Williamson has been killed: our former roll-caller & quite a decent Yank.

> [Literary aside continued] the homage which is paid to thee, as also

in the most real aspects of thy wide dominion, read no trophy of idle vanity, but a silent indication of the possible grandeur enshrined in thy nature; which realize to the extent of thy power,—"And show us how divine a thing, A woman may become." (The above contains as much <u>romance</u> as is compatible with <u>common sense.)</u>

Thursday, June 16, 1864

Letter from Father. Morning's paper brings news of another change of base on Grant's part, to the South side of James River: I rejoice at this, believing that the whole affair must now resolve itself into a question of <u>Generalship</u>. Also that Vallandigham has reappeared & made a speech at Hamilton. May the flames of civil war soon be lighted at the North, if, indeed, no other chance for peace remain! If during this Presidential campaign the Western people learn to value <u>their</u> <u>own</u> liberty & to appreciate their danger, all will be well, for them & for all.

Friday, June 17, 1864

"Claret & Olives, or From the Garronne to the Rhone"— not an <u>excellent</u> book, but very good <u>pastime.</u>[12] A letter to Father. A Glorious bath in the lake, according to recent orders, we are to be allowed this privilege (a block at a time) hereafter at stated periods.

[Literary aside] Every now & then we should examine ourselves; self examination is the key.
<u>Fielding's</u> <u>Ironical</u> <u>Definitions.</u>
<u>Patriot</u>—a candidate for a place.
Politics—The art of getting one!
<u>Knowledge</u>—the knowledge of the town
Virtue, Vice—subjects of discourse
Worth—power, rank, wealth
<u>Wisdom</u>—the art of aligning all three
Saturday, June 18, 1864
(fr. p. 153.) See page 375[13]

Sunday, June 19, 1864

Sultry as the middle of July in Louisiana—I wouldn't live on this island for the estate in fee simple of the whole thing. Letter from Rush, dated 16th.[14]

Monday, June 20, 1864

Police detail.

"Castle of Otranto,"[15] a book which I have long desired to read, but which does not come up to my anticipation. Had I read it ten years ago I would have been delighted with it, but my appetite for the marvellous has quite lost its zest.

Derivations
miniature, fr. minium, red-head
surname,—sieurnamie or lordname, an appellation derived fr. territorial property.
Algernon: al gerneset "of the whiskers," old norman soubrig't. Guillaume al germond was the 1st Lord Percy & came over with Will

Tuesday, June 21, 1864

A <u>small</u> <u>string</u> of "Fresh Fish"—eleven
Morgan's Men.
Read St. Pierre's "Indian Cottage" & finished "Gulliver's Travels': also began Sterne's "Sentimental Journey."
(fr. P. 170)[16]

Wednesday, June 22, 1864

Fremantle's Diary—("Three Months at the South") a very interesting book though such from extrinsic causes. Reading "Lady of the Lake" with Gavroche. Gold, in the morning paper quoted at 210. Good news in itself & a harbinger of better. Gen. Archer left to-day: some say for exchange; others, for retaliation (so called) I believe he himself was ignorant of his <u>destination</u>.
Rusticus exspectat dum defluat amnis.[17]

Thursday, June 23, 1864

Four prisoners this morning from Price's Army & above a dozen this evening from Gen. Johnston. A little later: about fifty more, recent captures from Inboden &c in the Valley. Fight this morning between the Dutch Jew & the Mannikin—Cur and Lice, nobody hurt: D.J. in the right, rather, though a good beating wouldn't be a backset to either. The yellow dog has taught himself to "fetch & carry,"—D.J. has chosen himself past master of the many issues, his proclamations, Jure divino.[18]

Friday, June 24, 1864

Mailed a letter which I wrote yesterday to <u>VBM.</u> Rec'd one fr Sister Mary. Wrote to brother <u>Rush</u>, but cannot mail my letter till after the mail comes in to-morrow.
An oppressively hot day.

[Literary aside] "What is it which threatens the permanence of the

union between the Northern & Southern States of the American Confederacy but a physiological fact that the soil & climate of the Southern States render them essentially agricultural; while those of the Northern States, combined with their geographical advantages as to seaports, dispose them in life naturally to the manufacturing & commercial. The whole character of the nation may be influenced by its geology, [illegible word] and geography."
 Gr. Arnold (1842)

Saturday, June 25, 1864
 On kitchen detail.

 [Literary aside] Coleridge on Shakspeare (characteristic)———There are three powers:—Wit, which discovers partial likeness hidden in general diversity; subtlety, which discovers the diversity concealed in general apparent sameness;—and profundity, which discovers an essential unity under all the semblances of difference.
 Give to a subtle man fancy and he is a wit; to a deep man imagination, and he is a philosopher. Add, again, pleasurable sensibility in the threefold form of sympathy with the ... in morals, the impressive in fancy and the harmonious in sound—and you have the poet. But combine all,—wit, subtlety, and fancy with profundity & imagination

Sunday, June 26, 1864
 "Rob Roy." Letter to Sister Mary. Small squad of prisoners; Morgan's company.

 [Literary aside continued] and moral and physical susceptibility of the pleasurable,—and let the object of action be man universal; and we shall have—O rash prophecy! Say, rather, we have—a Shakspeare![19]

 <u>A Singular Simple Distinction</u>
 Speaking of the "Mysteries" of the mid. ages & early reformation, Coleridge says—"As historical documents they are valuable, but I am sensible that what I can read with my eye with perfect innocence, I cannot without inward fear and misgivings pronounce with my tongue."
 Works, vol IV, p 32.

Monday, June 27, 1864
 Signed autographic testimonial of sympathy for Mrs. W. B. Mumford, banished from New Orleans — the subscribers binding themselves to deposit each ten dollars with the C.S. Sec. of Treasury for her benefit. This is the second paper I have signed and I must not forget to attend to them when I am

in Richmond. The other was the Barn & Horse Testimonial. Twenty Dollars to be deposited with — Williams opposite — Hotel to order of Col. Blackman.

Another squad of Morgan's men.

Tuesday, June 28, 1864

Since the thunder gust of night before last, the weather has been quite cool — this morning almost <u>cold</u>. More prisoners — fm. Morgan — 5 surgeons, and the rest, less than a dozen fm. Johnston.

> [Literary aside] Southern Fanaticism
> Capt. A. S. M., of Fla. says, that fifteen years of ago he rejoiced at & gloated over every account of railroad or steamboat accident at the North, where men, women, & children were killed. This man pretends to be a Christian, but is only a fanatic and a

Wednesday, June 29, 1864

Gen. Colemen's "Mustang Gray," miserable fustian as it is, I can only say <u>Peccavi</u>.[20] A letter from Father. Answered immediately.

> [Literary aside continued] worse fanatic than New England ever nurtured inasmuch as it is with him the result of no association of youth, nor inherited disposition, for his cousin is quite a gentleman. I think no one ever accused me of any leniency (in opinion) toward puritanism, yet, yet! it is to be loved & honored when compared with its sister, fanaticism of the South (of which I have known but two instances).

Thursday, June 30, 1864

See corrected version on p. 370[21]

JULY 1864

Friday, July 1, 1864

Nine more prisoners, Pillows command, no wonder <u>they</u> were captured. IV.[1]

Saturday, July 2, 1864

Read to-day in the August number of Blackwood for 1860, an excellent article entitled, "Lord Macaulay and Dundee" — a triumphant refutation of the slanders to which the great historical writer has lent the sanction of his honored name — slanders upon the fair fame of one of the noblest of modern heroes — the last of the Chevaliers.

> [Literary aside] In an old Moravian hymnal, marriage is included among their "Services of danger" for which the brethren must be prepared. "That like the former warriors each may stand ready for land, sea, marriage, at command. Life of Zin Zendorf

Sunday, July 3, 1864

"Owen Tudor," by the author of "Whitefriars" (whoever he be) an historical Romance and a very readable book — under the circumstances. An extensive structure built upon an exceedingly slight historical foundation.

> [Literary aside] Dido et Dux.
> "Venus urit venis et caco carpitur igni."
> "Sese ore ferens"—"haret laten lethalis anmdo"
> "Agnosco veteris vestigia flammae.
> "Talibus aggredibur Venerem Satumia dictis"[2]

Of good discourse, an excellent musician, and her hair shall be of what color it pleases God.[3]

Monday, July 4, 1864

The Yanks seem to be celebrating the day with as much gusto as though they were not striving to abrogate the great principle whose promulgation it is supposed to commemorate — viz "that the authority of all government depends upon the consent of the governed," and as if every single crime attributed in that document to the British government had not been committed by the Abolition government at Washington.

Tuesday, July 5, 1864

A Box of Good Things arrived to-day — Ham, eggs, new potatoes & green peas, all luxuries here and save the first, almost unknown. Reading Charles Reades "White Lies" — one of his earlier works, I believe, but written in his usual felicitous vein & very entertaining, especially to one in prison. This imprisonment has led me to resume (together with my camp life) the long discontinued habit of novel reading. For the four years previous to the war, I read very few novels. I never will read many of the poorer class of novels.

Wednesday, July 6, 1864

Letter from Sister Mary—

Sent "Harper & Brothers" 50 cts. for Thackeray's "Esmonds." I think it fairly problematical whether I shall ever receive the book or not, but if I do

I will be repaid for my trouble, for it is one which I have never read & Thackeray is one of my favorite authors, second only — among <u>Moderns</u>— i.e. contemporaries, to Bulwer. Alas, he is no longer a contemporary but is as much a part of the past as the great Fielding — whom he "in some sort" resembles.

Thursday, July 7, 1864

Detailed to sit up at Hospital last night. Read a semi-trashy novel (Seacliff) to keep me awake, or I should rather say turned over the pages and noted the startling denouement. Wrote a letter to Sister Mary.

> [Literary aside] Excepting "Rokeby" and "Harold the Dauntless" I have read gradually through Scott's poems: They do not please me so much as they used to,—my tastes seem to have undergone a change.

Friday, July 8, 1864

A letter to Mother.[4] "The Book of Esther," which seems to me to be a Rabbinical contribution to some Hebrew <u>Fasti</u>[5] and devoted to explaining the forgotten origin of some religious holiday. The anniversary of the surrender of Pt. Hudson, this day completes my twelvth month of captivity.

A few more prisoners this evening. Price & Jo. Johnston's cavalry corps send these delegates. The cavalry, indeed, seem to furnish not only the most numerous, but the least respectable representation in this prison.(cause bushwhack)

Saturday, July 9, 1864

England & The English," by Bulwer — a book wherein that great author appears in a new & pleasing aspect. I promise it another reading in better times. In many respects it is or seems — worthy of being a book of reference — not to go <u>ultra meam</u> crepidam,[6] I need only specify the Saxe-Weimar Classbooks, the Prussian educational system and — might <u>at</u> <u>present</u> add — his strictures upon the military system of Gt. Britain and comparison with those of Prussia & France.

Sunday, July 10, 1864

I am glad to find in the Second Volume (read <u>to-day</u>) such honored authority for the opinion I have long <u>clandestinely</u> entertained as to the superiority of Byron's dramas over his earlier & more popular works. Also, he takes a manifest view of another of my favorites, Shelley, and carefully discriminates that which, [The lower corner is torn off— missing a third of the page]

Monday, July 11, 1864

Finished Bulwer's very interesting work.

Glorious news this morning of a Confederate invasion of Maryland and a panic in Baltimore. The back of the rebellion is broken and the doomed confederacy must soon lose it Capital. This looks like [See note above]

Tuesday, July 12, 1864

Additional good news fr our Maryland raid — capture of Gen. Franklin. On kitchen detail. <u>Finished</u> <u>canopy-ing</u> <u>my</u> <u>bunk</u>, which though not hung with Gobelin or Arras yet presents a neat & comfortable appearance. "Picciola" by X. B. Saintine, a well written French novel, religio-botanical in its nature. It is devoted to the contradiction of what it assumes to be the leading tenet of unbelievers, viz "Chance is the Creator of all things." The book has been crowned by the Academy & seems worthy of the honor so far as style & language is concerned.

Wednesday, July 13, 1864

First Volume of Miss Martineau's "Western Travel" being an account of travel in the U.S. in 1834. An entertaining book despite its abolitionism or rather on acc't of that very abolitionism, for the author's extreme gullibility is decidedly asinine in "portions" of the work which would otherwise exasperate by their falsehood. One of her antislavery anecdotes turns upon the fact that the <u>Mississippi</u> between Kentucky and Arkansas is impossible to any swimmer!

Thursday, July 14, 1864

The Michigan has returned brought back, doubtless, by fears of an outbreak here.[7] I wish there was good ground for apprehension.

An envelope containing acknowledgment of money came in to-day, but the letter which <u>must</u> have accompanied it has not yet made its appearance. Gen. Franklin is said to have escaped while his guards (drunk, no doubt) were sleeping. Those miserable guerrillas disgrace the name of <u>soldier</u> — sleeping on post! Their officers ought to be dismissed, or then shot.

Friday, July 15, 1864

"Henry Esmond" arrived to-day — also an envelope addressed in Sister Belle's handwriting & endorsed "Letter contraband in length," which I disbelieve. Wrote to Sister.

[Aside] More Yankee Chivalry. A most foolish & groundless alarm took place tonight, outside, which was the occasion for the display of <u>Chinese</u> strategy of a high order. Just after taps several shots were fired into the pen (for what purpose is unknown) the bullets whistling audibly to us all,

Saturday, July 16, 1864

and sounding very familiarly. Immediately after, a Yank officer with a guard came in & was marching down the area when some one in the other end of our block shouted "Lie down!" Whereupon this gallant official halted his guard, faced them toward our block and then with heroic determination fired his own pistol over the house. Weren't we scared? The operation was repeated again at another block. Orders were shouted that no one would be allowed to leave the buildings

Sunday, July 17, 1864

until reveille. (but these were afterwards very slightly modified) The steamer's guns were run out, and everything was in commotion.————
Last night about 40 prisoners were brought in from various quarters, among them three of my messmates, old acquaintances—captured at a camp of instruction in W.N.C.—one of whom Capt. Long enters our mess. Finished "Esmond" & think it one of the best novels I ever read, or rather one of the most entertaining books, for its merits do not consist

Monday, July 18, 1864

in its excellence as a work of fiction, but in that vividness with which great men of the past are brought before us familiarly—Steele, Addison, Bolinbroke, Swift, Atterbury, & the Chevalier de St. Gevy. All appear upon the stage as men, with a full share of human weakness. Capt. Alfred Hudson, my old friend & gallant commander, thought this the best of Thackeray's works, and often wished for it for my perusal. Rec'd a letter fr. Bro. Rush yesterday. Our Maryland expedition has got off all its [illegible sentence].

Tuesday, July 19, 1864

Recd a package of papers from Father to-day, from one of which (a Telegraph) I learn that Dr. John McElwee resumes editorial charge of the Hamilton True Telegraph with the next number. The Doctor is one of the very few men left in my native State for whom I entertain a warm personal regard: he is a true man.

Wrote a letter to Bro. Wilse though I "wrote last."

[Literary aside] Rex est qui metuit nihil
Et hoc regnum sibi quisque dat." Sen.[8]

Wednesday, July 20, 1864

Last night we had a domiciliary visit from a squad of Yankees, their object & purpose are unknown.

Wrote an epistle to VBM & MM jointly, my two dearest friends. Rumors prevail to the effect that exchange is about to be resumed at some new point.

I hope there may be some foundation for this report but am not very sanguine. It has its origin in (or attributed to) the New York Herald. The first exchange "grape" we have had since the reopening of the campaign. Our attention having been absorbed by even more important subjects for rumor.

Thursday, July 21, 1864

A letter from Sister Mary which has already been answered. She is visiting at Mr. John G. Law's. The weather, which has been oppressively warm for a good many days back took, last night, one of those sudden turns for which this variable climate is famous, and is to-day almost disagreeably cold, too <u>cold</u> to be called <u>cool</u>, and by no means as pleasant as one would expect such weather to be at midsummer.

Friday, July 22, 1864

Weather still continues cool — A "Dixie Mail" is said to be outside — the largest ever rec'd here. I hope to receive a letter when it is distributed.

Am now re-reading Bulwer's "Harold," which I read, for the first time, a year ago in my redan[9] at Port Hudson, amid circumstances rather unsuitable for the full appreciation of the beauties of a literary work, & subject to many interruptions. I like the book as giving a fine sketch of the Norman Conquest, & one which I am disposed to regard as historically correct.

Saturday, July 23, 1864

Due letters only from the Dixie Mail came in to-day. The rest expected to-morrow.

Just after "taps" on the night of this day occurred an event which will long be remembered by those, who are prisoners here, nothing less than the wanton firing of a sentry into our block, without any provocation whatever, wounding two of my roommates (Inman & Dillard) rather seriously, one in the shoulder, the other in the arm. I suppose the

Sunday, July 24, 1864

pretext for this outrage was the reflection of the hospital light through our window, for it has been so reflected since the house was built, having been repeatedly mistaken for a light & ascertained to be a mere reflection. The fact is that the Yankee authorities give to their sentinels — and a lower, more abject & besotted class of creatures do not exist — discretion in these matters, & by constituting them judges of the infraction of orders in our part, power of life & death over everyone in the pen. There was not even a noise — beyond our ordinary conversation — in our room at the time of this cowardly outrage &

the two victims are as quiet & orderly as any two men can be. This is the 2nd time since the Veterans left that this block has been fired

Monday, July 25, 1864

into but the first time any one has been hurt. For the last week there has been firing every night, and if this is to last, we had better sell our lives dearly by an emente than be shot for amusement by these sneaking cowards.

The paper to-day brings important news, 1st Fighting in Atlanta, result so far favorable to the Federals, (It always is according to first reports) — and secondly; the superseding of Gen. Jo. Johnston by Gen. Hood in command of our Western Army. To me this bears the aspect of a Yankee forgery.

Tuesday, July 26, 1864

Yet it seems that it must be true, after all; since the addresses of both Generals are given in The Herald. Well, when all is known, it will prove to be all right, that I feel certain of. "Trelawny, Last Days of Shelley & Byron"— a very entertaining book, which, however does not give one a high opinion of the author. I recollect the first time I got hold on it, one summer evening in 1858, at Mr. Clark's, nor did I lay it aside until I had finished it, late at night. Have also been reading for the last few days a volume entitled "Entertaining Biography" composed of sketches originally published in

Wednesday, July 27, 1864

Chamber's Repository — Some of the sketches (e.g. Capt. John Smith, Mad. DeSèvigné, & The Dauphin) are good in themselves, but most derive their claims to my attention from the illustrious names of their subjects.

Rec'd The Time Telegraph, the first no. published under Dr. McElwee's supervision; the change is very marked. I am to receive the paper now regularly. Am reading "Diary in Turkish and Greek Waters" by the Earl of Carlisle; a very entertaining book,

Bath in Lake — 3rd opportunity.

Thursday, July 28, 1864

though on a somewhat hackneyed subject. Next to novels (and I have read all the good ones accessible to me,) I like Travels and Biography. They are not too heavy to be duly read & appreciated even in the din of our very noisy room. I am very anxious to lay hold on a copy of Don Quixote — There is one in "the bull-pen" but I can't find it. I should like to read it now above all other books. A letter from Brother Wilse; answered immediately. Sister B wrote me the same

Friday, July 29, 1864

day the papers were sent, but as the letter has not arrived, I suppose it has been confiscated.

> [Aside] On kitchen detail. Drums beat for roll-call at 5½ A.M. instead of 7½, this morning, this to enable the officers in charge of blocks to attend the reception of Gen. McPherson's remains. It was annoying to be roused so early but the reflection that the occasion is the loss of one of the ablest of the Yank Generals is consoling. 6 prisoners this evening from Forrest.

Saturday, July 30, 1864

Sister's letter came to hand to-day, also another number of the "Time Telegraph," the best, most outspoken paper I have yet read. A Dixie letter too, & what is better still, from VBM, who, it appears recently attempted to come through the lines, but was kept in custody at Ft. Monroe & then sent back to Richmond. The letter bore date May 26th. Reading Memoirs of Vidocq.[10] Interesting on acct. of his naïveté in confessing his rascalities, though I doubt its truth.

On Police Detail.

Sunday, July 31, 1864

Thirty-two prisoners came in last night from Gen. Hood's Army. Answered Sister Belle's letter & asked for some "Trak Fire" for the Lecti Cimices,[11] which annoy me very much, banishing sleep from my eyelids. For lack of other reading, I have been amusing myself by going over this, my diary. What an idle, unprofitable sort of life mine has been. Pleasure is not to be expected in prison, but under favorable circumstances I might have profited by

AUGUST 1864

Monday, August 1, 1864

the lessons afforded me for reading & study. When I reflect in my course of reading during this last few months, Falstaff's tavern is forcibly suggested and I think with Prince Hal, "O monstrous! but one halfpennyworth of bread to this intolerable deal of sack!"[1] One cannot enjoy life on the bare, solid necessaries alone, and sack & syllabub have their place as well as solid meat, only the proportion must not be and [illegible word] & besides much of my sack has been of very inferior quality, not "your good sherries."

Tuesday, August 2, 1864

Sixty-three prisoners brought in last night captured before Atlanta, though not all are recent captures.

Eleven sent away, Surgeons,— for exchange I suppose.

Wrote a letter to Bro. Rush to-day.

"Old Hill" & some of his official satellites were inside the pen this evening surveying & marking out sites for mess-halls, to be built for our accommodation, in order that the lower room, now used as dining room,

Wednesday, August 3, 1864

may be crowded with bunks thus making room for a large additional number of prisoners. Subscribed again to the circulating library — "War Pictures from the South" by one Estevan, who has been a Colonel of Cavalry in the Confederate Army. A German Adventurer, doubtless, who, not meeting with the appreciation to which he imagined himself entitled, went North & wrote this book in revenge. It is a vision of palpable falsehoods from beginning to end — so palpable as to be ridiculous.

Thursday, August 4, 1864

Thomas Hood's "Lylney Hall," an entertaining novel — and one which I began at Mr. Conner's at Mayhew Station in the M. & O. R.R. while I was detained at that place on ordnance duty one night in March 1862. I had not seen it since, until yesterday.

A small squad of prisoners brought in to-night, a very heterogeneous "lot" both as to time & place of capture & appearance. A light all night in our room by permission, M. Ruffin being very sick.

Friday, August 5, 1864

Rec'd back again to-day the letter mailed to Bro. Rush several days ago. I wrote on the back of a 'Rebellonian' Programme, thinking that he would like to see one & this was alleged (& must have been, since the letter was entirely free from anything possibly objectionable) as the reason for stopping my letter. I at once sat down & wrote the same letter, very nearly, over again on letter paper & trust that it may be supposed to go, this time.

Saturday, August 6, 1864

Thirteen prisoners from Gen. Hoods Dept. This evening a Lieut. Murphy of Tennessee effected his escape from the pen by getting in a wagon disguised in Yankee clothes & going out at the gate. The wagons are engaged in hauling gravel and are loaded & unloaded by Yankee soldiers who go back & forth in them. I hope he may succeed in getting off the island. Once on the mainland, he is safe.

Sunday, August 7, 1864

Rec'd envelope to-day fr Sister, endorsed "Letter contraband in sentiment & language disrespectful to letter inspectors." Wrote to Sister immediately, Her letters seem doomed never to reach their destination.

> [Literary aside] In one of Hawthorne's Twice-told Tales I find this & deem it appropriate to these times & <u>this</u> country. "Now is the day when every beggar gets on horseback. And is not the whole land like a beggar on horseback riding post to the devil?" (put in the mouth of an old loyalist in the days of '76.)

Monday, August 8, 1864

This has been an eventful day, Sixteen prisoners having gone out in the wagons, sometimes three & four at a time. All blue suits were put in requisition, and everyone who could procure the disguise was anxious to attempt escape, thus "overdoing" the thing. Among the last to go was Lt. Col. M. B. Locke, 1st Ala, to whom I gave a letter, devoutly hoping that he might be able to deliver it. First of the Seven had gone out at once, another who was in the wagon following, was detected & the game was up. The alarm was

Tuesday, August 9, 1864

given & the whole island vigorously searched and with such success that all were brought in, the last late in the night. We had a very strict roll-call in the evening, & a search for blue breeches, all of which when found were confiscated, though a part of our regular uniform. <u>Murphy</u>, however, is safe by this time, as many more might have been, if they had only exercised moderation.

> [Aside] Sent to Harper & Bro's for a copy of Lucretius, mailing the price in p.o. stamps. "Lovel The Widower" by Thackeray which is enough to recommend any day.

Wednesday, August 10, 1864

Two letters — from Father & Sister Mary. It seems that John T. Crenshaw (formerly overseer for Benj. Irby) is a prisoner at Point Lookout, Md. & has written to my Father — ignorant of the fact that I, too, am a prisoner. He was a very worthy, honest young man & I hope that his slight acquaintance with me may prove of service to him in his time of need. I answered Father's letter immediately.

"Two Millions" a satirical poem by the Author of "Nothing to Wear"[2]

Thursday, August 11, 1864

"The United States, Canada & Cuba," a book of travels by Hon. Amelia Murray — who brings to her task, — together with some British prejudice, much good sound old English Sense and a love of truth quite refreshing in these days of humbug. "The Pirates" begun. I did not think again to have recourse to the much honored & familiar "Waverlies:" but this came in my way & I accept it as a <u>waif</u>. A letter to Sister Mary

> [Literary aside] "If thou hast never been a fool, then be sure thou wilt never be a wise man" Thackeray

Friday, August 12, 1864

Half dozen prisoners <u>last</u> evening — Atlanta. General muster also in the middle of the afternoon — very tedious affair.

"The Amber Gods & c" by Miss Harriet Prescott,³ daughter of the great Historian — which fact may account for my reading the book. I don't think it's "<u>much</u>." A new Sutler has come in, & a new system is adopted, whereby we are deterred of the use of any kind

Saturday, August 13, 1864

of currency, inside — this Sutler using no checks. Old Hill had all the men assembled at roll-call & made a speech explaining the intricate manner of getting our money under the new dispensation.

Began F. D. Guerrazzi's "Beatrice Cenci," said to be one of the standard works of Italian literature,⁴ but (whether due to the poor effort of the translation, or to the fact that Shelley's magic pen had preceded the author in the field, I know not) I pity the literature which boasts such an assertion.

Sunday, August 14, 1864

Rec'd (yesterday) a small box from Bro. Wilse, containing a full supply of coffee, & also a letter from himself. Wrote to-day to Miss Nelly K. Brent, Georgetown, D. C.,⁵ in acknowledgement of a book (old vol.of magazine) sent me through her friend Maj. Saunders. Trying to read a work by M. T. Kryczynski, entitled Recovery of Poland, but as it is an attempt to write in English by one who cannot express himself in that language, I fear I shall derive no benefit from the book, for I shall lay it aside. Work on the

Monday, August 15, 1864   *P.J.N.O.*⁶

new mess hall is progressing notwithstanding the day, a proof, to my mind, that strong reinforcements are expected to arrive & that room must be made for them at once — Did succeed, by a great effort, in finishing The Pole's broken English # <u>To-day</u>: read the last of "The Amber Gods" stories — I retract my sneer against the authoress, though I do not admire her <u>style</u>. She possesses great command of language, but that is a <u>feminine gift</u>. Fifteen prisoners this evening; Western Army, — They are quartered upon the other two messes of our block — <u>We (M.2.)</u> will have to receive the next lot. "Omoo", a very interesting work by Herman Melville, but not so good as "Typee." It affords a Tahitian parallel to the missionary

Tuesday August 16, 1864

mildness of sway in the Sandwich islands, as recorded by Sir George Simpson —(Vide Supra)

> [Aside] Life of George Frederick Cooke by Wm Dunlap, (New York, D. Longworth, 1813.) An hour's hard digging this morning on "Sink detail." Wrote to Brother Wilse, but fear my letter may be destroyed as contraband, though I introduced the truth, very moderately. About half a dozen prisoners brought in, after dark in the rain—I know not where from.
> (Trans-Miss.)

Wednesday, August 17, 1864

On K. detail — 9 or 10 prisoners, Hood

The "Life of Cooke" finished — A very agreeable book full of incident & dramatic anecdotes connected with the great names of Macklin, Garrick, Kemble, Mrs. Siddons, & chiefly of Cooke himself, the successor of Macklin in Shylock & of Garrick in Richard, & the rival of Kemble. Historical Biography is always interesting to me, for the lives of the Great Actors, illustrate the Great Poet, and in this touch a chord of deep interest — This book is badly torn & many sheets omitted altogether, which is a drawback to a complete enjoyment of the rest. A bold attempt to escape made by a Maj from B.11 who went boldly to the gate attired as a Yankee major — The sergeant saw that he had not passed him in; no matter, somebody else did, & "you might pass me out," says Reb — Whereupon the officer is compromised by taking him before Col. Hill to whom he represented himself as Maj. Brooks of the 20th N. Y. Company come

Thursday, August 18, 1864

to visit some prisoners & that he had been admitted by the Major in charge of the yard. Hill interrogated him as to the location of his reg't &c, and finding all his questions promptly answered declared himself satisfied & entered into a friendly conversation, which was interrupted by the ringing of the boat bell. Reb jumped up declared he had forgotten & must go back to Sandusky, but it was now too late, so he accepted old Hill's offer of hospitality for the night. But the Yankee Yard-Major comes like a marplot[7] & in answer to Col. Hill's rebuke for not having informed Maj. Brooks of the hour of the boats departure, stands dumfounded & denys all knowledge of such man. Maj. B. returned to his old lodging in his shirt sleeves. + + + "Madeira, Portugal and the Andalusias of Spain"— author unknown, published Harpers, very agreeable reading, as even a tolerable account of life & sights in the

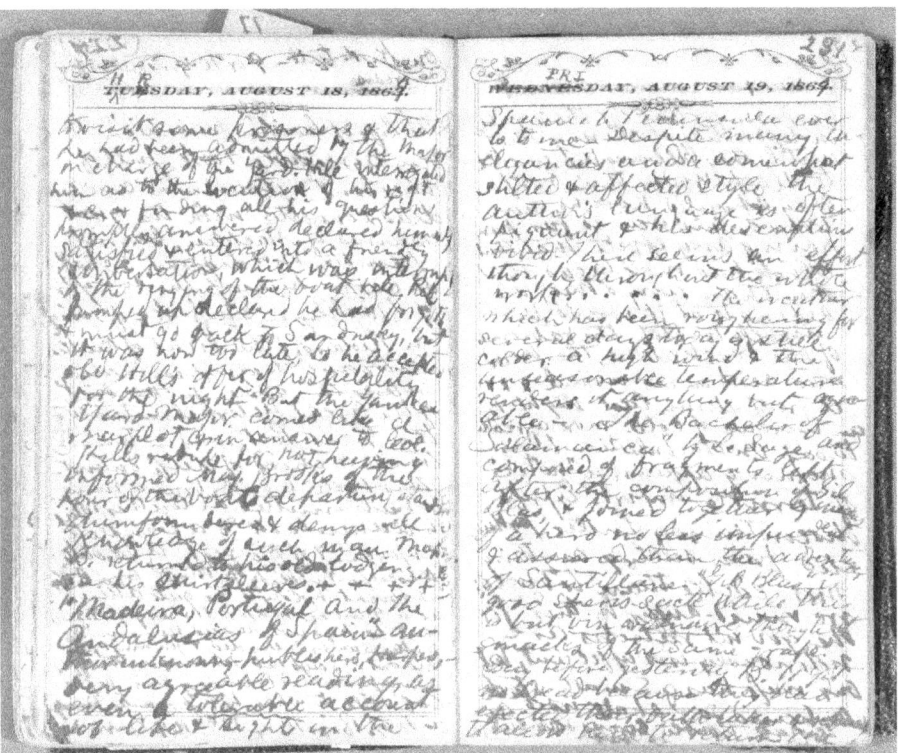

The blurred part of this page becomes clear when viewed in a mirror because it bled through from the other side of the page.

Friday, August 19, 1864

Spanish Peninsula ever is to <u>me</u>— Despite many inelegancies and a somewhat stilted & affected style, the author's language is often piquant & his description vivid — There seems an <u>effort</u> though, throughout the whole work....[8] The weather which has been <u>roughening</u> for several days, to-day is still colder: a high wind & the unseasonable temperature renders it anything but agreeable — "The Bachelor of Salamanca" by LeSage, and composed of fragments left after the composition of "Gil Blas," & joined together by means of a hero no less impudent & assured than the adventurer of Santillane. "Gil Blas" is good sheris-sack while this is but <u>vin ordinaire,</u> though it smacks of the same grape. Day before yesterday B.7 got no bread because they had ejected their oath taker & refused to allow him to return the

Saturday, August 20, 1864

Yard-Major cut off their rations indefinitely, declaring that until they allowed the wretch to sleep under their roof, they should have no more bread. This was so far from having any effect that their block had more bread that day than any other, so seeing that it would be useless to stop the rations of one block alone, the bread was sent in as usual x x x

A great storm last night & an increase of cold — more agreeable to-day. On the bulletin this morning appears a "notice" of terrible import. Express discontinued & Sutler prohibited from selling anything more edible than tobacco. We must suffer by this for the govm't rations are notoriously insufficient, but our mess has a small stock on hand so I shall not anticipate, trouble comes soon enough.

Sunday, August 21, 1864

A glorious day for me for I rec'd two Dixie letters from MBM & VBM respectively, good, long letters too — Such things incline to produce forgetfulness of the present & a happy feeling of self-satisfaction that interest is felt in one's fate by those he loves best. "Lucretius,"[9] also came safely to hand: in it I have a task before me, for it is altogether untrod open ground. Marrgate's Diary in America, Vol I, finished — Humbug like Miss Martineau but on more harmless subjects.

Monday, August 22, 1864

Mailed letter, — written yesterday, — to VBM. F'd Marrgate's diary — He says of Miss Martineau "her work is a strange compound of the true & the false" & I think the same may be said with equal justice of his own. Read in an old number of Blackwood, a most excellent critique of so much of Lord Macaulay's History of England as had been at that time — April, 1849 — published. His views of the causes of The Great Rebellion receive especial attention. This article was written by Sir Archi

Tuesday, August 23, 1864

bald Alison.

Borrowed to-day the Fifth Volume of Macaulay's History of England, — published since the commencement of the war, & of course new to me. It will be quite a treat. I begin it at once.

We have, at last, got rid of Muttonhead, as roll-caller; a Dutchman or rather German being substituted in his place. Anybody would be "an improvement" on old Mutton.

Wrote to M. B. M. If she & VBM only remain in Virginia until my exchange, I promise myself the pleasure of their company to Panola — but de Mulieribus non est disputandum.[10]

Wednesday, August 24, 1864

What delightful entertainment "The Caxtons" affords! How great the contrast between the characters of Uncle Roland & Mr. Caxton, & yet how perfect each in its kind? The book is one which I, at least, can read once a year and derive both instruction and amusement from every perusal. Now, when I am engaged in the pleasant occupation of reading it, I feel inclined to pronounce it Bulwer's best and Bulwer, to me, is the first of novelists.

Weather warm & Summer-like again,—not sultry but gentle.

Thursday, August 25, 1864

Finished V Volume of Macaulay, like its predecessors it is distinguished by that profound erudition, facile diction, prodigality of illustration and vivid and graphic power of description which render its author immortal among two <u>great</u> masters of our language. Those passages which relate to a standing army, and to The Danen Bubble are fine instances of his power. Alas that he (to use Alison's illustration) chose the bar of history instead of the bench, an advocate, when he might have decided as a judge!

Friday, August 26, 1864

Finished "The Caxtons"— read Biography of Lord Macaulay prefixed to his Fifth Volume.

A great storm to-day. Rumors of Exchange begin to pervade the air after so long a lapse into

comparative truthfulness. I <u>do</u> believe, however, that we will be in Dixie within two months, but what signifies that? for I have believed so almost anytime since my imprisonment. Four prisoners brought here to-day. Old captures, apparently, from hospitals.

Saturday, August 27, 1864

Grand match-game between the two base-ball clubs[11]; "Confederate" & "Southern," composed respectively of "Upper-endians" & "Lower-endians"— After a long & well contested game, the "Southern" club were victorious. The game afforded quite an exciting spectacle to us so unused to anything stirring. Weather turned cold again & so cold that coats, & in many instances greatcoats are quite in request. Obtained DeQuincey Autobiographic Sketches which I at once set about reading "Opium Eater" & "Suspiria" being remembered favorably.

Sunday, August 28, 1864

Rather unwell & "colicky"— Letter from Sister Mary, & two papers. Answered the letter immediately. The "Autobiographic Sketches" have no title to their name except a smack of the "Auto." I am much pleased with the book, except that there isn't enough of it & that it breaks off too suddenly. The chapters on the Irish Rebellions are instructive, that on "My Brother" is interesting & the final chapter contains the author's views on a subject on which

Monday, August 29, 1864

all men have views & but few correct ones viz. <u>Woman:</u> his exquisite appreciation of & reverence for the pure dignity of the womanly character (apart from vanities,) coincides with, & expresses my own. DeQuincey's style is pleasantly discursive, his matter irrelevantly relevant, and full proof of critical learning & cultivated taste. I finish the book to-day. Took morphine last night, & feel the effects of it now in the keen sensitiveness of my nerves to every slightest sound. Am better, otherwise. We are all intent on Chicago, today, & hopeful of "Peace" developments.[12]

Tuesday, August 30, 1864

Wrote a letter to Brother Wilse — The effect of stopping boxes &c is beginning to be felt — nearly all of the sub-messes are without bread for dinner, and hunger is beginning to be chronic. In three or four days at farthest the last of <u>our</u> supplies will be exhausted & then our little table will be on short [illegible word]

"History of the Florentine Republic and of the Rule of the Medici" by a Prof. Da Ponte, Univ. N. Y. City, Harper, 1833, a soi disant history,[13] written for a purpose, abounding in illogical

Wednesday, August 31, 1864

deductions which can only be called such <u>a non deducendo</u>.[14] The author is evidently a Carbonard, since he sees nothing in the character of Cosimo, the Pat. Patria[15] of Florence, but "atrocity," and calls the Pazzi plot for the assassination of Julian & Serevizo "a noble compact" — the Carbonari of to-day are ready to employ just such means to forward their schemes of doubtful utility, yet they are doubtless guided by patriotic motives, which was not the case with the Pazzi[16] — I am content with Machiavelli, Sisinendi, & R [?] and would rather err with them than accept the doubtful conclusions & revelations of their learned Theban, who is also a very dull, unentertaining writer.

SEPTEMBER 1864

Thursday, September 1, 1864

News of McClellan's nomination — I suppose he will do as well as anyone to bring about an exchange, for as for anything more, he is a <u>war democrat,</u> and all his <u>armistice</u> notions look to reunion, which can never be. "Travels & Adventures in Mexico" by a fellow named Carpenter, who, as a soldier, confesses himself a straggler, while as a man his reader convicts him of being a bully, beggar, liar, swindler & thief. It argues a fine state of morals in the public that such a book should be put forth with such innocent nonchalance. Why it is almost equal to Barnum's Autobiography — yet the Yankees are a very moral people. G.C.A? I read the

Friday, September 2, 1864

book on acct. of its subject, Mexico — and do not find myself paid for my trouble. I believe that Mexico under the govm't which has just been inaugurated there, will be a great, prosperous & constitutionally free country, however much I may sympathize with LaVeya & his sincere & patriotic, though mistaken fellow-theorists. A majority of the people (i.e. inhabitants, peons & all) may be opposed to a constitutional Empire, or any other form of govm't except anarchy, but I believe that Maximilian will have the support of that class of the people who ought to govern, i.e. the intelligent, educated classes, who rest their idea of freedom upon its true components. 2 or 3 prisoners this morning. According to our orders posted yesterday evening, the mail will go out but twice a week hereafter, Mondays, & Thursdays, and we are allowed to write but one letter each for each mail. A poor fellow belonging to one of our Ky. regts. was hanged outside, to-day, he having when at home on furlough murdered

Saturday, September 3, 1864

two of the Home Guard (who were doubtless endeavoring to arrest him. His name was Nichol: he may have brought himself within the military definition of crime, but it by no means follows that even this is the case, because he was sentenced by a Yank military commission. If his execution be as I half suspect, a flagrant outrage on humanity & the laws of war, I hope our govm't will retaliate. Wrote letter to Father yesterday for box; gave it to-day to Dr. Eversman, the Federal Surgeon who permits me to receive it on acct of my health. If he mails it, I ought to get the box next week. I have been under the influence of various drugs

Library subscription expires.

Sunday, September 4, 1864

for the last several days, but as I feel better in spite of them, I hope I have taken my last dose for this time. x x x The paper yesterday morning had a report, confirmed by Stanton's dispatch (if that can confirm anything) to the effect that Atlanta had fallen: and even went so far as to give a dispatch from the Gen. comdg the fed. forces in the place — Of course, we do not believe a word of this, though it may cause apprehensions. 15 or 20 prisoners this morning. Western Army, not recent captures. Wrote a letter to My Mother.

Monday, September 5, 1864

On Kitchen detail — A furious storm arose last night, & still rages, lashing the lake & bay into an ocean-like fury — day as bleak as December's dreariest in Mississippi. "Tennyson's Idylls of the King." I last read it four years ago: how great the contrast between now & then. On the banks of Fournile, one quiet summer's day, while my line being unattended in the clear water, I began it, & mused dreamily over its pages, thinking of one whom I loved even as Geraint loved

Tuesday, September 6, 1864

his fair Enid: then, after, my fishing excursion over, I had returned whence I came, and, called away from the book by the music of a laugh I well knew, left it where I lay — to the tender mercies of Bruno,[1] — who suddenly discovered a literary taste, — what a scolding I got for my carelessness! Oh the pleasure of those brief halcyon days of that pleasant visit North! Am I ever to experience its like again? I live in hope & bide my time. Gale continued during the whole of last night, & it still blows "great gusts." There now seems no chance, no doubt as to the Capture of Atlanta: — this is certainly a blow to us but after

Wednesday, September 7, 1864

so long a succession of successes we should not be disheartened by one reverse, however heavy a casual observer might think it. I hope the report of the death of Gen. Hardee may prove false, else the Confederacy has sustained the loss of another of her great & gallant leaders — not <u>great</u> like Lee, but <u>steady</u> as Massena, & unwavering in his patriotism x x x x x D'Israeli's "Coningsby," — I have read Thackeray's "Codlinsby" and recognize the excellence of his burlesque: it has taken the zest away from my reading of the <u>original</u>.

Thursday, September 8, 1864

Gen. Hardee not dead, — a Yankee lie. Morgan is said to have been killed, however: — a loss of a man & a patriot though not of a great commander. Wrote a letter to Father. Two letters to-day from Sister Mary & Bro. Rush. Supper this evening (i.e. slice of bread & cup of coffee) eaten in our new salle a manger. I do not know whether the new arrangement will be much worse than the old, or not; it <u>must</u> necessarily deprive us of some advantages, but rightly managed it might also confer new ones.

Friday, September 9, 1864

A white day: Three letters, M. VBM & Miss B. to whom I wrote several weeks ago. Dutch Hog and Peccary had a grand row to-day, wherein Peccary brushed his adversary's side slightly — with a pen knife — I believe. (Pecc.

est ille pastor dequoque bona dixi, nunc contradico.)² I suppose the affair had its origin in the Dutch Hog's denunciation of Pecc for refusing to believe some proposition which he (Apella the Jew)³ saw fit to declare oracularly as is his wont. Odom of this room "went out" this morning as a Yankee corporal and has not

Thursday, September 10, 1864

yet even been missed by our own mess. He was at great pains to prepare his plans, & they were perfected. May fortune attend him!

On Police detail — a small squad of prisoners brought in — I was greatly astonished by the entrance of an orderly with a note from Father, announcing his arrival outside, hoping by some means to obtain an interview — But all to no avail: The whole Yankee Government would doubtless be endangered by our conversing together. With the first note came 2 lbs coffee, ¼ lb tea, 3 lbs sugar

Sunday, September 11, 1864

and 1 ham — to which articles Dr. Eversman had limited my "application." Father however succeeded in sending in a trunk full of eatables (meal, grapes, apples & sweet-potatoes) to-day. I went upon the platform, Block One, & my Father stood in the walk about 300 yds dist't. Thus met Father & Son after 4 year absence: this was yesterday, & I know not whether sorrow or anger predominated — I felt both in a great degree. Father wrote in 4 notes, or letters. I wrote out 3 — He left the island at 6 P.M. On the whole since I have seen him to-day & my anger has toned down, I am glad he came, as it is some pleasure⁴

Monday, September 12, 1864

to see him so well, and he doubtless, is even better pleased than I am. I am glad that he does not know what kind of treatment we receive here, as he will of course, suppose it better than it is, & be comforted thereby. His notes acknowledge the courtesy of Drs. Eversman & Woodbridge, but that is not surprising from the reputation these officers have inside the pen. x x x Rose very early this morning & wrote letter to VBM. "<u>Vincenzo</u>," by J. Ruffino: a tolerably interesting Italian novel, which has been very fortunate in finding a translator who renders it into English as if he were <u>writing</u> it instead of adapting it from a foreign language. I like

Tuesday, September 13, 1864

it much better than I did Guerrazzi's Beatrice Cenci, although its author does not stand so high — I believe — as Guerrazzi....⁵

Finished First Book of Lucretius: I am delighted with him, though sometimes he shows too much of the philosopher (& that too, of an obscure philosophy) & too little of the poet for my taste. Among the many dicta he sets forth are to be found the germs of a truer philosophy than any other ancient, or at least any other Roman, dreamed of

Wednesday, September 14, 1864

Twenty five prisoners, private soldiers, from Camp Chase. A Translation — in the Continental Mag.— of Count Krasinski's "Undivine Comedy,"— mystical, obscure, yet containing much that is both sublime and tender, it reminds me somewhat of Goethe — but only as a Drummond light reminds one of the brightest star.[6] Moved my lodging to-day from the bunk I have occupied since Capt. Turner's departure to that vacated by Capt. Mosely who goes into a small room. Wrote to Sister Mary. Began Bulwer's "Zanoni" which I have long wanted.

Thursday, September 15, 1864

A letter from Sister, the first I have rec'd from her for many weeks.

I am delighted with "Zanoni" — It affords a strong contrast to Lucretius, which I read every morning: who knows that the old Horatian maxim does not apply to these two — In medio etc.[7] they are certainly extremes, each in his way. Shall finish, "Zanoni" to-morrow. I am half inclined to rate it as Bulwer's best.

Friday, September 16, 1864

Some one in the pen rec'd a letter from Odum to-day, stating his safe arrival in Canada: he has not been missed here as yet. About 42 prisoners left this evening for exchange: 36 on acc't. of sickness: the rest were Naval officers with one or two "special exchanges." Among the fortunate was Capt. J. C. Garland from our room, who came under the head of sick on acc't. of his one legged condition. Perhaps this augurs general change, but I fear not.

Saturday, September 17, 1864

{VBM}

Wrote, of course. The anniversary of what, I hope, may prove the most important event of my life, and as such ever memorable.

Elkins & another followed Odum's example this morning, & were safe on the boat when they were detected by the Sergt. who was looking for Odum who was missed for the first time at Roll-Call. Reading Coleridge's Notes on Shakspeare: his character of Hamlet pleases me more than any other &

— Albo dies simper notanda Capillo[8] —

Sunday, September 18, 1864

I believe is a newer approach to a full comprehension of the Great Poet. I transcribed his character of Shak. himself on p. 176.[9] I find a few very glaring inconsistencies in his notes, however, viz. After praising the poet for his full appreciation of the purity & elevation of the womanly character, the annotator, a little further on, reminds us "the resolve so to act "(i.e. Helena's determination of treachery in Mid. Night's Dream) is, I fear, likewise too true a picture of the lax hold which principles have on a woman's <u>heart</u>, when opposed to us; even separated from passion and motivation &c.— This is outrageous as is the defense of the ancient Lex mar obitae[10] in B. & F.'s "Custom of the Countries." I am loth, too, to give up "dear old Jack, honest Jack Falstaff," at the bidding of a metaphysical critic. Here is a sentence my heart re-echoes, "O, that detestable code that excellence cannot be loved in any form that is female, but it must needs be selfish!" That is in (Othello,) I have attempted C's prose before but always gave up in utter weariness; now, however, the choice of subjects is more fortunate & of interest to me—at least in this, vol. IV— General muster, strict search made for the missing—only result, a discovery that two instead of one were gone. Coleridge's Lectures, very meager, being published from notes taken by dif. Persons, also very obscure in many places. I am

Monday, September 19, 1864

best pleased with that on Cervantes.

Finished vol. IV of C's works—

Gunboat "got up steam" this evening & left hastily: hence a "grape." Go over to-night to sit up with Ruffin at the Hospital, he is very ill—Read "Macaria,"[11] of which, whatever may be said of its merits as a novel, I can truly say

Tuesday, September 20, 1864

that it interested, even affected me. It is evidently written from the heart & truly does it portray the state of Society in the South at the beginning of this war—nor is its tribute to the patriotism of our heroic women less deserved of commendation. I have book Sister Belle sent me fm. Father last week. As a novel I think it somewhat faulty but better than any woman's novel I have lately read. I read the first half to keep myself awake, but stayed awake to read the 2nd.

Surgeons examining sick, to be sent off—good omen, excitement outside—Yanks under arms; wish they had good grounds for alarm.

Wednesday, September 21, 1864

Finished 3rd book of Lucretius, began Coleridge's Table Talk & wrote a letter to Miss Brent. Rec'd from Miss B. copy of Demorest's Mirror of Fashion.

It seems from the paper this morning that two steamers have been captured by "Rebel pirates" on this lake, & that a design of attacking this place was entertained but abandoned. Hence the alarm, nor was it so groundless for if we had somebody to attend to the gunboat, we could soon overpower the garrison. An extra came in this evening containing a glowing acct.

Thursday, September 22, 1864

of a Yankee victory in the valley, & the rout of Early. If I mistake not this victory will dwindle down very considerably, when fuller acc'ts are published. The Yankees lie so, there is no believing anything they publish, at the first reading. Our arms have suffered a reverse; it would indeed be strange if such did not occasionally occur,— for it will be far — I opine,— from proving the "overwhelming defeat" of which the Yankee boast. Gen. Heintzelman, U.S. com. of exchange is "around"— I hope this is significant of better rations, if not of exchange

Friday, September 23, 1864

Lieut. Thos. Ruffin (4 N.C. Cav.) died about 6 A. M. He was a thorough gentleman and I regret his loss deeply. We have too few such, even among Confederate Officers. His life is given to his country as much as his who dies on the field of battle.

A letter from Sister. The night of this day will never be forgotten by any of the inhabitants of Block 5.— about 10 P.M. an Equatorial storm was accompanied by the fiercest gale of wind I ever felt; almost in

Saturday, September 24, 1864

an instant. Blks 4, 5, & 9 were roofless and their inhabitants flying for dear life, whither none seemed to know, for the air was filled with flying rafters & shingles. The roofs, almost entire, were moved a distance of 100 yds. The new dining room was blown away, trees fell & their branches strewed the pen. In addition to all this, the Yankees fired upon the fugitives for leaving their quarters, but why? 12 or 15 times, being much more moderate than I expected. Fortunately no one was killed. One soldier seriously injured (not gunfire) & many sprained & bruised. I escaped with a slight bruise on the hip. Our block is still roofless, & has careened over fearfully. Not a single block in the pen has any surer fastening than nails, the rafters & joists being not even moved.

Sunday, September 25, 1864

When the gale first arose I was sitting on the edge of my trunk, smoking, so that I was more fortunate than those who had retired — our retreat, though rather precipitate was effected in an orderly manner & in silence —

at one time the door was shut, but the crowd gave back a little to allow it to be opened. There was much less of panic than would have been in a crowd of citizens under the same circumstances. Once in the yard however, all was confusion & demoralization. The Yanks fired 15 or 20 shots, two broke through the Hospital & one struck B.5 (after our return.) The whole affair was worse than any battle could be — such is the general verdict. Moved to B.10 mid-storm yester evening. Wrote to Sister B. to-day.

Monday, September 26, 1864

Our removal to B.10 is likely to result in permanent residence — Maj. S. & Capt. L. came over yesterday from B. 11 where they sought shelter, & our mess is united again. "Society" is much better than in B.5 & the room, being closed, is much more comfortable. Ill to-day, colic, again took medicine but found not entire relief until late at night — Reading a book of comic stories, (Porter's Spirit of Zaine) & "Journal of Wm. H. Richansen, a Private in the Doniphan Expedition. The "letter" is highly amusing & ludicrous though it is not intended to be so. What soldiering? What discipline?

Tuesday, September 27, 1864

A horrible report, nothing less than the <u>surrender</u> of Early & Breckinridge was brought in last night: no one believed it, & the news this morning dispelled it entirely. For two nights past our slender stock of provisions has been preyed upon by thieves. Alas, that such things should occur among Confederate Officers! The Yanks fired a very mild salute of 100 guns over the victory in the valley — rather premature, as this morning's "news" has shown. I deeply regret the loss of Gen. Rodes,[12] but except his death & that of the brave

Wednesday, September 28, 1864

who fell, I see nothing so terrible in our late reverse. Brig. Gen. Goodwin who fell there was, last winter, Col. Goodwin of Block 8. Weather cold and unpleasant, yet we have no stove. This being a writing day, wrote to Bro. Rush with an appendix for Sister — Have sent up two applications for leave to rec. clothing from Father: one disapproved, the other remains unnoticed, though I asked for nothing disallowed by their orders — no danger of <u>my</u> asking Yankees for any <u>favors</u>. I shall try it again to-morrow.

Thursday, September 29, 1864

A general muster yesterday, someone having succeeded in passing the sentinels & being found outside nearly frozen fr. an attempt to swim the bay. He gave himself up I believe. Cold rain to-day. Weather very black, cold & disagreeable — Have lain up in my bunk all day, reading Hawthorne's "Our Old Home," and, in lieu of my lesson in Lucr, writing latin rhymes.

Hawthorne's sketches are very pleasing & graphic — delightful reading for such a day & such a place.

Friday, September 30, 1864

Yester-day we had no meat whatever, (none issued) but to-day we have each a ration of 9 ½ oz. including bone, — all foreleg and neck.[13] Truly we are drifting toward famine. <u>We</u> (our mess) have cornmeal left, and enough coffee to last for several weeks, and yet we are continually hungry. Those who are less fortunate eat rats but nothing short of absolute starvation could induce me to overcome my repugnance to these crea-

OCTOBER 1864

Saturday, October 1, 1864

tures which feed on the most loathsome garbage. Were they <u>barnfed</u> I should not long resist temptation of getting one "good meal" more. The authorities have openly reduced our rations (so that were they to give us all that we were <u>entitled</u> to, we wouldn't have enough) and this [illegible word]. Truly we will not starve, very little will suffice to sustain <u>life</u> but we now suffer from continual hunger.

Sunday, October 2, 1864

A letter from Sister Mary — A letter <u>to</u> VBM, of whom I dreamed of seeing last night as a venerable white haired old lady. Non accepi omen.[1] Reading, for two or three days back — with Gavroche — Mrs. Gordon's "Memoirs of Christopher North," a very pleasing & excellent work, the very faults of which are amiable. Mrs. Gordon is a daughter of the late Professor W. Have finished Hawthorne. Have neglected my Lucretius for three days, but will resume it to-morrow.

Monday, October 3, 1864

Finished Memoirs, & Reading an Essay on The Mass &c by Dr. England, Bp. of Charleston. I like to possess as much information on as many various things as possible, & like to obtain this at the very fountainhead. My <u>application</u> came back for the 3rd time. App'd by Col. Scovill (Supt) but disapp'd by Old Hill. It is quite hard not to be allowed to receive things from Father, when the regulations permit it, but not at all astonishing, I shall

Tuesday, October 4, 1864

try again to-morrow. x x Saw Scovill to-day; he told me that he couldn't imagine why my last application had been disapproved, & to try again, leaving off "tobacco & candles" which may be the reason — this I did. I suppose we are to be compelled to buy from the Sutler. Wrote to Father; letter will not go, however, till Thursday. A report of capture of Chafin's Bluff[2] by the U.S. Forces, which is not at all credited,—as no such report is apt to be

Wednesday, October 5, 1864

Said report proves false, or <u>worse</u>, for the Yanks seem to have suffered a severe repulse & considerable loss.

Wrote my letter to Father.

Mrs. Shelley's "Frankenstein," am rather disappointed in it—The Daughter of Godwin & Mary Wollstonecraft & wife of Shelley, ought better to have followed out her well-conceived, though terribly repulsive idea.

Thursday, October 6, 1864

Requisition came back, approved at last. Letter from Sister. Received fr Lt. Young, who seems very intelligent & well read & is an agreeable conversationalist—a volume of Macaulay Late Essays and Poems, several of which I have never before seen. Finished "Ad Patriae Vexillum, Carmen Militare." Began Macaulay by candlelight—"Fragment of a Nomads Tale"—would that it were more than a fragment. The essay on the Royal Soc. of Lit. shows that Macau. was sincere in his praise of Addison. "Athenian Revels" if concluded would about 50 sick left (for ex.) to-day, among them Dr. Seissons, & Maj. Moore of B.5[3]

Friday, October 7, 1864

be a most interesting work, but the introduction of the Eleut. Mys. of itself[4]—would preclude the possibility of continuation. On "The Wellington," an excellent burlesque: "Crowley & Milton," beautiful & clearly well worthy the pen of its great author, but also full of sophistry & specious pleading—in medio re, therefore on this question I take middle ground between Hyde & [illegible word] inclining rather to the former [illegible word] on the Italian writers &"Yankees" [illegible word] a non, to the very fine—William Pitt I have read before (as also I have Corv. & [illegible word] I shall not read it just now. Weather tonight very <u>gusty,</u> making us all as nervous as a [illegible word] child at the crackling

Saturday, October 8, 1864

Weather "turned cold" last night, & it has rained, hailed, snowed & sleeted, by turns all day. Very cold and disagreeable—Having a stove but no pipe, we rigged it up at the window (borrowing a few feet of pipe) & have had fire for the first time. 50 are in the room; not more than 8 can get around the stove—I have lain in bed, wrapped up, all day & have kept warm. Read Pitt & some of Dr. Arnold's Lectures on Modern History (which I <u>took</u> out of library yesterday, subscribing again.) I am pleased with them.

Sunday, October 9, 1864

A letter to Sister Mary. Room full of smoke, all day, from the stove. Reading very unedifying, though tearful (Arnold lectures continued) our beef ration to-day only purported to be 8 oz and was no more than 4.

[Literary aside] (cont'd fr. page 178)[5]
VII.
"I have seen falsehood veiled by the virginal cheek of a child. I have seen the immaculate meek Desdemona false; Imogene wanton; have seen Juliet faithless; and she, the chaste Ithacan queen, choose a swine from her suitors, and, from his embrace, rise to write to her [illegible word] that she pines for his face in a tender Ovidian strain."
"Strong necessity is supreme among sons of men"—Q. H. Sir.

Monday, October 10, 1864

Speaking of Historical Style (in Lect. VIII.) Dr. Arnold says, "If, on the other hand, it is always eloquent, rich in illustrations, full of animation, but too uninformative, & without the relief of simple & quiet passages, we must admire the writer's genius in a very high degree, but we must fear that he is too continually excited to have attained to the highest wisdom; for that is necessarily calm." Apply this to Macaulay.

Finished the "Lectures," to-day. Day before yesterday Capt. J. R. North (of Cha'ton, S. C.) left for special exchange (with 2 others.) He was steward to the prison hospital and was of great service to us all, at some sacrifice of his own interests. The sun is shining today!!

Procured an odd volume of the "Rambler:"—It was very well for just a reading. I regard it as very much inferior to the "Spectator," no. 70 contains

Tuesday, October 11, 1864

a singular opinion of woman for a professed moralist. Camillia in No. 105 is an amusing & not altogether unreal character. I know one, however, who playfully affects the Camillia, yet is "pure womanly," though I fear self-endearing, to achieve the perfection as she professes the excellencies of Tranquilla, (no. 119) This day has been a delightful one,—let this devil of a climate have its due. Harry Coleman (Miles Legion) came up to see me this evening, & broke down my bunk, which was

Wednesday, October 12, 1864

weakly supported. No one was hurt by the fall. A letter from Miss B.—answered to-day.

Reading "France, Social, Literary, and Political," by Henry Lytton Bulwer. A very interesting work (2 vols. 1834.) & a companion to his brother's similar work on England. A year ago, if I recollect it aright, I was in a casemate, at Ft. Columbus.[6] Better off, were I there now, though that casemate was a hard old place, only preferable to a distasteful parole. This book of Bulwer should be read in connection with Modern French History (one since the Revolution of '89) I marked the chapter on female influence —

Thursday, October 13, 1864

The book already graces the library of my Chateaux en Espagne. — Finished it to-day and took out Scott's Letters on Demonology & Witchcraft. The <u>Flour</u> <u>Question</u> is the subject of agitation "all over" the pen; it being reported that Scovill has said that those messes who may elect to receive flour in lieu of bread may do so. I fear that the change will be made on acct. of the few swaps gained, not thinking sufficiently of the difficulties in cooking & the unwhite sameness of half-sodden dough. Muster this morning; some knife & [illegible word] etc. found & some tobacco pilfered (from our room.)

Friday, October 14, 1864

Finished Dem. & Witchcraft. Two shots fired last night about 11 P.M., some say at rat-hunters, others at some room with a cracked stove. I heard the last bullet whistle. Have neglected Lucretius for several days, — not that it palls my taste (for I am still interested whenever I attempt it), but because my attention has been occupied with other things. Allan Cunningham's Lives of British Painters & Sculptors, — Early Painter & Hogarth + Here continueth to rot the body of Francis Charteris[7]; who by Arbuthnot furnishes one example of an unflattering epitaph; such a one, however, as is never gracious. —

My anniversary — arrived one year ago

Saturday, October 15, 1864

Sir Joshua Reynolds. — "In a footnote occurs an anecdote of Sterne's death & dissection[8] which I have never seen elsewhere & concerning whose authenticity am somewhat curious x x x, his body was sold by his landlady to defray his lodgings, & was recognized on the dissecting table by one who had caroused with him, & enjoyed his witty & licentious conversation." — This sentence is a specimen both of the style & matter of the author — "the great Earl of <u>Nottingham</u>" is spoken of as the destroyer of the Armada: besides, the work is wretchedly printed: yet I find it, withal tolerably interesting, inasmuch as I do not feel disposed to lay it aside with the first volume. "Benj. West" (cont. anec. of Presb. zealot attempt to convert Pope. "O [illegible word] cast not thou the kirk down on them for this abomination" — Henry II) and Henry Fuseli,[9] both entertaining sketches, though the latter

Sunday, October 16, 1864

contains a most ungentleman-like insinuation agst the character of Miss Wolstonecraft. Another letter from Miss B.; She is a very pleasant correspondent, & her letters give me a most favorable idea of her vivacity & cheerful disposition. Finished volume on Sculptors, having read all the sketches, except those of Milton & Bacon. "Nolebeus," "Mrs. Dames" & "Flaxman" interested me. This work is only entertaining (accdy to <u>my</u> notion of art) on acct of the subject matter: I consider the style detestable, though, for aught I know, my taste may be at variance with the decision of the critical world. Wrote to Sister.

Monday, October 17, 1864

On room detail; this is much better managed here than at Block 5,— the detail bringing water for all purposes,— except <u>bathing</u>, and wood, besides sweeping the room. Four General Officers, Trimble Beall Jones & Frazer, left to-day —(I hope) for exchange. Gen. Trimble is a fine old gentleman & a gallant officer, Beall will do well enough, Jones is an ex-officer, having left the service before his apptmt was confirmed & was captured as a civilian, Frazer will I trust be cashiered as soon as he arrives South; either as a traitor or a wonderful coward, perhaps both. "Akenside's "Pleasures Mag."— don't like it, but think I may 21 years hence. At night, (with Gavroche) Carlyle's "Chartism," the first of his works I ever succeeded in finishing. My taste must be changing for

Tuesday, October 18, 1864

I see much to admire in his nervous forcible style, humorously modulated with bathos. I tried "Sartor Resartus" once, & thought it —like P. R. Love's speech —"a pack of d —d nonsense." Perhaps I might think somewhat differently now. Yet, I am by no means, a Carlylist. "Past & Present," or — at least — a part of it, for the first volume is one not so good as "Chartism" and more <u>Carlylish.</u>— Rec'd by mail a pocket blank-book & other little things fr. Miss B. In it "Home, Sweet, Home" beautifully worked in petto on a card — Though I ate my whole allowance to-day, I am very hungry now. I have been in a state of chronic hunger for three weeks. Though <u>we</u> still have coffee, our meal we use very economically. I pity those who have none. + + +

[Literary aside] "Imbécile!" cried Mirabeau to his secretary, "ne me dites jamais ce bête de mot." It is a "blockhead of a word."

Wednesday, October 19, 1864

Finished "Autocrat of the Breakfast Table"— a book containing much that is fanciful, some commonplace, much that is old, new-draped & many striking & beautiful ideas of its own. 2d reading. Leigh Hunt's "Story of Rimini"— don't like it.[10] Immeasurably inferior to Dante's Episode, also to Parasina, though it ought not to be mentioned in the same sentence with Dante, beautiful & rhythmic as it is. — Then wrote a letter to my dear Mother. The silence of those at home troubles me. — A few "fresh fish"—first for a long time — Cavalry captures from Western Army. "Legend of Florence," tame, very tame.

> [Literary aside] "Delightful task, to rear the tender mind
> To teach the young idea how to [illegible word]
> To pour the fresh instruction on the mind,
> For loveliness
> Needs not the foreign aid & ornament,
> But is, when unadorned, adorned the most"
> (Thomson)

Thursday, October 20, 1864

No letter. "What can the matter be"—"Philip," by Thackeray. Codfish issued to-day, the dried lake fish were bad & disgusting enough, but this is (what seemed an impossibility), one step beyond.

> [Aside] Credo.
> All government derives its authority from the consent of the governed.
> All men should be absolutely equal before the law.
> All men have a right (not so much to be self-governed, as) to be well-governed. Universal Suffrage is a humbug. According to the spirit—as well as the letter—of the Constitution, the President should be chosen by electors, not by the people directly. These electors should be chosen by the legislatures—as in South Carolina.

Friday, October 21, 1864

Codfish for breakfast. Awful mess but better than nothing.
Snowed at night.

> [Aside] Caucuses, nominating conventions etc. have no place in the system of government, and only tend to cherish faction and to increase the influence of demagogues. Members of Legislatures and of the Lower House in Congress, and these alone, should be chosen directly by the people.
> The rights of citizenship should be granted only by special act of the Legislature,—and naturalization laws should be repealed. I would have our government a popular one, but the people should consist of the leading citizens. Populus should not include Plebs. The multitude is turbulent, the people should be conservative.

Saturday, October 22, 1864

Spent a few agreeable hours with Clark last night, staying till eleven o'clock & moistening our conversation with chocolate, & refreshing our grosser substance with bread & butter.—Clark, Jos. B. 18th Miss.—Jackson, Miss.—one of the most agreeable & intelligent men in this Prison. Rooms at hospital with Col. Woods (Steward vice Capt. McBeth.) He is one of the most companionable men I know—snow all gone.

> [Literary aside] Prosper Merimee:—Hist. of Pedro I, King of Castile & Chronicle of Chas. IX. Have these works been translated?

Sunday, October 23, 1864

A letter to Miss B.—A letter to Father. (Clark sends the former out for me, in his private mail.) Two Dixie Letters, one each fr. VBM & MBM. Very cheering, yet containing bad news, for these dear friends are soon to go to the Southwest, so that I fear I may not see them after exchange. I wish I could reply at once but cannot for several days yet. My Liberty will lose half her charms, if I cannot be permitted to see those whom alone I love dearly. Book of Judith.[11]

Monday, October 24, 1864

Box came to-day containing coat, vest, breeches, hat, shirts, underclothing, blanket etc. so that I am now very well provided for agst winter. A letter was in the box, but I shall not rec. it to-day, though it was almost in my hands. Submitted a <u>letter</u> to Dr. Eversman, he took it & I suppose will <u>cut it</u> down, as he did before, I cannot digest the food we get here, little as it is, & require (the Dr. says) vegetables etc. My list was 25 lbs. meal (or flour), 5 lard, 15 dr. fruit, ½ bu potatoes, 5 coffee, 8 sugar, 8 butter, 1 ham, 3 doz. eggs, crackers, & blk pepper. All of this may come; some of it will—nous verrons. Irving's "Conquest

(Letter was to Father)

Tuesday, October 25, 1864

of Granada."#

On Kitchen Detail—Literae quae hesterno die venerunt, hodie mihi advenerunt, Scripta est Mea Sorore.[12] An "allusion" called my attention to the needle-book which came in the box—

This has been the most delightful day of the year. "The Student; a Series of Papers" by Bulwer. A very small squad—not more than ½ dozen,—of prisoners came in. Our Western Army.

Wednesday, October 26, 1864

Wrote to Sister Belle—also to Harper & Bro. enclosing 75 cts—for a copy of <u>Plautus</u>.¹³ Fin. Conq. Granada. Find some of the essays in "The Student," both pleasing in themselves & interesting as affording a glimpse of the great mind of Bulwer, almost in his youth. In the Essay "On the Departure of Youth" is a passage, on Belief, which will please VBM — "Infidelity in Love" I accept as an explanation of the author's own Domestic infelicity. In the Essay on "The Passion for The Universal" is a tribute to, or estimate of the character of Milton, which

Thursday, October 27, 1864

is entirely new to me. Wrote again to Sister, by the <u>private mail.</u> Our mess removed to B.8 to-day (m.2) improving our condition by the change, which was brought about thru the influence of Capt. Eure. The room is much quieter even than our late one, & a <u>solitude</u> compared to B.5. There are, I believe, only 33 in the room. I have an excellent bunk, with a place for a window of its own. I shall improve it still more, though it is neatly papered etc now.

Thursday, October 28, 1864

Gav. & Capt. J. have each a bunk. Capt J; joins us in tete à tete, & we can read by one candle. Finished "Student," omitting conversations with Amts Stud in Ill Health which I remember hearing read (to Mrs A. at Ben. Irby's.) Thomsen's "Seaside," not disappointed in the book, though it comes embalmed in the frame of 100 yrs. Its diction chiefly pleases; few new thoughts, few original ideas, the character of the man shines thru the poet & deepens the reader's pleasure. A timid rider, he reviles the change aboard ship — or more likely afraid to discharge a piece — he condemns sporting & all this on grounds of humanity, while he speaks glowingly of the angler's "gentle craft." The heart of the foxhunters, is a fine specimen of mock-heroics, & reminds one of a picture, or, rather, seems

Saturday, October 29, 1864

to have been suggested by one. A good def. of <u>love</u> in Celadin & Amelia. "Damon & Misedorce," highly amusing & very characteristic of the age. Finish the book to-day. Begin Thackeray's Newcomes, expect to dally over it a long time. "History of France" by A.B. Edwards — a mere compend, & very concise, at that, yet useful as a "remembrancer!" For dinner, to-day, we had "<u>mush</u>" (made from our own meal) & a slice of gov't bread, each. To-morrow, however, we will feast on 8 oz. (each) of codfish — in lieu of pork. Hung up a blanket curtain before my bunk. Am enabled to enjoy quite a degree of privacy. O, what a luxury to be once more alone.

Sunday, October 30, 1864

Last night, after a bath, undried woolen undergarments — for the first time in at least 13 years, & I know not how many more. Rec'd a pkge of papers, addressed in Sister's hand. Wrote to VBM. It is a source of sadness to me that this dear friend (with MBM) has perhaps by this time increased that distance which already separates us, & that I may not be able to see her when I regain my liberty — Liberty, in itself, is of course greatly desired, but hitherto it has been doubly so on her account.

> [Aside] Day's ration: Bread & 8 oz. codfish.

Monday, October 31, 1864

Rec'd transfer, & answered at B.8 — M.2 this morning. We remain, however, at B.5 one day longer. Gen muster this morning, the Lt. Col. Comdg the Veteran Reserve here & left in comm'd by Hill's absence (Stumping State of Lincoln.) He is to Hill what King Stork was to King Log.[14] This morning, it being scouring day, the chairs were outside at roll-call, several in our (new) mess took seats in ranks. The New Col. ordered the Corp. to take those chairs away, & "knock down" those who refused to give them up. This without a preliminary word — Finished Edward's "France," instead of a compend., it is a summary. Lady Emmeline Stuart Wortley's Travels, cursorily read. Some of it interesting on acc't of subjects (Mexico, Sp.Am. &c) but the least said of the literary merits of the work, the better. No doubt the writer is a lady, but she certainly is not an author. Fin. Book V of Lucr.—

> [Aside] Rations—Beef, 10 ounces (even more bone than usual) & soup therefrom.

NOVEMBER 1864

Tuesday, November 1, 1864

A very pleasant day.— Sun shining brightly. As it is so little trouble, I attempt to mention all such days. M. Huc's "Recollections of a Journey through Tartary & Thibet," Vol. I. Very entertaining. I wish I had the second volume. Also borrowed fr. Col. Wood (& commenced reading) III volume of Lamartine's Hist. of Gironde (beginning "Thirty-first of May")[1] I will read the other volumes afterward. I have read this before. My sympathies are with The Gironde, though I have to ignore their advocacy (or at least, countenance) of the Death of Louis XVI.—

35 prisoners tonight. West.

> [Aside] For dinner, salt pork, sliced a superfacies, equal to ¾ that of this page,[2] with as much more left for breakfast. 3days rations pickled beef

issued—12 oz. a great improvement, though the bone weighs heavily. "They say" we are to have no more fish.

Wednesday, November 2, 1864

Wrote to MBM to-day—"Propria Quae Maribus & Box Tunnel" Chas. Reade—Began "Crescent & Cross" by Eliot Warburton. Episode of Charlotte Corday in Lamartine.³ I like his estimate of that heroine's character.

[Aside] The report (at first regarded as a mere rumor) of Gen. Archer's death has been confirmed. Doubtless, his long imprisonment had much to do, indirectly at least, in causing his death, which is greatly to be regretted. He was a gallant officer & a good man.

Thursday, November 3, 1864

A letter from Father—I wish I could hear oftener from my old home—letters have become very infrequent, yet I believe as warm a feeling, as ever, exists. Rec'd Plautus' Captives to-day.⁴ In Lam. Custine, Marie Antoinette, Last Days of Veryneaud etc. & Insurrection at Lyons. I like Thiers much the best: he is more reliable. Lescites, Lemielion, I cannot help regarding Lem. as a sort of literary Quack, though a harmless one. Cold weather, high winds, & driving rain. In the last 2 days, as many changes for the worse.

Friday, November 4, 1864

Finished Lucretius: I am very much pleased with "De Rerum Natura;" I think it the finest of the latin poems, the grandest achievement of the Roman Muse. Well has Bulwer pronounced the eloquence of Lucretius "like ebony, at once dark and splendid." His errors were those of his age, his greatness is his own. Many passages are obscured by the jargon of the school & the use of scientific or technical terms, but there is enough in the polished & melodious effusions of this preëminent Poet of the Garden, to constitute him henceforth one of my prime favorites. Wood was issued to-day, 1st time this week. Many rooms are as yet without stoves: Wood was withheld that we might be compelled to burn that which we were permitted to cut for ourselves a few weeks ago.

Saturday, November 5, 1864

Quite ill throughout this whole day, and from the middle of last night—cholic. Took much medicine in many doses. Also mustard plaster—all to no effect, so that I passed a day of suffering. Ate nothing. Attribute this attack to beans. Apropos. we receive 8 oz beans each for this week. The rations not accounted for in this record of the week were marked by issue of fr. beef 8—10 oz. Meat rations much improved this week, & fish discontinued—Thanks (on dit) to King Stork. Vive le Roi!

Monday,[5] *November 6, 1864*

Gens. Marmaduke & Cabell brought in last night, with three or four Colonels. Wrote to Father. Am puzzled by not hearing from Sister Belle, & from the Eversman Letter.

I don't like Lamartine's character of Robespierre, and I am more than inclined to doubt its accuracy. This book ought never to be read except by those who have read other & more reliable authors on this same subject. Went up to Clark's tonight where read 80 pages in Tytler's Universal History.[6] I hope to obtain the work & to read it throughout.

Monday, November 7, 1864

Library Subscription will expire (Oct. 7th)————

Cleared said subscription by returning "Crescent & the Cross"—a book "well enough in its way," evidently, "got up for market," yet containing many fine passages—the author's bigotry, too, is kept pretty well in hand & only peeps out occasionally, to remind the reader of its existence. Finished Lamartine's Gironde (Vol III.) A few "fresh fish"—home-loungers from Arkansas, I don't care whether these ever get away or not. There are too many such here already, though they do about as much good here as elsewhere. A Cloudless Day.

Tuesday, November 8, 1864

All-eventful election-day has come at last, and nature in honor of the event has put on her most somber—This day, which doubtless witnesses the suicide of a nation is fitly sad. It is none of our business, though, and really we owe the Yankees no sympathy if they are enslaved in their attempt to conquer us. As the schoolboys used to say, "it isn't our funeral."—

Fish issued again—2 days—Lake fish: not quite as red as cod. On Room detail. Letter fm Sister Mary.

Wednesday, November 9, 1864

Wrote to Sister Mary. "Bride of Lammermoor," the last "Waverly" I expect to read for many years. When I shall have finished "The Newcomes," I know of but few novels I care to read until I grow old, when I shall like my old favorites still—These are "Tom Jones," "Vanity Fair" (both of which I have read) "Vatliek etc."[?] "Caleb Williams," "Undine," & "Sintraia." I will, however, doubtless read many as I have done since my imprisonment—for want of better pastime. Very High Wind at night.

Thursday, November 10, 1864

Finished "Newcomes"—one of the most delightful books I have ever read. The Old Colonel—as a type of the true gentleman is only equaled, not surpassed, by Henry Esmond—

Lincoln is beyond a doubt elected. This is better for our country, though our own interests — as prisoners — would have been better served by McClellan. I am afraid we preferred him (Mc) for this selfish reason, and am glad the old Gorilla has leave to chatter on, though I <u>pity</u> our blind enemies.

Friday, November 11 1864

Out of reading. Began Plautus' Captevei. Also "Reproduction" in Dalton's Physiology, to which I get occasional access.

Renan Life of Jesus: don't like it as well as I did when I first read it. Too "Frenchy" & too much of a "trimmer" between Strauss (or Taylor) and Fleetwood. Not always "in medio tutissimus ibis."[7]

High winds again last night — all these from the South — don't prate to me about "the soft south" any more. Snowing to-night. Ground will be covered by morning. Bought 2 cans lobster (smuggled) @ 75 & 1 ½ lb. coffee @ 1.50. had enough for supper, cooking the lobster & our breakfast bread.

Saturday, November 12, 1864

Wrote (pr underground mail) to Sister — repeating most of my letter of Tue. which was miscarried — I tried another <u>office</u> this time. "Rogers' Table Talk" — a <u>readable</u> book: just such as one would read with pleasure on a Steamboat or R.R. It doesn't elevate one's opinion of Rogers himself. Snow melted — but renewed itself. And we are like to have a "heavy fall of snow" tonight.

[Literary aside] Porson considered "Gessners' Thesaurus" the best Dictionary of the Latin Language.[8]

Sunday, November 13, 1864

Ground covered with snow. Wrote a letter to My Mother — also one to Father concerning eatables — If Clark sees Fosters' book in time (tomorrow) & the list is approved the latter will be sent, otherwise, the former. More snow fell, & then all melted. Finished the book, Tytler's Universal History — I have ever been prejudiced against Universal Histories, but find this admirable in its arrangement and very interesting.

The Hospital Steward, whose book containing lists of articles appd &c, is the guide in issuing express matter.

Monday, November 14, 1864

Mailed letter to my Mother — Finished Renan — though I don't like it as well as I did when I first read it, yet I see much good in it. An act of "The Captives." — Plautus is delightful — very like Shakspeare's comedies in some things — Began John Stuart Mill "On Liberty." This <u>ought</u> to be a good book.

> [Literary aside] "A ruler who appoints any man to an office, when there is in his dominions another man better qualified for it, sins against God and against the State.
> Koran, af. Mill p 97.

Tuesday, November 15, 1864

Mill,—An Act of Plautus, Chap. in Physiology—and several old magazines (Atlantic Monthly.) Snowed last night, afterwards turned warm & we have had a "windy day." 40 prisoners brought in—Price's Army.

> [Literary aside] "The Great Truth has finally gone forth to all the ends of the earth, <u>that man shall no more render account to man for his belief, over which he has himself no control.</u> Henceforward, nothing shall prevail upon us to praise or to blame any one for that which he can no more change than he can the hue of his skin or the height of his stature. Henceforward, treating with entire respect those who conscientiously differ from ourselves, the only practical effect of the difference will be, to make us subject to the ignorance on one side or the other from [illegible word] finish by instructing them, if it be theirs; (324)

Wednesday, November 16, 1864

Mill Finished. The Book pleases me exceedingly: I promise it another perusal in better times. Letter from Miss B.—answered it but do not know whether I shall mail my letter or not. All depends on Foster's book. Reading in Irving's Wolfert's Roost to-night. Just 10 yrs. ago I was reading this book during my first session at M. U. The Sun shone clear during half this day: Quite a phenomenon! Our Thanksgiving day—but poorly kept.

Thursday, November 17, 1864

Finished Plautus' Captives—am very well pleased with it: wish I had his other five comedies.[9] Have now nothing else of the kind to read. Old Magazines, Blackwood, Putman & Household words—A good article in B. fm Apl. 1849 on Pedro the Cruel. Mailed the letter to Miss B. Day partially clear again, temperature mild, earth muddy, from rain last night.

> [Literary aside continued] Eng. under the House of Hanover, its History & condition during the reigns of the 3 Georges, Illustrated from the Saten & Caracatures of the day" by Thos. Wright, In 2 vols. Lindon, 1848—

Friday, November 18, 1864

Chap. In Physiology.—Old Magazines—(Art. on Ld. Costleragh in Nov.

1848, Blkwd — viewing the Irish Question from the <u>extreme other side)</u> Began Schlegel's Lect. on Hist. of Literature & Lord Brougham's Sketches &c. Lord B. views the Irish Question from another standpoint — He gives to Queen Caroline [illegible word] also though not fully. His translations are fine.

(321) ourselves if it be our own, to the end that the only kind of inhumanity may be preferred which is desirable among rational beings — the agreement proceeding from full conviction left, "the freest discussion" &c. Ld. Brougham "Inaugural [illegible phrase]

Saturday, November 19, 1864

A day of pain: Read nothing, ate nothing; colic again — the usual remedies with the usual want of success. Time, the healer of grief, is the only physician for colic. Henceforth I am a Pythagorean & foreswear beans as the [illegible word] of bloating, yet without them I must be hungry. Until I can be supplied with proper food I must continue to suffer from these attacks.

Sutler arrested — shop closed, & his assistant placed in confinement, General explanation is that he has been guilty of bringing in useless old things [illegible word]

Sunday, November 20, 1864

Read Tytler all day & Schlegel at night — A very pleasant day, as also was yesterday — two in succession! Mirabile dictu![10] — Episcopal service read at night in lieu of the usual prayer meeting — a good substitution. The Psalm was the 104 — the sublimest production of the Hebrew genius.

> [Literary aside] "Do anything in agitation for the interest of the state? Eschines is neutral.[11] Does anything go wrong & disappoint our expectations? Forth comes Eschines—as old fractures & cramps break out the moment any malady attacks the body."
> Demes DeCorona—N. G. Foste [illegible word]

Monday, November 21, 1864

Gave Dr. Eversman another letter, which will I hope be more fortunate than the last, which was lost <u>en route</u> to its address (i.e. Father.) Go on duty as <u>caterer</u> (a non caterendo) for the "ten" of which our mess forms half. My "tour" will last a week & will keep me busy all forenoon at the very least. Tytler, Schlegel & Lord Bro'm's translation of the Chersonese Oration.[12] Sutler opened this morning & resumed business, — Weather cloudy & cold.

Tuesday, November 22, 1864

A very busy day — drawing rations — could only get time to read one chapter in Tytler all day — At night, a lecture Schlegel & Ld. Brou'm's Dissertation on Ancient Eloquence. Rec'd back letter which I gave Eversman yesterday endorsed "Disapproved for reasons" — very unsatisfactory. I suppose I may as well make up my mind to face hunger manfully — weather very clear but colder than I have ever seen it elsewhere. A few — not more than a dozen prisoners — I know not whence

Wednesday, November 23, 1864

Another very busy day — on room detail, also, i.e. — "police." — Got our stovepipe at last & certain persons of mechanical genius at once commenced the construction of an oven, stone & mortar, upon which to place the stove. Now that we can place that article in its legitimate place in the center of the room — our room will be much warmer now. Only read a lecture in Schlegel — Shall not notice this or Tytler until I have finished, unless for some better reason than that they have merely been read. Gavroche got a box of eatables to-day, & I feel perfectly happy in the long unwonted fullness of satiety I enjoy tonight.

Small squad of prisoners.

Thursday, November 24, 1864

Wrote, late last night to Father. A letter fr Miss B. this morning. Finished "Sketches of Public Characters &c." — am pleased with it, on the whole. Some of the Sketches are certainly not by Lord Brougham, — This, the title page, permits one to assert while good taste would have forbidden such mention of his name as occurs were he the author. The Dissertations, many oral addresses, & Translations are very fine — so far as I can judge of their merit. Made my first assay at biscuit-making this evening — I don't like the business, & shouldn't relish the baker's trade — Breakfast will show with what success. Borrowed 1st & [illegible word] volumes of Lamartine Girondists. Shall read leisurely.

> [Aside] Sir William Hamilton,
> Etruscan Antiquities.
> Bryan Edwards, Hist. W. Indies—
> Beaufort's Bosnian Republic.

Friday, November 25, 1864

A letter from Father. A dozen prisoners brought in — Atlanta, I believe. A very bright, pleasant day. An election held in the pen for "agent," to distribute supplies sent by our government, & perhaps to go outside to purchase them. Choice fell on Col. Fitz, Cols. Murchison & Woods came next. I voted for the latter — I think it very unlikely that anything will come of it. Went up at "taps" to Clark's & read Tytler till 1 A. M. — Rare & glorious privilege, in this life of ours,— came back through the <u>rain</u>. Am highly pleased with Schlegel's view of Medieval civilization & antipopular notions as to its instruments & features.

[Literary aside] The Cnidian Venus of Praxiteles—known to the modern world as the Venus de Medici,—was modeled after the famous courtesan Phryna. (260 B.C.)[13]
On detail—digging for Hospital.

Saturday, November 26, 1864
Day cloudy, but tolerably pleasant. <u>Now</u> raining again however.

[Literary aside] <u>Origin</u> of <u>Certain</u> <u>Words</u>
I. <u>Pontiff</u>, Pontifex: Ancus Martius built a bridge across the Tiber connecting the city with Janiculum & gave the charge of maintaining & repairing the same to its <u>Priests.</u>[14]
II. <u>Capitol</u>, Capitoleum. In digging for the foundations of a Temple in the Tarpeian hills a human skull was found, hence the place was called Capitoleum.[15]
III. <u>Proletaire</u>, Proletarii, a name given to the lowest class of Roman citizens, as contributing to the support of the state only by raising progeny.[16]
IV. <u>Lusinun</u>; an expiatory sacrifice or ceremony performed at the conclusion of the census, every five years.
"Musically whining out the most grievous calamities"—Lucian—Dial. on Stage dancing (opera?)[17]

Sunday, November 27, 1864
Wrote a letter to Father. Last Day of my Detail: next week I will have more leisure.

[Literary aside] How I wish that <u>our</u> constitution had provided for some such temporary concentration of power as that granted by the Roman Senatus—consultum "Dent operam consules ne quid Republica detrimenti capiat"![18]

<u>Gladiators</u> <u>Oath</u>: "In verba Eumolpi Juravimus, uri, vinciri, verberari, ferroque necari, et quiquid aliud. Eumolpus jussisset tamquam optimi gladiatores et homines corpora animosque religiose addicimus"[19]

The Emperor Julian wrote "The systems of Pythagoras, of Plato & of the Stoics unanimously teach <u>that</u> <u>there</u> <u>are</u> <u>Gods;</u> that the world is governed by <u>their</u> <u>providence</u>, that their goodness is the source of every temporal blessing, and that they have prepared for the human soul a future state of reward or punishment."[20]

De Myst. Eleus. Warburton "Divine Legislation of Moses" & Cumberland's Observer v. 116[21]

"Nec recito cuiquam nisi amicis idque coactus." Hor.[22]

Monday, November 28, 1864

Breakfasted with Col. Jones (H.C.) — Finished first vol. of Tytler: his style is extremely inelegant — owing perhaps to printer & editor more than to the Author himself. I like the work for many reasons, chiefly because I have never read one of the kind which equals it. I don't like Universal History, as a branch of literature. It is too apt to be empirical.

[Literary aside] Les femmne sont très braves avec le peau d'autrui'—[23]

Zeuò estin ouranoò, Zeuò te ge ta panta[24]
Jupiter est quodcumque vides quocumque moveris.[25]—Chap LXXII Reade's C & H.

Tuesday, November 29, 1864

A delightful day, bright & genial as Mississippi herself can boast even on her most glorious autumn. Lamartine's character of The Duc d'Orleans grates harshly on all my convictions. He a patriot, forsooth! "Not all their florid prose or honied lies of rhyme, can blazon evil deeds or consecrate a crime,"[26] and to palliate & excuse is only less venial than to blazon & consecrate. M. de Lamartine will, however, in the course of his narrative doubtless write of this man in a different spirit, since I have observed an inconsistency in many of his characters, seeming to arise from instability in his own convictions.

Wednesday, Dec 7th

Manley & Johnston leave our mess to mess in their room down below.

Wednesday, November 30, 1864

Hill has been in command for several days: we hail his return as a deliverance from some few of our evils. Fin I vol. Lamartine, the trans (as I have remarked elsewhere) is a wretched one, yet there are beauties perceptible through it. Lam. is not a historian. Went up to Clark's, read Schlegel till 1 A.M. Wrote to Miss B. to-day. Weather mild enough, but nothing like yesterday; change wrought last night, with very high winds. Col. Wood's inscription I conjecture to be

ILEDECITO,[27] — easily understood.

DECEMBER 1864

Thursday, December 1, 1864

Have done nothing beyond the routine, or beyond what has already been recorded — i.e. Lamartine furnished my sole reading, & I have rec'd no letter, written nothing, seen nobody & almost <u>thought</u> nothing. Rer. dream. T — — J Rain at night, with a northerly wind, something of a phenomenon here where all breezes blow from one quarter.

> [Aside] Col. C. C. Blacknall 23 N.C. who was last winter a roommate of mine at B.5 recently died at Winchester of wounds rec'd in our Maryland Campaign. A brave & gallant officer–r. e. pace

Friday, December 2, 1864

The Military Situation has become critical and very interesting. Sherman threatens the inland towns of Georgia, while Hood is before Nashville. We all hope to see Sherman foiled & defeated, nor groundlessly, since by this time an army consisting in part, at least, of veterans must be in his front, while Breckinridge is in position to operate on his flank & Hood even if he accomplish nothing else, isolates him completely from the North. If he be utterly routed, then we may hope for exchange. Begin "The Wandering Jew." Rain again tonight.

Saturday, December 3, 1864

Letter from Sister Belle. Both my underground letters inflamed. She asks if "G — — e" is married: What a characteristic piece of feminine artifice this question masks! Worthy the notice of Thackeray's pen. Weather turns colder. Very high winds, from the old quarter — S.W. — shaking the house at every gust. I shall wrap up in my blanket like Ulysses when his winds were freed, & endeavor to sleep, resigned to the course of events. Even after I had got asleep, which was not till very late, —

Sunday, December 4, 1864

I was twice awakened by the increased violence of the wind, which shook the house like a tree. It will be almost a miracle if none of these blocks is blown down this winter. B.5 (the most rickety) is evacuated every high wind — I shall say no more on this subject. Wrote to Sister Belle. Finished, with the

2nd vol, Lamartine's Hist.of the Girondists. I am glad I have read it, though I am far from accepting it entirely. It is bien francais. A few days ago ½ doz prisoners brt in which I forgot to record + + + + + +

Monday, December 5, 1864

Finished "The Wandering Jew:" from a whole witch-caldron of horrors M. Sue brews his master-claim against the Jesuits,— horrors the most unnatural & revolting, impossible except to the imagination of a novelist. After the horrible, the sensual predominates, the artist presenting in the warmest tints, scenes seldom attempted in polite literature. There may be — accdg to my theory, there must be,— some good in his social philosophy, but the Jesuits, whatever they may have been when from the cabinets of kings they ruled the world, are now more sinned against than sinning. That this order has evolved very much evil, no one doubts, yet it produced St. Xavier. There is something truly admirable in the order. Of all religious educators, the Jesuit Fathers are the best. Evil & good mingle in this as in everything else — The struggle between [illegible word] & [illegible word] is unceasing, & each has influence in every soul. I am a Parsee in this. 107 prisoners brought in tonight: Franklin, Tenn. Our floor is covered with them. They are in good spirits, not in

Tuesday, December 6, 1864

the least demoralized. We got the best of the battle, evidently. It is to be regretted that new arrivals are not welcomed here with more courtesy & feeling: They meet with the cold shoulder. Selfishness has sapped all hearts, or perhaps — till now latent, is developed by circumstances. Schlegel's view of the Reformation is noteworthy. Begin "Cloister & the Hearth"——

> [Literary aside] "The Ancients may be considered as a rich common, where every person who hath the smallest tenement in Parnassus hath a free right to fatten his muse."

Wednesday, December 7, 1864

The which I find diverting, humorous, burlesque & mock-heroic — all this yet not without touches of feeling. Reade is the artist of feminine artifice (erratum — a few pages back for Thackeray, read Reade) not a great author, but a very entertaining one. Have — thro' kindness of Maj. Ridley — the promise of Prescott's Philip II "in a few days."

Had a bedfellow this night, Gen.Chany — De quo quae mala antea scripsi nunc revoco.[1] — refugee from B.6 on account of high wind. Weather changes, turning much colder. On room detail to-morrow.

Thursday, December 8, 1864

Bitter cold weather. A letter from Sister, berating me soundly on acc't of my last letter to Father. Well do I deserve her reproaches if I have even inadvertently wounded that noble heart. The fact is the one-page system compels one to crowd ideas together and in so doing mine have come to bear other constructions than that I gave them. I do blame Sister, however, for deeming me capable of willingly afflicting my honored & beloved Father, as well as for some of her expressions. Her letter shows her at once a good daughter (rara avis)[2] & a good sister — though somewhat unthinking in the excess of filial love.

Friday, December 9, 1864

Snowing but to no depth — weather more moderate, but tonight colder than ever with a piercing norther. A letter from Miss B. On dit: hereafter we are to be permitted to write three letters a week instead of two. Finished Schlegel. I like many of his views & believe him impartial — I do not [illegible word] myself jurare in ejus verba,[3] though — Moss & Bns, Philos. I wish to reread the book sometime, very poor translation. A man fell from B.12 platform and broke his skull, they say he is badly injured.

Saturday, December 10, 1864

Seven prisoners came in yesterday.—finished Lamartine's Cromwell: Don't like it. Don't think Lam. knows his own mind! Believe Cromwell to have been a hypocrite; his greatness is indisputable. Wrote to Father. Moved my bunk to that vacated by Maj. Johnston & Manly who have gone downstairs. Mine is occupied by two newcomers, Glover & Erickson 22nd Miss., who are thus my neighbors!! Glover told me that Barlow now is a Major. He well deserves such rank. Nothing to read tonight.

Sunday, December 11, 1864

Snowing, but the wind blows the snow away as fast as it falls. Bitter cold. New mail regulations, 3 letters a week, on Mondays, Wednesdays & Fridays. Also: express matter is to be opened inside and in presence of the parties interested. Had nothing to open when providentially I came upon mine. Disfranchised, book on Woman in Striving to be Masculine, she yet appears most womanly; the book is an amusing one and to a certain extent a good one. The author goes too far, Her vituperations of Proudhon are very amusing. My creed is that woman is not necessarily over, than equal with man, but, that, as society is constituted, she is in some respects his inferior, in others his superior. We "used up" the last of our coffee at supper. We will soon want again, I fear.

Monday, December 12, 1864

Mercury ranged last night as low as -21.5 degrees. Finished "Woman Disfranchised" (a Woman's Philosophy of Women) This Frenchwoman makes herself very ridiculous but there is in Section I of the chapter entitled "Love, its Function in Humanity" enough that is good & true to make amends for all her nonsense. Mail brought over on the ice — not in time for distribution to-day. "Dennis Duval"[4] — I wish it could have been finished —

Tuesday, December 13, 1864

Last night, or rather just after midnight I was awakened by a gun, followed by others fired rapidly, like the skirmishing that opens a battle. Then the alarm gun, followed after some time by three other rounds, one at least shotted. This was a gallant but ill-judged attempt to escape on the part of some 20 or 24 prisoners. One was killed, all who got outside were recaptured, some by citizens on the other side of the bay. Several had their clothes riddled. The night was clear & very light. Lieut. Bowles of Ky. was killed. Wrote a letter to Sister. Rec'd a London Society fr. Miss B. Attending roll-call in the cold is our worst annoyance now. It takes half an hour and one almost freezes.

Wednesday, December 14, 1864

Weather more moderate — Still very cold. Very hard-up for reading matter. I take up Ruffini's "Doctor Antonio." Fixed curtain before my bunk and at the foot, secluding me somewhat. The bunk at my feet, (my old one) is occupied by Lt. Glover, 22nd Miss — a new arrival — who tells me that Barlow is a Maj. of Artillery,— if merit alone were in demand, he would be a Brigadier General.[5] The 22nd having been one of our old brigade, under the cmd of Col. Bowen, Lt. G. knows our battery & its officers.

Thursday, December 15, 1864

Snowing again. A letter to Miss B.— Gens. Marmaduke, Cabell & Gordon leave for Ft. Warren. So much the better for them. The last, Brig. Gen. G. W. Gordon of Nashville, Tenn. has lodged & messed in our room since his arrival (from Franklin) Holding his rank from our Gov't, he is of course a gentleman. Further than this my limited acquaintance does not permit me venture further. He is quite young,— 28, I believe. Ruffini's Italian revolutionists are, I hope, more in accord with the truth than with the common idea. I detest Carbonari, but I love constitutional liberty and all who strive and suffer in its cause. Liberty is not monarchy — nor is it equality.

Friday, December 16, 1864

An order on the bulletin from Gen Bealle, announcing the perfection of arrangements to supply us with necessaries by our government & his appointment as agent. Also desiring to be informed of the wants of prisoners. In consequence an election is held to-day to choose another agent for this prison (Gen B. desiring that two should be selected.) in addition to Col. Fite.— the prison is almost unanimous: all want <u>something to eat.</u> I trust we may get it. Thaw to-day, weather very moderate.

Saturday, December 17, 1864

Thaw continues with a little rain. The Sandusky paper announces the coming <u>supercession</u> of Col. Hill in command here. I regret it: he has more of the milk of human kindness than any other Yank I have come in contact with. This is not saying much, but indeed, I honestly believe nearly all the brutality & all the inhumanity exercised toward us to be the result of explicit orders. He has said he was sorry we haven't enough to eat, but that he couldn't help it. Began TOM JONES[6] last night.

Sunday, December 18, 1864

A letter from Miss B.— answered at once. Reading Tom Jones: certainly the best novel in the language and one, in which I am able to discover new beauties at each successive perusal. Read also Harper's Catalogue; A [illegible word] feast of Literature,— Weather still is [illegible phrase] for the ice is not broken up in the bay. Am now "even" on the letters question,

Monday, December 19, 1864

And shall be able to reply to letters as they arrive— Thanks to the new arrangement, I now owe nobody— except her to whom I would rather write than to anyone else, but I know not where she is, and have but little encouragement to write. I have neglected this best friend for several weeks, waiting till I can learn her new address, but I am not afraid of my neglect being attributed to false motives— to forgetfulness. Finished T.J. What a pity the hero is made to like Lady Bellastiras' money. It spoils the whole character. On this point, I quite agree with Col. Newcome. Our old wind springs up at <u>night</u>, & cold ensues, of course. checking the book out fr library— Bulwer's Last Days of Pompeii—

Tuesday, December 20, 1864

A letter from Miss B. (in continuation). Papers from home, I wish they would <u>write</u>. What do I care for newspapers? A bright, pleasant— nay delightful,— day. Such as the whole year rarely affords in this murky, Beotian climate. Ordered fr Harper & Bros. by Moise "Schiller's Revolt of the Netherlands," price 100 ____

By an order posted to-day, we are allowed to receive books, except such as bear upon Military.

Wednesday, December 21, 1864

Science, or relate to the Geography, Topography etc of the U.S., <u>Mexico, The British Provinces & The West Indies</u>. Weather again colder, snowing. Col. Mike L. Woods, (Hospital Std) has a special exchange. I rejoice greatly at this for Col. W. is a gentleman & a true patriot, wherefore, since he is a man of much intelligence, he is necessarily a good officer. He made me a present of Lamartine's "Girondists." Bitter cold at night — Slept little —

Thursday, December 22, 1864

About three hundred prisoners, three Gen. officers, Maj. Gen. Ed Johnson, Brig. Gen. Smith & Cavalry Jackson. Hood was rather worsted it seems in the great battle — but routed by no means. Some of these prisoners are demoralized. Gen. Johnson is said to be — and to abuse his superiors — I hope the Yanks will keep him now. I write no letter, missing my first mail. On duty as caterer, Weather very cold.

Friday, December 23, 1864

18 more prisoners. "Roundabout Papers," delightful reading, What a genial, good man Thackeray must have been. Yet carpers call him cynical — H.S. Foots has resigned his seat in C. S. Congress. So much the better, that will be one crabber the less — he "died game," for his farewell speech — as reported in Northern papers — is one monster croak. The prisoners to-day bring more favorable reports — All is yet well with Hood.

Saturday, December 24, 1864

On room detail — Begin Sallust's <u>Catiline</u>[7] — never read this before. Bread very late, so that we take dinner & supper in one slice (with a little salt fish.) Christmas Eve! this thought gives me the blues, as it suggests reminiscences of better times. Dec. 24th, 1862: behold me saluting our glorious & beloved chief on review! Dec. 24th, 1864: see me pound beefsteak, for breakfast & a slim dinner next Monday or Tuesday!

Sunday, December 25, 1864

Began last night Carlyle's Frederick II — Rec'd to-day two letters, fr. my little sisters. A pleasant enough day — temperature mild — but an awful dull Christmas. I have the blues: I can't help it — this is not only Xmas, but the anniversary of my acquaintance with my best & dearest friend. God help her! Wrote two letters; one to Father — another to <u>her</u>. Shall mail the former to-morrow. 4 P.M.— Col. Woods has just gone — I have just bid him farewell — The only enjoyer of Xmas among 3000. I rejoice at his departure, yet I feel the sadder for seeing him go. Weather warm & cloudy.

Monday, December 26, 1864

One prisoner has certainly escaped in the last 3 days — perhaps more; The signal gun was fired yesterday but too late, the lucky wight has been gone 24 hours. Anyone may escape — now that the ice is strong — who has money enough to purchase the necessary accoutrements from the venal teamsters or others. With $50 I would not stay here many days. Weather quite warm — a thick, heavy fog all day; almost a Scotch mist. Express brought over. — à propos, for I forgot to record that I sent a letter to Dr. Woodbridge — now a clinic chf. surgeon etc — several days ago, & as it has not been returned I have some hopes of getting something to eat before many days.

Tuesday, December 27, 1864

Mild weather still continues. At this rate ice must break up before long. By an order posted yesterday, N. Y. News, Chicago Times, & Cinc. Enquirer are prohibited here. News of the Capture of Savannah, so direct too that it can not be doubted. The Army garrisoning it had withdrawn and, after all, our country's defenses are in the hearts of her soldiers — Mere strongholds or places which like Savannah have long since been rendered useless, may well be spared when they cannot be held except at great sacrifice of gallant men. Still this news is demoralizing to a few weak ones — as I hear, for I have seen nothing of the kind.

Wednesday, December 28, 1864

Mailed letter to VBM — written Sunday. Weather cold again, changed last night. Go off duty as caterer, will have nothing to do for two weeks — According to a Decree of Committee, we are all to double up — to make room for the recent arrivals. This will go hard with me, as I had marked out — as it were, — a course of solid reading for next year and can only ruin any advantage — in my bunk — which has a window of its own outward, — and a blanket-screen inward.

Thursday, December 29, 1864

Finished Catiline. Wrote to Sister Ida. Rec'd letter from Father, dated 25th with remittance (10.00) duly ack'd. Am to sit up at Hospital tonight — Miss. Relief Association Detail.

Friday, December 30, 1864

Finished "Reproduction," Dalton's Physiology — A fall of snow last night, but owing to the wind the ground is almost bare. Very cold. Sat up all night last, and am very sleepy to-day, but shall not lie down till bedtime, that I may enjoy <u>one</u> good night's rest. To-morrow I am to have a bunkmate, H. F., from B. 11. — I am fortunate, since there <u>must</u> be a doubling, to find one with the breeding & habits of a gentleman — for owing to paucity of blankets, nearly all the old residents have doubled long ago, & the new arrivals are not desirable

Saturday, December 31, 1864

as sleeping companions. Fetter moves in — Finish Vol III, Carlyle's Frederic Great with which I began the work. I like it much. Another case of smallpox, carried out to pesthouse yesterday, being the 2nd from the hospital. Determined, according to my custom to "see the old year out" I went up this night to Charles' room or rather the apothecary shop, where from 9 ½ o'clock to 4 A.M. the time passed in pleasant converse accompanied by a collation of which we twain partook with great gusto. May the next New Year find me elsewhere & may it find all I love in health & happiness.

January 1st, 1865

MEMORANDA

1 Turkey	Oysters
3 Chickens	Milk
Spare Ribs	Bread
Cakes	Butter
Pies	Peaches
Plums	Tomatoes
Pickles	Candies
Celery	Apples
Molasses	Candles
Bread	Butter
?	Steaks
Minced pies	Ham
Cakes	Cheese
Coffee	Sugar
Tobacco	

Notes

(I.) Col. Bullock was <u>severely</u> wounded while in com'd of his brigade, in the last Georgia campaign: Col. Blacknelle died of wounds rec'd at Winchester — in prison at that place.

(II.) Capt. Taylor died about 3 weeks after he got home predisposed to consumption his hardships were too much for him. Though he recognized his acquaintances, he still, to the last, thought himself at Johnson's Island.

(III) p. 229 [Wed. Aug. 17, 1864] The "Major" was <u>Capt.</u> N. C. Washington of B 1 (St. Louis)

(IV.) An exaggeration, he wasn't hurt much (p. 345)

(V) p. 348 [Mon. Dec. 12, 1864] I don't believe this: The Yank's Sergeant told it but I believe he lied, though it was very cold.

"De Morte Edwardi:

I.

Jampridem erat senex niger
(Haud dubito atque piger),
Qui solitus "Ned" vocari:
Et nihil erat laneum
In summum ejus craneum,
Ubi solet vegetare.

II.

Similes arundinibus,
Qui florent in fluminibus,
Et debiles exercendo
Huius erant digiti
Ut, prae servi rigidi
Casu, oculi videndo

III.

Defuerunt far edendo
Dentes, itaque depsendo
Non huic opus far:

Quam ob rem atque far et panem
Et quae pertinent ad sanum
Prohibuit quisque Lar.

IV.

Pastinum eius nunc depone,
Abjecto etiam ligone,—
Quae viris Faunus dedit.
Pariete nunc dependeat fides
Ornetur atque plectro aedes,
Nam silentium his insedit.

V.

Edwardo labor erit nullus
Nec ei dolor erit ullus
In saecula saeclorum:
Elysios campos nam advenit,—
Nobis coelum eum tenet
Ethiopum et bonorum

[See pages 62–63 of the present work for a translation.]

[Aside] Carceri militari
Ins Johnsoni Die,
Sept. IV

[In the next three pages Caldwell lists miscellaneous artillery information, then the Latin poem he has worked on and spread throughout the diary]

Ad Patriae Vexillum: Carmen Militare

I.

Ave bis cive, gloriae crux
Nostriae nationis lucida lux
Nostris animis lumen!
Quoties miles fortis,

In articulo mortis
Salutavit te numen?

II.

Mavortis diadema
Spei nobis emblema

The data are compiled in a range table showing by experience how far cannon-balls of a certain weight from a certain gun could be expected to travel. This is followed by a corrected version of the lengthy ode to the Confederate flag. The final version is at the end of the first diary. (See pages 208–209 of the present work for a translation.)

Pirfulgens in bellis
Aura tibi est gloria
Tuum coelum Victoria,
Gimmata crux stellis!

III.

Gloriosam in navem
Te Reipublicae avem
Sempiternum videre;
Tempestatem domantem
Et nimbum equitantem
Omne nefas terrare.

IV.

Durantibus annis,
Te fugiat tyrranis,
Liberatatis insigne!

Sia custos domorum
Lar atque focorum,
O cultra perdigne!

V.

O Patriae decus dulce
Corda nobis jam sulfulci
Intacta sint catenis!
Fortuimque adsis ori
Quibus bene fit mori
Sit illis quies lenis?

VI.

Pro patria moriuntur
Et morte nobis talluntur;
Adeint suepe memoriae?
Ex vitae perpaulis

Profecti sint aulas
Sempiternas victoriae.

VII.

In belli fulminibus
In leti grandinibus
Fulgentem tenes cursum,
Novae gentis natale
Sidus luce regule,
Per sanguen volens sursum!

VIII.

Manet quies amoena
Tibi, via serena
Per superum aera;
Tempestate superata,
Erit frons circumdata
Serta laudis sera.

IX.

Sanguinolentis ex undis
Tabo proelii immundis
Natio oritur nostra,
Atro videtur extare
Clarus ut Lucifer mare,
Per luminis claustra.

X.

Cito die cedat nox
Et sit dira tubae vox
Gaudio obscurata;
Et laetis carminibus
Dilectis virginibus
Fortium laus modulata.

XI.

Sanguinis campum aret bos,
Suter tumulo floreat flos,
Recens osculo novis
Vivida memoria fortis,
Unibis nec obsita mortis,
Haereat mentid in oris.

XII.

Oris libertatis impone
Vexillum sericum, coronae,—
Superbe illic pendeat?
Donec vocet bellum trux,
Tum stellata nostra crux,
Fulgore novo splendeat.

[Next:] "Some chronological data"
Troops at Greenwood by M Davis
29th Dec. 1862

Jan. 1863.
20th Leave G for [illegible word]
Feb. 14th Examined at Jackson.
Mar. 14th Bombardment of Pt. Hudson.
May 21st. Investment begins.
May 25. Fight in the woods.
May 27th Grand charge.
June 14th Greatest charge of all.
July 8. Flag of Truce [illegible words]
 " 9. Prisoners of war.
 " 15th Arrive at N. O.
Aug 15th " at Police Jail.

Sept 30–Oct 3rd Paroled a few hours daily to the city,
Oct 4. Leave N. O.
" [?] Reach N. Y. Harbor. Ft. Columbus.
Oct 13th Reach Johnson Island.

January 1865

Sunday, January 1, 1865

Capt. Youngblood brought me Don Quixote today: I have long desired to re-read this incomparable work, and know the pleasure which awaits me. Got from Clark Value's Ollendorf—am determined to review my French. A letter from Miss B. A letter to Sister Lizzie. Newspapers announce probability of an early exchange: a good omen for the opening year. *accepi.*[1]

Monday, 2.

Commence Carlyle's Hero-Worship. Our General officers, Maj. Gen. Johnson, Brig. Gens. Henry R. Jackson & Th. Smith left yesterday evening for Ft. Warren. A dozen or so prisoners brought in to-night from Ft. Delaware. They believe themselves *en route* for home, or Trans-Mississippi exchange. This is a bad stopping-place.

Tuesday, 3.

Weather "moderated" last night, & is to-day mild & cloudy. A letter from Father—announcing departure of box containing such of the articles as Dr. Woodbridge left on my list. Ham cut off, ditto molasses—all things *reduced* & all hopes of "candiouli divina tomacula porci"[2] utterly blighted! A letter to Miss B. Rec'd Schiller's Revolt of the Netherlands, by mail. Begin Gibbons, an abridgement, but better than nothing.

January, Wednesday, 4, 1865.

On Sink-digging detail. So busy attending to express all day—not constantly, but at intervals,—without any result, too, that I have almost *lost a day.* Missed my French. Trans-Miss officers, capt'd up to a certain date, are to be exchanged. Some were paroled to-day.

Thursday, 5.

Letter from Sister: VBM is at Canton, Miss. & has written to her—why not to me also! Doubtless *my* letter (that to me) has been miscarried. A letter *to* Father. Bothered myself again with "express" and with the same result. R. C. Jones fr. B.5 escaped the usual way—the 2nd this year: Col. Hunley being the first. They had money which will secure their safety. $100 offered for Jones by Col. Hill.

Friday, 6.

Box came: 25 lbs flour, 8 dried apples, 5 butter, 5 lard, 5 sugar, 3 coffee, 1 peck onions & some crackers. If my Father only knew he could have sent much more. This is very welcome & my hunger is once more appeased. Letter fr. Miss B. Snowing all day, but temperature wonderfully mild. High wind to-night, fr. *north* (Strange to say) and weather colder.

Saturday, January 7, 1865

Another case of smallpox in hospital to-day.[3] Finished "Heroes & Hero-worship." Like Shakspeare, Dante, Mahomet — not so his estimate of Cromwell — esp'y as comp'd with Napoleon — & Knox. He well calls the French Revolution "A Truth Clad in Hell-fire." Very cold to-day, but more moderate to-night with no wind.

Sunday, 8.

Col. Hunly, having been recaptured, returns. Begin Vol. II. Tytler's Universal History. Write a letter to Sister. Exchange "grapes" very prevalent. I begin to believe,— to *hope* more earnestly than ever. Trans-Miss officers are ordered to be ready to leave to-morrow. Do not feel the least hungry!——

Monday, 9.

Small-pox said to be spreading: somewhat of a panic begins to prevail: wholly uncalled for as I can see. Trans-Miss off. do leave, 180 of them, but none of my Police Jail acquaintances except Capt. Jordan: the others having been mis-registered as Port Hudson captures. Ventured *bean soup* at dinner. Ate no bean (consequence, colic: nox aerumnarum, laudanum, ether, camphor & mustard but no sleep till morn.[4]

Tuesday, January 10, 1965

(Commence I Vol. Carlyle's Friedrich II.) Well enough this morning: only a slight feeling of emptiness & a heaviness of eyelids. Snowed very heavily last night, but a northwind had swept the pen ere morning. Still blowing, & very cold for a N. wind. Disagreeable. Letter from Father. Letter to Miss B. Snow piled in great drifts.

Wednesday, 11.

Carlyle gives me — at last, — a clear idea of the origin & rise of the Prussian monarchy. It is to obtain this that I read the 1st vol., as it treats little of Frederic. It ceased snowing last night. Enough has fallen to cover the earth to a great depth, yet in many places it is bare, swept by wind. This is a very *cold* day, less blustering than usual though the old wind (S.W.) blows.

Thursday, 12.

Go on duty as "caterer" — i.e. prepare food for our mess, carry it to kitchen, draw rations etc. Made biscuits this afternoon, with tolerable success. Write to Father. Very high winds last night. Weather extremely cold, and roll-call a source of much suffering: needlessly, too, it seems to me.

Friday, January 13, 1865

Weather more moderate. Much to my joy, rec'd to-day a letter from VBM — dated Canton, Dec. 5th mailed N.O. Dec. 29th. I am not altogether desperate, since one friend, my dearest, still remembers me. No directions are given me how to direct my letters, which leaves me at a loss.

Saturday, 14.

Changes to-day: rain early last night, then snow, then terrible windstorm; this morning weather very cold again. A letter from Miss B. My app. for permiss. to rec shoes came back appd; only two trials. 1st time failed on acc't of pockethkfs, which are not considered necessary. (!)

Sunday, 15.

Letter to Father, enclosing application, which *was* the one including pkthkfs — that first sent out, of which I had despaired, since I know instances of those articles being confiscated. Snow. Chap. in Tytler, in M. Bailly; Theory in the Origin of Sciences in the East: the most remarkable thing yet found in Tytler. Make biscuits again; a complete success.

Monday, January 16, 1865

Very stormy last night. Big dinner to-day. Maj. S. doing the "extras," pie & biscuit, artistically & very creditably. Col Morris the guest. Go up to J. B. C.'s at night, play chess & talk till 2 P.M.[5] C. is one of the most companionable men, if not *the* most comp. man I know here.

Tuesday, 17.

Snow last night, continued to-day. A letter to Sister Belle: wrote for Dec'r Blackwood. Capt. Roberdeau brought me Burton's Anatomy for which I am much indebted to him. Wood scarce & room cold. Foote's arrest proves a fact. A fitting end, or *beginning* of it.

Wednesday, 18.

Finish Tytler's Universal History. The book abounds in the grossest mistakes but these I attribute to the Editor or the Printer, for some of them are such as no schoolboy, much less a Prof. of History, would commit. There is apparent a striving to be impartial which is highly commendable. Maj. Ridley brt me Philip II. Nores to supper, good biscuits.

Thursday, January 19, 1865

Write to Miss B. Go off duty. Begin History of Philip II (Prescott). Finish Don Quixote; edition (S. Andnis & Son) an emasculated one, & with both parts joined in one, yet the work is so cunningly done that had I not before read the complete work, I should scarcely have detected it. A plague on such doings. Thackeray says that he never knew the immorality of Shakspeare till he read a "Family Edition"— So with Cervantes.

Friday, 20.

Last night chess with C. till a late hour. Day remarkably pleasant, clear throughout. Finish Vol I Carlyle's Frederic Great. A new case of Smallpox— taken to the pesthouse— which is now within the enclosure, a few yds from our kitchen. Take up Burton's Anatomy of Melancholy.

Saturday, 21.

A printed order distributed, a bid to oath-takers — They are to have the upper blocks. Two letters, Sister & Miss B. Finished the Student's Gibbon— a plague upon all such abridgments! On the 19th a squad of recent captures came, among them a ci-derant lawyer from Holly Sprgs,[6] whom I desire to remember as demoralized. No Confed. Officer has any business to be so.

Sunday, January 22, 1865

Lt. Jus W Cross, of our "Co." detected in an attempt to escape this morning was subjected to the Yankee-like penalty of standing all day on a bbl-head. Honorable treatment for an officer! A letter fr. Father— answered at once. Among those capt'd in N [illegible word] lately was Lt. Col. Burke, 1st Mo. I found him to-day

(Monday, 23) and had him to breakfast with us *this* morning. He brings news of Barlow &c. He also says (& he knows,) that Yankees in Southern Prisons rec. the same rations with our own mess & only suffer for quarters; that officers may buy anything & that they are better treated than we, tho Winder is a brute & a disgrace to our service, he is the sole exception. Go up to C's to-night— play chess, then read till

(Tuesday, 24) at reveille, Sheridan's School for Scandal, The Rivals, & The Critic. It has been long since I read them last. Night cold & stormy, snow. This is the coldest day we have had this winter. A letter from Miss B. Wrote to her to-day. Finished Vol I. Philip II. I begin to hope again for a speedy

exchange nor do I know why. Wood of inferior quality & insufficient in quantity—Fires poor & room cold.

Wednesday, January 25, 1865

Last night, the coldest we have had according to *my* thermometer. Roll-call terrible. Manor came in yesterday to straiten rolls. My name wrong throughout. Perhaps this is an index pointing to exchange. Too cold to read with any pleasure. All huddle around the stove, news of new army bill

(Thursday, 26) proposed in our congress. This is the kind of reconstruction we need. The bill is much better than could have been expected from *civilians*. No more elections, for one good thing. Wrote a letter to Sister. Manor still busy correcting rolls—at the hospital. Roll called inside a great alleviation.

Friday, 27.

A letter from Sister containing 100 stamps. 18 "specials" left to-day, among them of my acquaintance only Lt. C. B. Trevilian, formerly of B.5 & Capt. J. Taylor, of our room. My express pkge—of which Sister's letter advises me ought to be here already but is not. Wood very scarce & weather very cold. Lights put out in our room a little after seven P.M., everybody going to bed to keep warm. *I* went to C's room and sat till bedtime. He beats me easily at chess.

Saturday, January 28, 1865

Weather somewhat moderated, but still very cold: cloudy, while the 3 days previous have been marvellously clear. One A. Shorter attempting to escape is subjected to the barrel punishment. I had thought Hill was more of an officer than to decree such a puerile punishment—to officers, too, prisoners of war.

Sunday, 29.

Letter fr. Miss B. Answered. Up to Clark's again last night. I believe I will be in Dixie by the first of April at least;—am so excited by my hopes that I can think & speak of nothing else. Roll called outdoors again. Warmer but still cold.

Monday, 30.

Shaved (or got shaved) for the first time in six months to have my picture taken. Day bright, springlike and beautiful. Oath-takers, some 25 in number, being moved to Block I. Not a single decent looking man among them & several convicted thieves. I hope

Tuesday, January 31, 1865

& believe that there will not be so much rascality among us in future.

This admitting such knaves to amnesty is an excellent thing for our service; I only hope all such will take it. Sat for my tin type with tolerable success. A letter to Sister. Gave rec't for express pckge but have not rec'd it yet.

FEBRUARY 1865

Wednesday, February 1, 1865

Rec'd shoes, socks & hdkfs. Excellent shoes. Oath-takers now number 42. I hope they will increase to 250 or 300 for out of our 3000 I think about that number ought to take the oath. They are lodged in the best rooms in the pen and given full soldiers' rations. Got my pic to-day. Vol IV. Carlyle's Frederic the Great — commenced yesterday. Mild weather still continues.

Thursday, 2.

Change in temperature last night — cold but not unseasonably so, or uncomfortable if we had enough wood which we have not. Fire out now (8 P.M.) & bed the only refuge. I shall go up to C's. A letter from Sister which I answered at once, enclosing in my letter my picture. Owe no letter now save to VBM whom I would gladly pay but cannot.

Friday, February 3, 1865.

Winds spring up yet weather is not very cold, if we only had wood enough. Seems to be a lull in exchange rumors. Much Jargon (in newspapers) about peace & recognition (probable) by France

(Saturday, 4.)

direct or acting thru some other "Latin" power. May be truth in it. Must come true some day, why not after 4th [illegible word] as well as another time? I hope nothing however. Winds very high (old S.W.) & night cold. No sleeping possible to me in my upper bunk, so I do not attempt it but go

Sunday, 5.

up to C's where I read & smoke with much comfort (nay felicity, so to speak) till reveille this morning. Achieving the conclusion of Carlyle's Vol IV & many favorite excerpts from Tennyson. Write to my Dear Mother. Wish I knew how to write to VBM; to her before all others.

Monday, February 6, 1865.

Commence II Vol. Prescott's Phil II. — A Letter fr. VBM. — old one, dated Augusta, Ga., Oct. 25th written en route west. She had been very sick, and I never knew of it. An excellent letter. I wish I could write with any prob. of my letters reaching her. Mrs. M. is at a Mr. Howerton's near Wolf Trap

Station on the Richmond & Danville R. R. I am requested to stop & see her when I

Tuesday, 7.

am exchanged. To be sure I will. Wrote to Capt. Goodwin, an old classmate in the Yank Army. Almost all yesterday we were without fire but this is wood-day. Wrote also to Mrs. Moon, which letter Col. H. C. Jones, 27th N. C. who leaves to-day, on special exchange is kind enough

Wednesday, 8.

to offer to leave at the very station. There are few officers here of whom I have as high an opinion as of Col. J.— or whom I would so gladly see exchanged. He left about 3 o'clock. Lt. John A. Stephens left also a few days ago: his exchange effected thru' his uncle, our Vice Pres't. Wood gives out again. Snow fell yesterday; still lies on the ground. Cold.

Thursday, February 9, 1865.

Go on duty again for our mess. Very busy since noon. Rec'd letter from Miss B. which I answered this evening. Home-folks are very negligent of me as far as letters go; haven't had a letter from any of them for a week.

(Friday, 10.)

News in "Sandusky" of a general exchange,— not "preliminaries" as we heard last year, but the exchange itself, & to go into effect immediately. Many doubt but *I believe*. After so many disappointments, I shall be able to say "I told you so" after all. A thaw. Letter from Miss VBM dated Oct. 18th.

(Saturday, 11.)

A letter from Brother Rush. He expects soon to go to Miami University to enter Sophomore. I hope he will do himself more credit by his conduct there than his brother did *himself.* Try a meat pie for dinner. Not a total failure, crust excellent, but pie not juicy enough. Finish Carlyle II vol. Have now read all of Frederic Great now out, an entertaining work & I believe, a veracious.

Sunday, February 12, 1865

Worst "blow" last night felt since the great unroofing. Much disquieting of sleep. Went to my usual refuge & remained till wind lulled, i.e. till morning. Finished Burton's Anatomy. A rare old book, well worth reading for the amusement it affords. Wit, Humor, Metaphysics & Pedantry. Wrote to Father.

Monday, 13.

Rucker & some other Brigade comdr bro't in. Wounded at Franklin.

Clark got a special. I know of no one whom I would rather see enjoy one, though I shall miss him very much though I

(Tuesday, 14.)

hope, not for long since the air is rife with rumors. Latest, 500 of the oldest captures are to leave soon. I hope this will include me. Letter from Father. Letter to Rush. Grapes multiply & flourish. Finish or nearly Prescott's Philip II with the III volume. Clark left to-day.

Wednesday February 15, 1865.

One hundred are to leave; sick & old captures *from* the States of Mo., Ky., Tenn., Ark., & La.—a most unfair way of sending off prisoners, though if kept up, it will get me out by reason of my having been captured while on duty with a La. Battery. Commence Kinglake's "Invasion of the Crimea," which I hope *not* to be able to finish also Pendennis, the first novel this year.[1]

(Thursday, 16.) A sudden change in the temperature from very cold to warm. Day pleasant, snow rapidly melting. Lt. Scott (La.) & Maj. Williamson (Tenn.), the latter a new inmate, driven from B.1 before the irruption of oath-takers. By the by, several days ago a party of oath-takers were detected in stealing on a large scale & Col. Hill is said to have ordered a C. M.[2] for them. What honors to their new country. Letter fr. Miss B—Letter to Father.

Friday, 17.

The hundred *left* yesterday. The weather changed again in the evening & again last night. Have returned Kinglake, find that I cannot read it now. Have an artillery drill book which I am "turning over" cursorily, hoping to have use for its contents before long. Rumor of 700 men to leave "in a few days." Hope I may go in the very next squad. Lt. Davis not executed to-day as ordered, sentence

Saturday, February 18, 1865

commuted to imprisonment during the war. Letter fr. Sister (d. 5th) containing Panola dates of Jan. 28th. *She* has heard fr. VBM: hope my letter will come soon. Also letter from Miss B. Busy re-reading Artillery Instructions & copying therefrom somewhat. Hope I may soon need this knowledge.

Sunday, 19.

Morgan who was stabbed by one Berry several days ago, has died in Hospital. Both from Ky. Berry has been ordered into close confinement (irons, some say) & will be tried. Write to Sister. The Squad of Trans-Miss officers get off at last. Shannon, Maj. Ridley &c I have come to have quite a

Monday, 20.

regard for the old, wild, (*Sauvage*) Major. I like him far better than any of his fellows. To-day 100 leave. Capt. Heard & Capt. Grave (Md.) the former of our room et praeterea nil,[3] the latter formerly a roommate, both here & at B.5. They are now taking captures up to July 1st in alphabetical order. The list doesn't quite get to Manley whom I would rather see go than anyone else. He goes next.

Tuesday, February 21, 1865

Finish "Pendennis," like it very much, wish I had time to read "Vanity Fair" again — perhaps I have, but I cannot read for excitement. A painful rumor that exchange has been stopped, which I will not believe.

Wednesday, 22.[4]

The anniversary of our independence. Celebrated by the *Yankees*, by a salute of 100 guns, over the recapture of Ft. Sumpter (previously evacuated, however). Manley was taken out & paroled yesterday, & will leave in the next lot. Thaw, so

Thursday, 23.

that I fear lest the ice may break up thus interfering with our delivery. Letter fr. Sister. Letter from Miss B. Letter to Miss B. Also remittance of $20.00 acknowledged, though the accompanying letter has not yet come in. This will be very useful to me in passing through the country for exchange.

Friday, February 24, 1865

300 left to-day. *Manly* in the 1st lot. Cherry, Dewees, Youngblood, Dillard, Capt. Davis and Thorp & Forester of this room — with last lot composed principally of Gettysburg prisoners. Letter fr. Mrs. C. A. Moon dated Feb. 6th. Very few letters could please me more than this from a lady whose friendship I value very highly indeed.

Saturday, 25.

The Sutler commenced to sell vegetables last Monday. A great relief to many who suffer from want of food. Three letters to-day, fr. Father, Sister & Miss B. Paroling still goes on. They say 300 are to leave Monday if the ice in bay permit.

Sunday, 26.

A March day, very stormy. Rain last night. Ice very weak but still continuous bet. here and Sandusky. The wind is in the right direction to blow it out, but doesn't seem to make much impression. A letter to Father. I wish it would either freeze solid again or clear out altogether. Delay may be dangerous to us.

Monday, February 27, 1865

Paroling still goes on. Maj. Saunders taken out & paroled. Also Sloan of our room. Nobody leaves & no present prospect of any doing so. Strong N. E. wind. Blowing, but freezing at night.

Tuesday, 28.

A thaw. I fear weeks may yet elapse ere I leave this accursed place. I long to be on my way. Letter fr. Sister. 2 photos of myself from picture sent ago. Also rec'd letter for Maj. Ridley which I must take care of for him. Wrote to Sister. Gibson, Paterson, Leslie, Pritchard fr. B.5. have been paroled. Capt. W. H. Johnston also.

Memo Pat's address E. D. PT will be Florence, Ala. after the war.

MARCH 1865

Wednesday, March 1, 1865

Paroling still goes on. Our list reached. Cater & Coleman taken out. No prospect of ice breaking up. On the contrary it seems more likely to strengthen as it turned very cold about dark, with piercing N.E. wind.

Thursday, 2.

Weather changed in the night, wind now from the South & everything is melting. What a climate. I wouldn't inhabit this island were it a solid coalfield in a lake of Petroleum. Letter from Father. Answered. Taken out and paroled. Am first on 5th hundred. I feel better now but wish the ice would clear.

Friday, 3.

Packed up, all ready to go. Waters of the bay visible for a long distance, though much solid ice still separates us from Sandusky. I am weary of waiting. Weather favorable till night when it blew up a snowstorm from just the wrong direction. Snow all night, not very cold however.

Saturday, March 4, 1865

Weather warm. Snow melting. No ice bet. the island & Cedar Point, where the light is. In a few more days, if no inauspicious changes interfere, we will at length bid farewell forever to this accursed place.

Sunday, 5.

Everything had to freeze up again last night of course, & large fields of ice to drift out into the bay. To-day, however, the thaw is resumed & I think the clear space is gaining perceptibly. Wrote farewell letter to Miss N. K. B. (E. B.) Snow fell last night, has fallen 26 times this winter.

Monday, 6.

Day bright & serene — weather worthy of "Dixie's" self. What is more to the purpose, the ice is melting, though not so fast as I would like. A bulletin posted this morning says that the first 300 are to leave as soon as the boat can pass, & they are accordingly ordered to have accts etc in order by 11 A.M. tomorrow.

Tuesday, March 7, 1865

A most vivid dream last night, such as I don't often have. Just as I got to Mr. Irbys, VBM had left for Memphis. It would be just my luck if something of the kind were to happen. Ice very stubborn yet yielding gradually. A letter to my dear Mother.

Wednesday 8.

After various changes in the state of the Bay, the boat was at last enabled to come over this evening. She made the second trip, & remained here all night. Wind N.E. & bay filling up again with floes. Turned warmer at night.

Thursday, 9.

Boat hurt herself somehow & remains here yet. Don't run. Weather turns colder again. A very murky fog this morning. Severe [illegible word] of cold. Go on duty again, "caterer." Letter from Sister. Answered. Am getting terribly impatient.

Friday, March 10, 1865

Weather very cold last night. Bay froze over again despite a very strong wind (W.S.W.) thus deferring our hopes of departure. As cold a day as I ever saw south of the Ohio River. Warmer in evening.

Saturday, 11.

Wind still violent; Sun shining brightly at roll-call for a few minutes. We had snow & sunshine together. Thawing somewhat, ice growing loose is being driven out by the wind, now S.W. "Sandusky" says. 600 of us are to leave as soon bay will permit.

Sunday, 12.

Wind changed to N.E. this morning, very cold. But about 1 P.M. to S.E. & evening warm & pleasant. The N.E. filled the bay with "Canada ice," but it is much broken. Paroling is still going on. 1000 are paroled. The Sutler is now allowed to sell everything not contraband.

Monday, March 13, 1865

Finished Life of Mrs. Siddons by Thos. Campbell,—a work which adds greatly to the reputation of the Tragic Queen without detracting from that of its author. Day mild, cloudy & calm, but N.E. wind has risen this ev'ng. Boat over again. I hope a "lot" may leave tomorrow.

Tuesday, 14.

Three hundred do leave. Among them Maj. S. & Capt. J. I am the sole lingerer of our general quarters, & I hope to go tomorrow. S., long my bunkmate, is a good specimen of that rare bird, the *gentleman:* I respect and esteem him but my heart does not *warm* toward him as toward Gavroche & J. I can assign no reason for this except that the two latter are more congenial, wh. means more amiable. Wrote to Father.

Wednesday, 15.

Pleasant day enough but nobody goes, all grapes "to the contrary notwithstanding"—up to Dr. Lewis' room. Traynor & I try Hasheesh, (tincture) take III drops without any perceptible effect the tincture must have been miserably compounded.[1] Shall try it again in form of extract, when practicable.

Thursday, March 16, 1865

Slept till after roll-call.[2] Day very boisterous, though it "opened" beautifully. The old adage "The Sun which shines at daybreak clear etc." Wind in gusts, occasionally hurricanish. I am weary-ennuyee to an un-paralleled extent at not being taken away. I hope to go to-morrow. Wrote to Father.

Friday, 17.

St. Patrick's day & no rain. A very violent storm at night, blowing down nearly the whole fence on the west side of the Prison, shaking the old houses & demoralizing the inmates to an extent unparalleled save by the great storm of Sept. 23rd. Verily I fear a high wind on Johnson's

Saturday, 18.

Island. Hope I may get away before the equinox. Bealle Express issued yesterday & to-day. I drew a pr. gray breeches. First thing I have rec'd from Confederacy

Sunday, March 19, 1865

for a long time. Dixie express also arrived. Pen flooded with good tobacco. I am growing more & more weary but see no certainty of getting off soon. Wrote again to Father, my last letter fr. Prison, I hope.

Monday, 20.

("Enoch Arden"—app'd.) Bulletin posted at least 300 gone tomorrow 1:30 P.M. My feelings may perhaps be imagined. Write to Mr. S. B. W. Rudder, New Orleans; a gentleman whom I shall never forget though I have neglected him long. Shall also leave a letter for Father.

Tuesday, 21.

Left Bullpen 2 P.M.— Sandusky after five — spent at Newark, what of the night was left. Much delay & irregular rushing. Crowded into box cars. Baggage examination merely formal. Guard ditto.

N. B. Beginning here — March 21 in *pencil* and I have *traced* in ink (Dec. 1918 IPC).[3]

March, Wednesday 22, 1865

After many stoppages (bad bridge) & much "lying over" reach Bellaire — C. O. R. R.— after night cross the river — jumbled in among machinery of stern wheel steamboat and are packed again into box cars — without seats at terminus of Balt. & Ohio R.R.

Thursday, 23.

Many delays as usual. Occasional glimpses of fine scenery but rare, as we are so shut up. Drew 10.00$. Reach Grafton about 10 P.M. Travel through the night with tolerable regularity. Snow in the mountains. Snow all night.

Friday, 24.

Cumberland at 7 A.M. Martinsburg at 7 P.M. Harper's Ferry about [blank space][4] P.M. very dark night nothing visible — Road very well guarded. All the bridges in many places the track fortified with block houses especially east of Cumberland.

March, Saturday, 25, 1865

Baltimore about 9 A.M.— Much waiting on track. Many elegant looking ladies, but they make no sign save by looks & nervous switching of hdkchs. Not allowed to accost us. To Ft. McHenry about 11 A.M. The ladies walking that our sick might ride Wrote to Sister

Sunday, 26.

in their carriages. This fort reminds me of Johnson's Island but in size much better accommodations. Among new arrivals there are 500 privates this morning fr. Camp Douglas, no quarters furnished them: huddled together & herded like sheep. Our qtrs. are not in the Ft. proper, but in old barrack in Patapko — cold sleeping.

Monday, 27.

Privates spent night outdoors. To-day — P.M. however — some wood was furnished them. Thought to leave to-day. Wrote to Mother. Hear we will not leave. Grape of big storm of fighting all along the line. God help the ladies of Baltimore. There's life in the old land yet — a faint spark — The city is environed with forts not for defense. I fear the fighting will interfere with exchange.

March, Tuesday, 28, 1865

Painful rumors of a suspension of exchange caused however without doubt, by the delay acting on the imagination of the timorous. Tonight the Sergt. came around to take letters saying that we were to leave for New York to-morrow A.M. & that there would be no time to mail letters.

Wednesday, 29.

"Fall in" at 10 A.M. aboard the Star, an old dilapidated sawmill-movement affair which I recognize as the 1st boat we rode on — transferred to "New York." 500 more privates fr. Camp Chase. a dreadful looking emaciated &c. Put us first in hold forward. Steamed to mouth of river after dark, cast anchor, lay all night.

March, Thursday 30, 1865

14 miles. Anchored in fog which doesn't abate. No shelter except shelter tents improvised out of our wet blankets [blank] wet. Rain [blank] impervious. Here we [blank] bound for Dixie [blank] skinned my hands [blank] ladder hand over hand to [blank]

Friday, 31.

Weighed anchor once last night, went ¼ mile then anchored again. Alternate rain & wind all night till 2 A.M. About 4 A.M. [blank] anchor. Rain all [blank] but no fog. Made Pt. Lookout about 12 m. Are there now. Anchored in mouth of Potomac [blank] oyster shack dragging along

APRIL 1865

April, Saturday, 1.

Moved a little distance up river to safer anchorage. Transferred to & packed in small steamboat — "The Kent." — landed at Pt. Lookout on verbal parole, assigned hospital quarters best I have had in Yankeeland. Shall sleep in bed to-night, first time in 27 months. No one knows how long we may be delayed here. The N. Y. State lies in sight. Table fare wretched.

Sunday, 2.

We are marched to meals 3rd table — What is left. Wrote to Mother to-day. Read Cris' "Poetic Principles" & King John, Collier's Edition e.g. "*Untread* the *Roadway* of rebellion." I want my Shakspeare to have all Shakspeare's mistakes & none of Mr. Collier's emendations though some sound well as "Shadowing his right under your wings of war." Painful rumors afloat.

April, Monday, 3. 1865

Richmond & Petersburg said to be in possession of enemy. A Yank Brig. Gen. distributing the grape visiting our wards "to demoralize." Faugh! If R. is taken I believe it has been done by Lee's withdrawal of troops to mass elsewhere. If so, Grant has been, I hope, severely beaten.

Tuesday, 4.

I now have a fear that our exchange may be postponed a long time, but believe & hope that some new point may soon be agreed upon. I had a little "fuss" with our impudent wardmaster. In all the other wards our party are well treated & politely. In this with great rudeness. Prisoners continually arriving from the front. They are not in the least demoralized

Wednesday, 5.

& do not believe the Richmond story though they say that all expect its evacuation soon. Doubtless it *has* occurred. They begin to give us clean plates at dinner instead of those used twice already, as heretofore. Here I can enjoy being alone by walking on the bay beach and finding a seat there. This approach to solitude is delightful after my life.

April, Thursday, 6. 1865

Gave us molasses for breakfast but the plates were so dirty that I couldn't eat though I hungered for it. — Wrote to Father to-day for money which I greatly need but which I had hoped never to receive again from my friends. I was as hungry when I rose from dinner as when I sat down. The quantity of food is insufficient. A cloudy day, a little rain, the first unpleasant weather we have had.

 A Chase — Hamet de Ford Fitz Hugh

Friday, 7.

Finished reading "Pilgrimage to Jerusalem & Mt. Sinae by Barm Geramb, Monk of the Order of La Trappe" a singular book, its author a good man, a devotte from under whose cowl traces of the helmet still visible. Hard up for reading. Shakspeare (Col. Locke's) stolen from under my pillow while we were at breakfast several days ago.

Saturday, 8.

Scouring day. Kept out of our room nearly all day. Not so in the other wards. Ventured bean soup at dinner impelled by hunger. I ran the risk — Perhaps it will not hurt me this time. Have nothing to read now but Lucretius & [blank] turned over the former; last night reading a fine passage here & there [blank] proves another conquest. Our army is still firm. Laus Deo[1.]

April, Sunday, 9. 1865

"The Poet's Journal" by Bayard Taylor — a book containing many beautiful things though some of the best are among the "various poems" at the end. For dinner to-day we had each a slice of bread, not larger than usual — only this & nothing more. Inspection — ordered to stand at attention scarcely [blank] Two small herrings for supper.

Monday, 10.

Dirty plates at dinner — If the news to-day (Surrender of Gen. Lee's Army) be true — & it is possible — we cannot hope to make a long stand E. of Miss. River. If we are only true to ourselves, it will be all right yet. Should the worst come — (&c for Mexico) we can hold out in Trans. Miss. for two or three years yet.

Tuesday, 11.

I believe the news — most of it — O for exchange! Our equivalents have been delivered & it must come. Then one more sight of VBM, a few campaigns in Trans Mississippi and *then*, if success come not, a home in a foreign land. Puritanic order against card playing, smoking etc. — O the blessed world of the Mayflower! A foretaste of subjugation. We are subjected to insults frequently. Vae victis.[2]

April, Wednesday, 12. 1865

Gloomy day. Called with Capt. R. H. Isbell to see a (KE fr. Brown — an educated man but an underling. A strong suspicion of "bombproof" about him. My *morale* is improving though my spirits are still depressed by Lee's surrender.

Thursday, 13.

Yet if our people but prove worthy of Freedom we will yet win it. O could we but imitate those bright, historic examples of fortitude & persistence all would be well. The rumor is that our beloved President has gone to Johnston's army. If this be so, it strengthens my hopes.

Friday, 14.

A rumor obtains that we are to be released on parole until exchange. Good for us individually but the worse for our hopes as the Yankees would not venture on any such step did they not feel certain of success. I cannot & will not believe that affairs are so bad as represented. "All must be well, if we are true to ourselves." Book II of the Dunciad (annotated)[3]

April, Saturday, 15. 1865

News of the assassination of Lincoln & Seward. A cowardly act, doubtless the work of some fanatic radical. Yet it will insure our independence for L's clemency dictated by L's policy was greatly to be dreaded. The radical Republican Johnson will give our people that union, which would have been wanting otherwise in desperate circumstances.

Sunday, 16. (Easter)

For breakfast — *two eggs* — unexampled liberality! No mailboat fr. Washington yesterday or to-day. Reading article on "U. S. as an Example" in Lond. Quarterly Jan. 1865 — Very good. Found Shakspeare. Anxiously am awaiting developments & new policy (*old* radical) in Johnson's inaugural.

Monday, 17.

Continual booming of cannons; no joy-guns these from vessels in the bay & river. Read 1 part King Henry IV — gathered some mussels yesterday — prepared them to-day for [blank] Long for a development of Johnson's policy. Hope he will inaugurate a reign of terror. Worse for us individually, it would save our cause. Let our people have no hope except in success & they will succeed.

April, Tuesday, 18. 1865

Letter to Sister — Am growing very anxious to rec. letters especially so to hear fr. Miss. fr. VBM. This latter indeed, is my chief source of anxiety. I fear I may have to go to some foreign land without ever bidding adieu to my best & most loved friend.

Wednesday, 19.

Do not think our affairs are yet hopeless. Gen. Johnston has not surrendered. Besides we have another army in the field. I do not believe that our nascent Confederacy is destined for the limbo of dead nations. She may flicker & burn low, but I believe the fire will live till again rekindled into a bright & enduring flame.

Thursday, 20.

Letter from Sister returned "Too long." Dirty plates — dinner too much for my over delicate stomach. I couldn't go it. 2nd part K. Henry IV. Heavy shower of rain.

April, Friday, 21. 1865

Very rancid pork with bread for dinner. Letter to Father. One month since our departure from the Island. How many events have happened in that time!

Saturday, 22.

To B. P. R._____As Johnston has not yet surrendered, I do not believe he has any idea of doing so. Joined by Forrest & the garrison of Mobil, he will have an effective army & will prove more than a match for Sherman.

Sunday, 23.

Cold weather. Late dinner, 2 P.M. Clean plates on all four tables for first time — owing to the state of things having been reported to the Chf. Med. Officer, we are to have our plates clean henceforth — Goldsmith's Sketch of Lord Bolingbroke.

April, Monday, 24. 1865

Finished Life of Shakspeare, preferred to Collier's Ed. (Jewell's) "Merry Wives of Windsor," I am growing to like some of the emendations. In some places I doubt not but that the genuine text has been restored to them but in this they are farfetched and puerile as "Tempest."

Tuesday, 25.

To the surprise of all we leave Pt. L. to-day. Embarking by means of the little "Kent" on the Str. *Weyposset* about 9 P.M. after much marching & countermarching, rollcalling &c. Weigh anchor about 10 P.M. for — no one knows where.

Wednesday, 26.

Make Ft. Monroe about 8 A.M. after a delay of about two hours. Reef in between the capes. All suppose Ft. Delaware to be our destination. So ends our hope of freedom. Are packed closely between decks — very uncomfortable — air almost stifling, out of sight of land nearly all day. Gunboat convoy bet. the bays, to render futile any attempt to take the

April, Thursday, 27. 1865

boat which might otherwise be done without losing a dozen men. Smooth sea, very little rocking & no pitching. This morning land on each hand, probably the Delaware capes. Enter the bay & land about 10 A.M. Searched — watches, oilcloths & canteens taken away. Enter pen about 1 P.M. Go out in evening to get baggage; lose arty. book. Find Dr. Hays. Sleep with Dr. Lewis.

Friday, 28.

Wrote to Father. Yesterday outside "Yes or No" proposed. Only about 12 yeses out of 314. Some have reconsidered since, learning the demoralization inside, where almost half said "yes" to the oath question. As for me "potius ruinam!"[4]

Saturday, 29.

Room in Field & Staff Barracks [illegible word] at Div. 27. After I get settled, think I shall like this prison better than Johnson's Island. Wrote to Father again on the parole question. News of Johnston's surrender. Demoralization intense among the weak-kneed. Lv. Dr [illegible words] If only could hear from VBM.

April, Sunday, 30. 1865

Letter to Mother. Day showery. Met [illegible word] Sledge, Jr. of Panola. Lieut. in Stark's Cavalry Regt. captd in Hood's campaign. Got fr. him all the news from my home. He has applied for the oath, doing so even before Johnson's Surrender. I have

MAY 1865

May, Monday, 1. (Dixie, June 26th)

no fault to find with him, but for my own part cannot even bring myself to consider the question so long as there remains a single organized comd. in the field. A concert tonight. Dr. Hays gave me a ticket: good way to pass off a few hours. Day very wet.

Tuesday, 2.

Letter to Sister — oath offered again & now, out of 2300 only 163 of us remain true. Those taking are to be sent home & I will have opportunity of writing to VBM. What is to become of the rest of us I know not — one thing certain, I have as yet felt no disposition to desert my colors — even after the close of the war I will rather accept exile were there no VBM.

May Wednesday, 3. 1865

Day pleasant & like a May day should be bright. There is much fishing in moat — small fish taken. Write a good long letter to VBM which Maj.

Sledge shall carry without knowing it. If I could only see her once more I feel that exile would lose its terror.— —

Thursday, 4.

Wrote Mr. Irby — also Mrs. Moon — latter to be sent by Logan. I begin to suffer somewhat from the insufficiency of my rations, though they are no worse here than were at Johnson's Island.— Only I have no money here & have to live on them alone.

Friday, 5.

(Quentin Durward)[1]
2 meals a day — 3 crackers & a small piece of meat at each, with a cup of soup at dinner — cooked for us, we being marched to the dining room. In other respects I like this prison much better than the Island. We have more liberty here, not being interfered with by the guard except only in

May, Saturday, 6. 1865

one corner of the pen. We may go where we will inside of fence & *when* we will. In this respect old Hill's rules afforded a great & painful contrast. Before we came Ft. Delaware was a bugbear — but, now, under

Sunday, 7.

like circumstances i.e. with like amt of money — it is the best prison I have seen as yet. Pt. Lookout cannot be termed a prison as we experienced it. Episcopal service & a sermon read. Prayer for President of the C. S.— Finished reading Anthony Trollope's "Three Clerks."

Monday, 8.

Letters to Sister & Capt. Long. Day warm — two showers — odors from the rear not like the gardens of [illegible phrase] in the room. Begin to have hopes of being set at liberty some day without taking the oath, or at least of being banished — were it not for VBM I would rather be banished than live in this "cursed" country.

May, Tuesday, 9. 1865

Wrote to Editor Freemans Journal inquiring concerning Mexican emigration scheme. I would take service under Max. with feelings of unmixed joy were it not for one only tie which still holds me to the South. Schiller's "Robbers," — stage translation — not so good as Elisar in Bohn's library — No letter though I fully expected one.

Wednesday, 10.

"Omne solum forti patria est, ut piscibus aequor"[2] is my motto as my

Mexican prospect gains head to my brain. Were it not for VBM I would go there surely—take service if I could & if I couldn't, why, I could do something else. "Rasselas"³—Cold weather.

Thursday, 11.

Weather sultry—Rain & thunder all evening—No letter from home. I fear that having a near relation in prison has lost its novelty, but my fears doubtless do my dear parents injustice though. L. who wrote the same day I did, & to a pt. in K more distant, recd an answer yesterday. Begin "Vicar of Wakefield."

May, Friday, 12. 1865

Weather very cold again this morning. No letter. I have the blues badly over this inexplicable silence. I little thought that prison life could last long enough to wear out the kindness of my kin, or that the time would ever come when I might complain of neglect. However, so mote it be.

Saturday, 13.

No letter yet. What can be the cause of this neglect? Reconciled myself to a bath in the foul moat-water inasmuch as no better can be had. I believe, after all, it is infinitely better than doing without the luxury of cleanliness.

Sunday, 14.

Take dinner with Capt. M. J. Alexander—(other guests Capt. Day & Lt. Band). Best dinner I have had this year. Feel an unwonted sense of delightful repletion, *chocolate*—which was most excellent. I have tasted *coffee* only once in a month. No mail to-day. I believe I am glad of it for I dread disappointment.

May, Monday, 15. 1865

(Wrote letter to Father.) Terrible news. Nothing less than the capture of our beloved President, whom I *honor* & respect first among mortals—Breckingridge escaped. They may subject Mr. Davis to the worst indignities but they cannot deprive him of the love of thousands of devoted men, nor can they deprive us of the privilege of being prouder of him in adversity than we were in his hour of glory.

Tuesday, 16.

A letter at last & a very welcome one fr. Sister, 15$ enclosed—No invitation to take the oath. No news fr. VBM. The President's capture is a subject of ridicule to the Yankee papers owing to circumstances with which it is invested but which I am persuaded will prove totally false.

Wednesday, 17.

Another oath panic, led by some of the best men here — Col. Steedmen et al. I do not really believe that the noes will exceed *fifty* when this paper has gone out. My time is no nearer than it was when Lee surrendered. While a military organization remains in the field, I am a Confederate i.e. while there is anything to cling to.

May, Thursday, 18. 1865

Drew in Sutler check 4.85 (15c. charged). Supped on that. Invested in a loaf of bread & a bottle of honey, being thereby enabled to regale myself after the manner of ancient royalty if we may believe the old heroic ballad. A letter fr. Father advising me to take the oath. Had just written.

Friday, 19.

Answered Father's letter to-day regretting the improbability of — at present — following his advice, but promising to do so as soon as the play is ended. Rec'd two letters forw'd fr. Point Lookout and containing twelve dollars in money. Change in weather — colder.

Saturday, 20.

Harry Coleman died this morning. (6 A.M.) A week ago he was the "heartiest" looking man in our room. He died a true Confederate — never having even considered the oath — pneumonia.[4] Whitewashing, all have to move out. Hurry in to escape rain. Stormy, unpleasant day. Wrote to Father in reply to Pt. Lookout letter. Am sorry he didn't wait awhile longer before wishing me to take the oath. Buy a ring & order 2.

May, Sunday, 21. 1865

Day unpleasant — shower of rain. Much "grape" owing to absence of newspaper. Feel unwell, lassitude & utter *"triflingness."*

Monday, 22.

Letter fr. Capt. Long at the Island. Arrival of Maj. Gen. Wheeler & Staff & of Cols. Johnston & Lubbock, Aides de Camp to the President. So thus at last we are able to learn the truth regarding his capture. Of one thing I am glad — I have not heard a single man express any belief in the assertion that he was in "disguise" when taken. More rain at night. Cols. L. & J. gave the true version.

Tuesday, 23.

Maj. Gen. Wheeler & staff left. Regaled myself on crust & onions a la Sancho. I have at length given up our cause as utterly hopeless: we may succeed hereafter, but *this* war is over! It only remains to come well out of it with a clean conscience & an untarnished *spirit* then to sit quietly down & keep my sword bright for a better time to come. Letter fr. Sister (Pt. Lookout).

May, Wednesday, 24.

Very cold (for season) last night. The Philadelphia Inquirer contains a long description of our President, his lady & companions — abusing them and uttering the coarsest remarks even concerning the ladies. How persistently the Yahoos contend that the Houyvayn-yhm is a brute![5] Characteristic. D — n. ed.

Thursday, 25.

Noes amt now to 40. The late proclamation of Southern Governors recognize the fact that the Confederate States Government has ceased to exist — Among them are Clark's of Miss. That I would be free to act upon as my allegiance is due primarily to my state were I not a soldier. Another recognition

Friday, 26.

of this fact is to be seen in the surrender of the "Stonewall" to the end as authorized. Another unpleasant rainy day. Wrote yesterday 2 letters — to Capt. Long at island & to Mrs. Lizzie Moon, Phila. I do not know that she is there, but [blank] address. No letters.

May, Saturday, 27. 1865

Very cold & disagreeable. No letter. No meat for dinner. It is painful to read the acct. of the insults & indignities to which our noble President is being subject. Manacled & in a dungeon! And he the brightest exemplar of manhood in this world.

Sunday, 28.

Warmer — but cloudy. Rain last night. Prisoners are being released very slowly — Twelve more taken out to-day — among them, Maj. R. R. Hutchison, formerly of Gen. Bowen's, late of Gens. Rodes, Ramsuns & Pigrams staffs. Service & Sermon to-day, indeed every Sunday.

Monday, 29.

Day very warm. Official announcement of Kirby Smith's agreement to surrender. I am now ready. There were more than forty of us left. A greater number than I expected. All are now willing as men can be who have no choice between evils. Wrote a letter to Father; recd one.

May, Tuesday, 30.

1865 Drew $11.90c — balance of my acct. Twenty-five called out this morning—Amnesty proclamation *but* a very ludicrous document, full of exceptions. Special application is now necessary in every instance. 28 called for tonight who are at liberty to

Wednesday, 31.

leave in the morning—Among them Capt. Alexander who however will not leave for several days, waits for spondulix.[6] Signed Mississippi memorial: also a paper signifying my willingness to take the amnesty. This is the date of my application as the paper got up the other day was not sent out. (+FINIS+)

JUNE 1865

June, Thursday, 1

An oppressively hot day. Capt. A. left in the morning. Our rations seem to get scantier. Hardtack. the poor fellows who have nothing else must suffer. Fast day. Sutler closed & no roll call. Can neither read nor write—dream & build air castles. Am at a loss to hear from VBM. Must see her on my release at all events.

June, Friday, 2. 1865

No mail—No meat. That issued at breakfast being entirely spoiled so that those at our table, at least, had to throw it away while none was issued at dinner. Six small crackers & a cup of soup.

Saturday, 3.

No letter—
Nothing.
"E'n where chains lie heaviest on the land, Souls may not all be fettered." Vespers of Palermo

Sunday, 4.

"Many a land arisen,
Hath bowed beneath the yoke, & then
as a stout lion rending silken bonds
And in the open field before high heaven
Won such majestic vengeance & hath made
Its name a power on earth."[1]

June, Monday, 5. 1865

Blank

Tuesday, 6.

Letter fr. Miss Carrie V. Haskell, No.1122 Arch St., Phila. Answered.

Wednesday, 7.

Blank

June, Thursday, 8. 1865

2nd Reading. Finished II volumes. Parton's Burr begun yesterday. Order for release of nine officers published.

Friday, 9.

Day very hot — 600 privates said to leave. Read Cuthbert Bede's Adventures of Verdant Green, a readable enough book. No letter. What can be the matter?

Saturday, 10.

Rain & Wind. Privates being released in numbers. Capt. Fellows released: this morning some other official specially

June, Sunday, 11. 1865

BLANK

No more Confederacy left! "Nothing left to cling to!" so Uncle Parks records that —[2]

Monday, 12.

Have taken the oath! That I should have lived to see this day! — Say we are to leave to-morrow morning. I don't want to go till I get some money but fear I may be forced to leave anyhow.

Tuesday. 13.

Arose at 4 A.M. Left Island at 7:30. Phil. 12:30. Found Mrs. H. waiting for me. Accpd. her home to dinner. Found Miss C. a very pleasant acquaintance & passed a few delightful hours. Thence to depot. Left on P.L.Q.R. 7 P.M. (Democratic clubs: Capt. Shaw: Money. I felt so awkward at first in co. I scarcely knew what to do; Old box address is old.

June, Wednesday, 14. 1865

Morning found us at Harrisbrg. which we left at 6 A.M. Took on a Federal Regt. this side encampment. F. at Altoona over mountains — Reach Pitts at 11 P.M. Go to a low lodging house where we are *over-run*. Have to wait here till tomorrow. 2 P.M.

Thursday, 15.

A whole day in the city of dirt & smoke & unbeautiful females. Leave at 6 P.M.

Friday, 16.

Reach Crestline at 8:30 A.M. Leave the party, take cars via Delaware for Springfield at 11:20. Reach Springfield 3, take broad gauge for Dayton, (ΣX) Hamilton before sunset—(Finis)[3]

[Many blank pages follow, but toward the end of the 1865 diary are various names and addresses of men, written by each man—in effect, an autograph book.]

J. L. Hughes, L. Co. C, 13th Ky Con, Lon Conn, Westenburg, Ky.

Frank A. Pope, Goodman, Miss.

L. B. Franks, New Orleans, La., Late a member of 16th La. Regt. C.S.A.

Hal Fetter, Lt. P.A.C.S. Address, Chapel Hill, North Carolina

Thos. A. Long, Capt & ACS PACS, Chapel Hill, N. C.

Richard B. Cater, Ex Lieut 1st Ala Regt, Selma, Ala.

Jno. D. Naynor, 1st Lt. 2nd J.C. Cleveland, Tenn.

Charles F. Bakin, Maj 3rd Chuki C.S.A. Carlg Indian Dep, [illegible word] Grand Saline

Reference: Cunningham & Co., Shaw & Co., Ft. Gibson, Chuki Nation

C. W. Lewis, Capt. 23 Ark Vol, West Point, Ky or Marion, [illegible word] Co., Ark.

A. A. Williamson, Capt Co F, 12th Miss Regt, Sardis, Panola Co, Mississippi

William Heays MD, Lt Co "B," C.S.A. 2nd Ky Cav, Residence: Covington, Kentucky

E. D. Jett, Capt 17th Ark Inftry, Home: Washington, Ark.

R. H. Isbell, Capt, V Ala Rg, Talladega, Ala

J. E. Nasen [?] Care: E. P. Rankin, New Orleans, La.

Jas. M. Murray, Lake Village, Chicot Co., Ark.

W. J. Alexander, Capt. 34th N.C., Address: Wilkesboro, N.C. or Memphis, Tenn.

Saml. D. Leslie, 1st Lieut. 8th Va. Supy, Hillsborough, Loudoun Cty., Va.

Jim. W. Lausdale, Lieut 23rd Ark Regt, West Point, Kentucky

P. Lynch Lee of Camden, Ark, Lt. Col. 15th Ark Rgt Inf.

Matt B. Shaw, Capt 1st Ark Bat, Grand Lake, Chicot Co, Ark.

J. E. Kelly, Lt Col 13th Va Cav, Suffolk, Nausunnos Co., Virginia

James P. Parker, Lt. Col. 1st Miss. Lgt. Arty. Reg.

Geo. U. Whiting, 1st Lt Co "C" 47th [?], Raleigh, N.Car.

Wm. P. Locke, Lt. Col. 1st Ala., Perote, Ala.

I. G. W. Steedman, Col 1st Regt Ala NaG, Allenton, Wilcox County, Alabama

R. Gillaud, 1st Lt — 1st Ala, Camden, Ala.

M. P. Wilrun, Maj. 1st Ark Battalion, Cambure, Ashley Co, Ark. Captured Port Hudson, 9th July, 1863

Henry G. Lewis, Major 32nd N. C., Scuppernong, Tyrrell Co, N. C. captu at Gettysburg, July 1863

W. R. Bond, Lt & ADC to 1 Ala Brig Gen Daniel, Scosland Nick, N. C. capt — Gettysburg, July 4th, 1863

Jno. Hines, Bowling Green, Ky. Care of L. L. Cook

[The following names are in Caldwell's handwriting.]

Mr. C. Houston, South Charleston

Otho L. Hayes, Delaware, Ohio

P. S. Myers, Byhalia, DeSoto Co., Mississippi (ΣX^4

(Tom McCracken $5.00) N.C.

N.C. Wheeler

Hawks

S.C. Simms

Mims

Ala. Pickett

Valley of Miss. Dr. Moneth

Miss. Naile

Va. Campbell

Fla.

Ga. White [illegible word]

12th Let. Chesnut, 4 Market

[The last two pages in the diary.]

1865

March

21st Leave Johnson's Island.

25th Arrive at Ft. McHenry.

29th Leave

April

1st Land at Pt. Lookout.

25th Leave Pt. Lookout.

27th Reach Ft. Delaware.

Last Page Major ?? Doubleyou

S. B. Rudder

N.O. La.

Mrs. Zoa A. Long

Chapel Hill N. C.

Appendix: Letters, Poems and Essays

Following are letters written to family members while Caldwell was in prison. Poems and three essays from The Overland Monthly.

Prison Letters from Parks

Police Jail, N.O.
September 11th 1863

Dear Father:

We are to sail from this port for New York, Fortress Monroe or some other place *day after tomorrow*. I hope for a speedy exchange though I had hoped to have heard from home while within the Federal lines. It may be, however, (and I greatly fear that *it is*,) that we are to exchange this prison for some other and to bid farewell to all hopes of seeing "Dixie" for a year or two.

My health is excellent and I daily grow more corpulent.

With love to Mother, Sisters & Brothers. I remain with all respect

Affectionately your son
J. P. Caldwell

P.S. I shall write from our next stopping place be it where it may.

Johnson's Island, O. Jan. 15, 1864

My Dear Brother Jo,

I rec'd your letter of the 10th inst., yesterday and was very pleased, both at hearing from you and at finding that you have so well progressed in your studies that you can write, compose and punctuate so correctly. You speak of having had bitter cold weather, but I think it could not have been nearly so cold as it was on this island: it astonished even the old inhabitants who declare that the weather was colder than it had been for sixteen years. I weathered it safely, however, and am now enjoying a temperature so mild that it almost seems the forerunner of opening spring. I am more so comfortably situated that I fear nothing from cold, and am prepared for the worst weather that may come. I fear that the papers, you allude to are mistaken, and that we will not have the pleasure of "going home" for many a long week yet. I hope, however, that my fears may be altogether without foundation, though I see no chance for so happy a disappointment. As long as I remain here I shall continue to write frequently — if permitted to do so, — but when I leave for the South communication will have to cease until the war ends, unless I should again be captured — a contingency by no means desirable, though very possible. I shall often think of home, and never let an opportunity of writing pass unimproved. Your messages to Frank shall be duly delivered — I wish I could say, *soon.* (Enclosed find a lock of hair for my dear Mother.) Write again & often, your letters shall never be neglected by your affectionate Brother.

J. P. Caldwell

B 5 — M 2, Apl 16th
My Dear Father; —

Your coming takes me quite by surprise, and right sorry am I to learn that it must prove of no avail. I would rather see you, and have a talk with you than anything else short of liberty, but I suppose it cannot be helped. I do not know what to write to you about, — I have so many questions I should so like to ask you. I suppose all were well when you left home? My health is about restored, I am obliged to you & Mother for your kindness — I will go up on the platform of Block Two *after* I receive another note from you where it may be permitted to us to get a glimpse of each other. As the messenger waits I will write no more now, but will proceed to set down a few questions to send you about various things — but I have neither heart nor mind to think of theses things when your are so near, & yet invisible —

Very affectionately
Yr loving Son —
J. P. Caldwell

I am so excited I can scarcely write!

P.S. — I have an old sabre outside — we were allowed by the "capitulation" to retain our arms — I suppose it is marked, at least, my name *was* placed on it when I gave it up on my arrival here — Please ask Col. Hill for permission to take it home with you to serve us both as a memorial —

[On the inside sheet of the letter is a note from Dr. Caldwell to his family, so they could read the letter from Parks as well.]

I have just returned from a visit to the Island, I went over at 12N — now it is 3 o'clock P.M. — at 4, one hour I will return. I sent the carpet sack in; and have returned for the trunk — the Doctor says he will send the eatables to the Rebel boy. I am in a great hurry, as this writing testifies.

Love to all
W. W. Caldwell.

P.S. I think I will get a glimpse of him — the Doctor says he will give me his *spyglass* for the occasion.

July 8th 1864.

My Dear Mother —

Today is the anniversary of the surrender of Port Hudson (though it was not occupied till the 9th) and completes the twelfth month of my long and wearisome captivity. I hope it may not last much longer and that, too, so confidently, that I expect to be in my own country and at my post again before the first of October. The box I lately rec'd was very welcome, & I feel thankful to all who had a hand in it. It contained several things which cannot be got here. We are living very well — for prisoners — but it is due to the Sutler's establishment. I do not know one single man (or mess) in the prison who lives upon the rations exclusively: this is very fortunate indeed and is owing to the friends so many of the prisoners have either in the United States, or within the lines of the U.S. Forces. It is really astonishing to witness the amounts of money rec'd here (by express) and the amount of business done by the sutler in such articles as he keeps. My own mess has got along very well and at a cost of not over $40.00 per month — butter and vegetables can always be had at the Sutler's, but for meat we depend upon "the govmt." Last winter there was nothing of this, and boxes were our only dependence. Now boxes are chiefly welcome as containing articles which the Sutler does not keep, or which have not yet come into the prison market. I am glad to rec. them, because they constitute a share in our housekeeping expenses. For my share of the *labor,* I get breakfast every morning — (formerly toast & roast potatoes — now toast, ham & coffee for regular dishes — the rest attend to the other duties. The bible & Hymn book duly rec'd: three of the former lie at all times within my reach, — I only wrote because I desired to read those books left out in the ordinary editions; I supposed the edition I wished would be easily obtained or I shouldn't have written. The hymnbook will do me no harm though it is entirely useless to *me* who am as unmusical as ever. I have just finished reading the *Book of Esther* which I had not read since I was a child. I do not wish, by this to make you think me religious (for I am not,) but merely to show you that I can find reading in the bible to interest me. I wish I could write more — Your Aff. Son, J. P. Caldwell.

U.S.Mil. Prison, — November 6th

Dear Father. Yours of Oct 30th was recd last Wednesday. The clothing came safely some days before and had been acklgd. It all suited very well and was admitted without demur. Nearly two weeks ago I gave Dr. Eversman a letter for you, accompanied by a certificate from Dr. Lewis: As he took the letter, I supposed he would send it. If he has not sent it I will trouble him with no more. I put down such articles as Dr. Lewis thought best, and followed his advice in offering my letter to Dr. E. — You ask if I rec. any help from others, I answer *no* — my friends in *Miss.* are too far from the point of interchange to help me in the present state of transportation in the south. Boxes only come from Va. & N. C. From no other place in the United States than *home* I would receive help. There must be some misapprehension about my request for 10$ — I *know* that it would not be agst orders to send that sum to my account here. However, I can get along without it very well at present. The money you sent was duly ackd, Thank you for it — also, for the stamps. Please do not apply *here* for any favors, whatever. My love to all — I write again Wednesday.

Affectionately yr. son
J. P. Caldwell

(B.8m2)

Johnson's Island Prison, February 2nd, 1865

Dear Sister: have just rec'd your last: I rejoice at the increased frequency of your letters. You can very easily write twice a week & thus make up for others to whom it is not so convenient. I have never allowed a letter from any of my brothers or sisters to remain unanswered a single day longer than absolutely necessary and I say it with satisfaction. You will find the picture enclosed: hope it may not be captured in transit. It is said to resemble me somewhat. I am, as you see, the picture of health: indeed, my health is better than it has been since my arrival — when it was perfect. Two months ago I looked like a different man. That you might have a natural picture I shaved for the first time in six months: could I have had two, I would have sent one bearded. Shoes, socks, & hdkfs rec'd: whatever else was in the box will reach me doubtless tomorrow — as reading matter & clothing come in thru different channels. I hope my name was legibly written in the Blackwood or whatever else was in the box. I did not know the so named *Col.* Johnson, nor does anyone else. A Johnson may have been released, but no *Col.* of that — or any other — name has been in those terms. I hope you do not know him either, for he is doubtless an impostor — not an unnatural character, by any means, but altogether consistent with the other. I would much like to have a better phot. of Mother than that sent me last winter. Tell her that I rejoice at the opportunity of sending my picture chiefly in her acct. — that she may come as near seeing her son as may be without an interview. My best love to her & to all the rest.

Lovingly, yr brother. J. P. Caldwell

POEMS

In Caldwell's papers is an undated poem that says, "Written while a Confederate soldier":

Day Dreams

1. My smoke wreaths are curling
   Like wind driven clouds
When moonlight our bright world
   In silver, enshrouds;
My thoughts, like the silvery clouds
   Flits swiftly away
Reminding that life
   Is but the dream of a day.
2. As day dreams are pleasant
   So bright and so brief,
The forest scarce blooming
   E'er the fall of the leaf.
3. Dum vivimus, vivamus
   While we live let us quaff,
To the bountiful giver
   Of joy and the laugh,
To gracious old Baccus,
The God of no pain;
Let us taste ere we cannot
The sweets of his reign.
4. Dum vivimus, vivamus
   While we live, let us live
Unmindful of care, unthinking of grief;
   When death on his pale horse
The reaper has come
   The grain is then garnered
      The labor then done.
5. This life then is over
   It's joys we forego
For pain or for pleasure
   For weal or for woe.

By Jas. Parks Caldwell

The following is the final rendering of the Latin poem about the flag, which had been written over a period of time, one verse at a time, and then transcribed to its final form here. The earlier versions that Caldwell scratched out were not shown earlier, but only referred to as they occurred. Ken Kitchell points out that there is no easy way to give an accurate translation that adheres to the way Caldwell's words fall into stanzas. A prose translation is therefore offered for each stanza. The rhyme scheme is AAB CCB but the lines contain a varied number of syllables. A stanza consists of two groups of three lines each, wherein the first two lines of each stanza rhyme with each other, but the last line of each stanza rhyme. Thus in stanza I we have "crux ... lux ... lumen ... fortis ... mortis ... numen."

Ad Patriae Vexillum; Carmen Militare

I

Ave bis cive, gloriae crux
Nostriae nationis lucida lux
   Nostris animis lumen!
Quoties miles fortis,
In articulo mortis
   Salutavit te numen?

II

Mavortis diadema
Spei nobis emblema
   Pirfulgens in bellis
Aura tibi est gloria
Tuum coelum Victoria,
   Gimmata crux stellis!

III

Gloriosam in navem
Te Reipublicae avem
   Sempiternum videre;
Tempestatem domantem
Et nimbum equitantem
   Omne nefas terrare.

IV

Durantibus annis,
Te fugiat tyrranis,
   Liberatatis insigne!
Sia custos domorum
Lar atque focorum,
   O cultra perdigne!

V

O Patriae decus dulce
Corda nobis *jam* sulfulci
   Intacta sint catenis!
Fortuimque adsis ori
Quibus bene fit mori
   Sit illis quies lenis?

VI

Pro patria moriuntur
Et morte nobis talluntur;
   Adeint suepe memoriae?
Ex vitae perpaulis
Profecti sint aulas
   Sempiternas victoriae.

VII

In belli fulminibus
In leti grandinibus
   Fulgentem tenes cursum,
Novae gentis natale
Sidus luce regule,
   Per sanguen volens sursum!

VIII

Manet quies amoena
Tibi, via serena
   Per superum aera;
Tempestate superata,
Erit frons circumdata
   Serta laudis sera.

IX

Sanguinolentis ex undis
Tabo proelii immundis
   Natio oritur nostra,—
Atro videtur extare
Clarus ut Lucifer mare,
   Per luminis claustra.

X

Cito die cedat nox
Et sit dira tubae vox
   Gaudio obscurata;
Et laetis carminibus
Dilectis virginibus
   Fortium laus modulate.

XI

Sanguinis campum aret bos,
Suter tumulo floreat flos,
   Recens osculo novis
Vivida memoria fortis,
Unibis nec obsita mortis,
   Haereat mentid in oris.

XII

Oris libertatis impone
Vexillum sericum, coronae,—
   Superbe illic pendeat?
Donec vocet bellum trux,
Tum stellata nostra crux,
   Fulgore novo splendeat.

The English translation of the Latin poem is not in the diary, but is added here from the work of Kenneth Kitchell.

To the Country's Flag
A Military Song

I

Hail, twice hail, cross of glory
Luminous light of our nation,
Light unto our spirits.
How many times as a brave soldier,
On the brink of death,
Saluted your majesty?

II

Crown of Mars,
Emblem of hope
Shining forth in wars,
Glory is your breeze,
Thou cross bejeweled with stars!

III

(Oh) to see you always glorious
Thou bird of the Republic,
Conquering the storm,
Riding on a cloud
Terrifying all that is unholy.

IV

As the years draw on,
Let the tyrants flee you,
Thou emblem of freedom!
May you be guardian of our homes.
Patron god of our hearths,
Thou who are worthy of worship!

V

Oh sweet adornment of the country,
Prop up now our hearts,
Intact, though in chains!
May you be before the face of the brave
And may you provide gentle rest
To those who have the blessed fortune to die!

VI

They die for their country
And they are taken away from us in death–
May their memories be ever with us!
From the trivialities of this life
They have set out for the halls of eternal victory!

VII

Amid the thunderings of war,
Amid the hail storms of death,
You hold the shining course,
Oh, birth of a new nation
Royal in your light,
Flying aloft through the blood.

VIII

Pleasant rest awaits you
On a calm path through the air above
The storm overcome
Your forehead will be surrounded
With a belated crown of promise.

IX

Out of the bloody waves defiled
With the plague of war
Our nation arises.
It seems to rise up bright
Out of the blackness as the morning star does
Out of the sea, through the barriers to light.

X

Let night give way quickly to day,
And let the somber voice of the war trumpet
Be drowned out by rejoicing.
And let the praise for the brave
Be sung by beloved maidens in joyful songs.

XI

Let the ox plow the fields of blood,
Let a flower, fresh with the kiss of dew
Bloom on the top of the grave.
Let the memory of the brave,
Let mention of the dead,
Linger on our lips
But not beset with shadows.

XII

Affix the silken flag on the altars of liberty,
Bystanders (?), and let it hang there proudly,
Until such a time as fierce war shall call;
And then our bejeweled cross
Will shine with splendor anew.

OVERLAND MONTHLY ESSAYS

SOME ACCOUNT OF A GREAT WESTERN POET
THE OVERLAND MONTHLY
Vol 2. — June, 1869. — No. 6.

To him who, from the studious retirement of philosophic speculation, carefully regards the various phases and manifold tendencies of our age, it appears one of reality, harsh and matter-of-fact — reverencing absolutely nothing but material success. The modern American man holds in utter contempt everything of doubtful advantage, not useful in itself or appraisable as money's worth, no matter how elevating or refining its abstract influence may be, and "cash payment" — or some fictitious substitute therefore — is fast becoming "the sole *nexus* between man and man."

Political Science has degenerated to an art, and is chiefly used as a subordinate means of money-getting. History is but a remorseless analysis, and Fiction runs on forgeries, dinners, and divorces. The drama has almost disappeared before the ballet, which, gorgeously disarrayed, leads the eye in close pursuit of the imagination; it is the era of base mimes, and sock and buskin have abandoned the stage from which more practical garments were preparing to flee. Poetry is turned into an advertising medium, or, preserving its formal identity, displays a monstrous pre-Raphaelism almost without light or coloring. Inspiration is no longer needed and poems are made to order; our bards, like Thomas Tucker, (whose metrical history whilom delighted our childish ears) sing for their suppers, and market their loves and their sorrows. Pegasus must henceforth be represented either as a pack-horse or as a velocipede, while the Muses remind us, only by the graceful distortion they practice, of the land of their birth.

Perhaps the clatter of machinery and the hum of trade deaden the intellectual perceptions; certainly, some such hypothesis is required to account for the insensibility of our generation to the merits of the great world-song which has been chosen for present consideration. A few hearts thrill beneath the influence of its matchless harmony, and recognize the tones of a master-singer, but scarcely a mark of attention has been bestowed by the public at large upon this most wonderful production of genius. Other works as great have met with similar neglect on their first appearance; even *Paradise Lost* had few admirers until Addison's time; true lovers of poetry must therefore derive what solace they may from the assurance that posterity will rightly estimate the treasure which we so palpably neglect. The poem in itself has all the elements of immortality; such songs bind ages together, and the day will yet come when the now forgotten author will be deemed worthy to be placed in "Fame's eternal bead-roll."

Perhaps, even, his country, in tardy atonement, may lay the corner-stone of a monument to his memory. When a new Renaissance shall come, its troubadours will delight to imitate the bard whom we in our barbarism almost despise, and his knightly devotion to his lady will be the inspiring theme of many a lay, but all less sweet than his own wild song of despairing love.

Believing that I shall confer a benefit on many readers who have never had their attention properly directed to the beauties of this great work, or their interest rightly awakened in the misfortunes of its heroic author, as well as inspired with a desire to aid in its transmission to posterity, I propose to venture a few remarks, not so much in the nature of criticism as of comment.

The poem is elegiac, and its form — that known as the ballad — at once the simplest and truest. Happily ignorant of the trills and fantastic *variations* of later times, the singers of old chose this form of song when they wished to speak to the heart. The scalds of the heroic North and the bards and harpers of the Celtic lands used its regular cadences, as well as the wilder dithyramb, in raising the Berserker madness, or exciting their picturesque chieftains to glory. Assuming a definite form in the Nibelungen Lied, it continued to improve until the legends of the Cid and the martial lay of Chevy Chase illustrated its fitness for the delineation of stirring scenes and tender emotions, but it has been reserved for our own day and our own nation to witness its attainment of absolute perfection in the *Lament of Joseph Bowers*.

The commencement of the poem is at once sententious and comprehensive, simply introducing the hero with only so much of remark as may enable the reader to enter into the sympathy of acquaintance with him, yet therein displaying a beautiful instance of fraternal affection and an example of exalted national pride, well calculated to inculcate patriotism. Considered in this light, the words derive additional grandeur from their very simplicity and directness:

> "My name is Jo Bowers,
> I have a brother Ike;
> I come from old Missouri,
> And all the way from Pike."

The direct self-assertiveness here illustrated, though but the natural result of our free institutions, is very rare among poets, who are, as a class, too much in the habit of assuming a supercilious modesty. A man's name is his *idea*— that by which the mind distinguishes him and maintains his identity. Heroes are often thus introduced by their celebrants, nor are instances wholly wanting of similar allusions to self on the part of the bard. Indeed, I am not sure that our author has not been to some extent influenced, though perhaps unconsciously, by the example of the great Mantuan, who commences his epic in this manner — in language, however, which the better taste of Mr. Bowers induced him to avoid:

> "*Ille ego, qui quondam gracili modulatus avena Carmen, et egressur sylvas.*"

The above passage might afford ground for a charge of plagiarism against a man of inferior intellect, but it is the privilege of genius to imitate what it also surpasses.

The poet's allusion to his dear native country, in the last two lines of the opening verse, is of so touching a nature that the unharmonious geographical application loses its monosyllabic harshness; yet, even in the use of a word so plain, he is able to bring to his support the distinguished authority of Virgil, who alludes in the Æneid to an inhabitant of the same country and uses almost the same word. I cite the passage, commending it as well to archeologists for the light it throws upon vexed questions of origin and discovery, as to those who love to trace even slight resemblances between great minds:

> "*Ipse Quirinali lituo, pavaque sedebat*
> *Succinctus trabea, lævaque ancile gerebat*
> Picus *equum domitor.*"

After this felicitous introduction of himself, the poet next gives us, in easy and graceful language, the argument of his work:

> "I'll tell you why I left thar
> And how I came to roam,
> And leave my poor old Mammy,
> *So far away from home.*"

The use of the broad provincialism at the end of the first line — as well as elsewhere throughout the poem — and the tender diminutive for *mother* will, doubtless, be objected to by critics who in over-niceness lose sight of the writer's individuality, and would have even patriotism and the enduring recollections of childhood yield to the requirements of arbitrary rules, but to me they seem to possess that quality of simple grandeur which marks the Doric odes of Pindar.

In the last line of the quatrain we find a conclusive demonstration of the immense superiority of the iambic measure for the delineation of pathos, and another great example is added to that of Burns, to the discomfiture of those ingenious pedants who maintain the necessity of employing the trochee in such cases.

In a few stirring stanzas we are now presented with the incidents which lead by a regular sequence to the denoument of the plot, and herein the colloquial style is used with striking effect to lend vivacity to the action of the work. Without violation of the unities, and with a high regard for poetical justice and inculcation of morality, the poet succeeds in rapidly introducing his personages, in changing the scene, in contrasting the alternation of liveliest joy and deepest woe — in short, in effectively displaying the workings of all the various emotions of the human heart.

The declaration of love, from which so many and dire evils follow, is plain and direct, and so natural and appropriate that it may well be cited as a model for practical imitation; it is only equaled by the consenting response which it unfortunately elicited:

> "I axed her if she'd marry me,
> *She said it was whack.*"

I cannot forbear noticing a resemblance which exists between the thought here presented and that clothed in more ornate language by Tennyson, in describing a similar scene, but advert to it without prejudice to that author:

> "Her deep '*I will*'
> Breathed like a covenant of God to hold
> Through all the worlds."

Without detracting from the rhetorical beauty of the language here employed, an impartial reader, in view of the great fact that Truth is grandest in simplicity, must award the palm to the energetic reply of the Pikian maid. Imagine for a moment the rapturous transport of the devoted Bowers at the sudden realization of his long-cherished hopes; a transport, alas! too soon to be tempered by the suggestions of prudence. The joy-bringing words are subsequently qualified, as, with an admirable spirit of forecast and the financial instinct so characteristic of our thoughtful virgins, the loved one breaks from a momentary forgetfulness of the requirements of society and suggests to her rapt swain the necessity of devising ways and means to meet them. But let the poet speak:

> "Says she to me: 'Jo Bowers,
> Before we hitch for life,
> You ought to get a little home
> To keep your little wife.'"

The unnatural suddenness of this proposition has been much censured, but it is admirably modified by the tender playfulness of the language which conveys it. The immediate effect upon the mind of the lover is a determined resolution to overcome all obstacles, to which he gives utterance in a declaration of his intention to brave the dangers of a distant land in the accomplishment of the wishes of his beloved. Then is her womanly heart melted by this ready acceptance of her terms, and overcome by a sense of the depth of love she has won; she vociferates an enthusiastic approval and accompanies applause with delightful rewards. But no language is so appropriate in setting forth the tender scene as that employed by the bard:

> "Says she to me, 'Jo Bowers,
> You are the man to win!
> Here's a kiss to bind the bargain'—
> *And she hove a dozen in.*"

"*Dozen*" is here put by synecdoche for a great but indefinite number, just as Homer uses *myriad*; nor is the poet to be censured for a resort to figure in this case, as accuracy of computation is not to be expected under the circumstances; the rapid succession no less than the ecstatic nature of the events would exert a paralyzing influence on the calculative faculty, and long before the bestowal of the complete number designated, the power of enumeration would be totally gone.

It was wise to forbear all attempt at description of the sensations which must have followed this luxuriant redundance of osculation; it is not well to provoke the imagination by glowing sensuality, and the writers — many of them men of genius, too — who use this method (a very indirect one) of indoctrinating their readers with the lofty precepts of morality, seldom achieve an enduring fame. It is to be regretted that Swinburne and others of his school have either neglected the study of the works of our author, or failed to follow his shining example.

We now have a masterly hiatus in the action of the poem, caused by the judicious omission of the final interview, which, with a refinement of tenderness seldom surpassed, is left to the imagination. Nor is the pilgrimage, with its wealth of adventure and vicissitudes, made the subject of an episode, but in his silence on this subject, I think — with all due deference be it written — that the poet erred. The greatest of bards must nod at times, and beside, were a work absolutely free from faults, it would become a skilful critic to interpolate them. In this case, however, the failure to notice what so directly and temptingly presented itself, is probably due to the reflection that an attempt to treat the theme fully would bring the writer into a comparison with Spenser, and even — from the requirements of his plot and similarity of his subject — render him liable to a charge of imitation; that great author having set forth a like journey in words which could but be to some extent adopted, as —

"A gentle knight went pricking o'er 'the plains.'"

For this reason, or some other equally valid, the scene is changed, not without some abruptness, to California, which was to witness the hopes and endeavors of the much-enamored man and to be immortalized in his pathetic lament over their disappointment and futility.

The facts, duly set forth, that our hero arrived, in an impoverished, or at least, impecunious condition, at the end of his journey is skillfully adduced to enhance the difficulties under which it was undertaken, while his industry and unwearied application, lightened only by thought of the dear one for whom he toiled, read us a lesson on the importance of maintaining an unyielding front against despondency; well hath Froissart declared that a knight hath ever double courage at need, when animated by a recollection of the looks and words of a beautiful and virtuous woman!

The description of mining operations, as carried on in those early days, lends something of a historic interest to the song, while the words used are forcible and appropriate. What can be finer for instance, than the poet's allusion to his own exertions, where he says that he —

"Went down upon the bowlders
Just like a thousand bricks"?

It is difficult to imagine the immense and crushing force which must have been put forth to justify such a comparison. This simile, though eminently apposite, has met with much condemnation, owing to a want of critical knowledge on the part of uncultivated readers. People who form their taste upon the quaint metaphors and little turns of wit so much in vogue in modern literature, cannot relish the simple beauties — of a much higher nature — with which our poem is so profusely embellished, and are apt to censure even the most just comparisons, when they are able to discover no surprising points of likeness.

There is no passage in the whole range of English literature more affecting in its pathos, or more beautiful in its severe simplicity, than the lines which conclude the retrospect, in which the singer indulges himself, and no critical reader would pardon their omission:

> "I worked both late and early,
> In rain, and sun, and snow;
> *I was working for my Sally,*
> *It was all the same to Jo."*

It is with heart-felt gratification that we recognize in a dull practical age, this sole type of the true hero, worshipping beauty by word and by deed — proudly referring to his wife as the exponent of his love.

The greatest creations of human genius seem to partake of the lot of humanity to the extent of possessing, in almost every instance, some well-defined trait of sadness, and the poem before us forms no exception to the melancholy rule. In fact, it were well to draw a veil over the *incidents* of the concluding verses of the ballad, but the attention is riveted in so marked a manner, that diversion is impossible; besides, as a work of art true to nature, the poem would be incomplete without its pathetic conclusion, being so unique that no part can be omitted, without leaving a chasm in the development of the leading idea.

In due course of time, perhaps, yet after the lapse of a period so long as to argue either culpable delays in the post-office department, or great indiscretion on the part of the lady Sarah, Bowers received a letter from his dear brother. In this, were the work purely one of fiction, the reader would commend the judgment with which Isaac, a character previously introduced for the purpose, is brought in as the *Deus ex machina*, but the impress of truth is too deeply stamped on every line to allow the mind to seek relief in criticism, from the flood of tender feelings which well to the surface, beneath a pen more potent than the rock-smiting rod of Moses, in the waterless wilderness.

The information which this letter contained was of the most distressing kind, and well fitted to paralyze the energies of a man less steadfast than lovers are apt to be. Sally, she to whom our hero had plighted his troth, and for whom he had encountered the perils of an adventure which few of his countrymen regarded as less than desperate, had proved false, and united herself in the holy bonds of wedlock to a butcher; this, too, under circumstances of great aggravations to the feelings of the slighted lover, since the locks, of his successful rival were of a hue popularly supposed by those who boast a different color to indicate a predominance of the animal over the intellectual qualities of the wearer. Not only had the bright visitant of our hero's dreams become the angel of another's household, but she had already experienced the joys and sorrows of maternity, and "baby lips would laugh away" any faint cloud of regret which might cross her brow, at the thought of him she had so cruelly deceived. The forlorn and deserted one dwells with peculiar sadness — more in sorrow than in anger — on the fact that the fond pledge of love which the false one had borne to the supplanting butcher was also distinguished by the color of its hair, not fully pronounced, it is true, but with an unmistakable tendency to furnish an instance of the hereditary nature of personal peculiarities; for the tender missive of condolence which had destroyed the happiness of a life, silent on circumstances of lesser importance,

> "Only said that the baby's hair
> Inclined to be red."

With this catastrophe the poem fitly closes. Of the effect produced by the fell tidings upon the sensitive nature of Joseph we know little, save that it awakened in him that latent power of poesy, to which our world owes its noblest lyric. Thus:

> "Out of every evil born of Time,
> God shapes a good for his eternity."

Turning from the work to its author, one cannot but regret that something definite is not known respecting his after life. The little known awakes a deep interest, and provokes a vehement curiosity to learn the rest. No character of pure fiction could excite so lively an interest. John Gilpin pleases us while he rides for our amusement, but when the circus is over the amused spectators turn their thoughts on other things, and none care to inquire what became of the sober London citizen, when he retired to the shades of private life. The same may be said of Mother Hubbard's dog. Not so with Jo Bowers, however, and the very depth of the interest felt in his behalf proves that he is no shadow. In respect to his subsequent career all is left to conjecture. He may have taken to drink, or some speedier means of self-elimination; he may have died with a broken heart; or he may not be dead at all. Most likely he returned to Pike, to dwell near the object of his enduring love, and he may, even now, occupy some lowly hermitage near her home. It certainly is not likely that he persevered in his efforts to amass wealth — else we should seek him now at White Pine — the "wealth of Ormus or the Ind" could bring *him* no solace. To the world's great loss, his harp, too, has been silent, or, at least, he has written nothing over his own name, and of the many unclaimed poems in circulation none is worthy of his genius. Many long thought that there could be perceived in the poems of Owen Meredith, a certain tinge of sadness which established his identity with Bowers; but long before the authorship of those poems was avowed, I had rejected the theory as unworthy, being unwilling to admit the possibility of such degeneracy in song.

The reader may reject with a feeling akin to scorn, the idea here adopted as to the *reality* of the writer and his identity with the character he personates. Certain German critics have asserted the non-existence of Homer, but all lovers of the true and the beautiful, who ignore the fetters of pedantic skepticism, continue to maintain the contrary doctrine. The case is a parallel one, and I shall as soon relinquish my belief in the grand old Smyrniote chanting his heroic lays to defray his travelling expenses through Greece, as abjure my devout faith in a veritable Bowers singing melodiously his own sorrows. The great work which bears his name has been more than merely edited; there is a certain touch of sincerity in its pathos which no editors, nor committee of editors, how able soever, could achieve, and it evinces a noble extravagance of fancy which must have had its source in deep feeling.

If we know little of the author's life, our posterity will know still less. The local allusions, from which we gather our all of information regarding him, will soon have grown obsolete; yet even to far future ages the poet will not be altogether a myth, but will stand in nearly the same situation which the great Grecian occupies in our estimation. To compare them rightly, imagine our system of civilization to have passed away and to have been succeeded, after a long interval of darkness, by another springing from a different race, how vague and inaccurate would then be the notions entertained by the antiquarians and literary encyclopedists of Coomassie and Timboo concerning our great poet. I am irresistibly tempted to quote an article on the subject which I have recently read in a dictionary of American Antiquities, prepared three thousand years hence by some learned pundits, expressly for the use of the State University of Ashantee. It reads as follows:

"JOBOWERS, a celebrated American poet, whose life is involved in great obscurity, and of whose works but a fragment has come down to us. He is supposed to have flourished during the ninth century before the commencement of our era, and seems to have been greatly neglected by his contemporaries, though after his death cities were named in his honor, and he was, by general consent, styled the Father of Lyric Poetry. He was born, according to the best accounts, in the city of Pike, and was probably of noble birth. Since the revival of learning, many attempts have been made to establish the locality of this once famous city, but without success. Some contend that the poet was of our race, but this is by no means evident; the subject is so intermingled with fable, and borders so closely on mythology that nothing can be accurately determined. All the traditions of that distant time clearly indicate the existence of a race of colorless men in the west, who are said to have attained a certain degree of civilization, though no traces of it are found within the historic period. The object of the poet's unfortunate attachment, however, was beyond cavil of a race resembling our own in complexion, at least, as the name, 'Salliblac' implies. She is supposed to have been a priestess of the god Rhino, whom the Americans worshipped, and to have furnished her lover with the original of his character of Minnehaha. California, the city to which the bard was exiled on account of alleged complicity with the Gunpowder Plot, was originally a colony of Pike. The chief theatre in America was called the Bowery, in memory of the poet, whose tomb was within its precincts, and the two chief officers of the finance were styled respectively Right and Left Bowers. This seems to us a singular way of honoring an author, but was not out of keeping with the customs of those barbarous ages. The best edition of the fragments of Jobowers is to be found in the American anthology, published at Timboo in 2722."

As the foregoing extract contains more truth than is nowadays found in writing of the sort, we may reasonably conclude that the new civilization which is to arise from the ruins of ours will not necessarily lead to the deterioration of the interests of humanity. It is pleasant to speculate, but one mustn't wander too far or too long from his subject.

It is not necessary here to allude to the view entertained by many learned and acute scholars, that our work is an allegory, presenting the continued strife between Ormusd and Ahriman, and celebrating the ultimate triumph of the Evil Principle in the person of the butcher, as the advocates of this theory are chiefly to be found among the divines, whose practical views of life and letters are apt to be affected by the scholastic nature of their studies. Others maintain that the ballad is but an adaptation, with slight change, of Italian opera; but it is far more likely that the *Lament* had been translated and dramatized, it being eminently suitable for such purpose.

In conclusion, I wish to call the attention of all who have at heart the intellectual interests of our people and the cultivation of a high literary standard on the Pacific coast, to the urgent need of some authorized edition of our poet. At present the public and posterity are alike dependent on occasional issues from music-publishing houses, full of errors and unaccompanied with the *variorum* notes which are requisite to render an edition complete. Will not our *literati* give this matter careful consideration?

Devoted to
THE DEVELOPMENT OF THE COUNTRY
THE OVERLAND MONTHLY
Vol. 4.—February, 1870.—No. 2.

THE RATIONALE OF SLANG

There is much lurking wisdom in the corruption of words, nor is it productive of any great evil, for words, if left alone, are apt to become corrupt of themselves. It almost seems that language is continually undergoing a sort of fermentation. But what is language? Wilhelm vonHumboldt best defines it as "the breaking forth of the power of speech, according to the mentalcast of a people;" and there really does seem to be something in the phonetic differences of tongues significant of the character of the nations which use them. The stateliness of the Roman; the volatile quickness of the Greek; the confused philosophy of the German; the coarse directness of the Celt, and the gabbling readiness of the Gaul, find echoes in the sounds of their respective tongues. English and Chinese are beyond the reach of inference.

The grammar of a language is supposed to embody or sanction all possible methods of using that language correctly: that is, in accordance with established precedents. But the mind naturally seeks relief from fetters which would chain it to a tread-mill path of expression through all eternity, and breaks for itself new paths. The most generally used of these is that by purists stigmatized as "Slang," but which may respectfully be defined as the spontaneous outburst of the thought-power become vocal. When genuine, it is no perversion of language, and rather a refinement than an innovation, consisting of old words in new senses, or new words in senses heretofore difficult of expression. It is spoken poetry, entirely dependent for its effect upon comparison and metaphor, and replete with invention—which is a truer test of song than rhyme or metre—and by its freshness carries us back to the childhood of the human race.

Grammar itself is but Slang agreed upon, while slang conceals the rudiments of future grammar. Call it a parasite, if you will: the mistletoe is greener than the oak, and enlivens the leafless winter of the trunk which nourishes it. Slang is the antithesis of pedantry and the illustration of history, while it often consists of words that say themselves, as it were, and thus enrich the language they are thought to deform.

The inventions of Slang, unlike the innovations of Neology, are spontaneous, and grow upward; they are found in all languages, but most abound in those of the Teutonic stock. The innate Norse love for the grotesque appears as plainly in the Gothic moldings of language as in the fantastic decorations of architecture. The mazy arabesque of the Saracenic order is, in like manner, the type and result of the intricate and aimless convolutions of Oriental subtlety.

I have termed Slang the illustration of history; but it illustrates much more. Give me the slang expressions of a people, and I will have some inkling, not only of their social habits, their customs, and their government, but even of their geographic and climatic conditions. Let a man say, disparagingly, of another, whose sagacity has been commended, "That's all very well, *but he has no back country,*" and I am at no loss to imagine the physical aspects under which his life has been cast. When I read, in the essays of a transcendentalist, of "the thin rinds of the finite," I do not need to be told that the author has been nurtured in a land of juicy melons or generous pumpkins.

Much of our English slang consists of antique expressions, long obsolete or dormant, but again, after the lapse of generations, asserting their native force. We continually find examples of this in the old English poets. Chaucer says, of the miller's wife:

"As any jay she light was and jolif,
So was her joly *whistle well zwette;*"

and of "Dorigen," in the "Frankeleine's Tale:"

"But natheless she must a time abide,
And with good hope must *let her sorrow slide.*"

He also speaks of "rime dogerel," and of a town yclept "Bob up and down," which almost rivals the unique nomenclature in vogue among our mining camps. But it is needless to multiply instances to prove that our colloquial barbarisms are the most ancient and pure of idiomatic expressions.

Slang may mix metaphor and confuse synonyms, but, if it be genuine, may still be understood at once. The word illustrates its own meaning, as the sound does, in some sort, "echo to the sense." A Southern General, more conspicuous for courage than culture, wishing to reprimand his "old regiment" for riotous conduct in a town of Tennessee, commenced by saying that he "felt deeply lagranged." The word thus accidentally coined has, throughout an extensive region, become a common expression for chagrin, and may, in time, find its way into the dictionaries, to the great perplexity of philologists. Words, at first considered as innovations, gradually — if there is worth in them — grow to form an integral part of the language. Much of what is deemed Slang by the present generation may become very good English in the course of a century. "You bet" may be the usual rejoinder of emphatic assent among English-speaking gentlemen, a hundred years hence: it already manifests an upward tendency. But the sudden introduction of new expressions by professed word-mongers is not to be tolerated, though a gaping public sometimes regards the new epithets with favor, especially if the inventor be a writer of established reputation.

There are many systems of deviation from the assumed standard which might be classed as Slang, were they not unworthy such denomination. The *argot*, or *flash*, of the swell-mob; the complicate and high-sounding political vernacular of the more blatant mob; the jargon of philosophy and criticism; the cant of religion; the technicalities of arts, when used beyond their scope — all that world of words with which the vulgar "talk shop," on all occasions — might be denounced, at one fell swoop, as Slang, were the meaning of that term wholly without moral restriction. But that is not Slang which has any ulterior purpose than emphases, or illustration. The dialect of thieves and vagabonds belongs to the world of slums and sewers — a pariah tongue — yet, as set forth in the pages of Bulwer and Hugo, or in the travesties of Maginn and Thackeray, it seems to possess much order, as well as Spartan force. This can not truthfully be said of the second species: political *argot* is the abuse of good words, such as "freedom," "patriot," "manhood suffrage," and other euphuisms. Vilely perverted on all sides, many time-honored words which once conveyed an infinity of meaning are fast falling into absolute disgrace. "Public interest" means the interest of our party. The Hon. Jeremiah Mander, whose silent abilities in committee-rooms have raised him to opulence, is a "patriot," and so forth; illustrations are readily found for each member of the category of what the South finely calls "the rabble-charming words which carry wild-fire wrapt up in them." Political Slang is not only wrong, but empty and frivolous. It is well for our people that so much of it is mere sound. The *vox populi*, whatever may be said of it, is often *vox et præterea nihil*. The jargon of philosophy would be Slang, were it intelligible enough: it is the Chinook of science, except in the relativity of conation required to use it.

Of religious Slang, or the *patois* of the *unco guid*, it is better not to speak otherwise than briefly. Much of it is cant; but the undoubted sincerity of many who use it, elevates it to a certain dignity, and induces its mention here. Perhaps I may be harshly judged as blasphemous, in classing the lingo of inordinate sanctity with profane utterances; but, to my mind, the Rev. Cream Cheese, though more harmless, is no better than Tartuffe. The accepted saints, the holy men whom the world reveres, have never been over-given to this phraseology. Beside, the pet phrases of each individual reader's own denomination — if he have one — are scrupulously excepted, and assuredly not intended to be alluded to. With this saving clause, it may still be permitted to call many religious expressions indefensible Slang. There is a large and varied class of them going through the whole range of literature and conversation, from the unctuous and habitual phrase of doctrine to which even urban clergy are somewhat addicted to that soft, enclitic sigh with which agrestic divines are wont to punctuate discourse

Other technicalities and professionalisms are below special notice, being generally more ridiculous than hurtful.

Nor are provincialisms to be considered as Slang: they might rather be called the foundation for future dialects — were it not for the continual intercommunication which prevents — like those which diversify conversation in England and Scotland. We Americans have nothing of the kind, though words in general use throughout the country attain in particular sections peculiar signification, or may be pronounced in a peculiar manner, but never assume the magnitude of a dialect. I remember an incident which occurred during the "Kansas excitement," tending at once to illustrate the importance of correct pronunciation, and conveying a moral. A stalwart, but illiberal Missourian was the proprietor of a ferry on the main track of emigration. Dreading the effect of an influx of New England innovators, he established a test which was satisfactory to him, though one can not but doubt its universal applicability. He kept, tied by the horns to a tree on the river-bank, one of the "milky mothers of his herd," and on the arrival of a customer, was wont to inquire whether he "saw that thar brute," and what he "mout call" the same. If the applicant "reckoned" it was *cow*, he could go on his way rejoicing; but should he "guess" it to be a *keow*, or, in a moment of hapless impudence, ask his questioner if he didn't s'pose everybody knew a *keow*, he must needs seek some other crossing-place, as well as depart under a heavy weight of malediction. Even so did the *sibboleth* of the sons of Ephraim betray them to their foes at the passage of the Jordan. Who says that history does not "repeat itself?" Each section of the country has peculiarities of this kind, but in none of them is the language of the educated classes affected by them. No other country so wide has so uniform a language.

It is wonderful that this is the case, considering the differences and various admixtures to be found in many of our States. Polyglot California, Texas with her Spanish, and Louisiana with her French, have enriched the language with new terms, but have not affected it "as used by the best writers and speakers." The misuse of adjectives is the most generally prevalent source of our deviations from correctness. Our "nice young man" may not be found over-nice, after all; and our "clever gentleman" is often anything but clever — indeed, this latter appellation is well followed by the more important and significant phrase, "and a good judge of whisky." This fault seems to result from that tendency toward hyperbole to which our intellects and imagination are so subject. We are eminently a poetic people, but vent our poesy in epigram. I have heard an old lady declare herself "powerful weak," and a landlord speak of the "transient public." In no part of the country is this disposition to exaggerate so manifest as in our own State. Every thing is so expansive, that ordinary modes of expression are too narrow to convey the ideas of our people. Last fall, while on a *pasear*, I saw, flying over the great Salina Plain, multitudes of large white geese, seemingly of a species unknown to me. Eager for information I accosted the first inhabitant I chanced to encounter, asking him concerning the name and the nature of the fowl. Of the former he knew nothing, but, on the latter point, expressed himself sententiously as follows: I shot one, the other day, and took it home; we b'iled it and b'iled it, but 'twas *tougher than the wrath of God."* I stood aghast at the idea of such toughness, as well as shocked by the profanity of establishing the Divine indignation as a measure of tenacity, but told my informant that it was well he had attempted to cook his goose by boiling, as it certainly would not have been friable. He smiles not, but, with a stolid countenance, assured me that I might safely hazard my physical existence upon the truth of *that* assertion. I rode on, musing. Our people excel the famed Orientals in the richness and vastness of their metaphorical expressions.

There are certain pure vulgarisms which are universally called Slang, to the discredit of the real article in the minds of the unthinking many. A few may be susceptible of defense, on the ground of origin: even "Let her rip"— the most vulgar of vulgarisms — doubtless originated in the expression of a tender desire for the repose of some departed loved one, having most probably been adopted from a monumental inscription frequently to be found in English and Continental cemeteries, by some one not an active member of the Academy of Inscriptions. It should be written "Let her R. I. P." so with "Putting on frills"— meaning, the assumption of unnecessary "style:" this must have arisen from the teaching of philosophy, that manners form the outer garment of man's individuality.

To this class of expressions, which are expressly excepted from any commendation implied in this article, belong the vulgar names and terms of endearment, derived from and representing gross material commodities: *e.g.,* "spuds," "hash," "rhino," "spondulix," and the legion of appellatives for alcoholic refreshments and other necessaries of life. This material Slang is brutalizing in its effect on the genius of a people, and destructive of the poetic principle which Slang should tend to foster. The "hands" in the barley-harvest are gathered on the porch, awaiting their meridian repast: a comely lassie, neatly clad and redolent with domestic odors, appears at the door. Her approach irradiates the swarthy faces and stolid features of the brown sons of toil; but, by a Circean word, she changes them to swine. What has the neat-handed Phyllis said? But one syllable — a magic one — "Grub." Alas, for the poetry of rural life!

Great is the power of words, and when the power works evil, or the idea is mean and sensual, let the word be unhesitatingly condemned; but when either a new word, or a new application of an old, increases the facility of expression, let us use it, remembering that all precedents were once innovations. Lord Bacon has pronounced it "as well to create a good precedent as to follow one."

Devoted to
THE DEVELOPMENT OF THE COUNTRY
THE OVERLAND MONTHLY
Vol. 5.—July, 1870.—No. 1.

THROUGH THE LOWER COAST COUNTIES

We — my partner and I — had long meditated an expedition to the "lower country," but were not quite ready to set out, when there came along one of those periodic fits of dread of epidemic to which country towns are subject, and forced us to quit business: to speak more correctly, business quit us, and we accordingly hastened our preparations.

The trip was to be a pure *pasear;* and we fondly introduced that charming word into discourse as often as we could, believing it to signify a sort of saunter on horseback, with unlimited liberty of deviation. According to our own theory, we were to become, for the time, a species of mounted vagabond, wandering at our own sweet will, yet always southward, and finding grass and water in abundance wherever we might wish to camp. The advantages of this method of travel are manifest to those who have never tried it: its evils we were to discover for ourselves.

Simple preparations are easily made. Horses were soon obtained at so low a price that we were almost ashamed to ride them, though we afterward found that it was far above their real value. The beasts were of the true California breed, and of the variety known as *plug*. That chosen by my comrade was a corpulent horselet, of a grayish color, beautifully dotted with the russet specks popularly supposed to resemble the marks of insect ravage, but in reality illuminating the surface like so many pustules of sunshine. The spirit of the animal was equal to his symmetry. I myself was doomed daily to surmount a Gothic structure of animated bones, the exterior of which was of a very uncertain hue. The bill of sale affirmed it to be *coyote;* and as I could not assert its likeness to any thing else, I was content to consider it *coyote*. Like the steed of Sir Hudibras,

> "The beast was sturdy, large, and tall,
> with mouth of meal, and eyes of wall."

And, according to the representations of his vender, his moral character was all that could be desired, though that worthy and conscientious dealer (after the transfer had been completed) enjoined certain cautions as to the peculiar mode of approach, and the special order of saddling and bridling, which the idiosyncrasies of the poor brute would render necessary.

Our baggage consisted almost entirely of provisions, and our camp-equipage of coffee-pot and tin-cups, which, with a soft, aromatic jingle, swung pendulous from my cantle; while a large camp-axe — which we were green enough to think needful — adorned the pommel, and finely illustrated to the beholder the similarity of appearance between the ancient crusader and the modern simpleton. We utterly scorned such Persian apparatus as frying-pan and oven, regarding the former, with its lethal flapjacks — and aided by that preparation of carbonate of potash, rightly called *sceleratus*— as the chief cause of the degeneracy of the American people; while for bread, we had abundance of the "hard-tack" which nourisheth heroes. In an older country, our progress through the village would have afforded a singular spectacle, and attracted canine and juvenile attention; but here we were wholly unnoticed.

The *pasear* began on one of the latter days of October, in early morning, while the fog was yet hanging, like a great drop-curtain, stretched between the mountains. From the town we were leaving, the road, by a gradual ascent, led to the foot-hills of the Santa Cruz Range, and steadily on with an increased grade to the mountains proper, up the rugged sides of which it seemed fairly to climb until it rested in the shadow of the giant redwoods. Occasional flowers still lingered in sheltered places, spared by the heat which had embrowned all the verdure of the valley: snowdrops there were, and roses in profusion; a species of wild honeysuckle occurred more rarely, with a flaming flower of unknown name, and a most delicate and fringe-like gorse. A short distance beyond the summit, with its inevitable tollgate, we came in sight of the sea. Far below us lay the open roadstead, which forms the north side of Monterey Bay, glowing warmly in the sunshine, and sending silver threads inland. Along the shores, straggling hamlets and isolated farm-houses lent variety to the picture, still further relieved by oak-groves and groups of hills in the near foreground. Lingering to enjoy the scene, we descended very slowly; then, deflecting southward, crossed the Pajaro, just as the tired sun was flinging himself into the ocean-fogs. Darkness found us near a ferry-house on an estuary of the bay, where we encamped, finding a *corral* and hay for our horses, and plenty of room outdoors for ourselves.

There is a sort of strange pleasure in sleeping again *sub Jove frigido*, after a listless life beneath man's wooden roofs, though one sinks into but a slight and fragile slumber when he has the continuous roar of the surf for a lullaby, and retains a dim and dreamy consciousness of every sound, from the faint rustle of the grass moved by the night-wind, to the monotonous *honk* of the wild-geese flying above: not to speak of a subdued, but anti-narcotic apprehension of centipedes, and the like.

Crossing in the ferry-boat next morning, a novel sight greeted my inland-bred eyes, as a seal popped up near by, regarding us with a degree of curiosity which did great credit to his intelligence, and looking for all the world like a bullet-headed little old gentleman with side-whiskers. He did not, however, remain long subject to inspection, but disappeared as suddenly as he had come. Before reaching Castroville, the road suddenly turns from the ocean, and tame and dreary downs fill the prospect on all sides. A new-looking wooden town stands where, but a few years ago, the solitude of the flats was all unbroken, and evinces a power of growth which elsewhere — even in our growing county — might be deemed wonderful; yet, a little farther on, Salinas furnished its parallel. Just beyond the latter place, we entered the extensive plain of the same name, covered with dry bunch-grass — a very unpromising kind of forage, yet relished by our horses, in whom exercise had developed alarming symptoms of starvation. Having resolved that pasturage was both excellent and abundant, we determined that our animals should "subsist on the country," even if we should be compelled to compensate for their light diet by giving them easy stages.

Early rising — doubtless a virtuous habit at all times — even becomes almost pleasant when one rises from a hard and uncomfortable, albeit romantic, bed. So at least it seemed, as our household affairs had been attended to before the sun appeared. We had breakfasted and were enjoying a smoke, when a visitor appeared — a stalwart, grizzled Ishmael — with a pack of dogs, palpably of the "yaller" variety, close at his heels. He was hunting ahead of his wagons, and thought he would drop in to inquire the news. Being very communicative, he at once proceeded to impart his past history. "I've ben movin,'" said he, "mighty nigh onto ten year, and 'spect to keep on movin' till I peg out." He was a veritable nomad, with all his wealth in his "train," which presently came up. I would have learned much more of this venerable man, had he not been admonished by a shrill voice (with a ring of absolute power in its tone) from the hindmost wagon, to "Stop his jawin,' and come along," which he accordingly did. Frequent encounters with emigrant-wagons form a notable feature of travel along any of the main lines of road. All we saw, however, were going in the same direction — southward. Our visitor was not, properly speaking, and emigrant, but rather a "mover" — one of that restless class, never content to remain long enough in a place to realize the fruits of his labors, and whose chief ambition is to "squat" on some piece of vacant land until he can sell his possessory claim to the owner of the title who will often suffer himself to be thus black-mailed, in order to avoid the litigation necessary to oust the squatter.

On across the Salinas plain, with the cheerful prospect of water only twenty-three miles ahead. The plain looked like an arid waste, the brown grass scarcely promising the cattle a respite from starvation; yet it was dotted on all sides with herds and flocks seemingly in good condition. For more than twenty miles north of the river not a single house appeared, and for a like distance south the only settlement was a stage-station. The river itself — a clear, but narrow stream, except during the rainy season — flows through a wide bed of sand, and between shores sparsely wooded for a short distance from its banks.

There being no pasturage near the river, we were compelled to seek it farther on. Carrying water on horseback, in a coffee-pot, may be picturesque, but I did not find it pleasant. At length, we found grass at a distance of about four miles, and made our *bivouac* under shelter of a plateau which rose to the westward, and in the midst of great numbers of vicious-looking Spanish cattle, which seemed to regard our proceedings with considerable interest. Here an unforeseen difficulty presented itself: no wood was in sight — not a tree, nor even a bush large enough to furnish timber for educational purposes; but Adolphus, fertile in expedients, and mindful of travel across the Plains, soon discovered a substitute, and we were enabled to prepare our frugal meal by aid of the fuel which it had pleased God, through the instrumentality of his meaner creatures, to scatter in profusion around us. What a wise and bountiful provision of Nature! Here, for the first time, I heard the *coyote*, and even saw the pale-green glare of his hungry eyes, as he hovered round at a respectful distance, attracted, doubtless, by the fragrant fumes of bacon. A furled banner of cloud — white, with smoke-tinted edges — hung between two peaks opposite our hill-side, and the moon rose grandly behind it, just in time to send with us to dream-land a bright picture of earth, as, heedless of Egyptian blight, we fell asleep beneath its rays.

On the following morning some of the disadvantages attendant on *pasearing* began to manifest themselves: want of water, frosty picket-ropes, intractable horses. My steed particularly distinguished himself by the extent and variety of his antics, and received on the spot — knighted on the field, as it were — the name of "Tribulation." (The gray had previously been christened "Socrates," from his personal pulchritude and philosophic temperament.) I began to realize the value of the treasure I had acquired, and to consider myself the possessor of an historic horse, being fully persuaded that he had long been known to fame. Bred by a Mr. Thompson, he became famous at an early age. Regarding his subsequent career, I can only conjecture that he was sold by that gentleman to some Celestial, who had enameled his left hind-quarter with several moral sentences from Confucius, which were still distinctly legible when I purchased him. Native horses are, at best, ungentle brutes —

though hardy, easily subsisted, and good travelers — and our hacks were among the worst specimens of the race.

Though the temperature of the morning had been rather cold, by noon the heat became almost oppressive — as it sometimes does, even in our climate — and we skirted along the dry river-bed, until we were nearly persuaded that the final parching-up had come and caught us away from home. At length, a long line of green bushes was descried ahead, and hailed as a sure indication of water; but, when we reached it, proved a row of large trees growing at the bottom of a deep crevice, extending for miles across the plain, and looking for all the world like a great crack in the baked earth in summer-time. Here a cruel suggestion of mint-juleps almost drove one of us to distraction, increasing thirst by mental *mirage*. But water was found at last — a running, or rather trickling stream, in what I have since learned to call a *cienaga*. Here, staking our horses on the green grass, we sat down, in helpless verdancy, to see them eat, when, by going up a few yards on the "bench," we would have found the ground covered with clover-burr: indeed, our animals had almost starved before we discovered that the burr was fit food for them.

After a rest, we entered a narrow valley between mountains, green on the one hand with bushes and, on the other, tawny with a furze-like grass. Live-oaks adorned the road-side with their dark-green foliage, and the duller white-oak, already speckled with dead leaves; there was laurel, too, along the foot of the mountains, with its rayed white flowers, like a mustang-magnolia, and a kind of Spanish moss — greenish, and shorter and slighter than the great trailers which festoon the southern forests. In the midst of the valley ran a stream margined with verdure, dotted with flowers, butter-cups in shape and cow-slips in color. Lured into a forgetfulness of time and distance, and shaded from the sun, we found ourselves ascending a divide, without much chance of reaching a camping-place on the other side before dark, yet too far to return; with horses both jaded and saturnine. After mistaking stage-lamps for camp-fires, and blundering into all the gullies in that region, we at last reached a *tienda,* in a state of indignant exhaustion. Here barley might be obtained, as well as whisky — villainous enough, as my comrade averred, "to kill all a man's relations;" but we were loth to depart from the programme, or to give up our cherished theory. We consulted our friend Ishmael, who had encamped near by, like a land-Noah, "with his wife and his sons, and his sons' wives," and many varieties of living things besides. In reply to an inquiry whether any pasture was to be found thereabout, the patriarch promptly answered, "Not a d — — bit; in fact, I might say, scarcely any." Compensated for the unpleasant news by the novel definition, we cheerfully purchased the barley.

During the whole of the next day our road led among low hills, evidently belonging to sheep-ranches, and grazed bare, affording no relief to the eye anywhere, except in the rose-patches, still green and finely mottled with scarlet seed-pods and large, wax-like snowdrops, contrasting like the mingled holly and mistletoe of Christmas decorations.

We found the San Antonio quite dry at the first crossing-place; yet, eight or ten miles higher up, it seemed a very respectable stream. Some of our California rivers are very like didapper ducks: going down and coming up just when and where they please. All day long, we kept up a fusillade with pistols at the quails, which fairly covered the hill-sides; and so on almost every subsequent day of our journey. His jaunty crest and more highly colored plumage give our quail the advantage over his Eastern congener; but I am inclined to think the superiority ceases with life, as his flesh is somewhat less juicy and delicate. This, considering the fact that he is esteemed as a California production, is rather surprising and difficult to understand.

On the following day, while passing over a very high range of hills, I discovered by the road-side a thicket of rough bushes, with dark-red bark and berries, the latter a little larger than the old-fashioned haws, and appearing so edible to the eye that, after making a short nuncupative will, I ventured to test their toxical qualities. As I consumed a considerable number, not only without ill-effect, but with positive relish, finding them of a pleasant, acrid taste, they were, doubtless, *manzanita*.

Crossing the Nascimiento, we entered San Luis Obispo County about noon, and left Monterey decidedly impressed with its extent, which is larger than that of several principalities of the old World, and more than one State of the New, and embraces within its area all kinds of soil and several distinct ranges of climate. A few miles beyond, we were caught by rain—the first of the season. The whole earth seemed to rejoice, and the brown dust to rise in impatient greeting to the first drops. I had never before been so struck with the apparent sensation of material objects. From a low range of hills the descent is easy to the old Mission of San Miguel, now deserted and desecrated—a *tienda* and stable being the only marks of human habitation. Yet it was once an outpost of Christian civilization and the home of a wealthy, though small and, perhaps, oppressive community. The ground must have been extensive, as the traces of their limits still show. The general plan remains visible, though the buildings have been almost wholly destroyed. But the incessant rain gave us no great facility for exploration, and we rode on, thoroughly discontented, past San Marcos, and turned aside through the open woods to seek a suitable place for making a night of it as best we might. We found it somewhere on the Paso Robles Rancho. Wood in plenty was furnished by the gnarled branches which lay around, riven from the trees by their own weight; but it proved a very sullen sort of fuel until coaxed by the sacrifice of a favorite book, which had been brought along with some vague idea of a possible want of something to read. Had it not been for that volume, no fire would have been kindled *that* night. As soon, however, as we began to feel somewhat independent of the elements, the rain ceased out of pure chagrin, as it seemed, and blankets were speedily spread under an oak; then, with a great fire blazing and crackling at our very feet, and silvering the pendent rain-drops and the hoary moss-beards swinging to and fro, we looked up through the twisted branches at the troubled sky, with its great patches of starry blue, and fell asleep.

To rise on a cloudy, murky morning from a spider-haunted slumber and find his horses lost, causes a sensation more romantic than delightful to the traveler. When after exploring an indefinite extent of territory, he at last catches them again — as we did ours — his pleasure is not without the important element of surprise. But a difficult problem arose from the necessity of finding the way back to camp. In an openly wooded country all trees look alike, and neither sky nor earth gave us the slightest indication. At last we blundered back somehow, and were, soon after, at Hot Springs, parboiling ourselves in pursuit of knowledge, with the temperature at 110° Fahrenheit, and emerged from the bath no longer skeptical on the subject of the deliverance of St. John.

On this day we bade a final farewell to the Salinas, along which we had been occasionally traveling for several days. The volume of water was much larger than where we had first crossed it, far below in its course, but the valley had narrowed to almost nothing — only a gorge serving as channel for the mountain streams. A succession of live-oak groves marked the route to Santa Margarita — a rolling land, beautifully wooded and well fenced, stretching for miles on both sides of the road, and looking not unlike ill-kept pleasure-grounds; and this, too, when the grass was "dry, and brown, and sere," — when all vegetation seemed to have felt the withering touch of summer: what may it not be in the beauty of spring? At night-fall — relying on false information of grass at a short distance — we persevered, and found mountains instead — the Santa Lucia; once among them it was vain to return — so we kept right on. It is but just to ourselves as a people, to remark that our deceitful informant was an Irishman. Californians are, of course, a model of Arcadian simplicity and rigid veracity — yet, sometimes, even their computation seems to have little to do with distance. The route lay over a made road, rugged and winding — often along precipitous ledges from which a false step would have been dangerous. Nothing could be seen but the sombre mountain-walls, and the pines fringing them against the sky; but the continuous babble of waters was audible, and we crossed one stream as it leaped forth in a cascade, far down into the darkness, forming a fine accompaniment to our execrations, and filling the night with the music of Nature and solitude. Becoming finally entirely belated, we halted to wait for daylight, and when it had come, descended into the smiling village of San Luis Obispo. This is the first group of houses one meets south of Salinas — a distance of over a hundred miles. Surely, there is room for more people and more homes in this land.

San Luis itself, judging from the number of billiard-saloons, was originally designed for a large population, and will be a city when they are "built up to." At the time of our visit the inhabitants seemed to consist principally of Mexicans, and the houses of *adobes*. Near town we met a queer wagon, with solid wheels — merely sections sawed from some great tree-trunk — and drawn by oxen with the yoke bound to their horns. The driver was a "Greaser," of course, and the whole equipage might be taken as no unfit emblem of Mexican civilization.

The chief attraction San Luis Obispo possessed for me was the old Mission, which casts and air of *quasi* antiquity about the place. Most of the buildings are disused and dilapidated, but the church, and the apartments in its immediate vicinity, are still in good repair. This Mission antedates American Independence by several years, and within its walls the old *padres* may have carelessly read the news, received by way of Spain, of the outbreak of the Revolution — little dreaming that the Anglo-Saxon people skirting the eastern ocean would, in less than a century, cross the wild desert to supplant them in the possession they had taken from the heathen for an inheritance.

A few miles south of the village we found a fine camping-place, beside a quiet stream at the foot of wooded hills; and we were soon enjoying our *café noir* with the marvelous zest which only an outdoor life produces. O, thou soft Sybarite, who requirest sugar in thine, at every station in life's journey, little dreamest thou what pleasure even the prepared insects known as ground coffee may yield to him who has earned his appetite! As evening approached, the stiff sea-breeze rushed furiously and unpleasantly through the gorges of the hills, and the fog began to roll over the summits, like smoke driven back from a long battery of guns. Long before midnight, however, the wind seemed to have spent its force, and all was still as a dead calm. In the night, and alarm was occasioned by the furious snorting of our horses, showing the presence of some exciting object; to us it furnished conclusive evidence of the presence of some wild beast — most likely a lion. But what if it should be a grizzly? As this question got itself asked, I carefully selected a convenient and accessible tree — in order to secure a better view — and then we repaired slowly to the pickets, where we remained until all became quiet again. In the morning we found, not a hundred yards distant from our camp — impressed in the soft sand of the stream-bed — unmistakable proof of a recent visit from a plantigrade wanderer, and vainly regretted the loss of so favorable an opportunity of killing a bear with our pistols.

Thence we traveled through a succession of beautiful and well-watered valleys, separated by low "divides," and shut in by high hills, either sparsely wooded or densely overgrown with *chemisal*. We could see no sign of human habitation — though herds of cattle and bands of horses were frequent, feeding on the bountiful clover-burr which forms the pastoral wealth of these valleys. Several *tule*-fringed lakes also met our view, but added nothing to the scenery, though they are doubtless picturesque enough in the emerald-setting of spring. Leaving these, we passed over bare, sheep-grazed hills, into other valleys — treeless, but well supplied with water. Then, gaining the table-land, we rode for several hours in full — but not very near — view of the ocean, until, by turning to the left, we lost sight of it again. At sunset the eastern mountains assumed a very peculiar appearance: rose-tinted, with the dry grass on their sides all aglow with soft radiance, while the jagged outlines of the cañon-clefts, and the scar-like traces of old land-slides, had the effect of gramarye. One could easily fancy that guardian *genie* had written in these weird runes the cabalistic announcement of hidden treasure. Then, wild-geese overhead, flying westward, their breasts bathed in the golden glow of the sunshine, already lost to us earth-dwellers — their voices faintly heard "falling dreamily through the sky" — brought to the hour another charm. After nightfall the wind again arose, and blowed disagreeably, but, before day, every thing was calm again.

We were awakened in the morning by the chattering of magpies, which appeared in countless numbers, and showed an entire disregard of our presence. I tried a shot at one, but as I had heard the flesh pronounced totally uneatable, missed him.

The Cuyamas River forms the boundary between the counties of San Luis Obispo and Santa Barbara. We found it a very small stream of muddy water, threading its way through a wide bed of sand. The valley showed an unpromising aspect, despite its reputation for fertility. The grass had been burned off, in anticipation of rain, which had failed to fall, and the bare earth lay charred beneath the pitiless sun. Here and there were scattered around numbers of those shantiform specimens of rural architecture which indicate recent "locations" by squatters. Some eight or ten miles up the river, an old sycamore tempted us to halt. The whirl of its falling leaves and the rustle of those fallen, brought back recollections of the Indian summer of our old homes. We had, by this time, entirely lost our way, on account of a rigid adherence to the map, and the variety of trails frequently occurring together. But it made little difference, as we knew the general direction, and cared nothing for time. Resuming our journey up the valley, we took the route which seemed nearest the proper course, leading southward beside a small and winding steam. Houses became frequent, and appeared neat and home-like, though small. Here we were overtaken by a Greaser boy, on his way to the *tienda* for the paternal supply of *aguadiente* [*sic*]. Him we assailed with successive volleys of book-Spanish, until a desultory conversation ensued. Being young and ignorant, he directed us rightly, and his historic name of Olivarez remains gratefully treasured up in memory. We had been skirting the foot of the San Rafael Mountains, and continued to follow their general direction, until we found a camping-place in a spot finely timbered with oak, and thronged with pigeons: these were larger than the familiar wild-pigeon of the "States," but doubtless a variety of the same species. Hence, we altered our course, and, by once more consulting our map, and carefully avoiding its precepts, we were enabled, after a half-day's wandering, to regain the stage-road, near the Mission of Santa Inez. A noble situation and picturesque view, combined with evident richness of soil and natural facilities for cultivation, here evince the taste, as well as the judgment, of the founders. A village of the same name stands somewhere in the vicinity, and a little farther on flows the Santa Inez River — almost as large as the Salinas, and with water of a crystal clearness; then, as if to exhaust entirely the resources of the name, the Santa Inez Mountains present themselves — a lofty range, and covered with dark-green bushes to its very top. A few miles beyond the Mission, the traveler enters Gaviota Pass. A Natural chasm, averaging about seventy-five feet in width, leads through the mountains, emerging within sound, and almost within sight, of the sea. Its sides are formed of walls of solid rock, nearly perpendicular for three hundred feet, and then sloping back steeply until they attain a height of nearly three thousand feet. The opposite faces appear to have been riven asunder to their bases by some great convulsion of Nature — some Titanic throe of the earth. For the distance of a mile the pass is narrow and rugged, and through it leaps and rushes a stream of water, as if trying, with its frequent noisy falls and mimic rock-encircled basins, to relieve, by sound and motion, the oppressive grandeur of gigantic desolation which would else prevail. Beyond the pass, the country is much broken, and consists of a mere strip between the mountains and the sea. In many places a strong bituminous odor pervades the air, and fields of asphaltum disfigure the earth, suggesting unpleasant proximity to subterranean agencies: again, however, herbs emit a minty fragrance, and flowers welcome us to the threshold of the South. It is a glowing land, rightly named *Calida Fornia.** The Santa Inez Range, terminating in Point Concepcion, forms its northern limit, and to this barrier is to be attributed much of the semi-tropical nature of the climate.

*[Original footnote:] If any doubt the correctness of this use of the term Fornia for a district of country, my authority may be found — Dr. Johnson's epitaph on Goldsmith, as given in "Boswell's Life:" " Natus in Hiberniæ Fornia Longfordiensis."]

All day long we rode through a houseless land, fairly alive with rabbits of both sizes, and the higher grounds perforated with gopher-holes. Verily, old Drake, or his chronicler, was correct in saying, "There be manie conies in this land." Occasionally a burrowing owl, startled by the tramp of our horses, would wing his flight back to his boarding-house, where, after pausing to survey us, he would hop into his hole as leisurely as might be; and we saw several *paisanos,* or road-runners — about the swiftest of running birds. The calm sea, clear sky, delightful temperature, islands dimly visible to the south-west — veiled in purple haze — the tumbling porpoises, and seabirds hovering or flitting about the water, all combine to make life like a dream, and the scene like an imagining. In the early morning, the heavens were more gorgeous than I had every seen them — except once, during an aurora: rivers of flame seemed to flow between lilac banks, and all the east was blazoned with heraldry — gold, and gules, and azure. The rising sun burnished away the glory, but replaced it with a stronger, through plainer brightness. The birds awoke, "all little birds that be;" myriad wings were seen fluttering, and myriad voices heard twittering, until the air was full of life and music. Wild-fowl were disporting themselves in a pond near by, and the eye, lifted from their gambols, could catch a glimpse of the stately sheen of ocean through the dark-green foliage. One suddenly awakened would have pronounced the season May. The poet's word came spontaneously to mind. It was

> "A goodly sight to see
> What Heaven hath done for this delicious land."

The towers of the Mission of Santa Barbara soon came in sight. The church is still in use, though built in 1786, and of such perishable materials. All the timbers used in the construction of the buildings are said to have been dragged across the mountains by the native converts; so that this Mission resembles the Taf [*sic*] Mahal, in being raised on a broad base of Indian fret-work. The town itself nestles quietly in a beautiful site, encircled by amphitheatric hills, and looking out on the boundless Pacific. Many of the houses are of *adobes,* giving rather a mean air to a part of the village, though in the American quarter there are pretty and pleasant-looking houses, among trees and flowers. Roses were blooming in profusion at the time of our visit, although it was the middle of November.

Just after leaving Santa Barbara, we overtook an old Mexican, who seemed to cast a longing look upon our camp-axe; so, accosting him and extolling its many useful properties, we intimated that we might be induced to part with it, on account of its weight, and would be content to receive payment in produce. A bargain was soon struck, the Señor contracting to deliver us two feeds each of hay and barley, and inviting us to the spend the night at his *rancho*. The invitation was promptly accepted, and I rejoiced at the long-coveted opportunity of witnessing the domestic life of these people. Our entertainer's family, as I observed at supper, consisted of his wife, a numerous progeny, one of his forefathers, (in whose expressive features I fancied signs of remorse for his part in the torture of Guatimozin) and a bandit-looking guest in a scarlet sash. To these may be added a little red bull, rather *blasé* in appearance, who seemed almost a member of the household. The supper consisted principally of *chile colorado*, and I was forced, out of politeness, to make such a meal as few civilized persons, since the days of Portia, had willingly regaled themselves with. The universal adaptation of *chile* as a condiment is truly astonishing. I am not entirely sure that they do not use it in coffee. The repast over, a conversation with our host elicited from us some very wonderful Spanish — that gentleman's knowledge of English being confined to one word, which he fluently pronounce *stichy,* and, when we confessed a shameful ignorance of our own language, translated by *diligencia*. Don Rafael had lived in California for ten years without making further progress. He had come hither from Sonora, and gave us a pathetic account of the causes of his emigration. These were chiefly *muchos Apaches;* and, I regret to say, the old man showed little Christian charity toward the poor savages, of whom he spoke in very forcible language. But his discourse soon became almost as prolix as the celebrated after-dinner conversation of his celestial namesake with our distinguished ancestor, and the inattention of his guests at length reminded him of the duties of hospitality. Therefore, with grave and ceremonious politeness, he escorted us to our chamber in the hay-stack, and put us to sleep with the bull. Next morning, dreading further torture from *chile,* we left our compliments with our fellow-lodger, and made haste to depart, without seeing our host or any of his family.

Near Rincon, the road descends to the shore and follows the beach for several miles, along the very edge of the water — so near that waves often break at the feet of the horses, and suggest the danger that might accompany any unusual flow of the tide, especially as the heights are in many places inaccessible, and everywhere so to horses. Strewn along the shore may be seen heaps of sea-weed, matted vines — bulbous, and brownish-yellow in color — undergrowth detached from some great submarine forest, and net-like, fibrous masses of tangled grasses, both brown and living-green. I saw none of those delicate and flower-like fringes which are gathered on the Atlantic shore. Perhaps the stimulating effect of our soil and climate on other vegetable productions extends even to the marine *algæ* along our coasts.

As we approached San Buenaventura, we heard a great shouting, accompanied with the blare of horns and a chorus of anvils in *extempore* cannonade; bonfires, too, blazed and flickered in the fitful wind. The native population were holding a wedding-feast with revelry and uproar. They had unfortunately — from some remissness, I suppose — selected the first day of the week for their celebration, and the mistake had not been discovered in time to be remedied.

Picketing the horses in a burnt district beyond town, we generously shared our crackers with them, and spent a cheerful night. At sunrise, we returned to visit the old Mission orchard, and see the wonderful olive and the giant pear-trees, and the three palms — those "strangers brought from burning lands, "and highly suggestive of Oriental fancies. The Mission church here humbly reproduces, in mud, the glories of the Saracenic architecture, though the irreverent swallows have added ornaments not specified in the original design — hundreds of gay, guiltless pairs having stuccoed the *façade* with their nests.

Having obtained the necessary misdirections, we left the main route, and steered our course toward the Santa Clara River, with intent to spend a day of glorious idleness upon its banks. The Santa Clara Valley, without question the loveliest I had seen, was like a haven of rest, lying entirely beyond the influence of the sand-laden wind which had annoyed us all day. The richness of the soil is evident to the eye, and the climate admits of the culture of nearly every thing, not excepting olives and the tropical fruits. Under the afternoon brightness it resemble one of the rich, sun-tinted pictures of Church, while, a little later, the fields of burning mustard raised a dense canopy of smoke, to join with the elemental cloud-muster. The fires burned luridly all night, lighting up the northern hills, and at times surging under the breath of the winds, and by their smoke-crowned expanse of flame — brilliant, but sombre — recalled the scenes of the *Inferno*. A great horned-owl overhead, moralizing on the picture, kept us awake to enjoy it.

Resuming our journey at a late hour, we rode fifteen miles through an undulating country to the outlying hills of the Santa Susanna, wholly ignorant of our relative whereabout to the stage-road, and entirely off the trail. This night we sat by a fire of mustard-wood, and listened to the screaming of the many-named beast, which is here called *lion*. Puma, panther, or cougar, would describe him better. The wild-mustard of this country must be of the Gospel variety, for it grows large enough to afford rest to the birds of the air in its branches. After killing a rabbit for breakfast, we climbed with some difficulty over a range of hills which appeared to be the home of eagles and hawks, (we saw one of the latter with a squirrel in his talons) and descended into another valley, where the ground was even enough to permit us to keep a straight course without a trail. The soil seemed fertile, and clover-burr was very abundant; but old skulls, visible almost everywhere, told the sad story of "the dry year," when even the burr-clover failed to yield its usual harvest. The Santa Susanna Mountains, in the shadow of which we encamped, showed outlines more fantastically shaped than any others I had seen. In the morning, we woke in the presence of the rainy season. Mists clave to the mountains, and the air seemed laden with moisture; then a slow, drizzling rain made it evident that the pleasant part of our journey was at an end, nor had we ridden an hour before the rain began to fall in earnest.

Before leaving camp, where I was afforded an opportunity of studying Spanish in a new form, by hearing a youthful swineherd revile his charge in the most unmeasured and dreadful terms, we had sought a neighboring *ranch-house* for the purpose of addressing letters penciled by the way. A big Mexican (Sancho Panza grown tall) came out to receive us, and with him a dog of ferocious aspect: a sense of personal danger so disconcerted me as to deprive me of the power of selecting my words correctly; and, while meaning to inquire respectfully whether his dog would *bite* or not, I outraged the worthy man's feelings by directing him to *grind* the faithful quadruped. After this failure, I gladly yielded the post of honor to Adolphus, who was less subject to terror. Entering the house, he transacted our business, while I remained without. Upon his return, a fearful interchange of compliments took place, which I noted down on the spot for future use:

(with painful hesitation)—"*Quedo muy agradecido á V., Señor.*"
Sancho Largo—"*Nada gracias, mi buen caballero.*" Then we went on our way rejoicing.

Passing the mountains at San Fernando, we traveled through a series of rough and broken hills, descending thence to the level of the plain and on to *aguas calientes,* where we dolefully waited for morning in the open oak-woods, listening to the melancholy voices of the *coyotes* behowling the moon. They sounded in such numbers that, in attempting to make a rough guess, I estimated them at 17,000,000. My more experienced comrade amended by leaving off the ciphers, and subsequent observations have led me to believe even his estimate an exaggeration.

Resuming our journey through the cold rain, made still drearier by the cloud-fields around the tops of the mountains, or piled in masses at the gorge-mouths, we hailed the first telegraph-poles on the road as evidences of our approach once more to comfort and civilization. Yet we plodded on until night-fall, when the gas-lamps of Los Angeles became visible, and we were soon at the end of our troubles.

Not here shall I essay to describe the impressions which brighter weather brought me of the City of the Angels, as she sits, dowered with wealth and decked with marvelous beauty, throned amid her groves and gardens, undoubted queen of all the southern land.

Notes

Latin and Greek translations and references are by Kenneth Kitchell, classics professor at Louisiana State University. Notes on Johnson's Island Prison are by Roger Long, an authority on the prison and its prisoners. Other notes are by George H. Jones, editor of this book.

Caldwell's Life

1. Most of the information in this chapter comes from Joseph Cookman Nate, *The History of the Sigma Chi Fraternity, 1855–1930*, vol. 4 (Chicago: The Fraternity, 1930). Used with permission.
2. Nate, *History of Sigma Chi Fraternity*, 2.
3. Nate, *History of Sigma Chi Fraternity*, 3.
4. Ibid.
5. Nate, *History of Sigma Chi Fraternity*, 4.
6. Note, Caldwell family archives.
7. Malaria can last a long time. Parks's case continued until 1864, as is well documented. His father, a physician, supplied the quinine, as doctors were also pharmacists at this time.
8. *The Confederate Veteran* 34 (1926): 45.
9. *The Confederate Veteran* 34 (1926): 45.
10. Nate, *History of Sigma Chi Fraternity*, 5.
11. Nate, *History of Sigma Chi Fraternity*, 9.
12. That did occur at Miami University on June 28, 1955, and the editor of this volume was there and spoke with a member who was present at Caldwell's 1905 speech.
13. *Sigma Chi Quarterly* (May 1912): 335.
14. This is a classic symptom of a heart attack.
15. *Sigma Chi Quarterly* (May 1912): 331.

Caldwell the Classicist

1. Within Caldwell's own lifetime, an influential report commissioned by the National Educational Association would recommend the abolishment of this rigid set of requirements. See *Report of the Committee of Ten on Secondary School Studies* (New York: American Book Company, 1894), 62f. Cf. the sample curricula in *Report of the Committee of Twelve of the American Philological Association on Courses in Latin and Greek for Secondary Schools* (Boston: Ginn & Co., 1899), 41.
2. Elvion Owen, "Caesar in American Schools prior to 1860," *Classical Journal* 31 (1935): 212–22.
3. Joseph Cookman Nate, *History of Sigma Chi Fraternity, 1855–1930*, vol. 4 (Chicago: The Fraternity, 1925f.), 3.
4. "Some Account of a Great Western Poet," *Overland Monthly* 2:6 (June 1869): 538–44.
5. Reference to letter in full in book.
6. Phillip R. Shriver and Donald J. Breen, *Ohio's Military Prisons in the Civil War* (Columbus: Ohio State University Press, 1964), 31.
7. The edition in question is H. A. J. Munro, ed., *T. Lucreti Cari, De rerum natura libri sex* (New York: Harper, 1861).

8. John Proudfit, ed., *The Captives: A Comedy of Plautus with English Notes for the Use of Students* (New York: Harper, 1863).

9. Carl J. Richard, *The Founders and the Classics* (Cambridge, Mass.: Harvard University Press, 1994), 19f; Meyer Reinhold, *Classica Americana: The Greek and Roman Heritage in the United States* (Detroit: Wayne State University Press, 1984), 221–49. *Report of the Committee of Ten*, 74; *Report of the Committee of Twelve*, 41.

10. Full citations are to be found in the notes to the diary.

11. That is to say, Euryalus would have been fine if he had not insisted on following his friend out on the night mission.

12. Nate, *History of the Sigma Chi Fraternity*, vol. 4, 6.

13. The version published here is taken verbatim from the facsimile of the sheet music published in 1848 by Millett's Music Salon of New York, reproduced in Richard Jackson, *Stephen Foster Song Book* (New York: Dover, 1974). For a recording, see "The Early Minstrel Show," New World Records, NW 338 Stereo, Number LP 10830, liner notes by Robert Winans (Wayne State).

14. Probably "hoe" cake. Other versions offer "corn" cake.

15. An alternate version offers, "When Uncle Ned died Massah took it very bad, The tears they run down like the rain. Ole Missus turned pale and she gets very sad, Cuz she never see Uncle Ned again."

16. "Iamdudum" in the earlier version of June 30.

17. On June 30, Caldwell wrote "solebat" and then wrote "solitus" above that.

18. As noted in the Latin text, the Latin is troubled here. My thanks to Professor Richard Warga, whose combination of expertise in Latin, paleography, and folk music was invaluable in deciphering parts of this poem. The line might also be translated, "His eyes were worn out from seeing."

19. Johann Matthias Gesner, *Novus linguae et eruditionis Romanae thesaurus* (Leipzig: Casp. Fritschii viduae et Bernh. Chr. Breitkopfii, 1749).

20. The text of the letter was supplied by George Jones, the editor of this volume, and appears to be a clipping from the newspaper, preserved by the Caldwell family.

21. The *Overland Monthly* began publication in 1868. A careful search of the three volumes that precede the date of the letter reveal that Caldwell was exaggerating here, apparently keeping up the joking nature of the piece.

22. Atellan farce was a popular but somewhat rude form of entertainment in ancient Rome.

23. Plutarch, *Life of Marius*, 40.5–9.

24. My great thanks to Professor Wallace McKenzie of Louisiana State University, who, on the barest of clues, pointed me to the original of the poem. The song is fully discussed by Richard Jackson, *Popular Songs of Nineteenth-Century America* (New York: Dover, 1976), 280–81. Jackson refutes any Civil War existence for the song and discusses its authorship.

25. He used "Lucifer" in the *Ad Patriae Vexillum*.

26. Nate, *History of the Sigma Chi Fraternity*, vol. 4, 12–13.

The Diaries

January 1864

1. The prison barracks were similar to barns, two-story, whitewashed frame buildings, with outside wooden stairways that led to the wide street.

2. That is, twenty degrees below zero.

3. Exact weather observations were not kept officially at that time, but various prisoner diaries generally agree with the temperatures indicated by Caldwell. According to prisoner memoirs written years later, it was even more frigid. With a stiff wind off Lake Erie, it certainly seemed colder, especially in barracks without insulation and short on firewood.

4. "Hodie frigoris dies est congelare testes simiae aeneae." "Today is cold enough to freeze the balls off a brass monkey." Although the writing is smudged, the reading is secure. The image of the learned Caldwell, huddled in bed against the cold, shakily writing this familiar bit of ribaldry in Latin is one of the earliest, but certainly not the last, glimpses we get of the intense humanity of his diary. This bit of scurrility is fairly uncharacteristic of Caldwell.

5. The escapees were from Block 10. Capt. W.M. Boyd of Virginia surrendered without making it off the island. The other

five escapees, led by Maj. John R. Winston of North Carolina, scaled the fence with a makeshift ladder and made it across the frozen bay to the Marblehead Peninsula. Lt. John Stakes of Virginia became separated from the others and was recaptured next morning at a farmhouse. The other four were Winston, Capt. Charles C. Robinson of Virginia, Capt. Thomas H. Davis of Virginia, and a possibly misidentified Capt. McConnell of Kentucky. The latter was forced to give up after two days in the cold. But the remaining three crossed the Detroit River into Canada, opposite Trenton, Michigan, and returned to the Confederate States through the blockade.

6. William Shakespeare. *Othello*, act 2, scene 1.

7. There were several Confederate officers named Taylor at Johnson's Island during this period. Caldwell occasionally refers to fellow prisoners by sobriquets he has coined but does not say why. This may be an example. Nicolas Chauvin was supposedly a soldier with a fanatic devotion to his commander, Napoleon, and to France. From this proper name is derived chauvinism, meaning excessively patriotic.

8. Caldwell's roommate in Block 5, Lt. Matthew Manley, 2nd North Carolina.

9. The proscribed length of all prisoner letters was one page of ordinary size containing no more than twenty-eight lines of handwriting. However, at the time Caldwell wrote this, longer letters could be sent if the prisoner was willing to pay extra to have the censors read them. The meaning here is clearly that Caldwell had written a letter of longer than one page.

10. Mollie Moon, the sister of the girl with whom Caldwell was in love, Ginny Moon. Mollie was ten years older than Caldwell.

11. Apparently Caldwell had received an express box of food before beginning his diary and presumably from family members in Hamilton, Ohio. The latest delivery of express boxes, according to other prisoner diaries, was on Christmas Day, 1863.

12. *Sandusky Commercial Register* or just *The Register* was a Republican newspaper, the only daily to which prisoners had full access.

13. The fruit of the grapevine, thus, rumor.

14. Another military prison for Confederates. Point Lookout was in Maryland.

15. Lord Mahon, Philip Stanhope, 1805–1875, an English historian; Lord Thomas Babington Macaulay, 1800–1859, best known for his *History of England* in five volumes; Clive of India, founder of the Empire of British India; Thomas Carlyle, 1795–1881, Scottish essayist and historian.

16. Caldwell's description of many-tongued rumor betrays his love of the classics, for he is paraphrasing Vergil's *Aeneid*, 4.175f., where the poet creates a brilliant picture of rumor, "Fama," as it runs about Carthage spreading the word about Dido's dalliance with Aeneas. Vergil describes Fama as a sort of feathered creature abounding with eyes and ears to gather information, and an equal number of mouths and tongues with which to spread abroad what it knows.

17. Maj. Joseph H. Saunders, 33rd North Carolina, had been severely wounded in the face during Pickett's Charge at Gettysburg. He was left for dead on the battlefield. Certain that he was lost, Saunders's family held a funeral at his home in Chapel Hill. Then a letter from Saunders at Johnson's Island reached his mother. He was a North Carolina farmer for many years after the war.

18. This may be another of Caldwell's unexplained nicknames for a fellow Confederate. When a prisoner went to the hospital at Block 6, his friends took turns acting as nurses.

19. Lt. S.P. Dougherty, 33rd Tennessee. Prisoners were led to believe they could be released immediately if they signed an oath of allegiance to the United States. Several tried to do so, with disastrous results. Dougherty was so badly treated that he had to be removed from the Bull Pen, lest prisoners kill him. Paroled on the island, he went to Sandusky without permission and was caught there. From jail he wrote a pitiful letter to Col. William S. Pierson, prison commandant, and was finally released as a harmless man.

20. An express box that had been sent to Caldwell.

21. In rolls and autograph books, Caldwell listed his residence as Panola, Mississippi, although he was a member of Watson's battery, a Louisiana command. He was in the Mississippi forces that were decimated at Shiloh, Tennessee, also known as Battle of Pittsburgh Landing, on April 6 and 7, 1862. This was a major battle of the Civil War in

which there were heavy casualties on both sides. The Confederates lost and retreated to Corinth, Mississippi. Caldwell later joined the Watson Battery of Louisiana. Thus "my state" refers to Mississippi. Clearly he no longer considered his native state, Ohio, his home.

22. William Shakespeare, *Antony and Cleopatra*, act 1, scene 5. Mandragora is a southern European plant with a branched root, once believed to have magical or soporific powers in a drink.

23. Water for drinking and cooking was usually supplied by two pumps near the Bull Pen fence facing Sandusky Bay. During very cold weather, the pipes froze. Then water had to be carried from a hole cut in the ice on the bay itself. Prisoners were occasionally allowed out in small lots, under guard, to secure bucketfuls of water.

24. The escape of Lt. Col. William H. Luse, 18th Mississippi, was mentioned in many prisoner diaries. Col. Pierson, the commandant, charged Luse's sutler account $10 for the expense of bringing him back from Newark, about 130 miles south of Sandusky. Prison officials tried unsuccessfully to determine Luse's method of escape. In time, several other prisoners, also dressed in Union uniform, would go off the island, and a few would make it back to the Confederacy.

25. Caldwell seems to have had little interest in religion. There were well-attended prayer meetings and preaching virtually every day throughout the prison. Several ministers had large flocks. Despite being surrounded by religious exercises, Caldwell seldom makes mention of them.

26. Confederate Maj. Gen. John S. Bowen was captured at the fall of Vicksburg, July 4, 1863. He was paroled but contracted dysentery and died on July 13, 1864, near Raymond, Mississippi.

27. William Shakespeare, *Hamlet*, act 1, scene 2.

28. Letter in Appendix dated January 15, 1864. This letter was saved by the family and given to William Smart sometime in the late 1940s, with this note on the stationery of the James Parks Caldwell Chapter of the United Daughters of the Confederacy, Chapter of Beverly Hills, California: "From the small packet of letters I'm sending a few out to you boys — for Uncle Parks took a great interest in young Sigma Chis who made a veritable shrine of his resting place in the old French Cemetery [sic] in Biloxi. Best wishes, I. C. J. Davis" [Isabella Caldwell Jones Davis, a niece of Caldwell's].

29. Union Brig. Gen. Alexander Shaler's brigade, Sixth Corps, Army of the Potomac. One of the regiments, the 122nd New York, would remain in Sandusky. The others (23rd and 82nd Pennsylvania, and 65th New York) were quartered on the island, near the prison. At this point Col. Pierson was effectively replaced as commandant by Shaler, with Brig. Gen. Henry D. Terry, headquartered at Sandusky, as the commander of all Union troops in the vicinity. The escape of the Winston party on January 1, plus the realization that in midwinter the prison was no longer on an island, precipitated the change.

30. William Shakespeare, *Hamlet*, act 1, scene 1 [paraphrase].

31. "forsan et haec olim meminisse juvabit." This is one of the more famous quotes from Vergil's *Aeneid* (1.203). Caldwell is most apt in putting it here. Translated, "Perhaps someday it will be pleasant to recall even these things." The words were said by Aeneas as a way to comfort his men after a shipwreck, when they were quite demoralized and all hope seemed lost. Aeneas, of course, went on to found a great new country at Rome, a hope surely not lost on Caldwell.

32. Johnson's Island mud was (and still is) all but legendary. The shallow clay soil over flat, Devonian limestone did not drain well, despite the fact that several ditches were dug, all leading toward the bay. Thousands of prisoners and guards tramping around in the area did not improve the situation. Planks and stone put down as paths were simply swallowed in the deep mire. Barracks floors were covered with the stuff, carried in on shoes.

33. The Hoffman Battalion, now expanded to ten companies and designated as the 128th Ohio Volunteer Infantry, would remain as guards on Johnson's Island and never be sent to the front. Prisoners, as might be expected, did not like the men of the Hoffman Battalion, many of whom were recent German immigrants. Members of Shaler's brigade were more respected, if only because they had fought as soldiers. Maj. Gen. George G. Meade was at the time commander of the Army of the Potomac, then at winter quarters in Virginia.

34. Novel by Charlotte Bronte.
35. Gavroche was a boy of the Paris streets in Victor Hugo's novel, *Les Miserables*. In this case Gavroche apparently applies to Lt. Manley, Caldwell's roommate and chess partner.
36. The heroine in *Les Miserables*.
37. By his sad fiancé.
38. William Shakespeare, *The Merchant of Venice*, act 4, scene 1.
39. Apparently added by Caldwell later.
40. This would be Virginia (Ginny) Moon.
41. Pen name of Bryan Waller Proctor, 1787–1874. Writer of popular sentimental poems.
42. "Iam satis terris nivis atque dirae, Grandinis miset Pater," The source of the quote is Horace *Odes* 1.2.1 and once more is very apt. These words represent the beginning of the poem, whose opening line reads, "Father Jupiter has sent enough of dire snow and hail onto the land." The poem was commonly read and memorized by students. Caldwell uses it here as a fitting commentary for the weather on Johnson's Island in January.
43. This rheumatism began in youth and continued throughout his life, incapacitating him in later years.
44. W.B. is Watson Battery (Louisiana) of which Caldwell was a member. Grenada and Vaiden are towns in Mississippi.
45. Historical novel with a Bavarian setting by Baroness Von Tautphoeus, who was Irish but married to the chamberlain to the King of Bavaria. In novels considered to be charming, she set out to explain German ways to the British reading public.
46. Lt. Col. Robert Bullock, 7th Florida.
47. Brig. Gen. James J. Archer, captured at Gettysburg, the first general in Lee's Army of Northern Virginia to be taken by Union forces.
48. The "upper-endions" were those from Blocks 1 to 5 along with Block 7. Block 6 was the prison hospital and did not count. The "lower-endions" were prisoners in Blocks 8 to 13. Caldwell, a resident of block 5, was an "upper-endion."
49. Capt. John R. Fellows of Arkansas, on the staff of Brig. Gen. William N. R. Beall. Years after the war, Fellows would be the district attorney for the city of New York.
Lt. Col. Junius I. Scales, 30th Mississippi; Col. Michael L. Woods, 46th Alabama; Lt. Col. Levin M. Lewis, 7th Missouri. Lewis was a much respected Methodist preacher, promoted to brigadier general in Trans-Mississippi sector after Appomattox. Obviously his field promotion was not approved by the Confederate Congress, then spread to the winds. Col. Charles C. Blacknall, 23rd North Carolina. Blacknall was severely wounded in the mouth and captured at Gettysburg. Promoted from major to lieutenant colonel, then colonel, while a prisoner. He was exchanged in March 1864 and killed at Winchester, Virginia, on September 19, 1864. Brig. Gen. Meriwether Jeff Thompson, Missouri State Guard, was one of the most colorful figures of the Civil War, despite the fact that he had few merits as a soldier. His memoirs, begun at Johnson's Island, were published in 1988.
50. Col. G. Troup Maxwell, 1st Florida Cavalry (dismounted), was a distinguished professor of medicine before and after the war. He is credited with having invented the laryngoscope. On most days while at Johnson's Island, he could be found in the prison hospital, tending to patients.
51. According to other Johnson's Island diaries, several prisoners were so badly wounded in the snowball fighting that they had to be treated at the hospital.
52. Prisoners took turns at doing the necessary chores for each block or barracks. The chores included cooking, carrying water, cutting wood, etc. Each morning the guards brought in axes and bucksaws for cutting firewood into lengths that would fit the stoves. The tool would then be picked up before dark. Wagons or sleds brought in large trunks and limbs from trees, and prisoners had to saw and split them.
53. "Dixie" mail was, as the name implies, from the Confederate States. Flag-of-truce boats exchanged mail bags, usually on the James River south of Richmond. Caldwell had no problem in sending letters to his family in southern Ohio, but writing to and receiving letters from his friends in Mississippi meant the correspondence had to go by "Dixie" mail. In addition to being slow, the process had other complications. U.S. Mails would not carry letters with only Confederate stamps affixed. Thus, people in the South had to secure U.S. postage as well as Confederate. Getting U.S. stamps was a problem

solved by prisoners enclosing the stamps with letters South. Often these uncanceled stamps were "lost" by Federal censors. At times prisoners were allowed to receive "Dixie" letters on a postage-due basis, i.e., without the U.S. stamp, but this privilege was sometimes withdrawn.

54. Libby was a prison for Union soldiers at Richmond. Several books had been published by released Libby prisoners, claiming that it was a hell-hole.

55. Verb sat. is a common abbreviation for an old Latin saw, "verbum sapientibus satis est," "A word to the wise is sufficient." Its original form, from the playwright's Plautus and Terence, was "dictum sapientibus." But in early textbooks, the less common "dictum" was changed to "verbum."

56. A thick and very hard cracker molded of wheat flour and water. A standard joke of the period was that a soldier once found a soft spot in the hard tack. It turned out to be a nail.

57. Probably Lt. H. Holland, 28th Virginia.

58. Lt. Col. Henry Carrington, 3rd Virginia Cavalry, and Capt. Robert McCulloch, 18th Virginia.

59. Another prison for Confederates on Delaware Bay.

60. "Credat Judaeus Apella, non Ego." Horace, *Satires* 1.5.100–101, "Let Apella the Jew believe that, not me." The words quite harsh to today's ears, stem from Roman anti–Semitism. The Romans believed the Jews to be very superstitious and this proverbial saying implies that a sophisticated race, such as the Romans, would never think things such as the Jews believe. It is interesting to note that recently, in the film *Tombstone*, one erudite gunfighter quoted the line, in Latin, to another.

61. Long narrative poem by Owen Meredith (Robert, Lord Lytton).

62. Coleridge, *The Ancient Mariner.*

63. Sir Walter Scott novels.

February 1864

1. Unless prisoners were sick in their bunks or had another good excuse, they were required to line up in front of their block each morning while the roll was called by Federal guards. Having bad shoes would not normally have been considered a sufficient reason to miss this exercise.

2. Capt. Alexander Moseley, 2nd Florida, like Caldwell a resident of Block 5. Although civilian visitors to the island were expressly prohibited, numerous exceptions were made, a few by President Lincoln personally.

3. In three volumes, published in 1841 by Samuel Warren, who held the "Mastership of Lunacy" for his most famous of all novels about the law and lawyers.

4. Patrial. From my father.

5. From the symptoms described, Caldwell was suffering from malaria, probably contracted in Louisiana.

6. Capt. Simeon E. Hamilton, 2nd Choctaw Cavalry, died of erysipelas. He was quite mad near the end of his life and once went screaming from the hospital onto the prison boulevard. See Caldwell's diary entry of June 4, 1864, for a description of the special wooden headboard erected for Hamilton. The diagnosis of erysipelas was made by observation. It was known as "Indian fire" in the 1930s (although it had nothing to do with Indians) and is now called a staph infection. Soap and water and support usually healed the patient then and an antibiotic does so now.

7. So far as can be determined, Maj. R.J. Durr was not a recognized physician.

8. William Shakespeare, *The Tempest,* act 4, scene 1.

9. The dose today is 5 grams, six times a day, for 10 days, sometimes supplemented by antibiotics. Thus, the 23-gram dose is not out of line. It should be kept in mind that the strength of quinine was variable. The ten-day therapy apparently was not followed.

10. *Psalms,* 116:11.

11. Capt. William N. Berkeley, 8th Virginia. Despite the strict ban on alcoholic beverages, the more devious prisoners always found a way around the rules. In 1862 and 1863, the prison sutler was a frequent supplier — until he was arrested. However, at the time Caldwell made this entry, the only sources would have been a guard or the hospital steward. The latter is most likely. All express boxes to prisoners were opened and checked for contraband, with any whiskey going to the hospital. The steward may have made a trade: whiskey for a prisoner's valuable watch, for example.

12. Lt. W.R. Bond of Gen. Daniel's staff; Lt. W.W. Apperson, 5th Texas Cavalry.

13. Capt. Frank Battle, 20th Tennessee.

14. Caldwell, of course, did not go, although it is not clear why, since he fit all the criteria. Thus, the escape plan on foot was never tried. Two prisoners did escape by jumping off the railroad cars while they were moving through the Pennsylvania mountains. Frank Battle was not one of the escapees. The rest of the Confederates aboard went to Point Lookout prison. A few would be exchanged shortly, while still others were sent on to Fort Delaware prison. Some became members of the Immortal 600. (These six hundred men were moved to Morris Island, South Carolina, where they were placed in an open-air cramped stockade as a human shield in front of the Union batteries at the siege of Charleston.) The plan had been to remove a good many more from Johnson's Island, but the boat had a difficult time crashing through the ice to Sandusky, and the next day the bay was frozen solid again.

15. Capt. William Barnes, 9th Battery, Georgia Artillery. Caldwell's bunkmate was Maj. Joseph Saunders of North Carolina.

16. Mother of Cosette in *Les Miserables*, although it is unclear what this had to do with a "series."

17. Matthew 10:22

18. "White Stone" refers to the ancients' belief in "white chalk day"—a lucky day. Caldwell might have in mind Horace *Odes* 1.36.10 as a source. Ancient Cretans, for example, used to drop a white pebble into their quivers for each good day they lived. Caldwell used the metaphor again on April 23.

19. *The Artillerist's Manual* (1863), by John Gibbon of the Union army. Normally such military works were contraband, since Caldwell, an artillerist himself, could use any knowledge gained against the Union if he were to be exchanged.

20. When cash was received, it was normally deposited into the prisoner's account, from which he could draw by purchasing items from the sutler. Prisoners were not permitted to have U.S. currency, lest it be used to bribe the guards or during an escape.

21. Battle had indeed been held in irons at Nashville prison, in retaliation for the alleged like-treatment of Capt. Shad Harris, 3rd East Tennessee Cavalry, a Union command. When Harris was removed from irons, so was Battle, but now both were back in irons. Battle was eventually transferred in irons to Fort Delaware and Fort Warren before being released late in the war. There were many references to the affair in the *Official Records,* Series II, Vol. 6–8. Battle survived for decades after the war and wrote numerous articles for *Confederate Veteran.*

22. "This country" was the United States. Judge Clark, a Copperhead, at the least, had fled to the Confederacy. Caldwell still believed at this point that he was about to be exchanged.

23. See January 1864, note 61.

24. "Hoc opus etc." Literally, "This work, and so forth." Caldwell may have a particular quotation in mind, but it is difficult to divine which one it is.

25. Ci-derant. Former.

26. A sutler maintained a store to sell provisions to an army camp or, in this case, a prison. In February 1864 the sutler store had been opened again, with Leonard B. Johnson as the new proprietor. Johnson was also the owner of the island and the man from whom it took its name. In order for a prisoner to buy so much as a postage stamp or envelope from him, Johnson insisted the customer first buy an unwanted lithograph of the prison for $3. When prisoner complaints reached Gen. Terry at Sandusky, he forced Johnson to give up the business practice and buy back all the unwanted pictures, much to the delight of Confederates. Whenever Johnson entered the stockade after that, he was met with wild cries of "Pictures!" from the Confederates.

27. George Eliot, the pen name of Mary Ann Evans.

28. There were three Brontë sisters who were English novelists: Anne, Emily, and Charlotte. Caldwell probably referred to Charlotte.

29. Caldwell's markings.

30. François Fénelon, 1651–1715, French bishop and author.

31. On February 22, not "yesterday" Capt. Benjamin L. Farinholt, 53rd Virginia, escaped as indicated. The east or bay gate had been opened so that a hundred prisoners could go out on the frozen bay to dip water from a hole in the ice. Farinholt made it all the way to Richmond. Another Virginian would escape by the same method on February 23.

32. Caldwell's "bunky" was still Maj. Joseph Saunders. There were two prisoners who could have been his foe. Lt. J.H. Sharp, 9th Alabama, or Capt. William Sharp, 4th North Carolina. Both lived in Block 5. Most likely it was the latter, who like Saunders, was from North Carolina. "Contemptible puppy" was a euphemism for son-of-a-bitch.

33. This was not only George Washington's birthday, it was the second anniversary of President Jefferson Davis's inauguration. He had been inaugurated at Montgomery, Alabama, February 18, 1861, when the capital was there. But when the government was moved to Richmond, there was a "final" or "ceremonial inauguration" on Washington's Birthday, 1862.

34. Capt. John R. Fellows of Arkansas, Gen. William N.R. Beall's staff, and Col. L.H. Lewis, 23rd Arkansas.

35. Confederate prisoners were angered by Federal celebrations on the holiday, as if George Washington were a Union saint. Claiming Washington as their own, prisoners held a counter-celebration. When the festivities became boisterous, guards were sent in to disperse the crowd.

36. Lt. Col. Osceola Kyle, 46th Alabama.

37. Isocrates. 436–338 B.C. Greek Rhetorician.

38. "'Nescire enim quid autem quam natus isi, acciderit, id est semper esse puerum.' Cic. Orat. 1.84." This is a slightly imperfect version of Cicero, Orator, 34.120. The line should begin: "Nescire autem quid ante" but is impressively close enough to the original if quoted from memory. Translated "Not to know what happened before you were born is to remain always a child," it is often quoted to support the need for the study of history. Although it is difficult to make out his notation, Caldwell seems to think it came from Cicero's orations. The number "1.84" can be read in other ways.

39. Famous Greek author of "The Sublime," literary criticism.

40. Friederich Kapp, German-American political writer. His biography of Gen. von Steuben was published in 1859. Von Steuben, a famous German general, was asked by Benjamin Franklin to come over to help the colonies in their war against England. He served with Gen. George Washington at Valley Forge and there was a monument erected to him in Washington D.C., in 1910.

41. Getting supplies to the prison with the bay frozen was no easy matter. Horse-drawn sleds were used. In this case, a horse plunged through the ice, and three drovers died in trying to extricate the horse. Hypothermia would have rendered them senseless in a very short time.

42. The remainder of this day was added later crosswise the page and continued the following day.

43. "Noctes coenaeque deorum." "Nights and feasts of the gods," a quote from Horace, *Satires* 2.6.65 and a wonderful example of Caldwell's ability not just to quote, but to quote aptly. In this piece the speaker is longing for simple food away from the frivolity and sumptuousness of the city, claiming that country meals of "faba ... simulque uncta satis pingui ... holuscula lardo" ("beans along with greens greased with some fat bacon") are the true feasts of the gods. For a man like Caldwell, missing southern cooking, the Horatian quote is absolutely perfect. The next line, in the diary, "quibus datur accumbere epulis" — "to whom it is granted to lie before the feasts" — would appear to be a cunning combination of the next line in the Horace passage, "quibus ipse meique ante Larem proprium vescor" — "[feasts] at which I and my friends eat, lying before my own household god" — with *Aeneid* 1.79, "tu das epulis accumbere divum," "it is you who grant the right to lie down at the feasts of the gods." It must be remembered that the ancients ate in a reclining position.

44. See January 1864, note 55.

45. Vida Supra. See above.

46. There were numerous competent physicians among the Confederate prisoners, but no one named Dr. Lewis is listed among them. He may have been a homeopath or self-styled medical man, not recognized by Dr. Timothy Woodbridge, the Federal officer in charge of all medical operations, and Col. Dr. I.G.W. Steedman, 1st Alabama, at this point the surgeon in charge of the prison hospital.

47. Dover's powder, a powder containing ipecac and opium, used to relieve pain and induce perspiration. Cinchona, the bark of the South American cinchona tree, was a source for quinine, used in treating malaria. Blue mass was calomel or mercurous chloride, a purgative compound, i.e., one that was supposed to induce a bowel movement. Blue

mass was a common treatment of the period, but one that probably caused more harm than good. With all these various medicines prescribed, it is no wonder that Caldwell feared he would be ill.

48. There was no prisoner by this name — probably another of Caldwell's nicknames for a roommate.

49. Capt. J.R. Carter, 8th Virginia. The new man in charge of the mess.

50. Capt. C.C. Knowles, 1st Alabama. Knowles had spent the summer of 1862 at Johnson's Island, having been captured at Fort Donelson. He was paroled and captured again at Port Hudson. It was Knowles who kept a list of all prisoners by block and mess numbers.

51. Various nicknames, obviously.

52. Intercalary days are those inserted into an imperfect calendar to make it come out "right" with respect to the solar year. So this was a leap year, and since Caldwell was using an 1863 diary that contained no page for February 29, he inserted the date at the bottom of the page for February 28. In early Roman times the calendar used was lunar and there were so many intercalary days that things were entirely out of hand, causing Julius Caesar to commission the reform of the calendar that eventually led to the calendar we use today.

March 1864

1. Charles Lever, prolific Victorian novelist and essayist.
2. That is, the American Revolution.
3. A prison in Boston Harbor.
4. Virginia (Ginny) Bethel Moon.
5. Delta Kappa Epsilon, a college fraternity. Caldwell evidently still considered himself a member.
6. "*Ingrata vice, rediit acris Hyems.*" The original version is "Solvitur acris hiems, *grata* vice veris et Favoni" and is the opening of Horace *Odes* 1.4, a poem Caldwell surely studied in school. Once more, however, we see Caldwell's learning tempered with humor. The literal translation is "Harsh winter is loosening its grip under the welcome change of spring and the wind Favonius," and the whole poem represents an ode of joy to the end of winter and the onset of warmer weather. March 5 must have been cold, however, for the author cleverly changes the text to read "Harsh winter has returned — a most *unwelcome* change!" Cf. June 2, 1864.

7. Formal complaints about the rations were filed by Maj. Gen. Isaac R. Trimble and Col. I.G.W. Steedman. There may have been other "petitions" as well.

8. William Shakespeare, *Macbeth,* act 5, scene 5.

9. Col./Rev. Levin M. Lewis had agreed to the visit from the northern minister, who promised not to preach on the evils of slavery. But when the visiting preacher arrived, he started passing out abolition tracts and railing at the Confederates on the subject, almost causing a riot. The northern preacher had to be removed by an escort.

10. Mr. Johnson, the sutler and island owner, had sold some prisoners a coal oil lamp, knowing that coal oil was or would soon be declared contraband. When he refused to take the lamp back, it was thrown at his head. There were no injuries. The culprit was never caught.

11. A few of those transferred to Point Lookout were exchanged at City Point below Richmond on the James River.

12. Sir Walter Scott.

13. There were sinks or privies behind all the prison blocks. These were long, frame shanties with rows of seats over a pit. The pits filled up frequently and the sinks had to be dug out or moved. It was most unpleasant but necessary work. Overflowing sinks would remain a problem until the prison was closed in 1865.

14. The jester in William Shakespeare's *The Tempest,* act 4, scene 1.

15. "*Fides et fiducia sunt relative,*" "Faithfulness and trust are interdependent."

16. Sir Walter Scott.

17. *Elsie Venner,* a novel set in New England, by Oliver Wendell Holmes.

18. By the Federal censors.

19. Lt. Col. Denman W. Shannon, 5th Texas Cavalry; Capt. Thomas J. Blount, Texas Artillery; Lt. H.A. Van Praag, 1st Alabama; Lt. J.M. Elkins, 3rd Texas Cavalry.

20. Although difficult to read, the Latin phrase is probably "et id genus omne" which means "and all that sort of thing." Caldwell might have been making up the phrase or might have been misquoting or adapting Horace *Satires* 1.2.2, where the Latin reads "hoc genus omne."

21. "Banished from Rome! What's banished, but set free from daily contact with the things I loathe." Catiline? 108 B.C.–62 B.C.

22. Despite the considerable efforts of Confederate diplomats in Europe, France would never recognize the Confederate States, nor would England, Spain, etc. It was hoped in Richmond that the blockade encircling the South would be broken once a major power recognized it and was eager to trade for cotton in the Confederacy.

23. "*Eheu effrenata iuventas,*" "Alas! Unbridled youth!" Caldwell was apparently recalling some previous wild celebrations of his past. The line is apparently not a direct quote, but made up for the moment. The language, however, is very reminiscent of Cicero, who was quite fond of the word "effrenata" and who would in his conservatism, surely have approved of the tone. A most appropriate quote for St. Patrick's Day!

24. The "sermons" are not religious. This refers to Horace's *Sermones,* or "Satires," which Caldwell might have quoted three days previously.

25. Catherine Ann Warfield published this Gothic novel anonymously as "A Southern Lady." Prolific and popular writer born in Natchez, Mississippi, in 1816.

26. Caldwell's sea voyage was from New Orleans to New York as a prisoner of war, just before coming to Johnson's Island. Apparently he became seasick in rough weather off Cape Hatteras.

27. If he took Dover's powders, he *was* an opium eater.

28. Eliot Warburton 1810–1852. British traveler and novelist.

29. This capitalized word is at the bottom of the page — meaning unknown.

30. Opium and morphine were duplicates, and a mustard plaster on a sore belly was worthless. There is little wonder that the patient had "nervous dreams."

31. A staff tipped with pine cone carried in Bacchic revels.

32. Caldwell wrote his mother on his birthday every year.

33. The new sutler was none other than Gen. Henry D. Terry's brother, an example of nepotism that would soon be overturned. Sutler Terry issued a flood of multicolored, pasteboard chits in various denominations, and even dollar bills. Food was to be sold by the sutler for the first time since the previous November.

34. Edward Bulwer-Lytton, English novelist, perhaps best remembered today for the opening line in his 1830 novel *Paul Clifford*: "It was a dark and stormy night." Most literary scholars today look upon Bulwer-Lytton as the quintessential "hack."

35. Caldwell was at Port Hudson, Louisiana, during its long siege and after its surrender was imprisoned in New Orleans, Louisiana, before being sent to Johnson's Island Prison.

36. Capt. W. C. Stevens, 16th Arkansas, captured at Port Hudson. He was sent to Point Lookout on April 22, 1864. This is the only Arkansas captain named Stevens or Stephens on the Johnson's Island rolls on the date Caldwell related the incident. Capt. Stevenson was a resident of Block 7, Mess 2. There were several officers from the 16th Arkansas in the same room, but none who outranked Stevens.

37. "*O tempora, O mores!*" The mere translation "Oh the times, oh the morals!" does not convey the emotion behind the quote, whose author is Cicero, *Against Catiline* 1.1.2. In this speech Cicero is deriding Catiline, who had hoped to overthrow the Roman government in 62 B.C. Cicero prosecuted him and in this famous passage calls on the heavens to witness the utter lawlessness of the times and an overall decay in public morality.

April 1864

1. Pathology of a malarial fever characterized by paroxysms that recur every other day.

2. "Versus Monachi, ap. Kames:

De planctu cudo metrum cum carmine nudo Mingere cum "bombis" res est saluberrima lumbis"

Quid significat "bombis," quid "cudo"? nonne iste "ferio, ut nummum"?

Quaestio Clerico propositurus [*sic*]....

Translation: "The monk's verses taken from Kames: 'Out of noise/lamentation I forge meter along with plain song." "To piss while you fart is very good for the loins.' What does 'bombis' mean and what about 'cudo'? Doesn't it mean 'I strike, as a coin'? This is a question that has to be put to a cleric."

Caldwell's entry consists of two parts. In the first he relates the lines and in the second he endeavors to understand them, a headache he shares with us, his later readers. It is reasonable to believe that the book from which the quotation is taken is the well-known *Elements of Criticism*, mentioned on April 10, just a bit later (Henry Home of Kames, *Elements of Criticism*, revised ed. [New York: A. S. Barnes, 1855]). Caldwell undoubtedly used the 1855 edition, and it is interesting to see how many of the quotes he writes down throughout his diary are also found in Kames. The book was first published in 1761 and had a long press run, providing several generations of readers with examples of the best elements of stylish writing available in several languages. As such, it is replete with quotations of various lengths in many languages. But despite carefully perusing each page of the book twice (and I am indebted to Professor Richard Warga for his selfless help in this endeavor), this quote did not present itself to me.

Let us take the two lines in order. Caldwell had trouble with the word "bombis," and asks what it might mean. The answer was difficult to obtain, for his writing at this stage is smudged and it was not until the original was located in a collection of medieval proverbs that the reading of "bombis" was assured. In fact, several versions of this folksy adage circulated in the Middle Ages (Hans Walther, *Proverbia sententiaeque Latinitatis Medii Aevi; Lateinische orichworter und Sentenzen des Mittelalters in alphabetischer Anordnung* [Gottingen: Denhoeck and Ruprecht, 1963–], 2:893 with cross references).

The second line eludes facile detection. Its translation, in fact, can vary rather a lot without a context into which to place it. Caldwell was correct in that "cudo" is used specifically for the act of minting a coin. In general, however, it merely means to strike and was frequently used in the Middle Ages to indicate the fabrication of poetry.

3. English novelist, 1824–1889. *No Name* was a densely plotted revenge thriller, and very popular.

4. Battle of Killiecrankie 1689. The Jacobites won the battle but Dundee was killed.

5. Nous verrons. We shall see.

6. *The Death of Wallenstein: A Tragedy in Five Acts*, by Frederick Schiller, translation from the German by Samuel Taylor Coleridge.

7. Et iam prima novo spargebat lumine terras
Tithoni croceum linquens Aurora cubile. (ir)

"And now Dawn sprinkled anew the lands with first light, leaving her saffron bed by Tithonus."

These lines appear twice in the *Aeneid*, at 4.584–85 and 9.459–60. The latter is most likely, as Caldwell was reading Book 9 at this stage.

"an sese medios moriturus in hostes
Inferat, et pulchram properet per vulnera mortem?"
"Euryale auden sum dextra; nunc ipsa vocat res."
Aeneid 9.400–01.

Caldwell turned to the Nisus and Euryalus story, at the point where Nisus sees Euryalus being killed (see April 12 and 25.) The poet lays bare Nisus's thoughts for us: "Should he hurl himself onto the enemy and die and should he hasten his glorious death through wounds?" This would seem to mark the beginning of Caldwell's reading of Vergil's *Aeneid*, a task he would pursue for many months to come. As we will see, his choice of Book 9, stressing as it does bravery and military comradeship, is no accident.

8. *An Overland Journey Round the World during the Years 1841 and 1842*. Simpson was governor of Hudson's Bay Company.

9. Pule Pulani. Hawaiian word for prayer or worship.

10. Dinah Craik, 1856. Ideals of the new middle class.

11. "Sedet aeternumque sedebit / verb. secund., qd seg." Although Caldwell's writing is very difficult to read at this point, the text seems to be a quote from Vergil, *Aeneid*, 6.617. Vergil is describing the Athenian hero Theseus, condemned to sit in the underworld, immobile in a chair of forgetfulness, forever. Caldwell might have felt as bored and hopeless as Theseus. Thus, the second line of the quote may not be "verb-etc." "Verb" might be "verg" for Vergil. The next three words elude decipherment, although they may represent in abbreviated form, "according to what follows."

12. "Lasciate agni speranza
Voi che entrate" — In Inferni portis
Dante sees these words posted over the gates of hell in the *Inferno*. "Abandon all hope who enters here." The last three words say, in Latin, "On the Gates of Hell."

13. "Scandit aeratas vitiosa naves / Cura:

nec turmas equitum relinquit/" is from Horace, *Odes* 2.16.21-22. "Care climbs on board brass-bound ships; neither does it leave the class of knights alone." Horace is warning against trying to make too much money in trade and, more generally, against putting too much faith in things temporal. The knights were a merchant class notorious for their focus on profits.

14. That quote apparently put Caldwell in mind of another, similar, bit of Horatian morality, "Post equitem sedet atra cura," or "Dark care sits right behind the horseman" (*Odes* 3.1.40). Once more Horace is decrying excessive ambition and warning that no matter what deeds we may achieve, bad luck may topple all. He ends, of course, by stating that no matter what happens over the years, his poems will survive, as indeed they have.

15. Caldwell had been reading the ninth book of Vergil's *Aeneid* (*see* April 8 and 25). It is worth noting that at this stage of the epic, Aeneas's army is fighting against overwhelming odds, a situation evocative of this late stage of the war. In reading these lines, Caldwell was struck by certain sentiments common to all bands of warriors, irrespective of when and where they fight. It is odd not to see another line from this book: "My mind has for long been astir to move to battle or to undertake some other great activity. It is not content with peaceful inactivity" (II. 187-88).

"His annis gravis, atque animi maturus Aletes;
di patrii, quorum semper sub numine Troia est,
non tamen omnino Teucros delere paratis,
cum talis animos iuvenum, et tam certa tulistis pectora."
Vergil *Aeneid*, 9.246-49

These lines are spoken by an aged member of Aeneas's band in response to a bold and brave offer of self-sacrifice on the part of some younger warriors, Euryalus and Nisus, who have volunteered to go out on a night raid, hoping to bring Aeneas back to the besieged Trojans.

"Then Aletes, grown old in years and wise in spirit said,
'Gods of our fathers, beneath whose protection Troy ever is,
You are not ready, it seems, to blot out the Trojans completely from the earth,
For you have brought forth this sort of spirit and such stout courage in our youth."

"Quae vobis, quae digna, viri, pro laudibus istis
Prarmia posse rear solvi? pulcherrima primum
Di moresque dabunt vestri" (IX)
Vergil *Aeneid*, 9.252-54

Aletes goes on to say, grasping the youths by the hand
"What rewards, gentlemen, could I possibly think worthy
To pay back such praiseworthy deeds? The gods
And your own characters will sooner provide the fairest of all."

"Multa patri portanda dabat mandata: sed aurae
Omnia discerpunt, et nubibus inrita donant."
Aeneid, 9.312-13

"[Iulus, Aeneas' son] gives many a command to be borne to his father, but the breezes Snatch them all up and give them, unfulfilled, to the clouds."

This brief quote speaks volumes, for it stresses a sense of futility. Even in the face of outstanding sacrifice such as that of Euryalus and Nisus, events often conspire to bring failure. These and similar thoughts must have been frequently in Caldwell's mind.

"Est hic, est animus, lucis contemptor; et istum
Qui vita bene credat emi, quo tendis honorem."
Aeneid, 9.205-6

As he ruminated over the cost of the war, Caldwell found a line in Book 9 that assures him it is all worthwhile:

"Here, here is a spirit that scorns the light of life and which thinks that
That honor, for which you strive, is well bought with a life."
"Te superesse velim; tua vita dignior aetas."
Aeneid, 9.212

"I would prefer that you survive; your age is more worthy of life." Here, in an epic from the Roman Empire, we find words that clearly must have been thought internally or spoken aloud, time and time again, on the battlefields of the Civil War as one soldier sacrificed himself for another. The reader who would understand this aspect of Caldwell had best read Book 9 of the *Aeneid* for him- or herself.

16. "non vinum, ut vinum, appetitur, sed tale

bonumque sic et vita, ut vita, est nil nisi bona: quod si (?)

est misera, ut vinum corruptum despiciatur

esse quidam, per se nec amandum nec fugiendum est"

"Wine is not sought as wine, but as a sort of good. So too is life, as life, sought as nothing other than a good. But if life is miserable, then let it be despised like spoiled wine. Existence is something which should neither be loved nor fled from in and of itself."

Caldwell's handwriting is rather tricky at this spot and not all words are clear. Moreover, this cannot be identified as a quote from any of Caldwell's major sources (e.g. Vergil, Horace, Cicero). Although the thought expressed is decidedly Stoic, the passage cannot be found in Seneca. The translation offered is a reasonably close approximation of what the author (is it Caldwell himself?) probably intended, but until the text is confirmed, no certainty is possible.

"Quippe habet hoc quamvis vilissima rerum, vermis,

Musca, lapis, cortex nihil est optabile adempta

Conditione boni, nisi est tale esse bonumque

Non vides cur optari cur possit amari."

"This, then, is how matters stand concerning even the smallest thing — a fly, a stone, a piece of bark. Nothing is desirable once the condition of goodness has been removed. Unless an existence has a certain sort of goodness to it, you do not see why it can be desired or loved."

This passage seems to be a continuance of the thoughts of the previous one. Again, the text is very difficult to read and a source is not apparent. The translation offered should be seen as more of an approximation. The phrase "vilissima rerum" is also found in Horace *Satires* 1.5.86, but that poem in no way resembles the present passage. The overall thought conveyed by this and the previous passage is evocative of Seneca *Epistles* 67, a Stoic reflection on suffering, but Caldwell was not quoting. It seems rather that he was creating his own bit of Stoic philosophy. If this is the case, it accounts for some of the obscure Latin used.

17. "Me, me, adsum, qui feci; in me convertite ferrum,

O Rutuli! Mea fraus omnis, nihil iste nec ausus;

Nec potuit; caelum hoc, et conscia sidera testor;

Tantum infelicem nimium dilexit amicum." Vergil *Aeneid*, 9.427–30.

"Turn your weapons on me, on me, oh Rutulians. I am the one who did it. The guilt is all mine. That fellow dared nothing, was capable of nothing. I swear this by heaven and the stars who see all. All he did was love his ill fated comrade too dearly."

Caldwell had resumed his reading of the *Aeneid*, Book 9, and was still focusing on the story of Nisus and Euryalus, two comrades who have gone out on a late-night mission amid great danger. Euryalus becomes lost. Nisus searches frantically for his friend and, when he finds him surrounded by the enemy, attacks. Amid his attack, he cries out the words quoted, trying to turn all the fury of the enemy upon himself to spare his friend.

"Volvitur Euryalus leto, pulchrosque per artus

It cruor inque humeros cervix collapsa recumbit:

purpureus veluti cum flos, succisus aratro,

Demisere caput! pluvia cum forte gravantur."

Vergil *Aeneid*, 9.433–37

"Euryalus rolls in death, and gore flows over his beautiful limbs and his neck, giving way, lies on his shoulders just as happens when a purple flower, cut down by the plow, goes limp in its death or when a poppy droops its head on its neck, weighed down by a chance flower."

Caldwell skipped two lines in the text and got to the description of the death of Euryalus, for the Rutulians, deaf to Nisus's pleas, run him through with a sword. Caldwell omitted line 436, but the translation includes it for continuity. The simile of the natural, tender flower being cut down by an instrument of mankind's "progress" is among Vergil's best, stressing, as often, the needless loss of life that attends war. "Purple" was a color of nobility for the Romans.

"Fortunati ambo! Si quid mea carmina possunt,
nulla dies umquam memori vos eximet aevo:
dum domus Aeneae Capitoli immobile saxum
accolet, imperiumque pater Romanus habebit."
Aeneid, 9.446–49

"Happy pair! If my verses can be of any avail, then no day will ever blot you out from the memory of time as long as the house of Aeneas has its place on the immovable rock of the Capitoline hill and the Father of Rome holds sovereign rule."

At this point in the poem, Vergil himself addresses Nisus and Euryalus. Nisus had rushed into battle upon seeing his friend die. Vergil sees in this scene the best and the worst of war. The death of fine youth is always to be mourned, but the bond among warriors and the selfless behavior it engenders are among the finest things mankind has to offer. By way of tribute, Vergil dedicates his verses to keeping their memory alive. He was undoubtedly gratified to see these lines affect Caldwell in a far different war at a far different time.

"Hic amor unus erat, pariterique in bella ruebant."—Vergil *Aeneid,* 9.182

"There was one love between them and they rushed headlong into war, together."

Apparently Caldwell went back and reread the entire scene, for he now put down a line from its earlier phases. Its presence here acts as a summation of all that he admired in the Nisus and Euryalus story.

18. Charles Reade, 1814–1884. English novelist-dramatist best known for *The Cloister and the Hearth.*

19. Quien sabe? Who knows?

20. "*Timeo Danaos.*" "I fear the Greeks." This is a partial quote designed to evoke the full quote from Vergil, *Aeneid,* 2.49, where someone, looking at the Trojan Horse, says "Timeo danaos, et dona ferentes," "I'm afraid of Greeks, even those bearing gifts." The implication is that Belding is not to be trusted, even when he offers to do something nice.

21. Battle of Mansfield, Louisiana.

22. "Tempora mutantur et nos mutamur in illis." "The times change and we are changed within them." Caldwell's memory was playing a bit of a trick on him here, for the line properly quoted is "Tempora mutantur nos et mutamur in illis." The meaning is the same either way. The quote is attributed to Lothar (Holy Roman Emperor 795–855), who, having been emperor, entered the monastery shortly before his death. According to one story, the original version of the quote read, "All things change and we too change in them." See Georg Büchmann, *Geflügelte Worte. Der Zitatenschatz des deutschen Volkes* (Berlin: Schreitersche,1918, 500). Thanks to Ulrich Schmitzer of Universität Erlangen-Nürnberg and Peter Green of University of Texas for their help with identifying the original source of this quotation. The question of where Caldwell first saw the quote remains open, although it was widely quoted.

23. "Tum super exanimum sese proiecit amicum
confossus, placidaque ibi demum morte quievit. (En. IX.)" *Aeneid,* 9.444–45

"Then he threw himself on top of the dead body of his friend, pierced through, and there at length he found his rest in death." Caldwell returns to the story of Nisus and Euryalus, quoting the lines where Nisus, having failed to save his friend's life, finds some solace in dying with him.

24. Sir Walter Scott.

25. "Aut tu, magne pater Divum, Miserere, tuoque
invisum hoc detrude caput sub Tartara telo,
quando aliter nequeo crudelem abrumpere vitam" *Aeneid,* 9.495–97.

News of Euryalus' death has come to his mother. Overcome with grief, she begs for death herself and here, addressing Jupiter, king of the gods, says, "But you, great father of the gods, have mercy on me and hurl this my hateful life down to Hell with your thunderbolt, for I am unable otherwise to break out of this cruel life." Surely Caldwell was thinking about the many mothers of his day who had similar feelings.

"Non illa virum, non illa pericli, telorumque memor"

"Femineo ululatu." (En. IX 490+)

Caldwell then jotted down two previous lines. The first, from *Aeneid*, 9.479, also describes Euryalus's mother's grief. It translates, "She was heedless of the men, heedless of the danger, heedless of the weapons." The next phrase, the mere fragment of a line, reads "femineo ululate." (9.477) and translates as "with feminine wailing." The onomatopoeia of this phrase may have caught his eye.

26. "Si cui videor non iustus, inulto dicere quod sentit, permitto" Hor.
(sed ubit —).
"If there is anyone to whom I might appear unjust, I give him permission to say what is on his mind without fear of reprisal." Caldwell switched from Vergil to Horace *Satires*, 2.3.189f. It is hard to know what caused him to write down this quote. Perhaps it represented the sort of freedom of speech he, a prisoner of war, wished he had.

27. See April 10 and April 12.

28. Caldwell was reading Shakespeare: *A Midsummer Night's Dream*, April 27; *Merry Wives of Windsor*, April 28; *Much Ado About Nothing*, May 8; *As You Like It*, May 10; *The Winter's Tale*, May 11; *Love's Labour's Lost*, May 14; *The Taming of the Shrew* and *Two Gentlemen of Verona*, May 15; *The Tempest*, May 21; *The Merchant of Venice* and *The Comedy of Errors*, May 22; *Troilus and Cressida*, May 24.

29. 1554–1586. Elizabethan statesman, soldier, and poet.

30. "Un home capable de faire des dominos avec les os du Saint Pere." "A man able to make dominoes from the bones of the Holy Father."

31. April 29 through May 2 are missing. Two pages are missing from the diary.

May 1864

1. May 2–4, 1863, in Spotsylvania County, Virginia. Called Lee's "Perfect Battle." The Confederates were victorious against the larger forces of Gen. Hooker. The victory was marred by the mortal wounding of Lt. Gen. Thomas "Stonewall" Jackson, a loss Lee likened to "losing his right arm."

2. Probably episcleritis, usually a superficial inflammation — not an infection.

3. Published in 1860. Said to be inspired by the sculpture, The Faun of Praxiteles. Generally regarded by critics as inferior to Hawthorne's other works.

4. Published in 1855. Subtitled *Sketches of the Court of Isabella II by Madame Calderón de la Barca*. Her husband was a Spanish diplomat.

5. On the qui-vive. On the alert.

6. Sir Walter Scott.

7. Federal prison in New Orleans.

8. The date was written in.

9. "Francais! Je n'ai rien a vous dire: vous avez Jure' de vaincre ou de mourir; faites votre devoir." "Frenchmen! I have nothing to say to you. You have sworn to conquer or to die: do your duty."

10. Nous verrons. We shall see.

11. Richard Porson, professor of Greek at Cambridge, 1792–1808. He was a brilliant scholar and wrote imitations of Horace and parodies. One story in a newspaper told how a friend had found part of a lost tragedy by Sophocles quoting a fragment of twelve iambic verses. Translated from the Greek, this proved to be a nursery rhyme: "Three children sliding in the snow" (*The Classical Journal* 28, No. 5 [February 1933]). Caldwell was fond of writing such things.

12. Opera by Meyerbeer.

13. Sir Walter Scott.

14. "Quoties vidi patrem tuum cubito emungentem." "How often I saw your father wiping his nose on his arm." The Roman poet Horace tells us that his father was a freed slave who collected the money at auctions. But the Roman biographer Suetonius (*Poet. frag.* 40), who preserves this quote, tells us that once, during a quarrel, a certain man cast the insult quoted here at Horace, intimating that Horace's father dealt in salted foods and was, in fact, an ordinary dock worker who blew his nose on his sleeve. (Thanks to Peter Green of the University of Texas for his help with this quotation.)

15. "Tout ça est bien gentil, mais qu'est qu'on fait de ça à la maison." "All this is very nice, but what can one do with it at home?"

16. The text of this riddle was put to an electronic discussion group of classicists. Professor David Meadows of McMaster and Wilfrid Laurier Universities located an interesting version of the riddle in the letters of Lord Chesterfield (1694–1773) to his son (Bryant, Mark, *Dictionary of Riddles* [London: Routledge, 1990], no. 403, p. 130). Unfortunately, Chesterfield cites no source and supplies no answer.

Despite the zealous efforts of many classicists, no single answer has arisen that evokes immediate agreement. They rightly point out that if the answer is one word (as it probably is) then we are confined to a ten-letter famous city from antiquity. The most likely candidates by far are Alexandria or Jerusalem, (spelled in the variant form, Hiero/usalem.) How one answers the individual clues may vary, for it is infinitely easier to compose such a riddle than to answer one. For more on the riddle, see the chapter "Caldwell the Classicist."

17. A standard piece of clothing for a soldier.
18. Sometimes used instead of "in."
19. ΤΟ ΠΡΣΠΟΓ & the ΤΟ ΚΑΛΟΓ . These two Greek words were stock phrases in Greek antiquity for "That which is fitting and that which is beautiful." The words symbolized all that was admissible in the good life.
20. Sprawled across the bottom of pages 144 to 146 of the diary (and thus cutting across May 24 through 26) is one of the oddest segments of the diary. It is entitled "FASTI JACOBI, or "James Chronicle." (James Parks Caldwell, no doubt.) What follows is written in Greek letters, but is clearly English and is definitely a narrative. Parts are quite illegible, and Caldwell's "spelling" is quite odd at times. But one can tell that the time of the play is Christmas and the opening scene is a library. After that there are scattered references to chess, molasses candy, and many repetitions of a word that can only be "love." It would be the work of many months to try to make more sense out of the passage, but the hints that we do possess are very tempting.
21. Capital A with decorated square around it.
22. A wealthy Cornish family.
23. This was the date of the Grand Charge at the Port Hudson Battle.
24. "et praeterea nil." "and nothing beyond this." Not a specific quote and repeated at February 20, 1865.
25. "Le premier des rois fût un soldat heureux." "The first of the kings was a happy soldier."

June 1864

1. "De toutes les bouffoneries la plus serieuse est le mariage." "Of all buffooneries the most serious is marriage." Figaro is the central character in the Beaumarchais plays *The Barber of Seville* and *The Marriage of Figaro or Day of Madness* and the operas by Mozart and Rossini.
2. "non ingrate." "not unpleasant." Not a direct quote of anything memorable, but the wording and context are reminiscent of March 5, 1864.
3. Caldwell appears to have composed this poem ("To Our Nation's Flag, Military Song") one verse at a time but crossed each one out (including this one). He then repeated the entire poem at the end of the diary of 1864.
4. Page in diary.
5. "Non iam, prima peto, Mnestheus neque vincere certo;
    quanquam o — sed superent, quibus hoc, Neptune dedisti —
    extremos pudeat rediisse; hoc vincite, cives,
    et prohibete nefas."
   "Abiit ael planes"

Caldwell now switched to *Aeneid*, 5.194–97, amid the famous scene that describes the funeral games Aeneas puts on for his father, Anchises. In context, amid the ship race, it represents the words Mnestheus uses to urge on his fellow citizens to pull harder at their oars. But out of context, it apparently read to Caldwell as an equally apt exhortation to his fellow citizens not to give up in their doomed war effort: "No longer do I, Mnesthesus, seek first place and neither do I strive to win even though it is shameful to come back last. No, let those win out, Neptune, to whom you give the privilege. Win this much, fellow citizens and ward off disgrace!"

6. "Emori nolo; me esse mortuum nihil estimo." "I do not wish to die. I think that when dead I will be nothing." The source of the quote is hard to place even with today's computer assisted searches. The thought of the quote is somewhat reminiscent of Socrates' last words as reported by Plato in the *Apology* and *Phaedo*, though the language there, of course, was Greek.
7. Confederate regiment.
8. Will Moon, brother of Ginny.
9. "O Utinam et Ego?" "O if only that were true and I?"
10. "Mentemque priorem expulit atque hominem toto sibi cedere iussit pectore. "This is a fairly obscure quote from Lucan's *Bellum Civile* 5.167–68. The scene occurs

when the god Apollo inspires his prophetess: "He expelled her former mind and her humanity and ordered her to give her heart entirely to him." This is Caldwell's only reference to Lucan. Was he reading the work, which, after all, dealt with a civil war, or had he picked up the quote secondhand? Might he even have remembered it?

11. Sir Walter Scott.

12. Written by Angus B. Reach (1852) and still in print.

13. This is verse II and part of verse III of the ode printed in full at the end of the 1864 diary. The page is crossed out on this date.

14. Remainder of the page—Latin poem, the rest of verse III and verse IV—all crossed out.

15. 1764 novel by Horace Walpole, generally regarded as first Gothic novel.

16. Verse V of the poem has been crossed out.

17. "Rusticus exspectat dum defluat amnis." "The hick is waiting for the river to run out of water." The source of this quote is Horace *Epistles* 1.2.42. There it is in a larger context, which says that a person who puts off the hour for beginning to live right is like a hick waiting until the river runs out. Here it would seem that Caldwell might merely be commenting on the prescience, or lack of it, of Gen. Archer.

18. "Jure divino." Probably to be taken with the previous phrase, indicating that "D. J." has made these proclamations by "divine law."

19. Caldwell always spelled Shakespeare as Shakspeare.

20. "Peccavi." "I have sinned."

21. Entire page Latin verse with big X through it.

July 1864

1. Another verse of the Latin poem.

2. "Venus urit venis et caco carpitur igni."
"Sese ore ferens"—"haret laten lethalis anmdo"
"Agnosco veteris vestigia flammae"—
"Talibus aggredibur Venerem Satumia dictis"

Caldwell was apparently now reading Book 4 of the *Aeneid*. Here, under the title, "Dido and the Leader" ("dux" is a common title for Aeneas), he lists four striking lines from the scene, in which Dido recognizes that she is irrevocably in love with Aeneas. Let us translate each in turn. "Volnus alit venis et caeco carpitur igni." (*Aeneid*, 4.2) "The wound (of love) feeds in her veins and she is seized with blind fire." "Quem sese ore ferens, quam forti pectore et armis!" (*Aeneid*, 4.11) "How noble he is in appearance! With what a brave chest! How noble in arms!" "Agnosco veteris vestigial flammae." (*Aeneid* 4.23) "I recognize the traces of that old flame," spoken by Dido to her sister Anna as Dido realizes that she is falling in love with Aeneas in spite of her vow never to love anyone other than her dead husband. "Talibus adgreditur Venerem Saturnia dictis." (*Aeneid*, 4.92) "With such words does the daughter of Saturn (Juno) approach Venus."

3. William Shakespeare, *Much Ado about Nothing*, act 2, scene 3.

4. See Appendix.

5. Fasti. Chronicle.

6. "Ultra meam crepidam." "Out of my field," literally "beyond my last." Caldwell was remembering an ancient proverb, "Let the cobbler stick to his last."

7. Union gunboat on Lake Erie.

8. "Rex est qui metuit nihil. Hoc regnum sibi quisque dat." Seneca, *Thyestes*, 388f.: "He is king who fears nothing. This is the kingdom which each person gives to himself." Seneca was a noted Stoic philosopher who also wrote gory tragedies. This particular bit of Stoic philosophy, from the play *Thyestes*, must have been particularly appealing to one who was imprisoned and whose every move was theoretically subject to another's control.

9. Fortification.

10. Vidocq was an eighteenth-century French crook turned cop. There is a modern day "cold case" club named after him.

11. "Lecti Cimices" are bed bugs, surely a plague in the conditions of the camp.

August 1864

1. William Shakespeare, *King Henry IV*, act 2, scene 4.

2. William Allen Butler (1825–1902). His popular, satiric poems were published in *Harper's Weekly*.

3. Harriet Prescott (1835–1920), a notable American writer of novels, poems, and detective stories.

4. Beatrice Cenci was a sixteenth-century beauty who murdered her father and was beheaded. Several poems, operas, paintings, plays and other literary works by illustrious talents such as Stendahl and Shelley have been composed about her. This one, by nineteenth-century Guerrazzi, was political.

5. Probably the Miss B. that Caldwell mentions quite a few times as a letter writer.

6. The meaning of these letters, which appear at the top of the page, is unknown.

7. Marplot. A person who mars or defeats a plot by meddling.

8. Caldwell's markings.

9. Caldwell wrote on August 9 that he had sent to Harper and Bros. for a copy of Lucretius, sending the price in "P&O stamps." The time it took to receive the book was therefore admirably quick. The edition in question is H.A.J. Munro, ed., *T. Lucreti Cari De rerum natura libri sex* (New York: Harper, 1861). On April 1, Caldwell had expressed an interest in reading Lucretius. As events turned out, Lucretius was to prove to be Caldwell's favorite ancient author.

10. "De Mulieribus non est disputandum." "One should not argue about women." Caldwell was playing off the sound of a famous old saying, "De gustibus, non est disputandum," "One should not argue over matters of taste."

11. Baseball was played in many prisons during the Civil War.

12. Chicago was hosting the presidential convention.

13. Soi-disant. So-called, self-styled.

14. "Deductions which can only be called such *a non ducendo*." That is, the deductions might be linked to the Latin word *deducere*, but in this case the etymology is false as they do not "lead from" anything, least of all a solid logical basis.

15. Cosimo de' Medici (1389–146), known as the Father of his Country.

16. The Carbonari were secret societies founded in early nineteenth-century Italy. The Pazzi plot was a 1478 conspiracy to end the hegemony of the Medici and enlarge the papal territory. On April 26, Giuliano de' Medici was stabbed to death during High Mass at the cathedral in Florence. Lorenzo de' Medici escaped with a wound. The enraged Florentines seized and killed the conspirators.

September 1864

1. His dog, no doubt.

2. "(Pecc. est ille pastor dequoque bona dixi, nunc contradico.)" "Peccary is that pastor/shepherd about whom I said good things, but now I take them back." Once more Caldwell was guarding against prying eyes by putting potentially negative comments in Latin. "Pastor" literally means "shepherd," but may well indicate a minister.

3. Apella the Jew is a symbol of credulous belief. See the note for January 28.

4. See Appendix for the exchange of letters from father to son on this occasion.

5. Caldwell's markings again.

6. A calcium light or stage "limelight": attributed to Capt. Thomas Drummond (1797–1840), English engineer.

7. The quote is hard to identify from Horace, based as it is on two words, "in medio." Perhaps Caldwell had in mind the proverb he quotes on November 11, "in medio tutissimus ibis." The quote is from Ovid, not Horace. But since Caldwell did not identify it in November, he might have confused its authorship.

8. "Albo dies simper natanda Capillo."

9. This refers to the page number in the diary, which is June 25, 1864.

10. The crabbed writing, very much hindered by "bleed through" of the ink, seems to read "Lex mar obitae," which would refer to a law. But further certitude is difficult.

11. A novel by Augusta J. Evans (1835–1909) about Confederate women in the Civil War.

12. Maj. Gen. Robert Rodes, one of the best Confederate division commanders.

13. See Appendix for letter from doctors to the authorities regarding the insufficiency of food and other health matters concerning the prisoners.

October 1864

1. "Non accepi omen." "I did not accept the omen." Caldwell meant that he rejected the implied aging of VBM in his dream. The Romans were quite superstitious and put a great deal of stock in such omens. Cf. Jan 1, 1865, where Caldwell noted a good omen for the new year and stated tersely, "accepi."

2. Chaffin's Bluff in Virginia.

3. This was written in the margin in tiny letters.

4. This is the Eleusinian mysteries and refers to the very important mystery religion and cult which existed near Athens at the town of Eleusis.

5. Refers to diary June 30, 1864, actually page 181. Another verse of the poem with large X through it. The final version is at the end of the diary.

6. Casemate: armored enclosure for guns in a warship or a chamber in a rampart, with embrasures for artillery. Fort Columbus was in New York Harbor; Caldwell was on his way from New Orleans Federal Prison to Johnson's Island.

7. He was said to be the inspiration for Hogarth's painting "A Rake's Progress."

8. Laurence Sterne (1713–1768), author of *Tristam Shandy*. This is a true story.

9. Benjamin West (1738–1820), an influential American-born painter with a wide reputation in Europe. Henry Fuseli (1741–1825) was a Swiss-born British Romantic painter.

10. Leigh Hunt (1784–1859), English poet. *Rimini* is the story of the legendary love of Francesca da Rimini and her brother-in-law, Malatesta, found in Dante's *Inferno*.

11. Book of Judith, in the Roman Catholic and Eastern Orthodox Old Testament. Judith, a beautiful widow, goes to the camp of the enemy general, Holofernes, and ingratiates herself. She decapitates him and takes his head to her countrymen. The Assyrians, having lost their leader, disperse. The story has shown up in Chaucer, Renaissance literature, paintings and sculptures, plays, oratorios, etc.

12. "Literae quae hesterno die venerunt, hodie mihi advenerunt, Scripta est Mea Sorore." "The letter which came yesterday got to me to-day. It was written by my sister."

13. The text in question is undoubtedly John Proudfit, ed., *The Captives: A Comedy of Plautus with English Notes for the Use of Students* (New York: Harpers, 1863). The book had originally been published in 1855 and was reprinted as late as 1870.

14. One of Aesop's fables. The frogs asked Jupiter to remove King Log, who they thought a tyrant. Jupiter sent them King Stork, who gobbled up the frogs.

November 1864

1. Girondins, a political group in 1791 that tried to promote progressive federalism against the Jacobins in Revolutionary France. They were eventually suppressed in 1793.

2. Less than 4 inches by 2 inches, very thinly sliced.

3. Charlotte Corday was executed in 1793 for the assassination of Marat, who was responsible for the Reign of Terror in the French Revolution.

4. Plautus's *Captivi*: Plautus was one of Rome's earliest authors, noted for his many comedies. The *Captives* is certainly an ominous choice of reading for Caldwell, himself a captive. This is apparently the book he sent for on October 26.

5. Actually Sunday.

6. Tytler's Universal History. From the creation of the world to the beginning of the eighteenth century.

7. "In medio tutissimus ibis." Taken together with the English, the thought is "You will not always travel safest in the middle of the road," apparently a criticism of the "trimmer" book that tries to walk the middle path between that of Strauss and Fleetwood. The quote is from Ovid, *Metamorphoses* 2.137.

8. Richard Porson (1759–1808). See May 1864, note 12.

9. In fact, twenty plays of Plautus have survived. Caldwell must have had a particular edition or collection in mind.

10. "Mirabile dictu!" "Wonderful to relate." This common Roman phrase was often used to teach the use of the supine.

11. Greek orator, born 389 B.C. Demosthenes defeated him in oratory and he went into exile.

12. An oration by Demosthenes.

13. Cnidian Venus of Praxiteles: Praxiteles was one of the most famous sculptors in antiquity and lived in the fourth, not the third, century B.C. Phryne, whom Caldwell correctly called a courtesan, was in fact Praxiteles' steady mistress.

14. Ancus Marcius was traditionally the fourth king of Rome. The later priesthood that was created to care for Rome's many bridges was headed by the "Pontifex Maximus," or "Chief Bridge-builder." The title eventually came to be associated with the Pope as the chief cleric of Rome.

15. The Tarpeian Rock or Cliff (not "hills") was located near the Capitol Hill of Rome. The etymology is tied in with the word for "head"—"caput," "capitis."

16. "Proletaire" is the French word for proletarian. "Proletarii" is the plural of the Latin noun that describe these people. As members of the lower class, it was thought that one of their main occupations was producing "proles," "progeny."

17. Lucian of Samosata lived in Roman times but wrote his works, most of which are dialogues, in Greek.

18. "Dent operam consules ne quid Republica detrimenti capiat!" "Let the consuls see to it that the Republic suffer no harm!" Caldwell referred to a device called the *senatus consultum* whereby, in times of crisis, the Senate gave the two consuls expanded powers with the sole enjoinder that the Republic should be spared harm.

19. "In verba Eumolpi juravimus, uri, vinciri, verberari, ferroque necari, et quiquid aliud Eumolpus jussisset tamquam optimi gladiatores et homines corpora animosque religiose addicimus" "We have sworn by the words of Eumolpus to be burned, conquered, beaten, slaughtered with the steel—and whatever else Eumolpus swore. We do this as if we, the best of gladiators and men, were assigning our bodies and souls faithfully to him." This oath has more the air of a nineteenth-century novel than of antiquity, but its source remains unclear.

20. Julian the Apostate, a fourth-century emperor, earned his name for returning the empire to paganism after its conversion to Christianity under Constantine. Several of his smaller works and letters are extant.

21. *De mysteriis Eleusinis* (see October 1864, note 3). Does Caldwell refer to a "modern" or an ancient work, such as that of Andocides?

22. "Nec recito cuiquam nisi amicis idque coactus." "I do not recite my works to any save my friends, and only then when forced to do so." Horace, *Satires*, 1.4.73

23. "Les femmne sont très braves avec le peau d'autrui." "Women are very good with the skin of others." Or women are fine as long as someone else has them.

24. "Zeuò estin ouranoò, Zeuò te ge ta panta." "Zeus is the sky, indeed, Zeus is everything." It is interesting that, like many students today, Caldwell left out the accents that are an integral part of Greek.

25. "Jupiter est quodcumque vides quocumque moveris." "Jupiter is whatever you see and anything by which you are moved." The name "Lucan" is scrawled between the two quotes but is quite hard to read. If Lucan, it is the epic poet who died under Nero's repressive reign and whom Caldwell quoted on June 12.

26. George Gordon, Lord Byron, *Childe Harold*.

27. "Not Latin."

December 1864

1. "De quo quae mala antea scripsi nunc revoco." "I now take back the bad things I said about this man previously." As he did before in the case of Peccary (September 9), Caldwell hides his change of mind beneath the Latin.

2. "Rara avis," "a good daughter." Originally a quote from Juvenal, *rara avis*, or "a rare bird" became proverbial, indicating a thing not commonly found. Caldwell used the English for this phrase once more on March 14, 1865.

3. "Jurare in ejus verba," "to swear allegiance to his words." Adapted from Horace, *Epistles* 1.1.14, "Not bound to swear allegiance to any master."

4. Thackeray.

5. Caldwell mentioned this on December 10.

6. Henry Fielding (1707–1754), the author of *Tom Jones*.

7. Sallust was a Roman historian who stressed the moral nature of history, using the Roman rebel Catiline as the target of his prodigious oratorical skills.

January 1865

1. "Accepi." " I accept." Cf. October 2, 1864.

2. Caldwell is apparently making up the Latin for a favorite recipe from his days of freedom. Though some of the words are made up, it would appear to mean "candied ham divine with tomatoes."

3. Smallpox is very contagious, but contemporary medical reports state that most smallpox cases were transfers from other prisons.

4. Caldwell was apparently treated by the block surgeon, not a trained physician. These medicines may have been worse than the disease. Laudanum is tincture of opium.
5. A.M., no doubt
6. In Mississippi, close to Caldwell's former home.

February 1865

1. *Pendennis,* by William Makepeace Thackeray.
2. Court-martial.
3. "and nothing further" Cf. May 31, 1864.
4. Tiny drawing of C.S.A. flag with stars and bars in upper left corner of this page.

March 1865

1. Hashish. A tincture is 10 percent alcohol; extract would be stronger. This is marijuana, cannabis, or hemp.
2. The hashish clearly was not so ineffective after all.
3. This note is by Isabella Parks Caldwell, sister of James Parks Caldwell, and the tracing is exactly similar to his handwriting, though some assumptions were made and the original can not be discerned in a few places.
4. [blank space] The words in some places had evidently faded too much for his niece to decipher — they are now gone completely — sometimes a word, a phrase, or several lines.

April 1865

1. "Laus Deo." "Praise God."
2. "Vae victis." "Woe to the conquered," Livy, *Histories* 5.48, reporting the words of the leader of the Gauls who besieged Rome in 387 B.C. After a siege of six months the Romans bought him off with gold. A Roman tribune complained that Brennus was using false weights to measure out the gold, but Brennus merely tossed his sword in the scale and said "Vae victis," or, in more modern terms, "Like it or lump it." His words obviously had resonance for Caldwell.

3. Dunciad, a literary satire by Alexander Pope, published anonymously in 1728. A poem to celebrate the goddess of dullness and the progress of her agents as they bring decay, imbecility, and tastelessness to the kingdom of Great Britain.
4. "Potius ruinam!" "As for me, I'd rather total ruin!"

May 1865

1. *Quentin Durward,* a novel by Sir Walter Scott.
2. "Omne solum forti patria est, ut piscibus aequor" "To a brave man every bit of soil is a fatherland, just as the deep (is home) to fish." Ovid, *Fasti,* 1.423. Ovid, having offended the Roman emperor, ended his days in exile in the far distant realms of the Roman Empire.
3. *Prince of Abyssinian,* a novella by Samuel Johnson, 1789.
4. Bacterial pneumonia proceeded to resolution or death in those days. There was no effective treatment, just individual resistance and luck.
5. The two "species" in *Gulliver's Travels.*
6. Money.

June 1865

1. This refers to the rebellion in Sicily in 1282 against Charles of Anjou. The insurrection began at the start of Vespers on Easter Monday, March 30, 1282, at the Church of the Holy Spirit outside Palermo, Sicily. Verdi's opera *The Sicilian Vespers* is based on this event. The poem is by Mrs. Felicia Hemans, a nineteenth-century poetess of England.
2. This note is written by Isabel Parks Caldwell — not *copying* Parks's own writing.
3. Thirteen pages from June 17, 1865, to September 3, 1865, have been carefully cut out of the diary, either by Parks or his sister. Another page is cut out from December 2 to December 7, 1865.
4. Records show that Myers was a member of Eta Chapter of ΣX at the University of Mississippi, which was founded in 1857.

Bibliographic Essay

A bibliography for a diary raises questions of what books may reasonably be cited. The personal narrative separates it from the wider experience described by more general works. But context can help illuminate text, so we have settled on four tiers of citation, a trajectory of perspective moving from the general, involving the nature of war, down to the particular, the warrior himself, James Parks Caldwell. At the broadest level are books on the nature of war as then understood, along with a modern treatise to give a sense of distance as well as kinship between the Civil War and our own troubled time. Next, we suggest some general histories of the Civil War, which will show the conflict as a whole, a view that Caldwell could not know. The third level consists of works on the politics of the border states, of which Ohio was one. Finally, the fourth level comes to Caldwell himself, and includes material by and about him. This system places Caldwell and his memoir in a sufficiently varied framework to establish a context for a prison diary by a Confederate officer who was born and educated in a free state.

The Nature of War

In the early nineteenth century, two books on the nature of war dominated discussion on how war should be conducted. Both arose from the extended Napoleonic campaigns. Baron Antoine-Henri de Jomini and General Carl von Clausewitz produced, in the same decade, reflections on what the new, that is Napoleonic, styles of war meant. Jomini and Clausewitz attempted to see war as a whole, in philosophical, strategic, and political terms, not just as tactics and techniques of command. Both understood war as a distinct political condition, constantly recurring but not permanent. Both discerned general principles of war, which applied always and stood above the welter of changing tactical and organizational details. Since the consequences of defeat and the fruits of victory were so serious, the study of war ought to be part of the standard business of statecraft.

We have also added a modern treatise on war, partly for the insights that contrast can bring, and partly to suggest that there are aspects of war that transcend even the technology of combat and the politics of conflict. In our own times, unlike the Civil War era, force "without stint or limit" is rarely useful for a major political and military power. Varied styles of war, from terrorism and guerrilla war to "psyops," political subversion and robot surveillance and attacks, have been added to the menu of military techniques available to commanders today. General Sir Rupert Smith advises caution, precision and delicacy in the use of force, but the principles of surprise, mass, dissimulation, speed, and position remain intact.

We suggest that the study of war as a political strategic category is a useful matrix within which memoirs of war and captivity may be placed.

De Jomini, General le Baron Antoine-Henri. *Precis de l'Art de la Guerre: Des Principales Combinasions de la Strategie, de la Guerre Tactique et de la Politique Militaire*, (Brussels: Meline, Cans et Copagnie, 1838). Jomini's treatise was an instant hit, and there were two English translations in the immediate Civil War period. Both were published in the United States. See de Jomini, *The Art of War*, trans. Major O.F. Winship and Lieut. E.E. McLean (U. S. A.), (New York: T.P. Putnam, 1854), and de Jomini, *The Art of War*, trans. Capt. G.H. Mendell and Lieut. W.P. Craighill (U. S. A.), (Philadelphia: J.B. Lippincott, 1862).

Clausewitz, Carl von. *Vom Kriege* (Berlin: Dümmlers, Verlag, 1832). A convenient modern edition in English is von Clausewitz, *On War*, ed. and trans. Michael Howard and Peter Paret (Princeton, NJ: Princeton University Press, 1984).

Rupert Smith. *The Utility of Force: The Art of War in the Modern World*. New York: Knopf, 2007.

The Civil War

There are hundreds of histories of the Civil War, by hundreds of authors, and all cannot be cited. We have chosen three authors, added an atlas, and suggest that these volumes will cover all but the most professional and/or compulsive desire to know the details of the war. All three authors combine vast detail about the war with a coherent overview of the battles, the armies, and the politics of the conflict. The reader can see how the war went, from Virginia where Robert E. Lee's victories gave Confederates hope, to the west, where the South knew almost constant defeat. As generals have always known, the "fog of war" obscures, often fatally, a contemporary overview of conflict, and history seeks, however imperfectly, to lift the fog a bit.

Foote, Shelby. *The Civil War, A Narrative, vol. 1: Fort Sumter to Perryville*. New York: Random House, 1958.
_____. *The Civil War, A Narrative, vol. 2: Fredericksburg to Meridian*, New York: Random House, 1963.
_____. *The Civil War, A Narrative, vol. 3: Red River to Appomattox*, New York: Random House, 1974.
McPherson, James. *Abraham Lincoln and the Second American Revolution*. New York: Oxford University Press, 1990.
_____. *What They Fought For, 1861–1865*. Baton Rouge: Louisiana State University Press, 1994.
_____. *This Mighty Scourge*. New York: Oxford University Press, 2007.
Nevins, Allan. *The War for the Union*, 4 vols. New York: Scribner, 1959–1971.
Woodworth, Steven E., and Kenneth J. Winkle. *Atlas of the Civil War*. New York: Oxford University Press, 2004.

Politics and Opposition in the Time of War

In antebellum America the freedom line ran along the Ohio River. Article 6 of the Northwest Ordinance (1787) had declared that states carved from territory north of the Ohio must prohibit slavery. Though free, the river valley states of Ohio, Indiana, and Illinois were tied economically and socially to the slave states to the south. Families owned land on both sides of the freedom line, and there were always slaves living and working across the river. At the same time, the Ohio River valley was a hotbed of abolitionism, from individuals whose houses along the river were stops on the Underground Railway to the fiercely abolitionist Lane Theological Seminary in Cincinnati. Politics and law reflected the nearness of freedom to slavery, and also the depth of emotion, and suspicion, that divided people on that social frontier.

Before the war, the Democrats had been the nation's majority party, strong in the north as well as the south. Although Lincoln carried every free state in 1860, there was still a substantial Democratic vote in the north. Democrats, in 1862, made substantial Congressional gains in the off-year election. Some Democrats in the north were Unionists, backing Lincoln and the war, while others, called Copperheads, openly supported the Confederacy. Many Copperheads were thought by their opponents to be too enthusiastic in their support for the Confederacy. In war, opposition is always suspect and easily equated with treason. Copperheads quickly came under suspicion of working, not just rooting, for the wrong side. In that environment, a decision in politics helped determine the future of one's life. The fighting ended but the legacy of war did not.

There seems to have been two major reasons the political and psychological split between the Copperheads and the Unionists (both Democratic and Republican) became so rancorous and bitter. The first was freedom, the freedom of states to secede, the freedom of states to manage their own society, and freedom from the military and political pressure to conform to a Unionist position. The second, and more important, reason was lack of freedom. Many supported slavery less as a good than as a necessity. Did an appropriate civil role exist for black people in the United States other than slavery? Many could not imagine black people as anything but slaves. A war against states' rights and to free slaves was unsupportable.

We have cited some works on Copperheads and opposition to Lincoln and the war. They are only a sample, but they do give some idea of the politics of opposition in time of war.

George, Joseph, Jr. "'Abraham Africanus I': President Lincoln Through the Eyes of a Copperhead Editor." *Civil War History*. 1968 (14:3): 226–239. Available online through JSTOR.
Gray, Wood. *The Hidden Civil War: The Story of the Copperheads*. New York: Viking, 1942.
Klement, Frank L. *The Copperheads in the Middle West*. Chicago: University of Chicago Press, 1960.
Silbey, Joel H. *A Respectable Minority: The Democratic Party in the Civil War Era, 1860–1869*. New York: Norton, 1977.
Stampp, Kenneth. *Indiana Politics during the Civil War*. Indianapolis: Indiana Historical Bureau, 1949.
Weber, Jennifer L. *Copperheads: The Rise and Fall of Lincoln's Opponents in the North*. New York: Oxford University Press, 2006.

Works about Caldwell and His Life

Bryant, Mark. *Dictionary of Riddles*. London: Routledge, 1990, no. 403, p. 190.
Büchmann. *Geflügelte Worte: Der Zitatenschatz des deutschen Volkes*. Berlin: Schreitersche, 1918, 500.
Cunningham, Edward. *The Port Hudson Campaign, 1862–1863*. Baton Rouge and London: Louisiana State University Press, 1963.
Fleming, William, Jr., ed. and comp. *One in Heart and Purpose: The Founders and the Founding of the Sigma Chi Fraternity From the Original Manuscripts of Joseph Cookman Nate, D.D*. Chicago: Sigma Chi Fraternity, 2009.
Foote, Shelby. "Echoes of Shiloh." *National Geographic*. July 1979, 106–111.
Frohman, Charles E. *Rebels on Lake Erie: The Piracy, The Conspiracy, Prison Life*. Columbus: Ohio Historical Society, 1965.
Gesner, Johann Matthias. *Novus linguae et eruditionis Romanae thesaurus*. Leipzig: Casp. Fritschii viduae et Bernh. Chr. Breitkopfii, 1749.
Guerrant, Edward O. *Bluegrass Confederate: The Headquarters Diary of Edward O. Guerrant*. ed. by William C. Davis and Meredith L. Swentor. Baton Rouge: Louisiana State University Press 1999.
Hewitt, Lawrence Lee. *Port Hudson, Confederate Bastion on the Mississippi*. Baton Rouge and London: Louisiana State University Press, 1987.
Hibbett, T.C. *College Days at Old Miami: The Diary of T.C. Hibbett*, ed. by William Pratt. Oxford, OH: Miami University, 1984.
Home, Henry, of Kames. *Elements of Criticism*. Rev. ed. New York: A.S. Barnes, 1855.
Jackson, Richard. *Popular Songs of Nineteenth-Century America*. New York: Dover, 1976. 280–81.
Jennings, Virginia Lobdell. *The Plains and the People,* 3rd ed. Baton Rouge, LA: Land and Land, 1989.
Meredith, Owen (Robert, Lord Lytton). *The Poetical Works*. New York: Hurst & Co., 1800s.

Morgan, Sarah. *The Civil War Diaries of Sarah Morgan,* ed. by Charles East. Athens, GA, and London: University of Georgia Press, 1991.
Munro, H.A.J., ed. *T. Lucreti Cari, De rerum natura libri sex.* New York: Harper, 1861.
Nate, Joseph Cookman. *History of the Sigma Chi Fraternity,* 1855–1930, vols. I and IV. Chicago: The Fraternity, 1930.
Owen, Elvion. "Caesar in American Schools Prior to 1860." *Classical Journal* 31 (1935).
Patterson, Edmund DeWitt. *The Civil War Journal of Edmund DeWitt Patterson,* ed. by John G. Barrett. Chapel Hill: University of North Carolina Press, 1966.
Proudfit, John, ed. *The Captives: A Comedy of Plautus with English Notes for the Use of Students.* New York: Harper, 1863.
Ransom, John L. *John Ransom's Diary.* New York: Paul S. Eriksson, 1963.
Reinhold, Meyer. *Classica Americana: The Greek and Roman Heritage in the United States.* Detroit: Wayne State University Press, 1984, 221–49.
Report of the Committee of Ten on Secondary School Studies. New York: American Book Company, 1894, 62f.
Report of the Committee of Twelve of the American Philological Association on Courses in Latin and Greek for Secondary Schools. Boston: Ginn and Co., 1899, 41.
Richard, Carl J. *The Founders and the Classics.* Cambridge, MA: Harvard University Press, 1994, 19f.
Shriver, Phillip R., and Donald J. Breen, *Ohio's Military Prisons in the Civil War.* Columbus: Ohio State University Press, 1964.
Smith, Ophia D. *Oxford Spy Wed at Pistol Point.* Oxford, OH: Cullen, 1962.
Walther, Hans. *Proverbia sententiaeque Latinitatis Medii Aevi; Lateinische orichworter und Sentenzen des Mittelalters in alphabetischer Anordnung.* Gottingen: Denhoeck and Ruprecht, 1963–, 2:893 with cross references.

Index

The Abbot 113
Ad Patriae Vexillum, Carmen Militaire 60, 149
Adam Bede 85
Adventures of Verdant Green 200
Akenside 152
Alamo 18
Alexander, Capt. M.J. 196, 199
Alexander, Capt. W.J. 201
Alhambra 112
The Amber Gods & c 135
Anatomy of Melancholy 178, 181
Ancient Mariner 107
Anne of Guerstein 80
Apperson, Lt. W.W. 83, 245n12
Archer, Brig. Gen. James J. 78, 123, 157, 243n47
Arnold, Dr. 149, 150
As You Like It 111
At Odds 77
Atlanta 131, 141
Attaché in Madrid 109
Autobiographic Sketches 139
Autocrat of the Breakfast Table 152

The Bachelor of Salamanca 137
Bailey 117
Bakin, Maj. Charles F. 201
Band, Lt. 196
Banks, Gen. Nathaniel 68, 106
Barlow, Maj. 167, 168
Barnes, Capt. William 83, 245n15
base-ball clubs 139
Battle, Capt. Frank 83, 84, 245n21
Battle in Virginia 110

Battle of Iuka 25
Beall (Bealle), Brig Gen. William N.R. 152, 168, 243n49
Beatrice Cenci 135
Beauvoir 41
Bede, Cuthbert 200
Behind the Scenes 109
Beldin, Maj. 104
Bell, Thomas C. 12
Berkely (Berkeley), William N. 82, 83, 244n11
Berry 183
Biloxi, Mississippi 36
The Birds of Killingworth 83
Bishop, Prof. R.H. 32
Blacknall, Col. Charles C. 78, 83, 165, 243n49
Blount, Capt. Thomas J. 94, 116, 247n19
Bond, Lt. W.R. 83, 202, 245n12
The Book of Esther 127, 206
Book of Judith 154
Book II of the Dunciad 192
Boston Puritanism 102
Bowen, Gen. John S. 19, 25, 75, 116, 168, 242n26
Bowles, Lieut. 168
Boyd, W.M. 118, 240n5
Breckenridge, John C. 19, 147, 165
Bride of Lammermoor 158
The British Provinces & the West Indies 170
Brougham, Lord 162
Buell, Gen. Don Carlos 25
Bullock, Col. Robert 78, 83, 172, 243n46
Bulwer, Henry Lytton 150

Bulwer-Lytton, Sir Edward 98, 99, 111, 112, 115, 130, 139, 144, 154, 169
Bulwer-Lytton, Lady Emily Elizabeth 109
Burke, Lt. Col. 179

Cabell, Gen. William 158, 168
Caldwell, Benjamin Rush (brother) 7, 34
Caldwell, Ida (sister) 7
Caldwell, Isabella (Bella) (sister) 7, 12, 21
Caldwell, Isabella H. Parks (mother) 7, 19, 20, 34
Caldwell, James Parks: admitted to the bar 30; buried in Biloxi 48; enlisted as a private 23; entered Miami University 9; graduated age Miami University 14; "Judge" Caldwell 45; and Latin 49, 51, 53, 54, 60, 61, 62, 66; malaria 18; Panola, Mississippi 16; prisoner in New Orleans 29; read law 16; reconstruction 29; as second lieutenant 23; sense of humor 61, 63, 65, 66; Sigma Chi speech 41–45; as teacher 17, 51
Caldwell, Joseph H. (brother) 7
Caldwell, Mary (sister) 7
Caldwell, Rebecca (sister) 7
Caldwell, Samuel Wilse (brother) 7
Caldwell, W.W. (father) 7, 15, 17
Caleb Williams 158

268 Index

California 30
Campbell 202
Campbell, Thomas 187
Captevei 159
Carlyle, Thomas 74, 152, 170, 176, 177
Carpenter 140
Carrington, Col. Henry 79, 244n58
Carter, Capt. J.R. 89, 116, 247n49
Castle of Otranto 122
Cataline 170
Cater, Richard B. 185, 201
The Caxtons 138
Chaffin's Bluff 149
Chancellorsville, Va. 109
Chany, Gen. 166
Chartism 152
Chauvin, Col. 73, 241n7
Cherry, G.O. 116, 184
Chilcut, J.W. 116
The City of the Czar 119
Claret & Olives, or From the Garonne to the Rhone 122
Clark, Judge James 16, 21, 30
Clark, J.B. 118, 154, 164, 172, 176, 178–181, 183
Cloister & the Hearth 166
Codlinsby 142
Coleman, Gen. 125
Coleman, Harry 150, 185, 197
Coleridge, Samuel Taylor 92, 144, 145
College Days at Old Miami 9
Collins, Wilkie 100
The Color Guard 79
Comedy of Errors 115
Comus 107
Confederate Veterans 37, 39
Coningsby 142
Conquest of Granada 154
Cooper, Daniel C. 12
Cordray, C.S. 118
Corinth 25
Cornwall, Barry 77, 92
Craney Island, Norfolk Bay 80
Crenshaw, John T. 134
Crescent & Cross 157
Cris 190
The Critic 179
Cross, Lt. Jus W. 179
Cunningham, Allan 151
Custom of the Countries 145
Cuyamas River 233

Dalton 171
Damon & Misedorce 155
Da Ponte, Lorenzo 140
Darien, or the Merchant Prince 96
Dartz, J. 117

Darwin, Charles 93
Davis, Isabella Caldwell Jones (niece) 7
Davis, Mrs. Jefferson 41
Davis, Pres. Jefferson 35, 36
Davis, Lt. 183
Davis, R.C. 117
Davis, Sam 40
Davis, Thomas H. 241n5
Davis, Capt. William Van 184
Dawson, C. 117
Day, Capt. 196
De Morte Edwardi 62
Demorest, Mme. 145
Dences, W.P. 118
Dennis Duval 168
De Quincey, Thomas 139
Dewees, Thomas 184
Dialogues on Eloquence 86
Diary in America, Vol I 138
Diary in Turkish and Greek Waters 131
Dickens, Charles 79
Dickey, Capt. Cyrus 106
Dillard, J.W. 116, 184
D'Israeli, Benjamin 142
Doctor Antonio 168
Don Quixote 176
Dougherty (also Daugherty or Docharty), Lt. S.P. 74, 241n19
Draughn, H.H. 116
Dunlap, Wm. 136
Duphy, T.H. 116
Durr, Major R.J. 82, 244n7

Earl of Carlisle 131
Early, Gen. Jubal 146, 147
Edward 156
Edwards, A.B. 155
Election day 158
Elements of Criticism 102
Eliot, George 86, 100
Elkins, Lt. J.M. 94, 118, 144, 247n10
Elsie Venner 93
England, Dr. 148
England & the English 115, 127
Enoch Arden 188
Entertaining Biography 131
Erickson 167
Ernest Maltraves 112
escapes and attempts 73, 87, 88, 128, 133, 134, 136, 143, 144, 168, 171, 179
Essay on the Mass 148
Essays on Clive & History 74
Estevan, B. 133
Eure, Capt. 155
Evans, Mary Anne *see* Eliot, George
The Everlasting Hills 109

Eversman, Dr. 141, 161, 162

Fair Maid of Perth 121
Fantine 83
Farinholt, Benjamin 245n31
Fasti Jacobi 54
Fellowes (Fellows), Capt. John R. 78, 87, 243n49
Fetter, Lt. Hal 172, 201
Fitz, Col. 162, 169
food 68, 73, 75, 76, 77, 79, 80, 82, 83, 84, 89, 91, 98, 99, 104, 105, 116, 120, 126, 140, 143, 148, 151–157, 159, 176, 177, 190–193, 195, 196, 199, 205, 246n43, 247n7
Forester 184
Fort Delaware 79, 85
France 156
France, Social, Literary, and Political 150
Frankenstein 149
Franklin, Gen. 128
Franks, L.B. 201
Frazer, Gen. 152
Frederick II 170
Frederick the Great Vol. I 179
Frederick the Great Vol II 182
Frederick the Great Vol. III 172
Frederick the Great Vol IV 181
Fremantle 123
Friedrich II, Vol. I 177

Gardiner, Gen. 23
Gardner, Maj. Gen. 68
Garland, J.C. 116, 144
Gaviota Pass 234
Geramb, Barm 190
Gibbon 84
Gibbons 176
Gibson, "Bob" 117, 185
Gil Blas 137
Gillaud, R. 202
Glover, Lt. 168
Glover, S.H. 117
Godolphin 115
Gold, J.E. 116
Goodwin, Brig. Gen. 147
Goodwin, Capt. 182
Gordon, Brig. Gen. G.W. 168
Gordon, Mrs. 148
Grame, Roland 113
Grant, Gen. Ulysses S 25, 122
Grave, Capt. 184
Guerrazzi, F.D. 135
Gulliver's Travels 123
Gunboats 145

Haley, Frank 117
Hall, H.H. 118
Hamilton, Capt. Simeon E. 82, 119, 244n6

Hardee, Gen. William J. 142
Harold 130
Harris, Capt. Shad 245n21
Hawks 202
Hawthorne, Nathaniel 108, 118, 147
Hayes, Otho L. 202
Hays, Dr. 194
health 18, 39, 40, 46, 77, 79–82, 85, 88–90, 95–97, 157, 161, 193, 259n4
Heard, Capt. 184
The Heart of Midlothian 92
Heays, Lt. William 201
Heintzelman, Gen. S.P. 146
Henry Esmond 126, 128, 129
Hero-Worship 176
Hickey, A. 117
Hill, Col. Benjamin 133, 135, 136, 148, 164, 169, 177, 183, 205
Hines, Jno. 202
History of England 1st Volume with Rufus Centuris 104
History of England, Volume V 138
History of France 155
History of Gironde Vol. III 156
History of Pedro I, King of Castile & Chronicle of Chas. IX 154
History of Philip II 179
History of Philip II Vol II 181
History of the Florentine Republic and of the Rule of the Medici 140
Hoffman battalion 76
Holland, Capt. H. 79, 244n57
Hood, Gen. John B. 131, 132, 165
Hood, Thomas 133
House of the Seven Gables 118
The Household of Bouverie, or the Elixir of Gold 95
Houston, C. 202
Huc, M. 156
Hughes, Lt. Col. J.L. 201
Hunley, Col. P.F. 176, 177
Hunt, Leigh 153
Hutchison, Gen. 106
Hutchison, Maj. R.R. 198

Idylls of the King 142
In the Tropics 109
Indian Cottage 123
Inman 117
Invasion of the Crimea 183
Iowa 14
Irby, Freeman B. 16, 17
Irving, Washington 112, 154
Isbell, Capt. R.H. 100, 201
Isocrates 88

Jackson, Brig. Gen. Henry R. 176
Jackson, Mississippi 34
James, G.P.R. 120
Jane Eyre 76
Jesuits 166
Jett, Capt. E.D. 201
Jobowers 218
John Halifax, Gentleman 103
Johnson, Capt. 76
Johnson, Col. 197
Johnson, Maj. Gen. Ed 170
Johnson Island Mud 76, 242n32
Johnston, Gen. Jo 131
Johnston, W. 116, 167, 185
Jones, B.H. 117
Jones, Gen. 152
Jones, Col. H.C. 164, 182
Jones, R.C. 176
Jones, Viva Warren 22
Jordan, Capt. 177
Jordan, C.S. 117
Jordan, Isaac M. 12
Journal of Wm. H. Richansen, a Private in the Doniphan Expedition 147
Journey Round the World 108

Kames, Lord 102
Kapp, Friedrich 88
Kelly, Lt. Col. J.E. 201
Kemper, Capt. Andrew 22
Kendrick 117
King Henry IV Part I 192
Kinglake, Alexander William 183
Knowles, Capt. Calvin 89, 247n50
Krasinski, Count Zygmunt 144
Kryczynski, M.T. 135
Kyle, Col. Osceola 88, 246n36

Lady Morgan's Diary 112
Lady of the Lake 123
Lamartine, Alphonse de 156
Last Days of Pompeii 169
Last Days of Shelley & Byron 131
Late Essays and Poems 149
Lausdale, Lt. Jim W. 201
Lectures on Modern History 149
Lee, P. Lynch 201
Lee, Gen. Robert E. 110, 112, 191
Legend of Florence 153
Legend of Montrose 95
Leila 111
Leonnes, a Tale of the First Crusade 88
LeSage, Alain-René 137
Leslie, S.D. 117, 185, 201

Letters on Demonology & Witchcraft 151
Lever, Charles 90, 96
Lewis, Capt. C.W. 202
Lewis, Dr. 194
Lewis, Maj. Henry G. 202
Lewis, Col. Levin M. 78, 87, 243n49
Libby Prison 79, 244n54
Life of George Frederick Cooke 136
Life of Jesus 84
Life of Mrs. Siddons 187
Life of Steuben 88
Lincoln, Abraham 3, 159, 192
Linginus 88
Lives of British Painters & Sculptors 151
Locke, Lt. Col. Wm. P. 201
Lockwood, William Lewis 12
Long, Capt. Thos. A. 198, 201
Long, Mrs. Zoa A. 202
Longfellow, Henry Wadsworth 83
Loring, Gen. W.W. 23
Los Angeles 238
Lovel the Widower 134
Love's Labour's Lost 112
Lubbock, Col. Thomas 197
Luce, Col. William H. 75, 242n24
Lucille 80, 85, 90, 94, 97, 98
Lucretia 99
Lucretius 56, 157
Lurtchell, W. 118
Lylney Hall 133

M. de Fenelon 86
Macaria 145
Macaulay, Baron Thomas Babington 74, 77, 104, 138, 149
Macpherson, James 100
Madeira, Portugal and the Andalusias of Spain 136
Mahon, Lord 74
Mail 78, 243n53
Manly (Manley), Lt. Matt 73, 94, 116, 164, 167, 184, 241n8
Manor (U.S.) 180
Marble Faun 108
Marmaduke, Gen. John S. 158, 168
Marrgate 138
Martineau, Miss 128
Martins of Cro' Martin 96
Maryland invasion 128
Maxwell, Col. G. 78, 243n50
McCarty, F.M. 117
McClellan, Gen. George B. 25, 140
McConnell, Capt. 241n5

McCracken, Tom 202
McCulloch, Capt. Robert 79, 244n58
McElwee, Dr. John 129
McKinley, Pres. William 41
McPherson, Gen. James B. 25, 132
Meade, Maj. Gen. George G. 76, 242n33
Melville, Herman 135
Memoirs of Christopher North 148
Memoirs of Vidocq 132
Merchant of Venice 115
Meredith, Owen 97
Merry Wives of Windsor 108, 193
Mexican emigration scheme 195
Miami University (Oxford, Ohio) 8, 9, 11, 12, 32
Midsummer Nights' Dream 108
Mill, John Stuart 159
Mill on the Floss 85
Miller, Newman 46
Milton, John 107
Mims 202
Mirror of Fashion 145
Mission of San Miguel 230
Mission of Santa Barbara 235
Mitchell, W.H. 118
Monastery 114
Moneth, Dr. 202
money 206
Monterey Bay 226
Moon, Ginnie 12, 16, 20, 21, 22, 23, 29
Moore, W.R. 149
Moreland, Capt. M.D. 120
Morris, Col. 178
Morte d'Arthur 113
Moseley, A.S. 116
Moseley, Capt. Alexander Moseley 81, 116, 244n2
Much Ado About Nothing 110
Munson 116
Murchison, Col. 162
Murphy, Lt. 133
Murray, Hon. Amelia 134
Murray, Jas. M. 201
Mustang Gray 125
Myers, P.S. 202

Naile 202
Nasen, J.E. 201
Naynor, 1st Lt. Jno. D. 201
The Newcomes 155, 158
Nichol, Ky. 141
Night & Morning 109
No Name 100
North, Capt. J.R. 150
Notes on Shakespeare 144
Novès, J.E. 116

Odum 116, 143
Ohio 34
Old Mortality 107
Old Uncle Ned 61
Oliver, C. 117
Oliver, J.B. 117
Ollendorf 176
Omoo 135
On Liberty 159
Origin of the Species 93
Our Old Home 147
Overland Monthly 30, 31, 32
Owen Tudor 126

Palmetto Academy 17, 19, 29
Panola, Mississippi 16, 17, 29
Parker, Lt. Col. James P. 201
Past & Present 152
Patterson, E.D. 185
Pendennis 184
Philip 153
Phillips, J.M. 117
Philpot 117
Picciola 128
Pickett 202
Pierson, Col. William S. 73, 241n19
Pilgrimage to Jerusalem & Mt. Sinae 190
The Pirates 134
Pitt, William 149
Plautus 159
Pleasures Mag. 152
Poetic Principles 190
The Poet's Journal 191
Pt. Lookout 74, 91, 92, 189
Pope, Frank A. 201
Port Hudson 26–29, 37, 38, 68, 69, 98, 106, 127, 205
Porter 117, 147
Prescott, Miss Harriet 135
Prescott, William H. 179
prison duties 76, 78, 79, 83, 84, 92, 95, 106, 115, 120, 122, 128, 132, 136, 142, 152, 161, 176, 178
prisoner arrivals 121, 123, 125, 127, 132, 133, 135, 141, 144, 156, 162, 166, 170, 176 183
prisoner departures 106, 177, 184, 185, 187, 188
Pritchard 185
The Professor's Story 93
Propria Quae Maribus & Box Tunnel 157

Quentin Durward 195
Quin, Joseph 117

Raitces, T. 119
Rambler 150
Rasselas 196

Rawlings, J.J. 117
Reade, Charles 105, 126, 157, 166
Reading habits 55
Recollections of a Journey through Tartary & Thibet 156
Recovery of Poland 135
Redout 117
Reid, Whitelaw 25, 45
Renan, Ernest 84
Reproduction 159, 171
Republican Party 3
Revolt of the Netherlands 169, 176
Richard, L. 117
Ridley, Maj. 166, 179, 183, 185
Riley, A. 118
The Rivals 179
Rob Roy 124
Robbers 195
Roberdeau, J.D. 178
Robertson, C. 116
Robinson, Capt. Charles C. 241n5
Rodes, Gen. Robert 147, 256n12
Rogers' Table Talk 159
Roland Cashel 90
Romola 100
Roosevelt, Theodore 46
Rosecrans, Gen. William 25
Roundabout Papers 170
Rucker 182
Rudder, S.B. 188, 202
Ruffin, Lt. T. 111, 116, 133, 145, 146
Ruffini, J. 143, 168
Runkle, Benjamin P. 12, 13, 23–25, 37
Rutledge 77

Saga of King Olaf 83
St. Pierre, Bernardin de 123
Saintine, X.B. 128
Sallust 170
San Antonio (river) 230
San Bernardino County 30
San Buenaventura mission 236
San Luis Obispo County 230, 232
San Marcos 230
San Rafael Mountains 234
Sanders, Maj. Joseph H. 74, 94, 116, 185, 241n17, 245n15
Santa Clara River 237
Santa Cruz Range 226
Santa Inez Mission 234
Santa Inez Mountains 234
Santa Inez River 234
Santa Lucia Mountains 231
Sartor Resartus 152

Index

Scales, Col. Junius I. 78, 243n49
Schiller, Friedrich 176, 195
School for Scandal 179
Scobey, Franklin Howard 12
Scott, Lt. 183
Scott, Sir Walter 114, 151
Scovill, Col. E.A. 148
Seaside 155
Seissons, Dr. 149
Sentimental Journey 123
Sermons by the Paulists 95
Seyton, Catharine 113
Shaler, Brig. Gen. Alexander 242n29
Shannon, Denman W. 94, 183, 247n19
Sharp 87, 106
Sharp, Capt. William 246n32
Shaw, Capt. Matt B. 201
Shelley, Mrs. 149
Shepard, J.A. 117
Shephard, E.C. 117
Sheridan, Richard 179
Sherman, William 165
Shiloh (Pittsburg Landing) 24–26
Shorter, A. 180
Simms, S.C. 202
Simpson, Sir George 108
Sintraia 158
Sketches by Boz 79
Sketches of Public Characters &c. 162
Sledge, Lieut. 194
Sloan 185
smallpox 172, 177, 179
Smith, "Governor" 106
Smith, Brig. Gen Th. 170, 176
snowball fights 77, 78
Spirit of Zaine 147
Stakes, Lt. John 241n5
State Papers 100
Steedman, Col. I.G.W. 197, 201, 246n46
Stephens, Lt. John A. 182
Sterne, Laurence 123, 151
Stevens 117
Stevens, Capt. W.C. 99, 248n36
Story of Rimini 153

Strange Story 98
The Student; a Series of Papers 154

Table Talk 145
Tales of a Wayside Inn 83
Taming of the Shrew 112
Taylor, Bayard 113, 191
Taylor, Capt. J. 172, 180
Taylor, Maj. 73; 241n7
Tempest 114, 193
Ten Thousand a Year 81
Tennyson, Alfred Lord 109, 113, 142
Terry, Gen. Henry D. 104, 242n29
Thackeray, William Makepeace 126, 134, 142, 153, 155, 170, 184
Thompson, Gen. Meriwether Jeff 78, 243n49
Thorp 184
Three Clerks 195
Three Months at the South 123
Tom Jones 158, 169
Tombstone (film) 53
Travels 156
Travels & Adventures in Mexico 140
Traynor 187
Trelawny, Edward John 131
Trevilian, C.B. 180
Trimble, Gen. Isaac R. 152
Troilus and Cressida 115
Trollope, Anthony 195
Tune, J.H. 117
tunnel 119
Turner, Capt. Henry 94, 105, 106, 113
Turner, Sir James 93
Turner's Memoirs 93
Two Gentlemen from Verona 112
Two Millions 134
Tyler 118
Tytler, A.F. 158

Undine 158
Undivine Comedy 144
United States, Canada & Cuba 134
Universal History 158

Vallandigham 122
Vanity Fair 158
Vergil 57–59
Very Hard Cash 105
Views Afoot 113
Vincenzo 143

Wallenstein 107
The Wandering Jew 166
War Pictures from the South 133
Warburton, Eliot 96, 157
Washington, Capt. N.C. 172
Waverly 110
weather 72, 73, 75, 76, 77, 79, 80, 81, 83, 84, 85, 86. 91, 92, 93, 94, 96, 97, 98, 99, 100, 102, 105, 107, 109, 111, 117, 118, 119, 121, 122, 123, 137, 138, 142, 146, 149, 159, 165, 167, 177, 178, 187
Western Travel 128
Wheeler, Maj. Gen. Joseph 197
Wheeler, N.C. 202
whiskey 82, 104
White, Edward Douglass 5
White, M.B. 116
White Lies 126
Whiting, 1st Lt. Geo. U. 201
Williams, J.B. 116
Williamson, Capt. A.A. 201
Williamson, Maj. 183
Wilrun, Maj. M.P. 202
Winder 179
Winston, Maj. John R. 241n5
Winter's Tale 111
Woman Disfranchised 167
Woodbridge, Dr. 143
Woods, Col. Michael L. 162, 170, 243n49
Woodstock 107
Wortley, Lady Emmeline Stuart 156
Wyoming 36

Young, Lt. 149
Youngblood, Capt. 176, 184

Zanoni 144

www.ingramcontent.com/pod-product-compliance
Ingram Content Group UK Ltd.
Pitfield, Milton Keynes, MK11 3LW, UK
UKHW041931140426
5217IPUK00014B/416